MySQL 8 Administrator's Guide

Effective guide to administering high-performance
MySQL 8 solutions

Chintan Mehta
Ankit Bhavsar
Hetal Oza
Subhash Shah

BIRMINGHAM - MUMBAI

MySQL 8 Administrator's Guide

Commissioning Editor: Amey Varangaonkar
Acquisition Editor: Aman Singh
Content Development Editor: Aaryaman singh
Technical Editor: Dharmendra Yadav
Copy Editors: Safis Editing
Project Coordinator: Manthan Patel
Proofreader: Safis Editing
Indexer: Tejal Daruwale Soni
Graphics: Tania Dutta
Production Coordinator: Aparna Bhagat

First published: February 2018

Production reference: 1140218

Published by Packt Publishing Ltd.
Livery Place
35 Livery Street
Birmingham
B3 2PB, UK.

ISBN 978-1-78839-519-9

www.packtpub.com

`mapt.io`

Mapt is an online digital library that gives you full access to over 5,000 books and videos, as well as industry leading tools to help you plan your personal development and advance your career. For more information, please visit our website.

Why subscribe?

- Spend less time learning and more time coding with practical eBooks and Videos from over 4,000 industry professionals

- Improve your learning with Skill Plans built especially for you

- Get a free eBook or video every month

- Mapt is fully searchable

- Copy and paste, print, and bookmark content

PacktPub.com

Did you know that Packt offers eBook versions of every book published, with PDF and ePub files available? You can upgrade to the eBook version at `www.PacktPub.com` and as a print book customer, you are entitled to a discount on the eBook copy. Get in touch with us at `service@packtpub.com` for more details.

At `www.PacktPub.com`, you can also read a collection of free technical articles, sign up for a range of free newsletters, and receive exclusive discounts and offers on Packt books and eBooks.

Contributors

About the authors

Chintan Mehta is a cofounder of KNOWARTH Technologies (www.knowarth.com) and heads cloud/RIMS/DevOps. He has rich, progressive experience in server administration of Linux, AWS cloud, DevOps, RIMS, and open source technologies. He is an AWS Certified Solutions Architect.

He has authored *MySQL 8 for Big Data* and *Hadoop Backup and Recovery Solutions*, and has reviewed *Liferay Portal Performance Best Practices* and *Building Serverless Web Applications*.

> *I would like to thank my coauthors. I would especially like to thank my wonderful wife, Mittal, and my sweet son, Devam, for putting up with the long days, nights, and weekends when I was camping in front of my laptop. Last but not least, I want to thank my mom, dad, friends, family, and colleagues for supporting me throughout.*

Ankit Bhavsar is a senior consultant leading a team working on ERP solutions at KNOWARTH Technologies. He received an MCA from North Gujarat university. He has had dynamic roles in the development and maintenance of ERP solutions and astrology portals Content Management that including OOP, technical architecture analysis, design, development as well as database design, development and enhancement process, data and object modeling, in order to provide technical and business solutions to clients.

> *First, I would like to thank the coauthors, reviewers, the wonderful team at PacktPub, and Aaryaman for this effort. I would especially like to thank my wonderful wife, Avani, for putting up with the long days, nights, and weekends. Last, but not least, I want to thank my mom, dad, friends, family, and colleagues for supporting me throughout the writing of this book.*

Hetal Oza an MCA from a reputable institute of India, is working as a lead consultant at KNOWARTH Technologies. She has rich experience in Java-based systems with various databases. Her 10 years of experience covers all stages of software development. She has worked on development of web-based software solutions on various platforms. She has good exposure to integration projects with web-service-based and thread-based architecture. Her knowledge is not bound to any single field because she has worked on wide range of technologies and tools.

It gave me immense pleasure to be an author of this book. First, I would like to thank my husband, Suhag, and my sweet son, Om, for putting up with me during the long days, nights, and weekends when I was camping in front of my laptop. Second, I would like to thank Chintan Mehta, who showed trust in me and provided this opportunity, and Krupal Khatri for his support. I would also like to thank the team at PacktPub for their great help.

Subhash Shah works as a principal consultant at KNOWARTH Technologies. He holds a degree in information technology from a HNGU. He is experienced in developing web-based solutions using various software platforms. He is a strong advocate of open source software development and its use by businesses to reduce risks and costs. His interests include designing sustainable software solutions. His technical skills include requirement analysis, architecture design, project delivery, application setup, and execution processes. He is an admirer of quality code and test-driven development.

I would like to thank my family for supporting me throughout the course of this book. It would have been difficult without them being a source of inspiration. Thanks to Packt Publishing, especially Aaryaman, for their smooth coordination and support. Thanks to fellow authors for being around all the time, for their dedication and commitment. Last but not least, thanks to my colleagues for all the support they have provided.

About the reviewers

Sahaj Pathak has been involved with backend technologies such as Java, Spring, Hibernate, and databases (MySQL, PostgreSQL, Oracle, and others). His experience also spans frontend technologies (HTML4/5, jQuery, AngularJS, Node.Js, JavaScript, and CSS2/3). He has speedy versatility with any technology and a sharp desire for consistent change.

He works at KNOWARTH Technologies as a software consultant where he deals with big enterprise-product-based projects.

Ravi Shah is a highly versatile IT professional with more than 5 years of experience of handling high-end IT projects, with competencies in conceptualizing and supporting critical IT frameworks and applications. He is a team player, a software engineer with a can-do attitude, and possesses phenomenal time management skills, and strong user focus. He has developed several web applications and mainly specializes in healthcare and insurance.

He is skilled in all phases of software development, an expert in translating business requirements into technical solutions, and devoted to quality, usability, security and scalability. His expertise mainly includes Liferay, Java, Spring, Struts, Hibernate, MySQL, Lucene, Angular, and Agile.

He is a good trainer delivering training on J2EE and the Liferay portal in his organization.

I would like to take this opportunity to express heartfelt thanks to KNOWARTH Technologies and Packt Publishing for giving me this opportunity. Also, I am very thankful to my parents for always supporting me in all possible ways.

Packt is searching for authors like you

If you're interested in becoming an author for Packt, please visit `authors.packtpub.com` and apply today. We have worked with thousands of developers and tech professionals, just like you, to help them share their insight with the global tech community. You can make a general application, apply for a specific hot topic that we are recruiting an author for, or submit your own idea.

Table of Contents

Preface

For any system, it is must to manage data in an organized manner. In a large-scale system, it is necessary to handle various configurations for security purposes. MySQL is one of the popular solutions used to handle enterprise-level applications. In this book, we will explain how to configure users, their roles, multiple instances, and much more.

Many organizations use MySQL for their websites or commercial products, and it's very challenging for them to manage data storage and analyze data in accordance with the business requirements. This book will show you how to implement indexing and query optimization for better performance. Along with this, we'll cover how scalability and high availability of the MySQL server can help to manage failure scenarios. In addition to that, replication and partitioning concepts are explained in detail with examples.

The book describes various features of MySQL 8 by targeting different levels of users, from beginners to database administrators. This book starts from the installation with a basic understanding of MySQL 8's concepts. The we proceed to administrative-level features with configuration. At the end of the book, you will have learned about very interesting functionalities, such as optimization, extension, and troubleshooting.

Who this book is for

This book is intended for MySQL administrators who are looking for a handy guide covering all the MySQL administration-related tasks. If you are a DBA looking to get started with MySQL administration, this book will also help you. Knowledge of basic database concepts is required to get started with this book.

What this book covers

Chapter 1, *An Introduction to MySQL 8*, serves as an introductory guide to MySQL 8. It briefly defines the core features available in MySQL and newly introduced or enhanced features of MySQL 8. In the later part of the chapter, we highlight the benefits of MySQL 8 along with real-world applications.

Chapter 2, *Installing and Upgrading MySQL 8*, describes detailed steps for installing MySQL 8 on different platforms. It also explains how to upgrade to or downgrade from MySQL 8.

Chapter 3, *MySQL 8 – Using Programs and Utilities*, introduces command-line programs for the MySQL 8 server and client. It also provides information on the available GUI tools with its configuration.

Chapter 4, *MySQL 8 Data Types*, focuses on a detailed explanation of MySQL 8 data types. It also explains data type categorization based on the types of content. We cover data types along with their properties in each category. We also cover storage requirements for data types.

Chapter 5, *MySQL 8 Database Management*, mainly explores the administration part of MySQL 8. This chapter covers components and plugin management, along with user and role management. In addition, it explains globalization configuration, caching techniques, and different types of logs available in MySQL 8.

Chapter 6, *MySQL 8 Storage Engines*, explains several types of storage engines and details of the InnoDB storage engine. This chapter provides information on custom storage engine creation, along with steps to make it pluggable in installed MySQL 8.

Chapter 7, *Indexing in MySQL 8*, explains indexing, along with the possible ways of implementing it. It compares types of indexing.

Chapter 8, *Replication in MySQL 8*, explains replication and the different types of replication available in MySQL 8. It also describes the configuration and implementation of replication along with different approaches.

Chapter 9, *Partitioning in MySQL 8*, explains the setting of several types of partitioning, selection, and pruning of partitioning. It also explains how to cope up with restrictions and limitations while partitioning.

Chapter 10, *MySQL 8 – Scalability and High Availability*, explains how to do scaling and how to handle different challenges during implementation. The reader gets an understanding of diverse ways to achieve high availability in MySQL 8.

Chapter 11, *MySQL 8 – Security*, focuses on MySQL 8 database security. This chapter covers general factors that affect security, the security of core MySQL 8 files, access control, and securing the database system itself. This chapter also includes details of security plugins.

Chapter 12, *Optimizing MySQL 8*, explains how to configure MySQL 8 for better performance. This chapter also describes use cases with a few performance results to validate. This will help you know various touch points to look out for when dealing with optimizing MySQL 8.

Chapter 13, *Extending MySQL 8*, shows how to extend MySQL 8 and add new functions, along with debugging and porting to MySQL 8.

Chapter 14, *MySQL 8 Best Practices and Benchmarking*, explains the best practices of using MySQL. It also explains various benchmarkings done for MySQL 8.

Chapter 15, *Troubleshooting MySQL 8*, explains many common and real-world scenarios of troubleshooting for MySQL 8.

To get the most out of this book

We recommend that you get some basic knowledge of MySQL (any version) and SQL commands before you start reading this book.

This book also covers practical scenarios and command execution, so if possible, install a tool for easy execution of MySQL commands.

Download the example code files

You can download the example code files for this book from your account at www.packtpub.com. If you purchased this book elsewhere, you can visit www.packtpub.com/support and register to have the files emailed directly to you.

You can download the code files by following these steps:

1. Log in or register at www.packtpub.com.
2. Select the **SUPPORT** tab.
3. Click on **Code Downloads & Errata**.
4. Enter the name of the book in the **Search** box and follow the onscreen instructions.

Once the file is downloaded, please make sure that you unzip or extract the folder using the latest version of:

- WinRAR/7-Zip for Windows
- Zipeg/iZip/UnRarX for Mac
- 7-Zip/PeaZip for Linux

The code bundle for the book is also hosted on GitHub at `https://github.com/PacktPublishing/MySQL-8-Administrators-Guide`. We also have other code bundles from our rich catalog of books and videos available at `https://github.com/PacktPublishing/`. Check them out!

Conventions used

There are a number of text conventions used throughout this book.

`CodeInText`: Indicates code words in text, database table names, folder names, filenames, file extensions, pathnames, dummy URLs, user input, and Twitter handles. Here is an example: "It will download `winMD5Sum.exe` onto your computer."

Any command-line input or output is written as follows:

```
CREATE TABLE working_days (
year INT,
week INT,
days BIT(7),
PRIMARY KEY (year, week));
```

Bold: Indicates a new term, an important word, or words that you see onscreen. For example, words in menus or dialog boxes appear in the text like this. Here is an example: "Click on the **Download WinMD5Sum** option on the page."

 Warnings or important notes appear like this.

 Tips and tricks appear like this.

Get in touch

Feedback from our readers is always welcome.

General feedback: Email `feedback@packtpub.com` and mention the book title in the subject of your message. If you have questions about any aspect of this book, please email us at `questions@packtpub.com`.

Errata: Although we have taken every care to ensure the accuracy of our content, mistakes do happen. If you have found a mistake in this book, we would be grateful if you would report this to us. Please visit `www.packtpub.com/submit-errata`, selecting your book, clicking on the Errata Submission Form link, and entering the details.

Piracy: If you come across any illegal copies of our works in any form on the Internet, we would be grateful if you would provide us with the location address or website name. Please contact us at `copyright@packtpub.com` with a link to the material.

If you are interested in becoming an author: If there is a topic that you have expertise in and you are interested in either writing or contributing to a book, please visit `authors.packtpub.com`.

Reviews

Please leave a review. Once you have read and used this book, why not leave a review on the site that you purchased it from? Potential readers can then see and use your unbiased opinion to make purchase decisions, we at Packt can understand what you think about our products, and our authors can see your feedback on their book. Thank you!

For more information about Packt, please visit `packtpub.com`.

1
An Introduction to MYSQL 8

MySQL is a well-known open source structured database because of its performance, easiness to use, and reliability. This is the most common choice of web applications for a relational database. In the current market, thousands of web-based applications rely on MySQL including giant industries such as Facebook, Twitter, and Wikipedia. It has also proven to be the database choice for **Software as a Service (SaaS)** based applications such as Twitter, YouTube, SugarCRM, Supply Dynamics, Workday, RightNow, Omniture, Zimbra, and many more. We will discuss this in detail in the *use cases of MySQL* section later in the chapter. MySQL was developed by MySQL AB, a Swedish company, and now it is distributed and supported by Oracle Corporation. MySQL carries a valuable history with it.

MySQL has continued to improve in order to become an enterprise-level database management system. MySQL 8 is expected to be a game-changer as today we are in the age of digitization. MySQL 8 is all tuned to serve many new use cases that in prior versions were difficult to achieve. Some of the use cases an enormous amount of data is produced are social networking, e-commerce, bank/credit card transactions, emails, data stored on the cloud, and so on. Analysis of all such structured, unstructured, or semi-structured ubiquitous data helps to discover hidden patterns, market trends, correlations, personal preferences.

"There is so much for each of us"

- James Truslow Adams

Let's take an in-depth look at MySQL 8 new features, benefits, use cases along with a few limitations of MySQL 8 after we have an overview of MySQL. This is going to be exciting, let's get prepared.

Overview of MySQL

Structured Query Language (**SQL**) is used to manipulate, retrieve, insert, update, and delete data in **relational database management system** (**RDBMS**). To make it simpler, SQL tells the database what to do and exactly what it needs. SQL is a standard language that all RDBMS systems such as MySQL, MS Access, MS SQL, Oracle, Postgres, and others use.

 RDBMS is the basis for SQL and for all modern database systems such as MS SQL Server, IBM DB2, Oracle, MySQL, and Microsoft Access.

SQL allows users to access data from MySQL and define and manipulate the data. To embed within other languages, you can leverage SQL modules, libraries, and precompilers, which can help you create/drop databases and tables, allow users to create the view, and stored procedures, functions, and so on, in a database. It can do various other operations such as allowing users to set permissions on tables, procedures, and views.

MySQL as a relational database management system

Data in a relational database is stored in an organized format so that information can be retrieved easily. Data will be stored in different tables made up of rows and columns. However, the relationship can also be built between different tables that efficiently store huge data and effectively retrieve the selected data. This provides database operations with tremendous speed and flexibility.

As a relational database, MySQL has capabilities to establish relationships with different tables such as one to many, many to one, and one to one by providing primary keys, foreign keys, and indexes. It can also perform joins between tables to retrieve exact information such as inner joins and outer joins.

SQL is used as an interface to interact with the relational data in MySQL. SQL is an **American National Standard Institute** (**ANSI**) standard language which we can operate with data such as creation, deletion, updating, and retrieval.

License requirements of MySQL8

Many industries prefer open source technology because of the technology's flexibility and cost-saving features, while MySQL has put its footprint in the market by becoming the most popular relational database for web applications. Open source means that you can view the source of MySQL and customize it based on your needs without any cost. You can download the source or binary files from its site and use them accordingly.

The MySQL server is covered under the **General Public License** (**GNU**), which means that we can freely use it for web applications, study its source code, and modify it to suit our needs. It also has the Enterprise Edition as well with advanced features included. Many enterprises still purchase the support contract from MySQL to get assistance on various issues.

Reliability and scalability

MySQL has great reliability to perform well without requiring extensive troubleshooting due to bottlenecks or other slowdowns. It also incorporates a number of performance enhanced mechanisms such as index support, load utilities, and memory caches. MySQL uses InnoDB as a storage engine, which provides highly efficient ACID compliant transactional capabilities that assure high performance and scalability. To handle the rapidly growing database, MySQL Replication and cluster help scale out the database.

Platform compatibility

MySQL has great cross-platform availability that makes it more popular. It is flexible to run on major platforms such as RedHat, Fedora, Ubuntu, Debian, Solaris, Microsoft Windows, and Apple macOS. It also provides **Application Programming Interface** (**APIs**) to interconnect with various programming languages such as C, C++, C#, PHP, Java, Ruby, Python, and Perl.

Releases

Here is a list of major releases of MySQL so far:

- Version 5.0 GA was released on 19th October, 2005
- Version 5.1 GA was released on 14th November, 2008
- Version 5.5 GA was released on 3rd December, 2010

- Version 5.6 GA was released on 5th February, 2013
- Version 5.7 GA was released on 21st October, 2015

Now it's time for the major version release--MySQL 8--which was announced on 12th September, 2016 and is still in the development milestone mode.

Core features in MySQL

Let's look back and quickly glance through some of the core features in MySQL. We will be discussing various features throughout the book in detail as we progress.

Structured database

Structured databases are traditional databases that have been used by many enterprises for more than 40 years. However, in the modern world, data volume is becoming bigger and bigger and a common need has taken its place--data analytics. Analytics is becoming difficult with structured databases as the volume and velocity of digital data grow faster by the day; we need to find a way to achieve such needs in an effective and efficient way. The most common database that is used as a structured database in the open source world is MySQL.

Many organizations use a structured database to store their data in an organized way with the formatted repository. Basically, data in a structured database has a fixed field, a predefined data length, and defines what kind of data is to be stored such as numbers, dates, time, addresses, currencies, and so on. In short, the structure is already defined before data gets inserted, which gives a clearer idea of what data can reside there. The key advantage of using a structured database is that data being easily stored, queried, and analyzed.

An unstructured database is the opposite of this; it has no identifiable internal structure. It can have a massive unorganized agglomerate or various objects. Mainly, the source of structured data is machine-generated, which means information is generated from the machine and without human intervention, whereas unstructured data is human-generated data. Organizations use structured databases for data such as ATM transactions, airline reservations, inventory systems, and so on. In the same way, some organizations use unstructured data such as emails, multimedia content, word processing documents, web pages, business documents, and so on.

Database storage engines and types

Let's now look at an overview of different MySQL storage engines. This is an important section that gives a brief of different database storage engines; we will be discussing this in detail in Chapter 6, *MySQL 8 Storage Engines*. MySQL stores data in the database as a subdirectory. In each database, data is stored as tables. When you create a table, MySQL stores the table definition in .frm with the same name as the table name. You can use the SHOW TABLE STATUS command to show information about your table:

```
mysql> SHOW TABLE STATUS LIKE 'admin_user' \G;
*************************** 1. row ***************************
  Name: admin_user
  Engine: InnoDB
  Version: 10
  Row_format: Dynamic
  Rows: 2
  Avg_row_length: 8192
  Data_length: 16384
  Max_data_length: 0
  Index_length: 16384
  Data_free: 0
  Auto_increment: 3
  Create_time: 2017-06-19 14:46:49
  Update_time: 2017-06-19 15:15:08
  Check_time: NULL
  Collation: utf8_general_ci
  Checksum: NULL
  Create_options:
  Comment: Admin User Table
1 row in set (0.00 sec)
```

This command shows that this is an InnoDB table with the column name Engine. There is additional information that you can refer to for other purposes such as the number of rows, index length, and so on.

The storage engine is the way to handle SQL operations for different table types. Each storage engine has its own advantages and disadvantages. It is important to understand each storage engine's features and choose the most appropriate one for your tables to maximize the performance of the database. InnoDB is the default storage engine when we create a new table in MySQL 8.

The MySQL server uses a plug-and-play storage engine architecture. You can load the required storage engine and unload unnecessary storage engines from the MySQL server with the help of the SHOW ENGINES command as follows:

```
mysql> SHOW ENGINES \G;
*************************** 1. row ***************************
  Engine: InnoDB
 Support: YES
 Comment: Supports transactions, row-level locking, and foreign keys
Transactions: YES
      XA: YES
 Savepoints: YES
*************************** 2. row ***************************
  Engine: MRG_MYISAM
 Support: YES
 Comment: Collection of identical MyISAM tables
Transactions: NO
      XA: NO
 Savepoints: NO
*************************** 3. row ***************************
  Engine: MEMORY
 Support: YES
 Comment: Hash based, stored in memory, useful for temporary tables
Transactions: NO
      XA: NO
 Savepoints: NO
*************************** 4. row ***************************
  Engine: BLACKHOLE
 Support: YES
 Comment: /dev/null storage engine (anything you write to it disappears)
Transactions: NO
      XA: NO
 Savepoints: NO
*************************** 5. row ***************************
  Engine: MyISAM
 Support: DEFAULT
 Comment: MyISAM storage engine
Transactions: NO
      XA: NO
 Savepoints: NO
*************************** 6. row ***************************
  Engine: CSV
 Support: YES
 Comment: CSV storage engine
Transactions: NO
      XA: NO
 Savepoints: NO
```

```
*************************** 7. row ***************************
     Engine: ARCHIVE
    Support: YES
    Comment: Archive storage engine
Transactions: NO
         XA: NO
 Savepoints: NO
*************************** 8. row ***************************
     Engine: PERFORMANCE_SCHEMA
    Support: YES
    Comment: Performance Schema
Transactions: NO
         XA: NO
 Savepoints: NO
*************************** 9. row ***************************
     Engine: FEDERATED
    Support: NO
    Comment: Federated MySQL storage engine
Transactions: NULL
         XA: NULL
 Savepoints: NULL
9 rows in set (0.00 sec)
```

Overview of InnoDB

InnoDB is the default storage engine broadly used out of all other available storage engines. It was released with MySQL 5.1 as a plugin in 2008. MySQL 5.5 and later has InnoDB as a default storage engine. It has been taken over by Oracle Corporation in October 2005, from the Innobase Oy, which is a Finland-based company.

InnoDB tables support ACID-compliant commits, rollback, and crash recovery capabilities to protect user data. It also supports row-level locking, which helps with better concurrency and performance. It stores data in clustered indexes to reduce I/O operations for all SQL select queries based on the primary key. It also supports FOREIGN KEY constraints that allow better data integrity for the database. The maximum size of an InnoDB table can scale up to 64 TB, which should be good enough to serve many real-world use cases.

Overview of MyISAM

MyISAM was the default storage engine for MySQL prior to 5.5 1. MyISAM storage engine tables do not support ACID-compliant as opposed to InnoDB. MyISAM tables support table-level locking only, so MyISAM tables are not transaction-safe; however, they are optimized for compression and speed. It is generally used when you need to have primarily read operations with minimal transaction data. The maximum size of a MyISAM table can grow up to 256 TB, which helps in use cases such as data analytics. MyISAM supports full-text indexing, which can help in complex search operations. Using full-text indexes, we can index data stored in BLOB and TEXT data types.

Overview of memory

A memory storage engine is generally known as a heap storage engine. It is used to access data extremely quickly. This storage engine stores data in the RAM so it wouldn't need I/O operation. As it stores data in the RAM, all data is lost upon server restart. This table is basically used for temporary tables or the lookup table. This engine supports table-level locking, which limits high write concurrency.

Important notes about memory tables are as follows:

- Because memory table stores data in the RAM, which has a very limited storage capacity; if you try to write too much data into the memory table, it will start swapping data into the disk and then you lose the benefits of the memory storage engine
- These tables don't support TEXT and BLOB data types, and it is not even required as it has limited storage capacity
- This storage engine can be used to cache the results; lookup tables, for example, or postal codes and the names of states
- Memory tables support B-tree indexes and Hash indexes

Overview of archive

This storage engine is used to store large amounts of historical data without any indexes. Archive tables do not have any storage limitations. The archive storage engine is optimized for high insert operations and also supports row-level locking. These tables store data in a compressed and small format. The archive engine does not support DELETE or UPDATE operations; it only allows INSERT, REPLACE, and SELECT operations.

Overview of BLACKHOLE as a storage engine

This storage engine accepts data but does not store it. It discards data after every INSERT instead of storing it.

Now, what is the use of this storage engine; why would anybody use it? Why would we run an INSERT query that doesn't insert anything into the table?

This engine is useful for replication with large number of servers. A BLACKHOLE storage engine acts as a filter server between the master and slave server, which do not store any data, but only apply replicate-do-* and replicate-ignore-* rules and write a binlogs. These binlogs are used to perform replication in slave servers. We will discuss this in detail in Chapter 8, *Replication in MySQL 8*.

Overview of CSV

The **comma separated values** (**CSV**) engine stores data in the .csv file type using the comma-separated values format. This engine extracts data from the database and copies it to .csv out of the database. If you create a CSV file from the spreadsheet and copy it into the MYSQL data folder server, it can read the data using the select query. Similarly, if you write data in the table, an external program can read it from the CSV file. This storage engine is used for the exchange of data between software or applications. A CSV table does not support indexing and partitioning. All columns in the CSV storage engine need to be defined with the NOT NULL attribute to avoid errors during table creation.

Overview of merge

This storage engine is also known as an MRG_MyISAM storage engine. This storage engine merges a MyISAM table and creates it to be referred to a single view. For a merge table, all columns are listed in the same order. These tables are good for data warehousing environments.

The table is used to manage log-related tables, generally. You can create different months of logs in separate MyISAM tables and merge these tables using the merge storage engine.

MyISAM tables have storage limit for the operating system, but a collection of MyISAM (merge) tables do not have storage limits. So using a merge table would allow you to split data into multiple MyISAM tables, which can help in overcoming storage limits.

Merge tables do not support partitioning. Also, you cannot partition a merge table or any of a merge table's underlying `MyISAM` tables in a different partition.

Overview of federated

This storage engine allows you to create a single database on a multiple physical server. It opens a client connection to another server and executes queries against a table there, retrieving and sending rows as needed. It was originally marketed as a competitive feature that supported many enterprise-grade proprietary database servers, such as Microsoft SQL Server and Oracle, but that was always a stretch, to say the least. Although it seemed to enable a lot of flexibility and neat tricks, it has proven to be a source of many problems and is disabled by default. This storage engine is disabled by default in MySQL; to enable it, you need to start the MySQL server binary using the federated option.

Overview of the NDB cluster

NDB cluster (also known as **NDB**) is an in-memory storage engine offering high availability and data persistence features.

The NDB cluster storage engine can be configured with a range of failover and load balancing options, but it is easiest to start with the storage engine at the cluster level. NDB cluster uses the NDB storage engine that contains a complete set of data, which is dependent only on other datasets available within the cluster.

The cluster portion of the NDB cluster is configured independently of the MySQL servers. In an NDB cluster, each part of the cluster is considered to be a node.

Each storage engine has its own advantage and usability, as follows:

- **Search Engine**: NDBCluster
- **Transactions data**: `InnoDB`
- **Session data**: `MyISAM` or NDBCluster
- **Localized calculations**: Memory
- **Dictionary**: `MyISAM`

The following diagram will help you understand which store engine you need to use for your requirement:

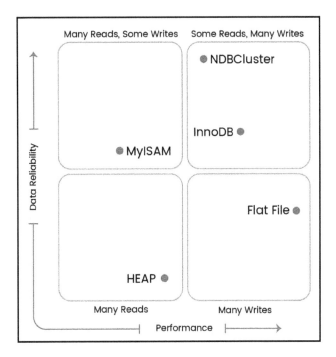

Now you have a better idea about various storage engines along with different use cases, which will help you to make a decision based on your needs.

It's time to move on to our next topic where we will look at delightful new features available in MySQL 8.

Improved features in MySQL 8

The MySQL database development team has recently announced its major release as MySQL 8 **Development Milestone Release** (**DMR**). It contains significant updates and fixes for problems that were much needed.

You might be wondering why it's 8 after 5.7! Were the intermediate versions, that is, 6 and 7, miss out? Of course not! Actually, 6.0 was preserved as part of the changeover to a more frequent and timely release, while 7.0 for the clustering version of MySQL.

Let's see some exciting features that have been introduced in this latest version, as depicted in the following diagram:

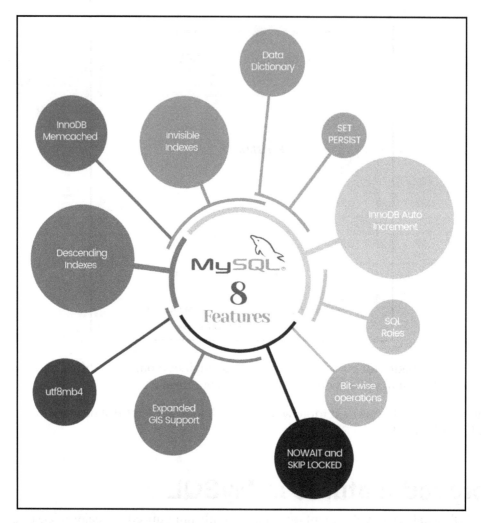

It's time to look at MySQL 8 features in detail, which makes us excited and convinced about the reasons for a major version upgrade of MySQL.

Transactional data dictionary

Up until the previous version, the MySQL data dictionary was stored in different metadata files and non-transactional tables, but from this version onwards, it will have a transactional data dictionary to store the information about the database. No more `.frm`, `.trg`, or `.par` files. All information will be stored in the database, which removes the cost of performing heavy file operations. There were numerous issues with filesystem metadata storage such as the vulnerability of the filesystem, exorbitant file operations, difficult to handle crash recovery failures, or replication; it was also difficult to add new feature-related metadata. Now this upgrade has made it simple by storing information in a centralized manner, and will have improved performance as this data dictionary object can be cached in memory, similar to other database objects.

This data dictionary will have data that is needed for SQL query execution such as catalog information, character sets, collations, column types, indexes, database information, tables, stored procedures, functions and triggers, and so on.

Roles

In MySQL 8, the privileges module has been improved by introducing roles, which means a collection of permissions. Now we can create roles with a number of privileges and assign them to multiple users.

The problem with the previous version was that we were not able to define generic permissions for a group of users and each user has individual privileges. Suppose if there are 1,000 users already existing that have common privileges, and you want to remove the write permissions for these 1,000 users, what would you have done in the previous version? You would have had to take the time-consuming approach of updating each user, right? Arrgh! That's a long, long task.

Now with MySQL 8, it is easy to update any change in privileges. Roles will define all the required privileges and this role will be assigned to those 1,000 users. We just need to make any privilege changes in the role and all users will automatically inherit the respective privileges.

Roles can be created, deleted, grant or revoke permission, grant or revoke from the user account, and can specify the default role within the current session.

InnoDB auto increment

MySQL 8 has changed the auto-increment counter value store mechanism. Previously, it was stored in the memory, which was quite difficult to manage during server restarts or server crashes. However, now the auto-increment counter value is written into the redo log whenever the value gets changed and, on each checkpoint, it will be saved in the system table, which makes it persistent across the server restart.

With the previous version, update of the auto-increment value may have caused duplicate entry errors. Suppose if you updated the value of auto-increment in the middle of the sequence with a larger than the current maximum value, but then subsequent insert operations could not identify the unused values, which could cause a duplicate entry issue. This has been prevented by persisting the auto-increment value, hence subsequent insert operations can get the new value and allocate it properly.

If server restart happened, the auto-increment value was lost with the previous version as it was stored in memory and InnoDB needed to execute a query to find out the maximum used value. This has been changed, as the newer version has the capability to persist its value across the server restart. During the server restart, InnoDB initializes the counter value in memory using the maximum value stored in the data dictionary table. In case of server crashes, InnoDB initializes the auto-increment counter value that is bigger than the data dictionary table and the redo log.

Invisible indexes

MySQL 8 provides you with a feature to make indexes invisible. These kinds of indexes cannot be used by the optimizer. In case you want to test the query performance without indexes, using this feature you can do so by making them invisible rather than dropping and re-adding an index. This is a handy feature when indexing is supposed to be dropped and recreated on huge datasets.

All indexes are visible by default. To make them invisible or visible, INVISIBLE and VISIBLE keywords are used respectively, as described in the following code snippet:

```
ALTER TABLE table1 ALTER INDEX ix_table1_col1 INVISIBLE;
ALTER TABLE table1 ALTER INDEX ix_table1_col1 VISIBLE;
```

Improving descending indexes

Descending indexes existed in version 5.7 too, but they were scanned in reverse order, which caused performance barriers. To improve performance, MySQL 8 has optimized this and scanned descending indexes in forward order, which has drastically improved performance. It also brings multiple column indexes for the optimizer when the most efficient scan order has ascending order for some columns, and descending order for other columns.

The SET PERSIST variant

Server variables can be configured globally and dynamically while the server is running. There are numerous system variables that we can set using SET GLOBAL:

```
SET GLOBAL max_connections = 1000;
```

However, such settings will be lost after server restart. To avoid this, MySQL 8 has introduced the SET PERSIST variant, which preserves variables across a server restart:

```
SET PERSIST max_connections = 1000;
```

Expanded GIS support

Until the previous version, it supported only one coordinate system, a unitless 2D place that was not referenced to a position on earth. Now MySQL 8 has added support for a **Spatial Reference System** (**SRS**) with geo-referenced ellipsoids and 2D projections. SRS helps assign coordinates to a location and establishes relationships between sets of such coordinates. This spatial data can be managed in data dictionary storage as the ST_SPATIAL_REFERENCE_SYSTEMS table.

Default character set

The default character set has been changed from latin1 to UTF8. UTF8 is the dominating character set, though it hadn't been a default one in previous versions of MySQL. Along with the character set default, collation has been changed from latin1_swedish_ci to utf8mb4_800_ci_ai. With these changes globally accepted, character sets and collations are now based on UTF8; one of the common reasons is because there are around 21 different languages supported by UTF8, which makes systems provide multilingual support.

Extended bit-wise operations

In MySQL 5.7, bit-wise operations and functions were working for BIGINT (64-bit integer) data types only. We needed to pass BIGINT as an argument and it would return the result as BIGINT. In short, it had maximum range up to 64 bits to perform operations. A user needs to do conversion to the BIGINT data type in case they want to perform it on other data types. This typecasting was not feasible for data types larger than 64 bits as it would truncate the actual value, which resulted in inaccuracy.

MySQL 8 has improved bit-wise operations by enabling support for other binary data types such as Binary, VarBinary, and BLOB. This makes it possible to perform bit-wise operations on larger than 64-bit data. No more typecasting needed! This allows the taking of arguments and returning results larger than 64 bits.

InnoDB Memcached

Multiple get operations are now possible with the InnoDB memcached plugin, which will really help in improving the read performance. Now, multiple key value pairs can be fetched in a single memcached query. Frequent communication traffic has also been minimized as we can get multiple data in a single shot.

Range queries are also supported by the InnoDB Memcached plugin. It simplifies range searches by specifying a particular range and retrieves values within this range.

NOWAIT and SKIP LOCKED

When rows are locked by other transactions that you are trying to access, then you need to wait for that transaction to release the lock on the same row so that you can access it accordingly. To avoid waiting for the other transaction, InnoDB has added support of the NOWAIT and SKIP LOCKED options. NOWAIT will return immediately with an error in case the requested row is locked rather than going into the waiting mode, and SKIP LOCKED will skip the locked row and never wait to acquire the row lock. Hence, SKIP LOCKED will not consider the locked row in the resulting set:

```
SELECT * FROM table1 WHERE id = 5 FOR UPDATE NOWAIT;
SELECT * FROM table1 FOR UPDATE SKIP LOCKED;
```

JSON

JSON support had been implemented in MySQL 5.7; it was well-acknowledged feature. In MySQL 8 it has added various functions that would allow us to get dataset results in JSON data format, virtual columns, and tentatively 15 SQL functions that allow you to search and use JSON data on server side. In MySQL8 there are additional aggregation functions added that can be used in JSON objects/arrays to represent loaded data in a further optimized way. The following are the two JSON aggregation functions that were introduced in MySQL8:

- JSON_OBJECTAGG()
- JSON_ARRAYAGG()

Cloud

In MySQL 8 a new option is introduced `innodb_dedicated_server`, which would be helpful for vertical scaling of the servers. It actually automatically detects the memory allocated to the virtual server and appropriately set MySQL 8 without any need to change configuration files. These would be very handy features considering the adoption of virtualization and cloud is there. In fact with this configuration, you might not even need to get shell access of server to edit the configuration files. You can do this with the new `SET PERSIST` feature that can set relevant configuration from the MySQL command line itself, which can enhance security further as you almost wouldn't need shell access of the server.

Resource management

MySQL 8 has come up with a wonderful resource management feature that will allow you to allocate resource to threads running on a server, which would be executed based on the resources configured for the group. Currently, CPU time is a resource that can be configured for a group. With this, you can tweak your workloads with virtual resource management within MySQL itself. MySQL will identify on startup numbers of virtual CPUs available and after that users with appropriate privileges can map the virtual CPUs with resource group and align thread management to these groups.

We expect to see more features by the time MySQL 8 is available for general use. Let us now look at benefits of using MySQL 8.

Benefits of using MySQL 8

Whether you are a developer or an enterprise, you would obviously choose one that provides good benefits and results when compared to other related products. MySQL provides numerous advantages as the first choice in this competitive market. It has various powerful features available that make it a more comprehensive database. Let's now go through some benefits of using MySQL.

Security

The first thing that comes to mind is securing data because nowadays data has become precious and can impact business continuity if legal obligations are not met; in fact, it can be so bad that it can close down your business in no time. MySQL is the most secure and reliable database management system used by many well-known enterprises such as Facebook, Twitter, and Wikipedia. It really provides a good security layer that protects sensitive information from intruders. MySQL gives access control management so that granting and revoking required access from the user is easy. Roles can also be defined with a list of permissions that can be granted or revoked for the user. All user passwords are stored in an encrypted format using plugin-specific algorithms.

Scalability

Day by day, the mountain of data is growing because of extensive use of technology in numerous ways. Because of this, load average is going through the roof. In some cases, it is unpredictable that data cannot exceed up to some limit or number of users will not go out of bounds. Scalable databases would be a preferable solution so that, at any point, we can meet unexpected demands to scale. MySQL is a rewarding database system for its scalability, which can scale horizontally and vertically; in terms of data, spreading database and load of application queries across multiple MySQL servers is quite feasible. It is pretty easy to add horsepower to the MySQL cluster to handle the load.

An open source relational database management system

MySQL is an open source database management system that makes debugging, upgrading, and enhancing the functionality fast and easy. You can view the source and make the changes accordingly and use it in your own way. You can also distribute an extended version of MySQL, but you will need to have a license for this.

High performance

MySQL gives high-speed transaction processing with optimal speed. It can cache the results, which boosts read performance. Replication and clustering make the system scalable for more concurrency and manages the heavy workload. Database indexes also accelerate the performance of SELECT query statements for substantial amount of data. To enhance performance, MySQL 8 has included indexes in performance schema to speed up data retrieval.

High availability

Today, in the world of competitive marketing, an organization's key point is to have their system up and running. Any failure or downtime directly impacts business and revenue; hence, high availability is a factor that cannot be overlooked. MySQL is quite reliable and has constant availability using cluster and replication configurations. Cluster servers instantly handle failures and manage the failover part to keep your system available almost all the time. If one server gets down, it will redirect the user's request to another node and perform the requested operation.

Cross-platform capabilities

MySQL provides cross-platform flexibility that can run on various platforms such as Windows, Linux, Solaris, OS2, and so on. It has great API support for the all major languages, which makes it very easy to integrate with languages such as PHP, C++, Perl, Python, Java, and so on. It is also part of the **Linux Apache MySQL PHP** (**LAMP**) server that is used worldwide for web applications.

It's now time to get our hands dirty and look at MySQL 8; let's start with the installation of MySQL 8 on a Linux platform in our case. We prefer MySQL 8 on a Linux operating system as that has been a common use case across many organizations. We will be discussing more installation in Chapter 2, *Installing and Upgrading MySQL 8*. You can use it on other platforms that MySQL supports, such as Windows, Solaris, HP-UNIX, and so on. Linux provides various ways to install the MySQL server, as follows:

- RPM package
- YUM repository
- APT repository
- SLES repository
- Debian package
- TAR package
- Compiling and installing from the source code

Limitations of MySQL 8

A coin has two sides; similarly, benefits of also using MySQL 8 would come along with a few limitations. Let us walk through a few areas of MySQL 8 now.

Number of tables or databases

The number of databases or tables are not a limitation for MySQL 8; however, the operating system file limit can be a limitation for MySQL 8. Storage Engine InnoDB is allowed to scale up to four billion tables as its peak number.

Table size

You may hit maximum table size limit, which is not restricted from MySQL 8; however, it may be because of operating system filesystem limits.

Joins

In a single join, one can use 61 tables, which can be referred. It is also applicable to the tables that are referenced in view definition. Joins that are part of subqueries and views are also considered to be part of the limitation.

Windows platform

There are few limitations when you have MySQL 8 used on the Windows platform:

- **Memory**: 32-bit architecture has limitation to use only 2 GB of RAM for a process.
- **Ports**: In case you have a high number of concurrency you might come across Windows platform limitation of having 4000 ports available for client connections in total.
- **Case-insensitivity**: The Windows platform doesn't have case sensitivity, which is why tables and databases need to be deliberately managed for case-insensitivity.
- **Pipes**: |, generally referred as pipe signs, they are not fully supported in Windows. You might come across them in a few scenarios while doing database administration activities.
- **Pathname separator**: MySQL 8 escape character is \, which is the pathname separator for Windows. Hence while using path separator you can double slash as "\ \" as an alternative for a pathname separator.

Table column count

The table column for each table in MySQL 8 has a limit of 4096 columns. It might vary based on a few other factors for columns count limit, as stated in the following section.

Row size

MySQL tables have a limit of 65,535 bytes for a row, although storage engines such as `InnoDB` are capable of supporting larger chunks.

InnoDB storage engine

Limitations on InnoDB storage engine are what we will talk about a bit more specifically as InnoDB now with MySQL 8 will play a prominent role.

Limitations of InnoDB storage engine

We will have a quick glance at a few of the limitations of InnoDB storage engine:

- The number of indexes supported can be maximum 64 for a table
- For tables that use compressed or dynamic row format; 3072 is the index key prefix length limit
- For tables that use compact or redundant row format; 767 is the index key prefix length limit
- Total columns in a table, which includes virtual generated columns, are limited to a maximum of 1,017
- 16 columns is the maximum permitted for multi-column indexes
- The combined InnoDB log file size cannot exceed 512 GB
- Maximum table size supported by InnoDB is 256 TB
- AdminAPI is not supported while using unix socket connections
- Multi-byte characters might give you unreliable aligned columns while formatting of results in InnoDB clusters

Restrictions

We will now have a quick glance at a few of the restrictions of the InnoDB storage engine:

- Delete from tablename: It doesn't actually delete the complete table, instead it deletes each row of the table one after another.
- Show table status: It wouldn't provide you accurate data all the time; it provides estimates.
- When counting rows, the number of rows provided by count(*) is not accurate because of concurrency; it would count only those counts visible to transactions currently available.
- If there is multiple analyze table queries executed, later one will be blocked until the first one gets completed.

- InnoDB keeps an exclusive lock on the index at the end associated with the auto_increment column.
- In a case the auto_increment integer runs out of the value; the following insert operations would show us duplicate-key errors.
- Foreign keys that are cascaded cannot activate triggers.
- There are a few column names reserved by MySQL that InnoDB uses for internal purposes. The following are a few such column names:
  - DB_ROW_ID
  - DB_TRX_ID
  - DB_ROLL_PTR
  - DB_MIX_ID

We might come across output shown in the following example in case of such reserved column names used:

```
mysql> CREATE TABLE chintan (c1 INT, db_row_id INT)
  ENGINE=INNODB;
ERROR 1166 (42000): Incorrect column name 'db_row_id'
```

- InnoDB locks are released immediately after the transaction is aborted or committed, which is held by a transaction.
- The addition of table locks are not supported, as locks are implicit to commit and unlock tables

Data dictionary

Let us have a look at a few known limitations of data dictionary:

- Individual MyISAM tables for backup and restore are not supported by merely copying the files.
- Manually created directories for databases are not supported by MySQL 8. For instance, using mkdir would have no impact on MySQL server data dictionary.
- DDL operations would take more time than expected because such operations are written to storage, undo logs and redo instead of .frm files as what we would have seen in prior versions of MySQL.

Limitations of group replication in MySQL8

It's now time to discuss a few limitations of group replication in MySQL 8:

- **Large transactions**: Transactions that result to GTID contents cannot be replicated between the rest of the members of the group if they're too large. It is suggested to use smaller chunks of data that cannot be replicated in around five seconds to group members to avoid failures.
- **Cluster from a group**: If you try to create clusters from an existing group replication setup it will result in an error as the instance would already be part of a replication group. This is noticed currently only in MySQL's wizard mode only; an alternative solution for the issue is to disable wizard mode.
- **Serializable isolation level**: Serializable isolation level is not supported when multi-primary groups are used, which is the default configuration.
- **DDL and DML operations**: If there is concurrent DDL and DML operations executed against the same data object but on different servers is not supported when multi-primary group mode is used.
- **Replication checksum**: Currently MySQL design limitations create restrictions of having replication event checksums.

Limitations of partitioning

We will be discussing limitations of partitioning in this section.

Constructs prohibition

The following are the constructs that are not allowed in expressions of partitions:

- Declared variables
- User variables
- Stored procedures
- Stored functions
- UDFs
- Plugins

Operators

There are a few operators that are not permitted in partition expressions such as << , >> , | , & , ~ and ^ . Results for arithmetic operators such as +, −, and * must have an integer value or NULL.

Tables

The following are a few specific areas that show us limitations of partitioning on tables:

- The maximum number of partitions supported by MySQL 8 for a table is 8192. This limit also considers sub-partitions.
- Fulltext index and search is not supported on partitioned tables.
- Tables that are temporary cannot be partitioned.
- Log tables can't be partitioned.
- Foreign keys are not supported on partitioned InnoDB storage engine.
- The data type of partition keys should be an integer column or can be an expression to an integer. Expression or column values may be NULL; however, expressions that include ENUM are not supported.
- Upgrading partitioned tables that have been partitioned by KEY would have to be reloaded, which stands true other than the InnoDB storage engine.

We have so far discussed overview, features, benefits, and a few limitations of MySQL. Let us now walk through the wonderful use cases of MySQL.

Use cases of MySQL

MySQL has many advantages because it has its foot in many industries and various use cases across the globe. The importance of MySQL doesn't depend only on how much data you have, it's rather what you are going to do with the data. Data can be sourced and analyzed from unpredictable sources and can be used to address many things.

Let's now look at use cases with real-life importance made on renowned scenarios with the help of MySQL:

The preceding figure helps us understand where MySQL is serving various industries. Though it's not an extensive list of industries where MySQL has been playing a prominent role in business decisions, let's now discuss a few of the industries.

Social media

Social media content is information, and so are engagements such as views, likes, demographics, shares, follows, unique visitors, comments, and downloads. At the end of the day, what matters is how your social media-related efforts contribute to the business.

One notable example is Facebook, where MySQL had been used extensively. On top of MySQL where petabytes of data was used to serve likes, shares, and comments. Facebook has developed the `RocksDB` storage engine on top of the MySQL `InnoDB` storage engine, which leverages many advantages of InnoDB storage engine as Facebook wanted to primarily focus on storage optimization. Though currently MySQL is still used largely for other common applications.

Government

The era of MySQL has been playing a significant role in government too; government bodies have been using MySQL extensively because of splendid return on investments and promoting open source. In fact, the government sector is carrying out a huge number of implementations of MySQL worldwide.

This may come as a surprise to you; US Navy uses MySQL for its critical flight planning activities. There are various activities such as weather conditions, flight plans, fuel efficiency, maintenance of flights, and many more that are being tracked with the help of MySQL as the database. It's a no-brainer that it needs to run 24x7 with full redundancy; MySQL was able to achieve this serving US Navy aircraft across the globe.

Media and entertainment

YouTube is also one of the prominent users of MySQL. Anytime you watch a video on YouTube it gets data from a relational database or a blob store using MySQL. YouTube also uses Vitess; a project that was released by YouTube to frontend MySQL. Vitess helps to do lots of optimization and acts as a proxy to serve each database request using MySQL. MySQL replicas are heavily used in YouTube's implementation; leveraging MySQL caching was one of the other prominent factors for YouTube.

Fraud detection

When it comes to security, fraud detection, or compliance, and precisely if your solution helps you in identifying and preventing issues before they strike, then it becomes a sweet spot for business. Most of the time, fraud detection takes place a long time after the fraud has occurred, when you might have already suffered loss. The next steps would be obviously to minimize the impact of fraud and improve areas that could help you prevent this from being repeated.

Many companies who are into any type of transaction processing or claims use fraud detection techniques extensively. MySQL helps to analyze transactions, claims, and so on in real time, along with trends or anomalous behavior to prevent fraudulent activities.

PayPal is one of such use cases that has built fraud detection system using MySQL. PayPal has more than 100 million active users, which is distributed to US, Japanese, and European data centers. High-availability for such use cases is a key criteria along with performance, which MySQL has been able to deliver as expected.

Business mapping

Netflix has millions of subscribers; it uses MySQL for running its billing systems. The core billing system of Netflix on MySQL is a prominent backbone for any business. Netflix has billions of rows of data concurrently updated and of consisting data since its inception two decades ago. Compliance was one of the key factors along with migration from Oracle with minimal downtime; both of these were achieved with MySQL and has been expanding tremendously every other day.

E-commerce

Uber is one of the other well-known customers of MySQL. Uber had been growing enormously worldwide, and scalability, high-availability, and return on investments were a few of the important criteria to be worked upon. Uber uses MySQL as its primary database for its known private car transportation service. Uber heavily uses schema less database architecture as its backend as a layer on MySQL.

There are many real-world MySQL use cases that have changed humanity, technology, predictions, health, science and research, law and order, sports, e-commerce, power and energy, financial trading, robotics, and many more. MySQL is an integral part of our daily routine, which is not evident all the time, but yes, it plays a significant role in what we do in many ways.

Summary

In this chapter, we started with an overview of MySQL along with major features of the MySQL database and explored the newly added features in MySQL 8. After this, we took a deep dive into exciting new features of MySQL 8 along with benefits of using MySQL for your business applications. We understood MySQL 8's current limitations and restrictions, which is important for us when performing the implementations. Finally, we glanced through a few impressive use cases from the real world that play prominent roles in our daily routine, and they all use MySQL as their database.

In the next chapter, we will learn detailed steps for installing MySQL 8 on different platforms. The chapter also covers methods to upgrade or downgrade from MySQL 8, and they will all be discussed in detail.

2
Installing and Upgrading MySQL 8

In the previous chapter, we provided an overview of MySQL along with MySQL 8's new features, use cases, and limitations. MySQL is very flexible in terms of platforms, such as RedHat, Fedora, Ubuntu, Debian, Solaris, Microsoft Windows, and so on. It has the support of an API to connect with different languages, such as C, C++, C#, PHP, Java, Ruby, and many more. For any programming platform, the most important and monotonous task is to set up the environment with the necessary software tools. That won't be the case for MySQL 8, as this chapter is focused on setting up the environment with MySQL 8.

This chapter explains MySQL 8's installation steps in detail with the necessary prerequisites. Separate installation steps are provided to set up MySQL 8 on various platforms. The chapter also covers methods to upgrade to or downgrade from MySQL 8.

We will cover the following topics in this chapter:

- The MySQL 8 installation process
- Post-installation setup for MySQL 8
- MySQL 8 upgrading
- MySQL 8 downgrading

The MySQL 8 installation process

This section will guide readers in MySQL 8 version selection, where to get MySQL 8 from, and how to install MySQL 8. It also explains the post-installation steps required for setup. This chapter provides information on how to upgrade or downgrade from MySQL 8.

General installation guide

MySQL 8 is available on many operating systems with different versions. The MySQL 8 release is managed in two ways:

- **Development release**: This has the newest feature but is not recommended for use in production
- **General release**: This is a stable release and users can use it for release in production also

Naming conventions are followed in each release of MySQL 8, which indicates its status. Each release name consists of three digits and an optional suffix. For example, **mysql.8.1.2-rc**. The numbers are interpreted as follow:

- The first number (**8**) indicates a major version of the release.
- The second number (**1**) indicates a minor version of the release. A combination of major and minor numbers describes the series of the release.
- The third number (**2**) indicates the version within the release series. It is incremented on each bug fix release.

The most recent version of the release is the most preferable for use. The suffix given in the example indicates the stability of the MySQL 8 release. The MySQL 8 release follows three suffixes:

- **Development Milestone Release** (**dmr**): MySQL 8 follows the milestone model, where each milestone indicates thoroughly tested features.
- **Release Candidate** (**rc**): A new feature might get released in this version but the aim is to fix bugs within the previously released features.
- **Absence of a suffix**: This indicates **General Availability** (**GA**) or production release. This release is stable and passed through earlier stages. It is reliable and suitable for use in production.

As described, preceding each release is the DMR, followed by the RC, and finally the GA release status. Now, after deciding the MySQL 8 version for the installation, it's time to select the distribution format.

The binary distribution is recommended for general-purpose use. It is available in native formats for many platforms. For example, the RPM package for Linux and DMG package for OS X.

Downloading MySQL 8

To get MySQL 8 from the official site, refer to the following URL: `http://dev.mysql.com/downloads/`. MySQL also provides a mirror site: `http://dev.mysql.com/downloads/mirrors.html`. When you reach the download page, you can see the version selection tab at the bottom side of the page, where two tabs are displayed:

- **Generally Available (GA)** release
- Development release

Based on the previous section, select the suitable version from the list and click on the **Download** button.

Verifying the package integrity

This is a stage where the downloaded package is available and ready for the installation. It's an optional step, but we recommend it to avoid errors during the installation process. There are three different ways available to check integrity:

- Using MD5 checksums
- Using cryptographic signatures
- Using the RPM integrity verification mechanism

Using MD5 checksums

This is the simplest way to check integrity and requires little effort. The MySQL download page itself provides an MD5 checksum, which is unique for each MySQL product. After downloading MySQL 8, we just have to make sure that the checksum of the downloaded file matches with the checksum provided on the download page. There are many tools available for different operating systems to compare checksums. Here, we are providing an example of MD5 checksums using the command line and using one graphical tool, named winMD5Sum, for the Windows operating system.

Perform the following steps for the command line execution:

1. Download the utility from `http://www.fourmilab.ch/md5/`
2. Unzip the file under `E:\Softwares` location

3. Go to the command line and execute the following command:

```
E:\Softwares\md5>md5.exe
E:\Softwares\mysql-installer-community-5.7.19.0.msi
2578BFC3C30273CEE42D77583B8596B5
E:\Softwares\mysql-installer-community-5.7.19.0.msi
```

Perform the following steps for the graphical tool execution:

1. Open the link: http://www.nullriver.com/index/products/winmd5sum.

2. Click on the **Download WinMD5Sum** option on the page. It will download winMD5Sum.exe on to your computer.

3. Run the downloaded Install-winMD5Sum.exe and install it on your local machine.

4. After successful installation, open the **winMD5Sum** tool. This opens one dialog box where you have to select the downloaded MySQL.msi file.

5. Click on the **calculate** button. This will calculate the MD5 checksum of the downloaded file.

6. Enter the MD5 checksum available on the MySQL download page in the **compare text** box and press the **compare** button.

Using cryptographic signatures

This technique of integrity verification requires a public GPG build key. This key is available from the http://pgp.mit.edu/ URL. Once the build key is downloaded, you have to perform the following steps:

1. Import the build key
2. Download the desired MySQL 8 package and its related signatures from the MySQL site

 Make sure the MySQL package name and its downloaded signature file name are the same. Both the files must be placed under one common storage location.

3. Now, its time to execute the following command for verification:

```
cmd> gpg --verify package_name.asc
```

For Microsoft Windows, some GUI tools also available for integrity checks. One of the most popular is `Gpg4win`. To perform the same check on Linux, we have commands available because the RPM package itself contains a GPG signature and MD5 checksum. Execute the following command to verify the package:

```
cmd> rpm --checksig package_name.rpm
```

This technique of verification is more reliable than the MD5 checksum but it is very complex and requires more effort for integrity checks.

Installing MySQL 8 on Microsoft Windows

MySQL is available for both 32-bit and 64-bit versions. There are different ways available to install MySQL 8 on Microsoft Windows. The most common approach is to use an installer, which installs and configures MySQL 8 on your local system.

 Before installing MySQL Community 8.0 Server, make sure that the Microsoft Visual C++ 2015 redistributable package has been installed on the system.

MySQL 8 either runs as a standard application or runs as a Windows service. Use it, as the service enables users to control and measure operations using the Windows service management tool. Three major distribution formats are available for each platform:

- **Installer distribution**: This includes the MySQL 8 server along with other products such as MySQL Workbench, MySQL for Excel, and MySQL Notifier. An installer is also useful for upgrading products into other versions.
- **Source distribution**: As the name implies, this contains all the source code along with all the supported files. The Visual Studio compiler is required to make it executable.
- **Binary distribution**: This distribution is available in ZIP file format. It contains all the required files except the installer. The user has to unpack the file into a selected directory.

Windows-specific considerations

Before installing MySQL 8 on Microsoft Windows consider following points:

- **Antivirus software**: As we know, antivirus software uses the fingerprinting technique, which will consider rapidly changed files as a potential security risk. In MySQL 8, there are some directories that contain MySQL 8 related data and temporary tables information and are updated frequently. So, there is a possibility that antivirus software will consider those files as spam. This will also impact performance.

  Antivirus software provides configurations to exclude some of the directories, so it is recommended to exclude the MySQL 8 data directory and temp directory. MySQL 8, by default, stores temporary data into a Microsoft Windows temporary directory. To change this default configuration in MySQL 8, refer to `my.ini` file's `tempdir` parameter.

- **Large table support**: Use MySQL 8 on NTFS or any new filesystem to support large tables whose size is more than 4 GB. For these larger tables, the user has to define the `MAX_ROWS` and `AVG_ROW_LENGTH` properties at the time of table creation.

MySQL 8 installation layout

Microsoft Windows, by default, considers the `C:\Program Files` directory for the MySQL 8 installation. However, we have a choice for the directory selection at the time of installation. Whatever the location of the installation, the subdirectory structure after installation remains same. For the Microsoft Window layout, refer to the following table:

Directory	Contents of Directory	Notes
`bin`	**mysqld** server, client and utility programs	
`%PROGRAMDATA%\MySQL\MySQL Server 8.0\`	Log files, databases	The Windows system variable `%PROGRAMDATA%` defaults to `C:\ProgramData`
`examples`	Example programs and scripts	

include	Include (`header`) files	
lib	Libraries	
share	Miscellaneous support files, including error messages, character set files, sample configuration files, SQL for database installation	

You can learn more about this topic at `https://dev.mysql.com/doc/refman/8.0/en/windows-installation-layout.html`.

Choosing the right installation package

There are multiple options available for package formats while installing MySQL 8 on Windows. MySQL provides a facility to debug the installation process using **program database (pdb)** files. These files are available in a ZIP distribution:

- **The installer package**: This is a wizard-based process and is easy to use. The installer package is available for 32-bits only but can install MySQL 8 on the 64-bit configuration also. It does not contain the debugging component of MYSQL; we have to download it separately in the form of a ZIP file. The installer package is available in two different formats:
    - **Web Community**: As the name implies, this is available for web installation. It means the Internet is required for the installation using the web community. Its size is approx 19 MB. Its name is defined as MySQL-installer-community by the appending version.
    - **Community**: This package format is used for offline installation. Its size is approx 301 MB. Its name is defined as MySQL-installer-web-community by the appending version.

An installer is the most common way for MySQL product installation and upgrade.

- **The Noinstall Archives**: This is a manual installation process that contains files for the incomplete installation package. As it is a manual process, no GUI is available. The user has to manually install and configure MySQL 8 and other products if required. Unlike the installer, it provides two different files for 32-bit and 64-bit configuration in a ZIP format.

The MySQL 8 installer

The MySQL 8 installer is mainly used to reduce the complexity of the installation process along with the management of MySQL products running on the Windows platform. In the product list, we can consider:

- MySQL servers
- MySQL applications
- MySQL connectors
- Documentation and samples

The MySQL 8 installer has two editions :

- **Community Edition**: This can be downloaded at `http://dev.mysql.com/downloads/installer/`. As described in previous section, both Web Community and Community package formats are available for the installer.

- **Commercial Edition**: Refer to `https://edelivery.oracle.com/` to download the Commercial Edition. The Commercial Edition contains all the products that are available in the Community Edition along with the following products:
  - Workbench SE/EE
  - MySQL Enterprise backup
  - MySQL Enterprise firewall

Initial setup information

As mentioned previously, the installer will guide a user through the wizard. Once we start the installer in our host machine it will detect already installed MySQL products and consider them in a list of products to be managed. The following are the steps that are required in the initial setup of the installer:

1. **MySQL installer licensing and support authentication**: This is the step where the user must accept the license agreement before starting the MySQL 8 installation. After accepting the terms, the user is allowed to add, update, or remove MySQL products. In the Commercial Edition, credentials are required to unbundle products and must match with the user's Oracle account in the support site.

2. **Choosing a setup type**: This is the step where the user must select MySQL products for installation. The installer also provides the option of a predefined setup, which contains a set of MySQL products. So, you have the flexibility of selecting one setup type as per your requirements. The following are some setups available in the installer.

3. **Developer default**: This installs the version of MySQL 8 server that was selected at the time of download:
   - MySQL server
   - MySQL shell
   - MySQL router
   - MySQL Workbench
   - MySQL for Visual Studio
   - MySQL for Excel
   - MySQL notifier
   - MySQL connectors
   - MySQL utilities
   - MySQL documentation
   - MySQL samples and examples

4. **Server only:** This installs only the MySQL server.

5. **Client only**: This is the same as the developer default setup type, except it does not contain the MySQL 8 server or any client-specific package added to it.

6. **Full**: This installs all the available products of MySQL, such as `mysql-server`, `mysql-client`, `mysqladmin`, and a few more.

7. **Custom**: This option installs only those products that are selected by the user from the catalog. Here, the user has the freedom to choose only the required products, rather than installing the complete bundle of products.

8. **Path conflicts**: When the hosting system already contains a MySQL product and the user is trying to install a different version of that MySQL product on the same path, then the installer will show a path conflict error in the wizard. The installer enables the user to take action on the path conflict in the following ways:
   - Choose a different location using the **Browse** button from the wizard
   - Choose a different setup type or version by custom selection
   - Overwrite the existing folder by moving on to the next step
   - Cancel the wizard steps, delete existing products, and start the installer again

9. **Check requirements**: Each MySQL product has a `package-rules.xml` file attached to it, which contains all the prerequisite software lists. During the initial setup, the installer will check the availability of the required software and prompt the user to update the host in case of missing requirements.

10. **MySQL installer configuration files**: The installer configuration files are located at `C:\Program Files`. The following are the configuration file details:

File or Folder	Description	Folder Hierarchy
MySQL installer for Windows	This folder contains all of the files needed to run MySQL installer and `MySQLInstallerConsole.exe`, a command-line program with similar functionality.	`C:\Program Files (x86)`
Templates	The `Templates` folder has one file for each version of MySQL server. `Templates` files contain keys and formulas to calculate some values dynamically.	`C:\ProgramData\MySQL\MySQL installer for Windows\Manifest`
`package-rules.xml`	This file contains the prerequisites for every product to be installed.	`C:\ProgramData\MySQL\MySQL installer for Windows\Manifest`

`produts.xml`	The `products` file (or product catalog) contains a list of all products available for download.	`C:\ProgramData\MySQL\MySQL installer for Windows\Manifest`
`Product Cache`	The `Product Cache` folder contains all standalone `MSI` files bundled with the full package or downloaded afterward.	`C:\ProgramData\MySQL\MySQL installer for Windows`

Reference: `https://dev.mysql.com/doc/refman/8.0/en/mysql-installer-setup.html`

Installation workflow

The MySQL installer follows a workflow for each product:

1. **Product download**: The installer will download all the required product MSI files into the `Product Cache` folder.
2. **Product installation**: The installer manages the status of each product by **Ready** | **Install** | **Installing** | **Complete**.
3. **Product configuration**: This phase uses a step-by-step configuration process for products. The installer will change the status from **Ready** | **Configure**.
4. **Installation complete**: This finalizes the installation and the user can start using the application after the installation.

InnoDB cluster sandbox test setup

There are two options available for high-availability implementation in MySQL 8, using the installer:

- **Standalone MySQL server / Classic MySQL replication (default)**: This option configures multiple servers manually or uses the latest version of MySQL Shell to configure the `InnoDB` cluster.
- **InnoDB cluster sandbox test setup (for testing only)**: This is also known as the sandbox cluster. This option allows you to create an `InnoDB` cluster on the local system for testing only. The MySQL installer toolbar provides configurations for a number of instances in `InnoDB` clustering.

Cluster nodes run on different ports. After configuration, click on the **Summary** tab to get the port details of each cluster.

Server configuration

The MySQL installer performs some basic configurations for the MySQL 8 server, including:

- The installer will create a `my.ini` configuration file for the MySQL 8 server. File contents will be decided as per the selected options of the **installation process**.
- By default, the installer will add the Windows service for the MySQL 8 server.
- The required default installation and data paths of the MySQL 8 server will be provided by the installer.
- The installer will create some user accounts with roles and permissions for MySQL 8 server. It can create a Windows user with limited privileges to the MySQL 8 server.
- Using **Show Advanced Options,** MySQL installer allows for defining custom paths for logging options. For example, you can configure the separate path for an error log, show a query log, and much more.

The following server configuration is required for MySQL 8:

- **Server configuration type**: Based on the server configuration type, system resources will be assigned to the MySQL 8 server.
- **Development**: By considering the host as a personal workstation, it configures MySQL 8 to use the minimum amount of memory.
- **Server**: As servers, some other applications are also running on the machine, so it will configure a medium amount of memory.
- **Dedicated**: In case of a dedicated machine for the MySQL 8 server, this option configures the maximum use of available memory for the MySQL 8 server.
- **Connectivity**: This option indicates the connection for the MySQL 8 server. The following options are available:
    - **TCP/IP**: This option enables TCP/IP connection with MySQL 8. Users are allowed to define the port number along with the firewall setting for the port on the network access.
    - **Named pipe**: This option allows you to define the pipeline name for the connection.
    - **Shared memory**: This allows you to define the memory name for the MySQL 8 server.
- **Advanced configuration**: This configuration enables additional logging features which will manage logs in individual files. Users are allowed to configure paths for individual files. For example, configuring a custom path for a binary log.

- **MySQL Enterprise Firewall**: This option is used for the Commercial Edition only. Check the **Enable Enterprise Firewall** option to enable the firewall.
- **Accounts and roles:** Accounts and roles are used to manage access rights for the users. During the installation process, the MySQL installer allows you to set root account passwords and user accounts.
    - **Root account password**: It is required to enter root password during the installation process. The installer will check the password strength and give a warning if there is a violation of a predefined policy.
    - **MySQL user accounts**: This is an optional step where a new MySQL user account defines with existing user roles. Predefined roles have their own privileges.
- **Windows service:** The MySQL 8 service can be configured in the following two ways:
    - **Configure as a Window service**: This is the default option selected during the installation process. It further provides two options:
        - **Start service on system startup**: This option is selected by default and will start the MySQL 8 service automatically at system startup.
        - **Run Window service as**: This option allows attaching the user account with the MySQL 8 service. By default, the system account is selected where the service is considered as network service. With a custom user, it first sets privileges for the user by using the "local security policy" in Microsoft Windows.
    - **Configure as an executable program**: This deselects the Windows Service option during the installation process.
- **Plugins and extensions**: This step is available for a new installation. If the user wants to upgrade from an older MySQL version, then the user needs to choose the **Reconfigure** option in the MySQL installer.
- **Advance options**: To enable this option, select the **Show advance configuration** check box in the **Type and Networking** step. This option enables the user to define a specific path for log files, such as an error log, a general log, a slow query log, and bin log.

- **Apply server configuration**: Once all the configuration has been done by the user in the MySQL installer, click on the **Execute** button to make it available. When the installation has been completed by pressing the **Finish** button, the MySQL installer and all the MySQL installed products are available in the Windows Start menu.

MySQL installer product catalog and dashboard

This section contains details on how the **MySQL installer** handles product catalogs and manages dashboards.

The **product catalog** is a component where a list of all the released MySQL products is available, which support Microsoft Windows. The MySQL installer updates the catalog on a daily basis and the option is also available for the manual update of the catalog. The product catalog performs the following actions to manage the list:

- Populate the available products list on a regular basis
- Check for the product's update as installed in the host

The product catalog lists all the products that are available in the development, general, or any minor release.

The **MySQL installer dashboard** provides the facility to manage MySQL products installation in the host workstation. The following are the ways to manage products using the dashboard:

- The MySQL installer provides a configuration to update the catalog at specific time intervals. The user can enable or disable automatic updates by the configuration. The dashboard shows a special icon at the product level when its new version is available.
- The user can manage products with the following actions:
  - **Add**: Use to download and install one or more products.
  - **Modify**: Use to add or remove features in installed products.
  - **Upgrade**: Use to upgrade products. Make sure the checkbox is selected at the product level for upgrading in the **upgradeable products** pane.
  - **Remove**: Use to uninstall products from the populated list.
- The dashboard provides the reconfiguration feature, where the user can change already configured options and values. After applying changes, the MySQL installer will stop the MySQL 8 server and restart it again to make them available.

- The dashboard provides the facility to download the products catalog without upgrading it. The **Do not update at this time** checkbox is available to check current changes related to products without downloading. To perform this functionality, select the checkbox and click on the **catalog** link.

MySQL installer console

The MySQL installer includes the `MySQLinstallerConsole.exe` file, which provides the functionality to execute commands using Command Prompt. This functionality is installed by default during the initial installation of the MySQL installer. There are some commands available to manage MySQL products. To see the details of these commands, execute the `help` command.

MySQL 8 installation using a ZIP file

To install MySQL 8 using a ZIP archive, perform the following steps:

1. **Extract install archive**: In this step, select a specific directory for the extraction of the installed MySQL 8 archive. Microsoft Windows by default installs it into the `c:\mysql` location. At the time of the installation process, make sure the logged in user has administrative rights.

Make sure no MySQL service is running during the installation of MySQL as a Window service.
During the command execution type -- install first and then specify -- default –file option; otherwise, the `mysqld.exe` file will start the MySQL 8 server.

2. **Create option file**: The option file is the place where the user can configure commands related to MySQL 8. This file is referred to by MySQL 8 on every server startup. In Microsoft Windows, when the MySQL 8 server starts, it searches for an option file in the Windows directory and in the MySQL 8 base directory. Mainly `my.ini` and `my.cnf` files are used as option files and they are in plain text form.

With the Windows operating system:

1. To get `Windows` directory, refer to the `WINDIR` environment variable.
2. `my.ini` is available at the default location of MySQL server installation.
3. Path names in options file are specified using forward slashes rather than backslashes. If you want to use backslashes then double them.

As mentioned, the option file is the same as a normal text file; the user can modify it using any text editor. Consider an example where the MySQL 8 installation directory and data directory are at different locations. In this case, the user must mention the location of both the directories in the options file under the `mysqld` section:

```
[mysqld]
# set basedir to your installation path
basedir=E:\\mysql
# set datadir to the location of your data directory
datadir=E:\\mydata\\data
```

Remember, a ZIP archive does not initialize data directory. To initialize data directory and populate tables in the MySQL 8 system database, the user has to execute the `initialize` command. This process will be covered in the later section on post-installation.

3. **Select server type**: The following two servers are available for Microsoft Windows in MySQL 8:

Binary	Description
mysqld	Optimized binary with named-pipe support
mysqld-debug	Like mysqld, but compiled with full debugging and automatic memory allocation checking

MySQL 8 supports TCP/IP on all Microsoft Windows platforms with pipes. But the default option is in normal mode because the pipes option has a performance impact. It slows down the overall performance. You can learn more about this at: https://dev.mysql.com/doc/refman/8.0/en/windows-select-server.html.

4. **Start MySQL 8 server**: This step describes how to start the MySQL 8 server for the first time. It can be started using the command line or as a Windows service. To start it using the command line, execute the following command. Assume that MySQL 8 is installed under the E:\MySQL\MySQL Server 8 folder:

```
E:\> "E:\MySQL\MySQL Server 8\bin\mysqld"
```

After the execution of the preceding command, the user can see a list of messages that help the user to identify an error if one exists. The last two lines in Command Prompt are displayed as follows. They indicate that the MySQL 8 service has started and is ready for the server-client request:

```
mysqld: ready for connections
Version: '8.0.4' socket: '' port: 3306
```

The user can omit the console for error logs because MySQL 8 is maintaining logs in separate log files under a data directory with the .err extension. When starting the MySQL 8 server, the user has to execute same command each time, using Command Prompt. To stop the MySQL 8 server, execute the following command:

```
E:\> "E:\MySQL\MySQL Server 8\bin\mysqladmin" -u root shutdown
```

Initially, when MySQL 8 is installed, the root account password is not set. After first starting the MySQL 8 server, the user has to set it manually. Steps to set the password are described in detail under the post-installation section.

The path of mysqld and mysqladmin may vary depending on the installation location of MySQL 8. If the password was set on the root user of the MySQL 8 server then execute the command with the -p option and provide a password for successful execution.

5. Set the environment variable for MySQL 8. As mentioned in the preceding section, we have written the command with the complete path of the MySQL 8 server installation. To simplify this command, we have to define the environment variable for MySQL 8 in Microsoft Windows by performing the following steps (in Windows 10):
    1. Right click on **My Compute** and select **Properties**:

        1. Click on **Advance system settings.**
        2. Click on the **Environment Variables** button available at the right bottom side.
        3. Go to **System Variables** section and find the **PATH** variable.

4. Select the **PATH** variable and click on the **Edit** button.

5. A new dialog box opens; click on the **New** button and enter the path of the MySQL 8 server installation up to the `bin` file location. For example, `E:\MySQL\MySQL Server 8\bin`

6. Press the **OK** button in all the related dialog boxes to apply this change in Windows.

After applying the environment variable, the user is able to execute any MySQL command in Command Prompt without giving the complete path of MySQL 8.

6. **Start MySQL 8 as a Windows service**: It is recommended to use MySQL 8 as a Windows service because it will start when Windows starts and stop when Windows stops. There is no need to start the MySQL 8 service explicitly in this case. Use the Microsoft Windows services utility to manage the MySQL 8 service. To install the MySQL server as a service, use the following command:

```
E:\> "E:\MySQL\MySQL Server 8\bin\mysqld" --install
```

This command has the following options for additional arguments:

- If we are not defining a service name, then the command will consider the default service as **MySQL**.

- Use the `-- default -file` argument to specify the option file name, which contains the service name

- The user can also use the `--local-service` option followed by the service name

Use the following command to set the MySQL service as a Window service and refer to the file `my-opts.conf` as the option file to refer to the MySQL 8 configuration:

```
E:\> "E:\MySQL\MySQL Server 8\bin\mysqld" --install MySQL --defaults-file=E:\my-opts.cnf
```

So far, we have discussed the MySQL 8 service as a Windows service but there is a command available with the `--install-manual` option to start MySQL 8 without the Windows service. To remove the MySQL 8 service, use the `--remove` command, as follows:

```
E:\> "E:\MySQL\MySQL Server 8\bin\mysqld" --install-manual
E:\> "E:\MySQL\MySQL Server 8\bin\mysqld" --remove
```

Installing MySQL 8 on Linux

For MySQL 8 installation on Linux, various solutions are available. The user can choose any of the distributions for his requirement. Th following are the different distributions and among them, three of which are described in detail:

- Installation using the `Yum` repository
- Installation using the `APT` repository
- Installation using the `SLES` repository
- Installation using the `RPM` package
- Installation using the `Debian` package
- Installation using Docker
- Installation using the Native Software repository
- Installation using Juju

Installation using the Yum repository

Perform the following steps to install MySQL 8 using the `Yum` repository:

1. Download the `Yum` repository from the `http://dev.mysql.com/downloads/repo/yum/` link.
2. Select the MySQL package for your installation.
3. Execute the installation command to add the MySQL `Yum` repository into your `local` repository:

    ```
    shell> sudo yum localinstall package_name.rpm
    shell> yum repolist enabled | grep "mysql.*-community.*"
    ```

    Replace `package_name` with the actual name of the RPM package. After installation, execute the second command to check whether the `Yum` repository has properly installed.

4. **Select Release Series**: The MySQL Yum repository contains various series of releases for the installation. Execute the following command to check the list of the available series:

```
shell> yum repolist all | grep mysql
```

In the MySQL Yum repository, the latest GA series was enabled by default for installation but apart from that other development series are also available in the disabled state. For the development series installation, execute the following two commands to disable the GA release and to enable the require development series:

```
shell> sudo yum-config-manager --disable mysql57-community
shell> sudo yum-config-manager --enable mysql80-community
```

Another way of defining the release series is using the manual entry in the repository file. For example, add following entry into the/etc/yum.repos.d/mysql-community.repo file:

```
mysql80-community]
name=MySQL 8.0 Community Server
baseurl=http://repo.mysql.com/yum/mysql-8.0-community/el/6/$basearch/
enabled=1
```

Here, `enabled=1` means enable this series and `enabled=0` means disable this series. Yum allows only one enabled sub-repository for one release at a time; if multiple release series are enabled then only the latest series will be selected by the Yum repository. After saving the changes in the configuration file, execute the following command to check that the correct sub-repositories have been selected or not:

```
shell> yum repolist enabled | grep mysql
```

5. **Installation of MySQL 8**: Execute the following command:

```
shell> sudo yum install mysql-community-server
```

It will install the MySQL 8 server with all its dependencies, such as the client, the character sets for client, and the required libraries.

6. **Start MySQL 8 server**: The first command will start the MySQL service and the second command shows the current status of the MySQL service:

```
shell> sudo service mysqld start
shell> sudo service mysqld status
```

During the initial startup, the following tasks are performed:

- The server is initialized
- The SSL certificate and key files are generated in the data directory
- The plugins name `validate_password_plugin` is installed and enabled
- A super account is created

Installation using the RPM package

RPM packages are available from the Yum repository and SLES repository for MySQL 8. It is the recommended way of installation for MySQL 8. RPM packages follow the `packagename-version-distribution-arch.rpm` syntax, where distribution and arch indicate the Linux distribution and processor respectively. The RPM package is a bundle of all the required packages and they are dependent on one another. The RPM package follows the same steps as discussed in the Yum repository installation. In the RPM-based system, the MySQL service is not automatically started. To start it manually, execute the following command:

```
shell> sudo service mysqld start
```

As with other installations, the RPM package installation also creates files and directories in the system on following path :

Files or Resources	Location
Client programs and scripts	`/usr/bin`
mysqld server	`/usr/sbin`
Configuration file	`/etc/my.cnf`
Data directory	`/var/lib/mysql`
Error log file	For RHEL, Oracle Linux, CentOS, or Fedora platforms:`/var/log/mysqld.log` For SLES: `/var/log/mysql/mysqld.log`
Value of `secure_file_priv`	`/var/lib/mysql-files`
System V `init` script	For RHEL, Oracle Linux, CentOS, or Fedora platforms:`/etc/init.d/mysqld` For SLES: `/etc/init.d/mysql`

Systemd service	For RHEL, Oracle Linux, CentOS, or Fedora platforms: `mysqld` For SLES: `mysql`
Pid file	`/var/run/mysql/mysqld.pid`
`Socket`	`/var/lib/mysql/mysql.sock`
Keyring directory	`/var/lib/mysql-keyring`
Unix manual pages	`/usr/share/man`
Include (`header`) files	`/usr/include/mysql`
Libraries	`/usr/lib/mysql`
Miscellaneous support files (for example, error messages, and character set files)	`/usr/share/mysql`

Installation using the Debian package

`Debian` packages are available for the MySQL APT repository or from the MySQL Developer Zone's download area. Each MySQL component has its own `Debian` package for the installation but a tarball bundle is prepared to combine different `Debian` packages into a single bundle. The tarball naming convention is `mysql-server_MVER-DVER_CPU.deb-bundle.tar,` where MVER represents the MySQL version, DVER indicates the Linux distribution version, and CPU indicates the processor. To install MySQL 8 using the `Debian` package, perform the following steps:

1. Download the required tar package from the MySQL site.
2. Unpack the package with the following command:

   ```
   shell> tar -xvf mysql-server_MVER-DVER_CPU.deb-bundle.tar
   ```

3. The `Libaio1` library may be required, so execute the command for the library installation:

   ```
   shell> sudo apt-get install libaio1
   ```

4. Execute the command for the pre-configuration of the MySQL server:

   ```
   shell> sudo dpkg-preconfigure mysql-community-server_*.deb
   ```

This is the process implemented before installation, which applies on the set of `Debian` packages and other packages that use `debconf` with their config script to examine the system. During this process, the system will ask for the root user password of the MySQL 8 installation.

5. Install the dependencies required for the MySQL 8 installation:

```
shell>sudo apt-get -f install
```

The MySQL 8 configuration files are available under the following path in the `Debian` package:

- Configuration files are stored under `/etc/mysql`
- The data directory is stored under `/var/lib/mysql`
- Binaries, libraries, and headers are stored under `/user/bin` and under `user/sbin`

Post-installation setup for MySQL 8

Post-installation is a process that describes the basic steps or configuration that the user has to perform after MySQL 8 installation.

Data directory initialization

In previous sections, we have seen different methods of MySQL 8 installation. Some of the methods will automatically create a data directory for MySQL 8. For generic binary distribution and source distribution, data directory creation is a must. Data directory initialization is performed by either of the following two commands:

```
E:\> bin\mysqld --initialize
E:\> bin\mysqld --initialize-insecure
```

Either of these commands can be chosen based on the user's requirements to generate a random initial password or not. These two commands can be used by the user, regardless of the platform for the data directory initialization. Initializing is a way in which random initial root passwords will be generated. In the case of `initialize-insecure`, no password will be generated.

Another option is to specify the installation directory and data directory by using command line arguments, as shown in the following command:

```
E:\> bin\mysqld --initialize --basedir E:\mysql --datadir :\mydata\data
```

The user can also specify these directories in a separate file, known as the Option file, under the mysqld parameter. This configuration is described in detail under the Option file section in this chapter. When the user executes either of the commands, mysqld performs the following steps in the execution:

1. It checks the existence of the data directory

2. The MySQL 8 server creates a system database and its table, grant tables, help tables, and time zone tables

3. It initializes a system tablespace with data structure for InnoDB tables

4. The root@localhost superuser account and other reserved accounts will be created

Securing the initial MySQL account

This section explains how to assign a password to the root account during the first execution of the MySQL 8 server on the workstation. When the user installs MySQL 8 using the installer in Windows or using the Debian package in Linux, the installation process provides the option to enter a password and assign that password to the root account by itself. But with the RPM package, the random password is generated for the root account which is written into the server log file during the installation process. The initial root account may or may not have a password. To assign a password at the initial stage, use either of the following procedures:

- If the root account has a random password:
    1. Look in the server log files to get an auto-generated password.
    2. Connect to the MySQL 8 server with the auto-generated password by executing the following command:

```
shell> mysql -u root -p
Enter password: (enter the random root password here)
```

- Set the new password for the root account:

```
mysql> ALTER USER 'root'@'localhost' IDENTIFIED BY 'newPassword';
```

- If the root account has no password:
    1. Connect with the MySQL 8 server without a password:

```
mysql -u root
```

    2. Set the new password for the root account:

```
mysql> ALTER USER 'root'@'localhost' IDENTIFIED BY 'newPassword';
```

After assigning the new password, you have to use the new password whenever you want to connect with MySQL 8.

Starting and troubleshooting MySQL 8 services

This section explains how to start the MySQL 8 server and how to troubleshoot problems during the start process. After successful installation of the MySQL 8 server on the Linux system, execute the following command to start the MySQL 8 service:

```
shell> sudo service mysqld start
```

To check in detail whether the service has started or not refer to the log file. You can use the status command to check the status of the MySQL 8 service:

```
shell> sudo service mysqld status
```

After getting a message of the service starting/running, you can connect with MySQL 8 by using the following command:

```
shell> mysql -uroot -p
```

The preceding command prompts for the password, so enter the password and press the *Enter* key. The MySQL prompt will be displayed where you can enter `mysql` commands for execution. During the execution of the preceding commands, some common problems may arrive, so here we will present the following troubleshooting suggestions:

1. Check into the `log` files to find the exact error that occurred during the service startup. As mentioned in the previous section, the `error` file and `log` files are located under the data directory. Its naming conventions are `host_name.err` and `host_name.log`. By reading the last few lines of the file, you can identify the problem that occurred during the last command executed.

2. Check that the required port/socket is available. The following errors will indicate that the required ports and sockets are not available for use, meaning that they are in use with other programs. To identify this, track all the problems by disabling the service. Another reason is your firewall settings are blocking the access of the required port, so modify the firewall setting and give permission to the required ports:

   - **Can't start server**: Bind on the TCP/IP port: the address is already in use
   - **Can't start server**: Bind on the Unix socket

3. Defining the specific parameters into the `Option` file is recommended. If the parameters are not define into the file then MySQL 8 will consider the default parameters, so refer to all the available parameters provided by MySQL 8 before using it.

4. Verify that the `data` directory path and permission are properly defined or not. This directory is used as the current directory for MySQL 8. To find the currently set path of the data directory, execute the `mysqld` command with the `--verbose` and `--help` command. If the `data` directory is located at a different place other than the MySQL installation directory, then use the `--datadir` option with the `mysqld` command. For permission, you will get an Error code 13, which indicates the permission denied error. To overcome this issue, change the permission of the required files and folder. Another way is to log in with the root user, but this is not possible in all the scenarios, so the first approach is recommended to overcome the permission issue.

Executing commands to test the server

After performing the preceding steps, now your MySQL 8 service has started and has connected with a specified user. Now, it's time to check your MySQL 8 server works satisfactorily or not by executing the following basic commands:

```
shell> bin/mysqladmin version
```

This command lists all the information related to the installed MySQL server, which contains its version details, protocol version, and much more. Execute the following commands after connecting with MySQL 8 to check that information has been properly retrieved from the server:

```
mysql>mysqlshow
mysql>mysqlshow mysql
```

The first command shows the list of databases available in the server. Lists may vary as per the system, but `mysql` and `information_schema` must be available in the list. The second command lists all the tables created under the `mysql` database.

Upgrading MySQL 8

In previous versions of MySQL, the data dictionary is stored in the file-based system while in MySQL 8 it is stored in the data dictionary structure. So, the up-gradation process will move the file-based structure into the data dictionary structure. Up-gradation into MySQL 8 is possible from the MYSQL 5.7 GA version, which means from 5.7.9 or higher. For non-GA versions of 5.7, up-gradation is not possible. Before starting the up-gradation process, the following points need to be understood.

Upgrading methods

Two methods are in use for up-gradation that are differentiated by their implementation method. Let us discuss these methods in detail.

In-place upgrade of MySQL

As the name implies, this is a process where we replace the existing old version package of MySQL with a newer version. Before starting, make sure the old server has stop and after replacing the package, restart the MySQL 8 server on the existing data directory with the mySQL upgrade.

Perform the following steps for in-place upgradation:

1. With an encrypted `InnoDB` tablespace, rotate the master key with the following command:

    ```
    ALTER INSTANCE ROTATE INNODB MASTER KEY;
    ```

2. Configure the shutdown parameters with the `innodb_fast_shutdown` command:

    ```
    SET GLOBAL innodb_fast_shutdown = 1; -- fast shutdown
    SET GLOBAL innodb_fast_shutdown = 0; -- slow shutdown
    ```

3. Shut down the old MySQL version, using the following command:

    ```
    mysqladmin -u root -p shutdown
    ```

4. It is the up-gradation process where the user will replace the old package with the new MySQL 8 package.
5. Start the MySQL 8 server, using the existing `data` directory.

    On the server startup, it will check for `data` dictionary tables. If they are not present then the server creates tables in the `data` directory, and populates metadata and processes with its normal startup sequence. If these steps are successfully executed then the server performs cleanup by creating the `backup_metadata_57` directory. In addition, the server renames events and proc tables into `event_backup_57` and `proc_backup_57`. If this step fails then server will revert all the changes.

6. After successful completion when MySQL 8 has started, execute `mysql_upgrade`:

    ```
    mysql_upgrade -u root -p
    ```

7. After up-gradation, shut down and restart the server to check whether all the changes have been applied or not.

Logical upgrade for MySQL 8

Export or take a dump of the old MySQL version. Install the new MySQL 8 version and load the dump file into the new MySQL 8 version with the MySQL upgrade. Perform the following steps to apply the logical up-gradation:

1. Use the `mysqldump` command to export the data:

    ```
    mysqldump -u root -p --add-drop-table --routines --events --all-
    databases    --
        force > data-for-upgrade.sql
    ```

    The `--routines` and `--events` options are used to include stored routines and events in the dump file and define these options explicitly to get an effect.

2. Shut down the old MySQL server.
3. Install the new version of MySQL 8.
4. Initialize the `data` directory:

    ```
    mysqld --initialize --datadir=/path/to/8.0-datadir
    ```

5. Start the MySQL 8 server with the new `data` directory:

    ```
    mysqld_safe --user=mysql --datadir=/path/to/8.0-datadir
    ```

6. Load the SQL dump file into the new `MySQL` database:

    ```
    mysql -u root -p --force < data-for-upgrade.sql
    ```

7. Upgrade MySQL with the following command:

    ```
    mysql_upgrade -u root -p
    ```

Upgrading prerequisites for MySQL 5.7

Before starting up-gradation, perform the following checks to avoid failure during later stages:

1. Execute the following command to check there is no absolute datatypes or function:

    ```
    mysqlcheck -u root -p--all-databases--check-upgrade
    ```

2. Check for native partitioning support, using the following command:

```
SELECT TABLE_SCHEMA, TABLE_NAME
FROM INFORMATION_SCHEMA.TABLES
WHERE ENGINE NOT IN ('innodb', 'ndbcluster')
AND CREATE_OPTIONS LIKE '%partitioned%';
```

This command will list tables that use the storage engine which doesn't support native partitioning. After executing the preceding query, if any table is found then remove the partitioning on the table and change the storage engine, as shown in the following command:

```
ALTER TABLE table_name ENGINE = INNODB;
ALTER TABLE table_name REMOVE PARTITIONING;
```

3. Make sure MySQL 5.7 does not contains any table which is used as a data dictionary in MySQL 8.

4. Check that the foreign key constraint name doesn't contains more than 64 characters, using the following code:

```
SELECT CONSTRAINT_SCHEMA, TABLE_NAME, CONSTRAINT_NAME
FROM INFORMATION_SCHEMA.REFERENTIAL_CONSTRAINTS
WHERE LENGTH(CONSTRAINT_NAME) > 64;
```

5. Make sure MySQL 5.7 doesn't contain features that are not available in MySQL 8, for example:
   - If a table used a storage engine that is not supported by MySQL 8, so was altered with the supported storage engine
   - A configuration change where you use an option or variable that is not available in MySQL 8

MySQL 8 downgrading

Downgrading is the reverse process of up-gradation, where we will move from a higher version of MySQL to a lower version of MySQL. In this section, we cover how to downgrade from MySQL 8 to MySQL 5.7. A downgrade that does not support a version skip means that downgrading from MySQL 8 to MySQL 5.6 is not supported. Within the same series where a version skip is supported means you can downgrade from MySQL 8.z to MySQL 8.x by skipping the MySQL 8.y version. First, we will explain some basic points that need to be understood before starting downgrading.

Downgrading methods

An in-place downgrade means shutting down the new version of MySQL 8, replacing its binaries or packages with the old version of MySQL. Restarting the old version means MySQL 5.7 on the existing data directory. This downgrade method is supported between GA versions within the same series. Perform the following steps for an in-place downgrade:

1. Shut down the newer version of MySQL 8.
2. After the shutdown, remove the InnoDB redo log files from the data directory to avoid downgrade issues:

   ```
   rm ib_logfile*
   ```

3. Position the older version of MySQL in place of the newer version binaries or package.
4. Start the downgraded version of MySQL by specifying the data directory, using the following command:

   ```
   mysqld_safe --user=mysql --datadir=/path/to/existing-datadir
   ```

5. Execute the mysql_upgrade command:

   ```
   mysql_upgrade -u root -p
   ```

6. Shut down and restart the MySQL server again to check if all the changes have been applied or not.

 For MySQL installation based on APT, SLES, and the Yum repository installations, in-place downgrades are not supported

Logical downgrade

Take a dump of all the tables using mysqldump in the new version. Install the new version of MySQL 8 with the new database and load the old version dump into the new database. This downgrade is also supported within the same GA release series and for the release level. MySQL 8.0 to 5.7 downgrade is supported using the *logical downgrade* method.

To perform the logical downgrade, follow these steps:

1. Take a dump of the database, using the following code:

```
mysqldump -u root -p --add-drop-table --routines --events
--all-databases --force > data-for-downgrade.sql
```

2. Shut down the MySQL server, as shown here:

```
mysqladmin -u root -p shutdown
```

3. Initialize the new data directory to the older MySQL version, using the following code:

```
mysqld --initialize --user=mysql
```

4. Start older MySQL with the new data directory, using the following code:

```
mysqld_safe --user=mysql --datadir=/path/to/new-datadir
```

5. Load the dump into the older MySQL sever, as shown here:

```
mysql -u root -p --force < data-for-upgrade.sql
```

6. Execute the mysql_upgrade:

```
mysql_upgrade -u root -p
```

7. Restart the server to apply all the changes, using the following code:

```
mysqladmin -u root -p shutdown
mysqld_safe --user=mysql --datadir=/path/to/new-datadir
```

Manual changes required before downgrading

This section describes some of the changes that need to be executed manually by the user before downgrading:

- **System table changes**: MySQL 5.7 manages individual tablespace for system tables while in MySQL 8, system tables were migrated into a single tablespace file known as mysql.ibd. So, before downgrading to MySQL 5.7, move the system table back to the individual tablespace files with the following commands:

```
ALTER TABLE mysql.columns_priv TABLESPACE=innodb_file_per_table;
```

```
      ALTER TABLE mysql.component TABLESPACE=innodb_file_per_table;
      ALTER TABLE mysql.db TABLESPACE=innodb_file_per_table;
      ALTER TABLE mysql.default_roles TABLESPACE=innodb_file_per_table;
      ALTER TABLE mysql.engine_cost TABLESPACE=innodb_file_per_table;
      ALTER TABLE mysql.func TABLESPACE=innodb_file_per_table;
      ALTER TABLE mysql.general_log TABLESPACE=innodb_file_per_table;
      ALTER TABLE mysql.global_grants TABLESPACE=innodb_file_per_table;
      ALTER TABLE mysql.gtid_executed TABLESPACE=innodb_file_per_table;
      ALTER TABLE mysql.help_category TABLESPACE=innodb_file_per_table;
      ALTER TABLE mysql.help_keyword TABLESPACE=innodb_file_per_table;
      ALTER TABLE mysql.help_relation TABLESPACE=innodb_file_per_table;
      ALTER TABLE mysql.help_topic TABLESPACE=innodb_file_per_table;
      ALTER TABLE mysql.innodb_index_stats
TABLESPACE=innodb_file_per_table;
      ALTER TABLE mysql.innodb_table_stats
TABLESPACE=innodb_file_per_table;
      ALTER TABLE mysql.plugin TABLESPACE=innodb_file_per_table;
      ALTER TABLE mysql.procs_priv TABLESPACE=innodb_file_per_table;
      ALTER TABLE mysql.proxies_priv TABLESPACE=innodb_file_per_table;
      ALTER TABLE mysql.role_edges TABLESPACE=innodb_file_per_table;
      ALTER TABLE mysql.server_cost TABLESPACE=innodb_file_per_table;
      ALTER TABLE mysql.servers TABLESPACE=innodb_file_per_table;
      ALTER TABLE mysql.slave_master_info
TABLESPACE=innodb_file_per_table;
      ALTER TABLE mysql.slave_relay_log_info
TABLESPACE=innodb_file_per_table;
      ALTER TABLE mysql.slave_worker_info
TABLESPACE=innodb_file_per_table;
      ALTER TABLE mysql.slow_log TABLESPACE=innodb_file_per_table;
      ALTER TABLE mysql.tables_priv TABLESPACE=innodb_file_per_table;
      ALTER TABLE mysql.time_zone TABLESPACE=innodb_file_per_table;
      ALTER TABLE mysql.time_zone_leap_second
TABLESPACE=innodb_file_per_table;
      ALTER TABLE mysql.time_zone_name TABLESPACE=innodb_file_per_table;
      ALTER TABLE mysql.time_zone_transition
TABLESPACE=innodb_file_per_table;
      ALTER TABLE mysql.time_zone_transition_type
TABLESPACE=innodb_file_per_table;
      ALTER TABLE mysql.user TABLESPACE=innodb_file_per_table;
```

In MySQL 8.0.2, the storage engine of six system tables changes from MyISAM to InnoDB. Their names are `columns_priv`, `db`, `procs_priv`, `tables_priv`, and `user`. So, before downgrading, change the storage engine of these tables by executing the following command. Apply the same command for the remaining tables:

```
ALTER TABLE mysql.columns_priv ENGINE='MyISAM'
    STATS_PERSISTENT=DEFAULT
```

In MySQL 8.0.2, `mysql.user` table was changed by adding two tables, so, before downgrading to MySQL 5.7, drop those columns from the table:

```
ALTER TABLE mysql.user drop Create_role_priv;
ALTER TABLE mysql.user drop Drop_role_priv;
```

- **InnoDB changes**: Before starting in-place downgrading, shut down MySQL using the `innodb_fast_shutdown` option. Shut down the server with `innodb_fast_shutdown=0`. Removing the redo logs is recommended for in-place downgrading.

Summary

To choose the proper software with its version for development is an important phase, right? In this chapter, we understood how to select the proper version of MySQL 8 by understanding its version pattern. We also learned the execution steps of MySQL 8 installation using the installer and command line in Microsoft Windows. For the Linux platform, we installed MySQL 8 using the Yum repository, RPM package, and Debian package. Post-installation describes the basic configuration to start with MySQL 8. Finally, we explained how to upgrade and downgrade from MySQL 8 with execution steps.

In the next chapter, we will learn about various programs and utilities available for MySQL 8. It mainly focuses on how to use these programs for MySQL 8 along with command-line executions.

3

MySQL 8 – Using Programs and Utilities

In the previous chapter, we installed MySQL 8 and got to know alternative ways to install MySQL 8. We also learned how to migrate and upgrade to MySQL 8. The following are the summary topics explained in the previous chapter:

- MySQL 8 Installation
- Post Installation Setup
- MySQL 8 Upgrading
- MySQL 8 Downgrading

In this chapter, the reader will learn about various programs and utilities available in MySQL 8. The reader will also get to know how to use programs and utilities in MySQL 8. The reader will learn about using command-line programs used in MySQL 8. The reader will learn the syntax for the program and how they are being used with specific options to perform specific operations. The following is a summary of the topics covered in this chapter.

- Overview of MySQL 8 programs
- MySQL 8 command-line programs
- MySQL 8 client programs
- MySQL 8 administrative programs
- MySQL 8 environment variables
- MySQL GUI tools

Overview of MySQL 8 programs

There are various different programs in the MySQL installation. A brief overview of these programs is covered in this section. Upcoming sections will cover a detailed description for each of them and the description will have its own invocation syntax and options to perform the operation.

Most of the MySQL distribution will have all these programs, apart from those that are platform-specific; for example, server startup script not used in Windows. RPM (Red-hat package manager) distributions are very specialized and are part of the exceptions to all programs available in distributions. What is specialized about RPM distributions? Well, they have different programs for different operations; for example, one program will be executed for the server, a second program will be executed for the client, and so on. If it looks like one or more programs is missing in your installation, then don't worry. See Chapter 2, *Installing and Upgrading MySQL 8,* for information on the types of distributions available and what is included in them. It might be the case that the distribution which you have does not include all the programs and you need to install an additional package.

Each of the MySQL 8 programs will have their own options, but most of them will have a --help option that can be used to retrieve descriptions about all the options that the program has. For example, try mysql --help on the command line (that is your shell or Command Prompt).

The description on the first few lines will have specific version information about MySQL that is installed along with operating system and license information. The next line will start with Usage : mysql [OPTIONS] [database], that is, a syntax of the program command usage, and later lines describe the options available to be used along with them as per the usage description. This was just a glimpse of what we will be looking at: program details with options, their usages and default options, overriding default option values on various command-line programs, client programs, administrative programs, and so on.

For detailed information about executing programs and specifying program options in the command line see the *MySQL 8 command line programs* section, which will be followed by a list of installations, client and server start up, and other utility programs.

MySQL programs in brief

Let us start with the MySQL server programs first!!

`mysqld` is the first program, also considered to be the main program for MySQL installation. It works with several scripts to help with starting and stopping the server. The following are the programs divided into categories based on their operational scope:

- Startup programs
- Installation/upgradation programs
- Client programs
- Administrative and utilities programs

Startup programs

The startup programs are the programs that are used during MySQL start up and initiate the required background services based on the configuration.

- `mysqld`: This is the MySQL server daemon. All the other client programs interact with the database using this server program. It must be started and be running at all times except for maintenance.
- `mysqld_safe`: This is one of the server startup program scripts and attempts to start the `mysqld` program.
- `mysql.server`: Another server startup program script, which is used in those systems, uses V-style run directories containing scripts. It starts system services at particular run levels. It calls `mysqld_safe` to start the MySQL server.
- `mysqld_multi`: As the name suggests, this is a startup program script to start or stop multiple MySQL servers on the system.

Installation/upgradation programs

The programs regarding the operations of installation and upgradation are listed here with their respective usage:

- `comp_err`: This program is used to compile error message files from error source files and it is used during the MySQL build or install operation.
- `mysql_secure_installation`: This program is used to update the security configuration in order to enable security during installation of MySQL.

- `mysql_ssl_rsa_setup`: As the name suggests, this program is for generating `SSL` certificates and key files and `RSA key-pair` files, if those files are missing and are required to support secure connections.

- `mysql_tzinfo_to_sql`: This program gets the content of the host system zone info database (files describing time zones) and loads the information in the time zone tables of MySQL.

- `mysql_upgrade`: As the name suggests, it is used for upgrade operations. It checks for any incompatibility and makes repairs if it is necessary. It also updates the grant tables with any changes in new versions of MySQL.

Client programs

The client programs are among the programs that are commonly used to connect to the MySQL database and perform different query operations:

- `mysql`: This is the most commonly used program. It is an interactive command-line tool for executing SQL statements directly or using a file in batch mode. Detailed information is followed in the next *MySQL 8 command line programs* section.

- `mysqladmin`: This is the program responsible for performing various administrative operations, such as creating or dropping databases, flushing tables, reloading grant tables, reopening log files, and much more. The program is also used to retrieve information from the server, such as version, process, and status.

- `mysqlcheck`: This is the client program used for maintenance of tables, performing analysis, checks, repairs, and optimizing tables.

- `mysqldump`: This is the client program that dumps the MySQL database to a file in text, SQL, or XML formats. It is commonly known as a database back up program.

- `mysqlimport`: This is the client program that imports text files into respective tables using `LOAD_DATA_INFILE`. It is also commonly known as the data import program.

- `mysqlpump`: The client program which dumps MySQL database into SQL file.

- `mysqlshow`: The client that shows information of databases, tables, columns, and indexes.

- `mysqlslap`: This is the client program that is used to check client load capability for the MySQL server. The program mimics multiple clients accessing the server.

Administrative and utilities programs

The following are the programs that perform various administrative activities. They are depicted along with some of the utilities which help in administrative operations:

- `innochecksum`: The program for the `InnoDB` offline file checksum.
- `myisam_ftdump`: The utility program gives information of full-text indexes in `MyISAM` tables.
- `myisamchk`: The program used to check, describe, repair and optimize `MyISAM` tables.
- `myisamlog`: The utility program for processing a `MyISAM` log file contents.
- `myisampack`: The utility program that produces smaller read-only `MyISAM` tables through compression.
- `mysql_config_editor`: The utility program that enables authentication credentials storage in an encrypted and secure login path file named `mylogin.cnf`.
- `mysqlbinlog`: The utility program that can read binary log file statements. In the event of a server crash, a binary log file executed statements can be big help.
- `mysqldumpslow`: The utility program that can read and summarize the contents of a slow query log.

Environment variables

The MySQL client programs that communicate with the MySQL server using libraries use the following environment variables:

- `MYSQL_UNIX_PORT`: This variable is responsible for the default Unix socket file which will be used for connecting to a localhost
- `MYSQL_TCP_PORT`: This variable is responsible for providing the default port number and is used in TCP/IP connections
- `MYSQL_PWD`: This variable is responsible for providing the default password.
- `MYSQL_DEBUG`: This variable is responsible for providing debug trace options during debugging operations
- `TMPDIR`: This variable is responsible for providing the directory where the temporary files and tables will be created

For a detailed list and uses of environment variables in programs, see *MySQL 8 environment variables* section. The use of MYSQL_PWD is insecure.

MySQL GUI tool

The MySQL Workbench GUI tool, provided by Oracle corporation, is used in the administration of MySQL servers and databases, for creating, executing, and evaluating queries. It is also used for migrating schema and data from other relational database management systems to be used with MySQL. There are other GUI tools, including MySQL Notifier, MySQL for Excel, phpMyAdmin, and many more.

MySQL 8 command-line programs

In the previous section, we went through various types of programs provided by MySQL 8 and outlined their usage in brief.

In this section, we will look at command-line programs and learn about executing programs from command lines. We will take a detailed look at the provision for options and how they can be utilized for the administration.

Executing programs from the command line

Executing programs from the command line (shell or Command Prompt) is one of the most used forms of administration in MySQL. Plenty of programs have been added along with options for administration.

Executing MySQL programs

To execute a MySQL program, enter the program name followed by options or any other arguments required to tell the program what you want it to do. Following are some sample executing commands. Here shell> represents the command interpreter. Typical prompts will be c:>\ for a Windows machine with command.com or cmd.exe as the command interpreter, $ for a Unix machine with sh, ksh or bash as the command interpreter, and % for a Mac machine with csh or tcsh as the command interpreter:

```
shell> mysql --verbose --help
```

```
shell> mysql --user=root --password=******** mysampledb
shell> mysqldump -u root personnel
shell> mysqlshow --help
```

There are nonoption arguments, arguments without any leading dash, giving supplementary information to the program. As an example, if you see the second line of the preceding example, it has a third nonoption argument with a database name `mysampledb`, so the command `mysql --user=root --password=******** mysampledb` tells the `mysql` program that you wanted to use `mysampledb` as the database name.

Arguments beginning with single or double dash (`-`, `--`) are used for specifying the program options. Specifying the program options indicates the type of connection the program will connect to the server or will affect the mode of operation. Syntax for the options are explained with details, see the *Specifying options for programs* section.

Connecting to the MySQL server

In this section, we will explain how we can establish connection to the MySQL server. We will be using client programs for connecting to the MySQL server. For connecting to the server program, we need some information to specify the `hostname`, `username`, and the `password` of the MySQL account because we need to tell the client program which host the server is running in and the associated username and password. Although there will be default option values associated to these options, you can override the option value whenever it is necessary. For example, consider using the common client program `mysql`:

```
shell> mysql
```

In the preceding program, no option has been specified but the following defaults will be applied automatically:

- Hostname default value applied as `localhost`
- Username default value applied as per the login name (ODBC name in Windows or Unix login name)
- If the `-p` or `--password` option is not specified along with the program, then it will not send any option value to the program
- The first non-option argument is considered as the default database name for the `mysql` program and if no such option is specified, then `mysql` does not select any default database

The principles applied to the client program `mysql` are also applicable to other client programs, such as `mysqldump, mysqladmin,` or `mysqlshow`. Now let us see the example client program connecting with arguments of a specific option value:

```
shell> mysql --host=localhost --user=root --password=mypwd mysampledb
```

As you can see in the preceding example with specific option values, the host is to be considered as the `localhost` and the user value is provided as `myname`. The password is also specified and, finally, a non-option argument is specified that tells the program to use `mysampledb` as the default database name.

Specifying options for programs

In the earlier section, we have seen how program options change the operation mode based on argument values specified for the option in the client program. Here we will look at several ways to specify options for MySQL programs. These include:

- Providing the options on the command line followed by the program name. This is the common way of providing options but it will be applied specifically to the execution of the program at that time only.
- Providing the options in the options file that is being read by the program before it starts execution. This is the common way for providing the options that you want the program to use each time it executes.
- Providing the options in the environment variables. By using this method, you can also specify options that you want to apply every time the program is being executed. In general practice, using option files is commonly used for this purpose but specifying option values in the environment variables is also very useful in some cases; for example, when running multiple MySQL instances on a Unix system.

The MySQL program checks which options are to be given first by examining the related environment variables, then it processes option files, and then it considers option arguments in the command line. Thus, the command-line options have the highest precedence and the environment variables have the lowest. However, there is one exception that applies and that is the `mysqld-auto.cnf` option file in the data directory processed last, so it takes higher precedence to the command-line options.

Options on the command line

With the command line program options, follow these rules:

- Options are followed by the program name.
- Option arguments begin with a single dash or double dashes, depending on if they are using the short form or the longer form of the option name.
- The option name is case sensitive. For example, –V and –v are both valid as they are the respective short forms for --verbose and --version, thus stating different meanings to the program.
- Options can also take a value followed by the option name. For example, –h localhost or --host=localhost tells the client program to take the localhost as the hostname.
- With a short option that takes a value, the value can follow the option letter immediately or the single space between the two will also work. The only exception to this rule is when specifying the MySQL password option.
- With the long option that takes a value, the value and name can be separated by the = sign.
- (-) and (_) can be used interchangeably within the option name, such as--skip-grant-table or --skip_grant_table. Both are valid and work the same way but the underscore cannot be used in place of a leading dash.
- An option value taking a numeric value can be used with a suffix of K, M, or G to indicate a multiplier of 1,024 with lowercase or uppercase. Consider the following example where the command is telling the mysqladmin program to ping the server 1,024 times and sleep for 10 seconds for each ping:

```
shell> mysqladmin --count=1k --sleep=10 ping
```

- For filename options values, avoid using the ~ meta character because it will not be interpreted as per expectation.
- Option values containing spaces must be enclosed by quotation marks when a value is specified on the command line.

Modifying program options

Some of the options are of the `boolean` type and control a behavior that can be turned on or off. Let us consider, for an example, the `mysql` program. It supports the `--column-names` option that controls displaying the first row of the column names in the first line of query results. In order to disable the column names, the following specifications will work for us:

```
--disable-column-names
--skip-column-names
--column-names=0
```

As you can see in the preceding example, the `=0 suffix` and the `--skip` and `--disable prefixes` have the same effect. It is also applicable when turning the option on with the `=1` suffix and the `--enable` prefix.

If the option is specified with the `--loose prefix`, and if the option specified does not exist, the program will issue a warning instead of exiting.

For some of the programs, the `--maximum prefix` is available to be used with the option name for specifying the limit. It can also be used with environment variables.

Modifying options with files

Most of the MySQL programs can read startup options from the option files, also sometimes called **configuration files**. It is a very convenient way of providing the options that are commonly used and once specified you need not specify them each time you execute the program. To check whether the program reads option files, use the `--help` option. For example, consider the `mysqld` program, which should use `--verbose` and `--help`, if it reads option files. The help message will indicate which option file it looks for and for which option group:

> The MySQL program with the `--no-defualts` option does not read any option files apart from `.mylogin.cnf`. If the server program started with the option `persisted_globals_load` system variable disabled then the program does not read the `mysqld-auto.cnf` file.

The majority of the option files are plain text files that can be created and edited by any text editors. Exceptions among those files are `.mylogin.cnf`, which has login path options, encrypted by the `mysql_config_editor` utility program.

MySQL checks option files for Windows and Unix systems in specific order and follows the precedence that starts from reading global options, such as in the Windows system:

- `%PROGRAMDATA%\MySQL\MySQL Server 8.0\my.ini` and `%PROGRAMDATA%\MySQL\MySQL Server 8.0\my.cnf`
- `%WINDIR%\my.ini` and `%WINDIR%\my.cnf`
- `C:\my.ini` and `C:\my.cnf`
- `BASEDIR\my.ini` and `BASEDIR\my.cnf`
- The file specified with `--defaults-extra-file`, if any
- Login path options in `%APPDATA%\MySQL\.mylogin.cnf` (client program only)
- For system variables persisted with `SET_PERSIST` or `PERSIST_ONLY` (if it is the server program) in `DATADIR\mysql-auto.cnf`

Similarly, in Unix systems it follows the following order of precedence for reading option files:

- `/etc/my.cnf`
- `/etc/mysql/my.cnf`
- `SYSCONFDIR/my.cnf`
- `$MYSQL_HOME/my.cnf` (server program only)
- The file specified with `--defaults-extra-file`, if any
- `~/.my.cnf` for user-specific options
- `~/.mylogin.cnf` for user-specific login path options (client program only)
- For system variables persisted with `SET_PERSIST` or `PERSIST_ONLY` (if it is the server program) in `DATADIR\mysql-auto.cnf`

In the preceding options, ~ refers to the current user's home directory.

Empty lines in option files are ignored, along with comments. Comments can be specified using # or ; characters and # can start in the middle of any line as well.

group

`group` is the name of the program or group for which options are to be set. They are not case sensitive. Once a group line is added to the option file, all the following lines apply to the named group until another group line is specified or at the end of the option file.

opt_name

This is similar to the --opt_name in the command line turning on the named optimization.

opt_name=value

This is similar to the --opt_name in the command line but in place of the value, you can specify the value with spaces, which you cannot in the command line.

Include directives

It is possible using !include directives in the option files to include another option file and !includedir to search for specific directories to check for option files. For example, !include /home/dev/myopt.cnf and !includedir /home/dev, for directories. The only thing that MySQL does not consider is any order during the directory search.

Any option files to be used in the !includedir directive on a Windows system must end with the .ini or .cnf extension and in Unix systems they must end with .cnf.

Command-line options affecting option file handling

Most of the MySQL programs support option files. As they affect option file handling, they must be given in the command line and not as part of an option file.

In order to make them work properly, they must be given before other options. Some of the exceptions are as follows : --print-defaults might be used immediately after --login-path, --defaults-file, or defaults-extra-file.

--no-defaults and --print-defaults are also used to modify option file handling.

Setting program variables with options

Many MySQL programs have internal variables that we can set during runtime operations using the SET statement and also using the same syntax by which we specify option values. This will work when the program is started. For example, if we use the option value syntax then we have to specify like this: shell> mysql --max_allowed_packet=16M. To specify the runtime option using the SET, we can specify like this: mysql> SET GLOBAL max_allowed_packet=16*1024*1024.

To find out if the option variable syntax is correct, you can go to `mysql` and use the following: `mysql> show variables like 'max%'.`

Setting environment variables

In Command Prompt, we can set environment variables which will affect the runtime execution of the program, or can be set to affect future executions permanently. They can be set up in the startup file or by using the interface provided by the system. A list of environment variables that can affect the MySQL programs are given with details in the *MySQL 8 environment variables* section.

To specify values for the environment variable, the syntax will be based on the underlying command interpreter. For a Windows system, you can set the user variable using the following syntax:

```
SET  USER=your_user_name
```

For a Unix system, it depends on the shell, so you will need to use following syntax if using `sh`, `ksh`, `zsh`, or `bash`:

```
MYSQL_TCP_PORT=3306
export MYSQL_TCP_PORT
```

If using `csh` or `tcsh`, use `setenv`, which will get the shell variable available to the execution environment:

```
setenv MYSQL_TCP_PORT 3306
```

The commands to set environment variables that are executed will immediately affect the program in execution but if you wanted to get the environment variable to persist, you need to specify it on the interface provided by the system or you may set it up in the startup file that the command processor uses at startup. On Windows, this can be set up from the control panels option to set environment variables and in Unix, this can be set up based on the command-line processor you use. For `bash`, you need to put the value in `.bashrc` or `.bash_profile` and for `tcsh` use `.tcshrc`.

Server and server-startup programs

There are specific programs provided by MySQL which you need to execute first in order to make MySQL work correctly. In the following sections, we will look at the server programs and related startup programs that can be used with several options as per your requirement.

mysqld - the MySQL server program

The MySQL server is a daemon program. All other programs connect with the database through this server, so it should be running at all times. The daemon program usually gets started from a script called `mysqld_safe`. The program script is required, as it sets the appropriate environment variables and executes the `mysqld` program with the required arguments `-option` values.

Options

The following are the options briefed in detail for various options available from command line:

- `-?, -I, --help`: Displays the usage information of the program.
- `-# debuglevel, --debug=debuglevel`: Sets the debugging level as specified.
- `-b directory, --basedir=directory`: Specifies the base directory used to determine all other related directories.
- `--big-tables`: Used to allow large result sets. They are saved as temporary results in a file.
- `--bind-address=ip-number`: Specifies the IP address the server will bind it to.
- `-h directory, --datadir=directory`: Specifies the directory where the database data files are stored.
- `-l [logfile], --log[=logfile]`: Add various log information, which includes connections and error information. If an argument is not provided, then `hostname.log` is used as the log file, and here `hostname` is the name of the server machine.
- `--log-isam[=logfile]`: Adds changes to the data (ISAM) files in logs. If an argument is not provided, then `isam.log` is used as the log file and the log generated by this option can only be read and manipulated with the `theisamlog` utility.

- `--log-update[=number]`: Logging the database updates info. The log file gets named as `hostname.num`, where the `hostname` is the name of the server machine and the `num` is the argument to the option or generates a unique number if the argument is not specified.
- `-L=language`, `--language=language`: To specify the language (English, French, German, and so on) for the server.
- `-n`, `--new`: To enable new routines (and possibly unsafe routines).
- `-S`, `--skip-new`: To disable/enable new routines (and possibly unsafe routines).
- `-O variable=value`, `--set-variable variable=value`: To specify and set value for the variables
- `--pid-file=file`: To get the name of the file having the **process ID** (**PID**) of the running server. The default value for the file is `hostname.pid`, where the `hostname` is the server machine's name.
- `-P port`, `--port=port`: To specify the network port number.
- `--secure`: To enable network security checks. But this reduces database performance.
- `--skip-name-resolve`: To specify using only IP numbers (not names) for the connections. This increases the network performance.
- `--skip-networking`: To disable network connections, with only local access being allowed.
- `--skip-thread-priority`: For giving all the threads the same priority.
- `-Sg`: To disable access checking. This allows all the users full access to all the databases.
- `-Sl`: To specify not to perform thread locking.
- `--use-locking`: To enable thread locking.
- `--socket=file`: To specify the filename for the Unix socket.
- `-T`, `--exit-info`: Used to display debugging information during the shutting down of the server.
- `-v`, `-V`, and `--version`: To show the version information of the server.

mysqld_safe - MySQL server startup script

This is the most recommended way to start the MySQL server in a Unix- based system as it adds a few safety features, such as logging information to error log if any error occurs at runtime and restarting the server if there is an error.

In some of the Unix platforms, MySQL installations from RPM or Debian packages include the systemd support to manage MySQL startup and shutdown operations and so mysqld_safe is not installed on those systems.

mysqld_safe attempts to execute mysqld and to override the default behavior to specify the name of the server that you wanted to execute. The option to specify the directory using --ledir is also available so that mysqld_safe will look for the server in the directory. Most of the options in mysqld_safe are also available in mysqld and if the specified option is unknown to mysqld_safe then it gets passed on to mysqld. mysqld_safe , which reads out all the options from the mysqld, server, and mysqld_safe sections in option files. For backward compatibility, mysqld_safe also reads safe_mysqld sections but you should rename such section to be on the current one that is mysqld_safe.

As stated previously, there are very common options specified in both mysqld and mysqld_safe, so some of the options are excluded in the following list of options:

--core-file-size=size

To specify the size of the core file which mysqld should create.

--ledir=dir_name

If mysqld is not able to find the server, then use this option to specify the path name of the directory in which the server is located. This option can be used only on the command line, and not in option files. On platforms that use systemd, the value should be given in the value of MYSQLD_OPTS.

--mysqld-safe-log-timestamps

This option is to specify the format for timestamps in the log output produced by mysqld_safe.

--mysqld=prog_name

To specify the server program name contained in the ledir directory that you want to start. If mysqld_safe cannot find the server, use the --ledir option to specify the pathname to the directory where the server with the specified name is located. This option is only accepted on the command line, and not from the option files.

--open-files-limit=count

The number of files which `mysqld` can open.

> **--plugin-dir=dir_name**

To specify the path and name of the plugin directory.

> **--timezone=timezone**

This option is to set the `timezone` environment variable to the given option value, depending on operating system time zone specification formats.

> **--user={ username | user_id }**

Run the `mysqld` server as if you have the name of the user. Specify the `user_name` or specify the numeric `user ID` as `user_id`.

mysql.server - MySQL Server startup script

This is the server startup script that is used on MySQL distributions of Unix/Unix-like systems. It uses `mysqld_safe` for starting MySQL the server program. The program is also used in systems using `V-style` run directories containing scripts. It starts system services at particular run levels.

> **basedir=dir_name**

To specify the path of the MySQL installation directory.

> **datadir=data_dir**

To specify the path of the MySQL data directory.

> **pid-file=file_name**

To specify the pathname along with the filename in which the server writes its process ID.

> **service-startup-timeout=seconds**

To specify in seconds how long to wait for confirmation of the server startup. If the server does not start within this time, `mysql.server` exits with an error indication. The default value for the option is 900 seconds and a value of 0 means not to wait at all for startup and providing negative values means to wait forever (there should not be a timeout).

mysqld_multi - managing multiple MySQL servers

mysqld_multi is designed for managing several mysqld processes that listen for the connections on different Unix socket files and TCP/IP ports. It can also start or stop the server and report its current status.

mysqld_multi searches for the group named mysqldN in my.cnf or in the file provided as the --default-file option. Here N can be any positive number. This number is referred to as the option group number, that is GNR. Group numbers separate option groups from one another and are in arguments to mysqld_multi to specify which server is to be started,stopped, or the status requested for. Options in this group are the same as we use in the [mysqld] group used for starting mysqld.

To execute mysqld_multi, the following syntax is used :

```
shell> mysqld_multi [options] {start|stop|reload|report} [GNR[,GNR] ...]
```

In the preceding syntax, start, stop, reload (stop and restart) and report refers to the operation to be performed. Based on the GNR list values specified, you can perform targeted operations on single or multiple servers.

> Please make sure that the data directory for all servers is fully accessible to the Unix account by which the specific mysqld process is started. Do not use a root account unless you know exactly what you are going to do with it.

Installation programs

The programs discussed in this section are used during the installation process or when upgrading the MySQL, so make sure you understand it correctly before doing any modifications on the program.

comp_err - compiling the MySQL error msg file

This creates the errmsg.sys file which is used by mysqld to identify the error messages and display individual error codes. comp_err is normally run automatically when MySQL is built. The errmsg.sys file is compiled from the text file located in MySQL distributions at sql/share/errmsg-utf8.txt. It also generates sql_state.h, mysqld_ername.h, and mysqld_error.h header files.

`comp_err` has several options and can be retrieved using the `--help` option in the previous command.

mysql_secure_installation - improving MySQL installation security

The program has ways to enable and improve the security of the MySQL installation, including:

- Setting passwords for `root` accounts.
- Removing `root` accounts that can be accessed outside the `localhost`.
- Removing anonymous accounts.
- Removing test database privileges that permit anyone to access databases that start with names `test_`.
- Execute the `mysql_secure_installation` command without any arguments if you want normal usage with the local MySQL server. It will ask you further to check which actions to perform.
- The `validate_password` plugin can be used to strengthen password checking. If the plugin is not already installed, it will ask you to install and once installed and enabled, it can validate for the password.

Execute `mysql_secure_installation` with the following syntax:

```
shell> mysql_secure_installation [options]
```

You can use the `--help` option here and retrieve a list of other options whenever required.

mysql_ssl_rsa_setup - creating SSL/RSA files

As the name suggests, this program is for generating SSL certificates and key files and RSA key-pair files, if those files are missing and files are required to support secure connections. `mysql_ssl_rsa_setup` can also be used to create new files if any of the existing ones have expired.

The `Openssl` command is used by `mysqlssl_rsa_setup`, so using it is necessary to have `OpenSSL` installed on your machine. To generate these files automatically by the server, it can use MySQL distributions compiled using `OpenSSL`, which is another way to generate `SSL` and `RSA` files.

Execute `mysql_ssl_rsa_setup`, as shown here:

```
shell> mysql_ssl_rsa_setup [options]
```

Use the `--help` option here and retrieve a list of other options if required.

 Using `ssl mysql_ssl_rsa_setup` lowers the barrier to `ssl` and makes it easier to generate the required files but the files that are generated are self-signed, which is not very secure. You can consider obtaining a CA certificate from the respective authority.

mysql_tzinfo_to_sql - loading the timezone tables

This program gets the content of the `host system` zone info database (files describing time zones) and loads the information in the time zone tables of MySQL. If the system does not have a zone info database, you can use the downloadable package with `POSIX` standard `timezone_2017c_posix_sql.zip` and non `POSIX` standard `timezone_2017c_leaps_sql.zip` from `https://dev.mysql.com/downloads/timezones.html`.

`mysql_tzinfo_to_sql` can be executed in the following different ways:

```
shell> mysql_tzinfo_to_sql tz_dir
shell> mysql_tzinfo_to_sql tz_file tz_name
shell> mysql_tzinfo_to_sql --leap tz_file
```

After running the `mysql_tzinfo_to_sql` program, it is highly recommended to restart the server so that it will not use any previously cached `timezone` data.

mysql_upgrade - checking and upgrading MySQL tables

As the name suggests, this is used for upgrade operations. It checks for any incompatibility and makes repairs if it is necessary and also updates the grant tables with any changes in new versions of MySQL. It also updates the system tables so you can take advantage of any new privilege or compatibility that might have been added in the newer version.

 Before performing an upgrade always backup your current MySQL installation.

If `mysql_upgrade` finds that a table has possible incompatibility, it performs a table check and attempts repairing the table, and if it cannot repair it, it will ask for a manual table repair.

`mysql_upgrade` should be executed each time MySQL is upgraded. It communicates directly with the MySQL server and sends the required SQL statements to perform an upgrade.

Once we run `mysql_upgrade`, we should restart the server. If any changes made to system tables are taken into effect, before running it, you should make sure the server is running.

Execute `mysql_upgrade` with the following syntax:

```
shell> mysql_upgrade [options]
```

You can use the `--help` option here and retrieve a list of other options whenever required.

MySQL 8 client programs

The MySQL 8 client programs are the programs that are commonly used to connect to the MySQL database and perform different query operations.

The programs information detailed in the following subsection includes `mysql`—command line tools with many commands and related options and configuration for `logging`, `mysqlcheck`, `mysqldump`, `mysqlimport`, `mysqlsh`, `mysqladmin` and so on.

mysql - the command-line tool

This is the most commonly used program. The command-line tool is used for executing SQL statements directly or using a file in batch mode. It has support for both interactive and non-interactive modes. In this section, we will look at the mysql command line and the various options, commands, logging, and other related programs.

mysql options

mysql is a command line tool that has been provided for a long time and so it has plenty of options to get your work done. The following is the table of options with formats and descriptions:

Format	Description
--auto-rehash	Enables automatic rehashing
--auto-vertical-output	Enables automatic vertical result set display
--batch	Do not use the history file
--binary-as-hex	Displays binary values in hexadecimal notation
--binary-mode	Disables \r\n - to - \n translation and treatment of \0 as end-of-query
--bind-address	Uses specified network interface to connect to MySQL server
--character-sets-dir	Directory where character sets are installed
--column-names	Writes column names in results
--column-type-info	Displays result set metadata
--comments	Ascertains whether to retain or strip comments in statements sent to the server
--compress	Compresses all information sent between client and server
--connect-expired-password	Indicates to server that client can handle expired password sandbox mode
--connect_timeout	Number of seconds before connection timeout
--database	The database to use

`--debug`	Writes debugging log; supported only if MySQL was built with debugging support
`--debug-check`	Prints debugging information when program exits
`--debug-info`	Prints debugging information, memory, and CPU statistics when program exits
`--default-auth`	Authentication plugin to use
`--default-character-set`	Specifies default character set
`--defaults-extra-file`	Reads named option file in addition to usual option files
`--defaults-file`	Reads only named option file
`--defaults-group-suffix`	Option group suffix value
`--delimiter`	Sets the statement delimiter
`--enable-cleartext-plugin`	Enables cleartext authentication plugin
`--execute`	Executes the statement and quit
`--force`	Continues even if an SQL error occurs
`--get-server-public-key`	Pathname to file containing RSA public key
`--help`	Displays help message and exit
`--histignore`	Patterns specifying which statements to ignore for logging
`--host`	Connects to MySQL server on given host
`--html`	Produces HTML output
`--ignore-spaces`	Ignores spaces after function names
`--init-command`	SQL statement to execute after connecting
`--line-numbers`	Writes line numbers for errors
`--local-infile`	Enables or disable for LOCAL capability for LOAD DATA INFILE
`--login-path`	Reads login path options from .mylogin.cnf
`--max_allowed_packet`	Maximum packet length to send to or receive from server

`--max_join_size`	The automatic limit for rows in a join when using `--safe-updates`
`--named-commands`	Enables named `mysql` commands
`--net_buffer_length`	Buffer size for TCP/IP and socket communication
`--no-auto-rehash`	Disables automatic rehashing
`--no-beep`	Do not beep when errors occur
`--no-defaults`	Reads no option files
`--one-database`	Ignores statements except those for the default database named on the command line
`--pager`	Uses the given command for paging query output
`--password`	Password to use when connecting to server
`--pipe`	On Windows, connect to server using named pipe
`--plugin-dir`	Directory where plugins are installed
`--port`	TCP/IP port number to use for connection
`--print-defaults`	Print default options
`--prompt`	Set the prompt to the specified format
`--protocol`	Connection protocol to use
`--quick`	Do not cache each query result
`--raw`	Writes column values without escape conversion
`--reconnect`	If the connection to the server is lost, automatically tries to reconnect
`--i-am-a-dummy, --safe-updates`	Allows only UPDATE and DELETE statements that specify key values
`--secure-auth`	Do not send passwords to server in old (pre-4.1) format
`--select_limit`	The automatic limit for SELECT statements when using `--safe-updates`
`--server-public-key-path`	Pathname to file containing RSA public key
`--shared-memory-base-name`	The name of shared memory to use for shared-memory connections

`--show-warnings`	Shows warnings after each statement if there are any
`--sigint-ignore`	Ignores SIGINT signals (typically the result of typing *Control+C*)
`--silent`	Silent mode
`--skip-auto-rehash`	Disables automatic rehashing
`--skip-column-names`	Do not write column names in results
`--skip-line-numbers`	Skips line numbers for errors
`--skip-named-commands`	Disables named mysql commands
`--skip-pager`	Disables paging
`--skip-reconnect`	Disables reconnecting
`--socket`	For connections to localhost, the Unix socket file or Windows named pipe to use
`--ssl-ca`	Path of file that contains list of trusted SSL CAs
`--ssl-capath`	Path of directory that contains trusted SSL CA certificates in PEM format
`--ssl-cert`	Path of file that contains X509 certificate in PEM format
`--ssl-cipher`	List of permitted ciphers to use for connection encryption
`--ssl-crl`	Path of file that contains certificate revocation lists
`--ssl-crlpath`	Path of directory that contains certificate revocation list files
`--ssl-key`	Path of file that contains X509 key in PEM format
`--ssl-mode`	Security state of connection to server
`--syslog`	Logs interactive statements to syslog
`--table`	Displays output in tabular format
`--tee`	Appends a copy of output to named file
`--tls-version`	Protocols permitted for encrypted connections
`--unbuffered`	Flushes the buffer after each query
`--user`	MySQL username to use when connecting to server

`--verbose`	Verbose mode
`--version`	Displays version information and exit
`--vertical`	Prints query output rows vertically (one line per column value)
`--wait`	If the connection cannot be established, wait and retry instead of aborting
`--xml`	Produces XML output

Reference : `https://dev.mysql.com/doc/refman/8.0/en/mysql-command-options.html`

To get more information on individual options, use that option along with the `--help` option.

mysql commands

Each of the SQL statements that you issue are sent to the server for execution. There is also a list of commands that `mysql` itself interprets. To get the list of all those commands, type `\h` or `\help` at the `mysql>` prompt.

Each of the commands have both long and short form that can be used; except short form cannot be used in multi-line comments. The long form is not case sensitive but the short form command is case sensitive.

help [arg], \h [arg],\? [arg], ? [arg]

The help `arg[]` command is used to display help messages, along with listing all the available commands in `mysql`.

charset charset_name, \C charset_name

To change default charsets, issuing the `SET_NAMES` statement.

clear, \c

To clear the current output or previous query results from the command line.

connect [db_name host_name], \r [db_name host_name]

To reconnect the server by providing `database` and `host_name` arguments.

edit, \e

To edit the input statement currently provided.

exit, \q

To exit the `mysql` command line.

prompt [str], \R [str]

To specify a string and reconfigure it with the `mysql` prompt.

quit, \q

To exit the `mysql` command line.

status, \s

This is used to check for the status of the server connection that is currently being used.

use db_name, \u db_name

To specify using the provided `db_name` as the default database.

mysql logging

The `mysql` program can do logging as per the following types.

On Unix systems, it writes the logs to the history file with the default name `.mysql_history` in the home directory.

On all platforms, if the `--syslog` option is provided, it writes the statements to the system logging implementation. On Unix, it is `syslog`, on Windows, it is event logs, on Linux distributions, it often goes to the `/var/log/message` file.

mysql server-side help

To get server-side help from `mysql` , the following syntax is used.

```
mysql> help search_string
```

If you provide any argument after the help command, `mysql` uses that argument for searching the string for accessing server-side help from the MySQL reference manual content. If there is no match for the searched string, the search operation fails and it appears as follows:

```
mysql> help me
Nothing found
Please try to run 'help contents' fro a list of all accessible topics
```

If `search_string` matches multiple contents of a topic, then it shows a list of matching topic items. A topic can also be used as `search_string` and looks for the entry for the topic. It also contains the wildcard character `%` and `_` , which have the same meaning for matching operations performed by the `LIKE` operator.

Executing sql from text files

The `mysql` client is generally used interactively but it will also allow you to execute SQL statements from a file. In order to do so, create a `text_file`, which contains several statements that need to be executed, as follows:

```
shell> mysql db_name < text_file
```

Instead if `USE  db_name` is kept as the first statement of the `text_file` then you can skip specifying the `db_name` from the command line:

```
shell> mysql < text_file
```

If already using the `mysql` connection, then use the source or `\.` command:

```
mysql> source file_name
```

By using the `--verbose` option, each statement gets displayed just before the result produced by it.

mysqladmin - client for administering a MySQL server

`mysqladmin` is the client for administrative operation. It can be used to check the server's configuration, connection status, drop and create database, and much more.

The execution syntax for the `mysqladmin` command is as follows:

```
shell> mysqladmin [options] command [command-arg] [command [command-org]]
...
```

`mysqladmin` supports plenty of program commands, starting from `create db_name` to create new database with name `db_name`, `debug` to get debug information, `drop db_name` to drop a database, `flush-xxxx`, where `xxxx` can be replaced with logs, hosts, privileges, status, tables, threads, and so on. `kill id` to kill the server thread or multiple threads, `password new_password` to set a new password, `ping` to check the server's availability, `shutdown` to stop the server, `start-slave` to start replication on a slave server, `stop-slave` to stop replication on the slave server, `variables` to display server system variables and their respective values.

`mysqladmin status` commands give results with values of uptime, threads, questions, slow queries, opens, and flush tables with relevant information.

Along with the command list, there are options that come in handy when retrieving specific information from the server. Such information can be retrieved using the `mysqladmin --help` command.

mysqlcheck - a table maintenance program

This program is used for table maintenance. It checks, repairs, optimizes, or analyzes tables.The program can be time consuming, particularly for largesized tables. `mysql_upgrade` uses the `mysqlcheck` command for checks and repair of all the tables. The `mysqld` server must be running to use the `mysqlcheck` command.

`mysqlcheck` uses CHECK TABLE, REPAIR TABLE, ANALYZE TABLE, and OPTIMIZE TABLE in a convenient way for the user. If the table repair fails by `mysqlcheck` then a manual table repair is required.

The following is the execution syntax for the `mysqlcheck` command :

```
shell> mysqlcheck [options] db_name [tbl_name ...]
shell> mysqlcheck [options] --databases db_name ...
shell> mysqlcheck [options] --all-databases
```

`mysqlcheck` has a special feature that is the default behavior of checking tables. It can be changed by renaming the binary, such as renaming `mysqlcheck` to the `mysqlrepair` program by creating a copy of `mysqlcheck` and adding a symbolic link to `mysqlcheck` , after which `mysqlrepair` can repair tables instead. This also works with the `mysqlanalyze` and `mysqloptimize` options to make them the default operation for the `mysqlcheck` command.

Similar to other administering programs, this program also have many options that can be used to get specific information, and by using the `mysqlcheck --help` command, a list of options can be retrieved.

mysqldump - a database backup program

This program is a utility program used for making a logical backup by generating a set of SQL statements which can be executed to reproduce the original database table data and object definition. It dumps one or more database for backup or may transfer to another SQL server. It can also generate data output in different formats, such as CSV, XML, or other delimited text files.

Performance and scalability

It should not to be considered as a fast or scalable solution for backing up large amounts of data. The backup takes some time and restoring data can be very slow, as SQL statements involve index creation, disk I/O for insertion, and so on. It can retrieve and dump table data row by row; otherwise it can take a whole table and buffer it in the memory for dumping it.

The following is the execution syntax for `mysqldump`:

```
shell> mysqldump [options] db_name [tbl_name ...]
shell> mysqldump [options] --databases db_name ...
shell> mysqldump [options] --all-databases
```

There are more than 25 options available for modifying the operation of the `mysqldump` command and they can be retrieved by using the `mysqldump --help` command. Specific modifications can be used in this command for debugging options, help options, connection options, DDL options, and so on, based on your requirement.

mysqlimport - a data import program

This client program provides the CLI interface to LOAD_DATA_INFILE SQL statements. The majority of the options correspond to the clauses of the LOAD_DATA_INFILE syntax.

The execution syntax for mysqlimport is as follows:

```
shell> mysqlimport [options] db_name textfile1 [textfile2 ...]
```

Options for the commands can be specified on the CLI or in the [mysqlimport] or [client] group of the options file as per your requirement. It provided options to retrieve and modify import operations for the data, such as using a different delimiter format, debugging, forcing the path of a file, providing default values, ignoring and locking tables, and so on, which can be retrieved by using the mysqlimport --help command.

mysqlpump - a database backup program

This program is a utility program used for making a logical backup by generating a set of SQL statements that can be executed to reproduce the original database table data and object definition. It dumps one or more databases for backup or may transfer to another SQL server.

mysqlpump has the following important features :

- Parallel processing of databases and objects in databases, which speeds up the dump processing
- More control over which database objects and databases to dump
- Dump user accounts data to account management statements rather than inserting data into the system database
- The capacity to create compressed output
- Showing the progress indicator
- Dump file reloading; for InnoDB tables it adds indexes after rows are inserted

mysqlpump dumps all the databases, as specified explicitly specified in the following code:

```
shell> mysqlpump --all-databases
```

To dump multiple databases, specify --databases followed by the database names to dump. You can also specify --exclude-databases= followed by database names not to dump. There are many options to be used for dumping databases or objects, such as for specifying exclusion or inclusion of databases options, applicable for objects such as tables, triggers, routines, events, users, and so on, if they support multiple option entries:

```
shell> mysqlpump --include-databases=db1,db2 --exclude-tables=db1.t1,db2.t2
```

The preceding command dumps databases db1 and db2 but it will exclude table t1 from the database db1 and table t2 from the database db2.

mysqlpump uses parallelism to achieve the concurrent processing and it can be between databases or within a database. --default-parallelism=N specifies the default number of threads used in the queue created by the program and the value of N is 2 by default. --parallel-schemas=[N:]db_list sets up the processing queue as per the database name list provided. Thus, additional queues and the number of threads can be controlled.

mysqlpump does not dump performance_schema, nbdinfo, or sys by default but can do so by specifying the --include-databases option and similarly it also does not dump the INFORMATION_SCHEMA.

mysqlsh - the MySQL Shell

The advanced command line client and editor for MySQL is the very well known MySQL Shell. It has capabilities for scripting in Python and JavaScript. When connected to the MySQL server using the X Protocol, the X DevAPI can work with documents and relational data. It includes the AdminAPI, which enables you to work with an InnoDB cluster.

MySQL Shell has many options associated with it, but the important ones are listed as follows:

```
--port=port_num, -P port_num
```

The TCP/IP port number to use with port_num. The default port is 33060.

```
--node
```

Creates a node session to a single server using the X Protocol and is deprecated in 8.0.3.

```
--js
```

Starts JavaScript mode.

    --py

Starts Python mode.

    --sql

Starts SQL mode.

    --sqlc

Starts SQL mode in ClassicSession.

    --sqln

Starts SQL mode in NodeSession.

    --sqlx

Starts SQL mode by creating an X protocol connection.

    --ssl*

Options beginning with `--ssl` specify connecting the server using SSL and also finding certificates and SSL keys. It works the same way as for the MySQL Server and it accepts SSL options : `--ssl-crl`, `--ssl-crlpath`, `--ssl-mode`, `--ssl-ca`, `--ssl-capath`, `--ssl-cert`, `--ssl-cipher`, `--ssl-key`, `--tls-version`.

Other options not listed can be retrieved using the `mysqlsh --help` command.

mysqlshow - showing database, table, and column information

This is the client mainly used to quickly check which databases, their tables, columns, and indexes exist or not. It provides an interface to some of the SQL `SHOW` statements.

The execution syntax for the command is as follows:

```
shell> mysqlshow [options] [db_name [tbl_name [col_name]]]
```

By executing the preceding command, you will get information about the databases, tables, or columns for which you have privileges:

- A list of databases is shown if no database is given
- A list of all matching tables in the database is shown if no table is given
- A list of all the matching columns and column types in the table is displayed if no column is given

 In the previous command execution, if you used the SQL wildcard character (*, ?, %, _), then names that are matched by the wildcard are displayed. * and ? wildcard characters, if given, are converted into SQL % and _ wildcard characters. It might create confusion when trying to display a column with a table or a column name with _ in the name, it displays only names matching the pattern, but it can be fixed easily by adding an extra % at the end of the command line as a separate argument.

The program has many options to get the desired information by using specific option arguments. A few of the important ones are given as follows:

    --character-sets-dir=dir_name

Specifies the directory name where character sets are installed.

    --compress, -C

If both the client and the server support compression, all the information sent is compressed.

    --enable-cleartext-plugin

Enables the `cleartext` authentication plugin.

    --get--server-public-key

Requests the RSA public key from the server required for key-pair-based password exchange. Also, if a client connects to the server using a secure connection, RSA-based password exchange is not needed and is ignored.

    --keys, -k

Displays table indexes.

```
--ssl*
```

Specifies options starting with `--ssl` to connect to the server using an SSL connection by using certificates and SSL keys.

Many other options not listed here can be retrieved by using the `mysqlshow --help` command.

mysqlslap - load emulation client

This is the diagnostic client program that is used to check client load capability for the MySQL server. The program mimics multiple clients accessing the server.

The execution syntax is as follows:

```
shell> mysqlslap [options]
```

There are many options available to modify the command in execution, some of them, such as `--create` or `--query`, provide a way to specify SQL statements or files with statements with specific delimiters.

`mysqlslap` runs at three different stages :

1. Creating table, schema, and optionally stored programs or data to test. It uses a single client connection only.
2. Running the load test. It uses multiple client connections.
3. Cleaning up (dropping tables if specified earlier, and disconnecting). It uses a single client connection.

For example, creating our own query statement with 20 clients and 100 selects to each of them will look as the following `CLI` :

```
mysqlslap --delimiter=";" --create="CREATE TABLE t (i int);INSERT INTO t
VALUES (21)" --query="SELECT * FROM t" --concurrency=20 --iterations=100
```

`mysqlslap` can also add or create a query statement of it's own, as shown in the following code block:

```
mysqlslap --concurrency=7 --iterations=20 --number-int-cols=2 --number-
char-cols=2 --auto-generate-sql
```

Here, `mysqlslap` will build a statement with a table of two `INT` columns and two `VARCHAR` columns and seven clients querying 20 times to each of them. It also supports specifying statement files for creating and querying separately and running the load test. It provides many such alterations in load testing execution with options that you can check by executing the `mysqlslap --help` command on the command line.

MySQL 8 administrative programs

This section describes different administrative programs along with some utilities that will help in doing administration operations such as performing check sum, compression and extraction, and so on.

ibdsdi - InnoDB tablespace SDI extraction utility

This is a utility program that extracts serialized dictionary information from `InnoDB` tablespace files. Serivalized dictionary information that is SDI data will always be present in all persistent `InnoDB` tablespace files. It can be run on file-per-table on tablespace files and general tablespace files, system tablespace files, and data dictionary tablespace files, but using a temporary tablespace or undoing a tablespace is not supported.

`ibd2sdi` can be used while the server is offline or at runtime. It reads uncommitted data of SDI from a specified tablespace and undoes logs and redoes logs that are not accessible.

Execution for the `idb2sdi` will look like the following command line:

```
shell> ibd2sdi [options] file_name1 [file_name2 file_name3 ...]
```

`ibd2sdi` also supports multiple tablespaces but does not run on more that one tablespace at a time as the `InnoDB` system tablespace. Specifying each file will work as follows :

```
shell> ibd2sdi ibdata1 ibdata2
```

`ibd2sdi` outputs SDI data in JSON format.

There are many options available for the program which can be retrieved using the `ibd2sdi --help` command.

innochecksum - offline InnoDB file checksum utility

This is a checksum utility for InnoDB files. It reads InnoDB tablespace files, calculates checksums for them, and compares them with stored checksum values. If the comparison fails, it reports error with damaged page details. It was developed to verify integrity of the post-power outage but it can also be used after copying the files. It is very useful in the event of any damaged page found when running InnoDB. It will shut down the running server, so to avoid any production issue due to damaged pages.

If a tablespace file is open, it cannot be used by innochecksum. The execution syntax for the command will look as the following:

```
shell> innochecksum [options] file_name
```

innochecksum command also has few options to display information of the pages being verified and can be retrieved with innochecksum --help command.

myisam_ftdump - displaying full-text index utility

This is a utility for displaying information about MyISAM tables and FULLTEXT indexes. It will scan and dump the entire index, which can be a slow and lengthy process. If the server is already running, then you need to make sure to insert a FLUSH TABLES statement first.

Execution for the myisam_ftdump command will look like the following code block:

```
shell> myisam_ftdump [options] <table_name> <index_num>
```

In the previous example, table_name should be the name of the MyISAM table with the .MYI index extension.

Suppose the test database has a table named mytexttable with the following definition:

```
CREATE TABLE mytexttable ( id INT NOT NULL, txt TEXT NOT NULL, PRIMARY KEY
(id), FULLTEXT (txt) ) ENGINE=MyISAM;
```

The index created on id is 0 on FULLTEXT index and on the txt it is 1. If the working directory is the test database directory, then execute myisam_ftdump as follows:

```
shell> myisam_ftdump mytexttable 1
```

`myisam_ftdump` can also be used to generate a list of index entries in order of frequency of occurrence as follows (the first line in Windows and the second line for Unix systems):

```
shell> myisam_ftdump -c mytexttable 1 | sort /R
shell> myisam_ftdump -c mytexttable 1 | sort -r
```

`myisam_ftdump` also has several options that can be retrieved by using the `myisam_ftdump --help` command.

myisamchk - MyISAM table-maintenance utility

`myisamchk` is a command line tool for getting information about database tables, checking, repairing, and optimizing non-partitioned `MyISAM` tables. It works with `MyISAM` tables.

`CHECK_TABLE` and `REPAIR_TABLE` statements can also be used to check and repair `MyISAM` tables.

Execution for the `myisamchk` command is shown in the following code block:

```
shell> myisamchk [OPTIONS] tables[.MYI | .MYD]
```

 Before running the `myisamchk` command, you must make sure that any other program is not using the tables. Otherwise, it will display warning message saying: **warning: clients are using or haven't closed the table properly**. To do this effectively, shut down the MySQL server or lock all tables being used by `myisamchk`.

This program has many options to perform table maintenance.

myisamlog - displaying MyISAM log file content

This program is a utility for processing content of a MyISAM log file. When starting the MySQL server, use the `--log-isam=log_file` option.

Executing the `myisamlog` command uses syntax as shown in the following code block:

```
shell> myisamlog [options] [file_name [tbl_name] ...]
```

The default operation is marked as an update and if recovery is done all writes, updates, and deletes are done and errors are counted only. `myisam.log` is the default log filename.

The program has some options used to specify offsets, recovery, open a number of files, and a few more, which can be retrieved by using the `myisamlog --help` command.

myisampack - generating compressed, read-only MyISAM tables

This is a utility program that compresses `MyISAM` tables. It compresses each of the columns in tables separately and compresses the data file by about 40% to 70%.

MySQL preferably uses the `mmap()` function to do memory mapping on compressed tables; otherwise, it uses normal read/write file operations.

`myisampack` does not support partitioned tables.

Once tables are packed, they become read only.

Stopping the server and then going for compress tables is safe way to perform the compress operation.

Execution syntax for `myisampack` looks like the following block on the command line:

```
shell> myisampack [options] file_name ...
```

Specify the index file name with or without the `.MYI` file and also add the `pathname` if you are not in the database directory.

After compressing a table with `myisampack`, you should use `myisampack -rq` to rebuild the indexes of the compressed table. It supports some of the common options, such as versioning, debugging, and so on along with specific compression checks, such as `--test`, `--backup`, `--join=big_tbl_name`, `--silent`, and so on. If you want to check in detail, you can execute the `myisampack --verbose --help` command on the command line.

mysql_config_editor - MySQL configuration utility

This is a utility to store and update the authentication credentials in an encrypted login pathfile with the name `.mylogin.cnf`.

For further details, use the `mysql_config_editor --verbose --help` command to execute on the command line.

mysqlbinlog - utility for processing binary log files

This program is a utility for processing a server's binary log files. The binary log files contain events data which describes modifications to database content. The server writes such content to the file in a binary format. In order to get them in to a readable (text) format, the `mysqlbinlog` utility is used.

`mysqlbinlog` can also be used to display the content of relay log files written by a slave server during the replication setup because the format for the relay log and the binary log files are same.

Execution for the program syntax is as shown in the following code block:

```
shell> mysqlbinlog [options] log_file ...
```

There are several options that modify the format of the output and usage of `mysqlbinlog`. They are listed as follows:

- It can be converted into a hex dump format that contains byte position, event timestamp, and type of the event that occurred
- It also provides a row event display format that displays data modifications information in the form of pseudo-SQL statements
- It is also used for making a backup of the binary log files by providing the required option values, such as a path for the backup file and type or format of the output in the backup
- When you connect to the MySQL server using `mysqlbinlog`, it provides a specific server ID to identify itself and requests binary log files from the server

The program has some common options which are not mentioned but can be retrieved using the `mysqlbinlog --help` command.

mysqldumpslow - summarizing slow query log files.

The program is a utility that helps in reading the log contents of slow query log files, containing queries taking a longer time to execute. It parses MySQL slow query log files and prints out the summary of the query content.

It generally groups queries that are similar, apart from particular number or string data values. It abstracts those values and display a summary output using N and S, respectively. The -n and -a options are used to modify abstraction behavior of the value.

Execution of the program in the command line syntax is as shown in the following code block:

```
shell> mysqldumpslow [options] [log_file ...]
```

You can modify the output by using some options, such as limiting the number of result -t N , where N is the number of query results to be displayed. -s stands for sort type by query time, lock time, or by rows count, and -r for reversing the sort order.

MySQL 8 environment variables

In this section, we will look at the number of environment variables that are used directly or indirectly for different MySQL programs, changing their behavior with the use of environment variables.

Options provided on the command line take precedence over values specified in the option files and on the environment variables, and similarly values in options take precedence over the environment variables; so in most cases, it is preferred to use an option file instead of environment variables to modify the behavior.

The following is the list of environment variables and descriptions for the variable:

- CXX: The name of your C++ compiler for running CMake
- CC: The name of your C compiler for running CMake
- DBI_USER: The default username for Perl DBI
- DBI_TRACE: Trace options for Perl DBI
- HOME: The default path for the mysql history file is $HOME/.mysql_history

- `LD_RUN_PATH`: Used to specify the location of `libmysqlclient.so`.
- `LIBMYSQL_ENABLE_CLEARTEXT_PLUGIN`: Enables the `mysql_clear_password` authentication plugin
- `LIBMYSQL_PLUGIN_DIR`: Directory in which to look for client plugins
- `LIBMYSQL_PLUGINS`: Client plugins to preload
- `MYSQL_DEBUG`: Debugs trace options when debugging
- `MYSQL_GROUP_SUFFIX`: optional group suffix value (such as specifying `--defaults-group-suffix`)
- `MYSQL_HISTFILE`: The path to the `mysql` history file; if this variable is set, its value overrides the default for `$HOME/.mysql_history`
- `MYSQL_HISTIGNORE` : Patterns specifying statements that mysql should not log to `$HOME/.mysql_history`, or `syslog if --syslog` is given
- `MYSQL_HOME`: The path to the directory in which the server-specific `my.cnf` file resides
- `MYSQL_HOST`: The path to the directory in which the server-specific `my.cnf` file resides
- `MYSQL_PWD`: The default password when connecting to `mysqld`; using this is insecure
- `MYSQL_TCP_PORT` : Default TCP/IP port number
- `MYSQL_TEST_LOGIN_FILE` : Name of the `.mylogin.cnf` login path file
- `PATH`: Used by the shell to find MySQL programs
- `PKG_CONFIG_PATH`: Location of the `mysqlclient.pc pkg-config` file
- `TMPDIR`: Directory in which temporary files are created
- `TZ`: This should be set to your local time zone
- `UMASK`: User-file creation mode when creating files
- `UMASK_DIR`: User-directory creation mode when creating directories
- `USER`: Default user name on Windows when connecting to `mysqld`

`MYSQL_TEST_LOGIN_FILE` is the pathname for the login path file that is created by `mysql_config_editor`.

The `UMASK` and `UMASK_DIR` variables are used as modes instead of masks.

It is necessary to set `PKG_CONFIG_PATH` if using pkg-config for building MySQL programs.

MySQL GUI tools

There are many MySQL GUI tools available for performing various operations, starting with creating databases to performing daily administration tasks.

MySQL Workbench

MySQL Workbench is a graphical tool to work with the MySQL server and databases. It fully supports MySQL versions 5.1 and above. In this section, we will briefly discuss the capabilities of MySQL Workbench.

Five main function provided by MySQL Workbench are as follows:

- **SQL development**: This creates and manages database connections, and configuration for connection parameters. It executes SQL statements using the built-in SQL editor and it replaces the standalone application query browser provided earlier.
- **Data modeling**: This creates models of database schema graphically, with reverse and forward engineering between two different schema as well as on a live database. It provides a comprehensive table editor, with easy to use facilities for editing tables, columns, triggers, indexes, options, inserts, partitioning, routines, views, and privileges.
- **Server administration**: This creates, maintains, and administers server instances.
- **Data migration**: This allows migration from PostgreSQL, SQLite, Sybase ASE, Microsoft SQL Server, and other relational database management system objects, tables, and data to MySQL. It also facilitates migration from earlier versions to the latest release version.
- **MySQL Enterprise support**: This provides enterprise level support for the product; for example, MySQL Enterprise backup, MySQL Audit.

MySQL workbench is available in two different editions, the Commercial Edition and the Community Edition. The Community Edition is provided without any cost. The Commercial Edition provides additional features, such as database documentation generation.

MySQL Notifier

MySQL Notifier is a simple tool used to monitor and adjust the status of local/remote MySQL server instances. It is an indicator which is placed in a system tray. It is installed with the MySQL installer itself.

MySQL Notifier acts as quick launcher with list actions clubbed together that can be act and monitored very easily from the system tray itself and along with that it keeps monitoring based on specified interval and notifies on status change.

MySQL Notifier usage

MySQL Notifier stays in system tray and provides one click option for MySQL status and maintenance. Followings are important usage of MySQL Notifier.

- MySQL Notifier provides start, stop, and restart of MySQL Sever instances
- MySQL Notifier configures MySQL server services and automatically detects and adds new MySQL server services
- MySQL Notifier monitors both local and remote MySQL instances

Summary

In this chapter, we dived deep into the ocean of commands that are used for almost all the activities for the MySQL server, starting with installation, server start up, client programs to administrative programs, and several utility programs to cater for different purposes on a routine basis for database administration. The chapter also provided a working knowledge of making database backups and importing the databases with or without specific tables.

The next chapter will focus on MySQL 8 data types in detail. It will categorize data types based on their content types and it will describe properties in detail for each of the categories and storage level details that should be kept in mind during table and column design.

4

MySQL 8 Data Types

In the previous chapter, we learned how to use MySQL 8 command-line programs and utilities to perform various operations on the MySQL 8 database. It is always good to have hold on command-line tools. It provides flexibility to work in non-GUI environments. The focus of this chapter is data types. Isn't it fascinating to know the type of data the programming language supports or the storage engine can store? It is a fundamental feature of any programming language or database. At the same time, it is the most ignored topic, as well. The majority of programmers don't spend enough time assessing the storage requirements for `variables` used in a piece of code. Actually, it is extremely important to understand the basic and custom data types that the database supports, which is why this chapter exists.

The following is a list of topics to be covered in this chapter:

- Overview of MySQL 8 data types
- Numeric data types
- Date and time data types
- String data types
- JSON data type
- Storage requirements for data types
- Choosing the right data type for columns

Overview of MySQL 8 data types

All standard SQL data types are supported in MySQL. These data types are classified in a few categories, such as numeric types, string types, date and time types, and the JSON data type. When we assign a data type to a column, certain conventions must be followed. These conventions are necessary for MySQL to allow values to be stored in a column:

- **M** denotes the maximum display width for integer types. For floating point and fixed point types, it is the total number of digits that can be stored. For string types, it is the maximum length. The maximum value allowed depends on the data type.
- **D** is applicable to floating points and fixed point types. It denotes the number of digits after the decimal point. The maximum allowed value is 30, but must be less than or equal to M-2.
- **fsp** is applicable to date and time types. It denotes the fractional seconds precision, which means the number of digits following the decimal point for the fractional part of seconds.

This overview is brief so that the detailed descriptions of the features of each data type can be covered in topics to follow.

Numeric data types

The MySQL 8 numeric data types include integer or exact data types, decimal or approximate data types, and bit data types.

By default, REAL data type values are stored as DOUBLE. If we have set the REAL_AS_FLOAT flag on MySQL, REAL data type values are stored as FLOAT. FLOAT occupies less space compared to DOUBLE.

Integer types

All standard SQL integer types are supported by MySQL.

The following is a table describing the required storage and range for each integer type. Along with standard integer data types, MySQL also supports TINYINT, MEDIUMINT, and BIGINT:

Type	Storage (Bytes)	Minimum Value	Maximum Value
		Signed / Unsigned	Signed / Unsigned
TINYINT	1	-128	127
		0	255
SMALLINT	2	-32768	32767
		0	65535
MEDIUMINT	3	-8388608	8388607
		0	16777215
INT	4	-2147483648	2147483647
		0	4294967295
BIGINT	8	-9223372036854775808	9223372036854775807
		0	18446744073709551615

Reference: https://dev.mysql.com/doc/refman/8.0/en/integer-types.html

The range of signed numbers includes both -ve and +ve numbers, whereas the range of unsigned numbers includes +ve numbers only.

The following is the column declaration for the unsigned integer column:

```
CREATE TABLE employees
(salary INTEGER(5) UNSIGNED);
```

INT and INTEGER can be used interchangeably. But consider if we declared a column as:

```
CREATE TABLE employees
(id INT(255));
```

The maximum value that an INTEGER column can store is either 2147483647 (in case of a signed INTEGER) or 4294967295 (in case of an unsigned INTEGER). 255 here defines the visible length of a number. On the one handed, it is impractical to display a number 255 digits long. On the other hand, INTEGER supports 10 digit numbers as a maximum value. So, it will be converted to INT(11) in the preceding case. Now, this raises another question: if the number of digits for a maximum integer number is 10, then why should it be converted to INT(11) and not INT(10)? The reason is that one digit is kept for storing the sign.

ZEROFILL is an attribute which indicates that the number value should be prefixed with zeros if the length of the number value is smaller than the length of the column. The CREATE statement demonstrates a way to declare a column with the ZEROFILL attribute. The following is an example:

```
CREATE TABLE documents
(document_no INT(5) ZEROFILL);
```

We specified the value to be stored as 111; it will be stored as 00111 if we provided the ZEROFILL option.

Fixed point types

Fixed point types represent numbers with a fixed number of digits after the decimal or radix point. MySQL has DECIMAL and NUMERIC as fixed point, or exact, value data types. These values are stored in a binary format. Fixed point data types are useful, especially in storing monetary values in multiplication and division operations. The value of a fixed point data type is an integer number scaled by a specific factor, according to the type. For example, the value of 1.11 can be represented in fixed point as 111, with a scaling factor of 1/100. Similarly, 1,110,000 can be represented as 1110, with a scaling factor of 1000.

The following code block demonstrates the declaration of a DECIMAL data type:

```
CREATE TABLE taxes
(tax_rate DECIMAL(3, 2));
```

In the preceding example, 3 is the precision and 2 is the scale. An example value could be 4.65, where 4 is the precision and 65 is the scale:

- **Precision**: Denotes the number of significant digits stored for the values
- **Scale**: Represents the number of digits after the decimal point

Precision and scale define the range of values that can be stored in the column. So, in the preceding column declaration, `tax_rate` can store values falling between -9.99 and 9.99.

The syntax for defining the `DECIMAL` type in standard SQL is as follows:

```
DECIMAL(M)
```

In MySQL, this is equivalent to:

```
DECIMAL(M, 0)
```

Declaring a column with `DECIMAL` is equivalent to `DECIMAL(M, 0)` in MySQL.

 In MySQL, 10 is the default value for `M`, if it's not provided.

The maximum number of digits supported for the `DECIMAL` type is 65, including precision and scale. We can limit the number of digits on values which can be entered for a column by using precision and scale. If a user enters a value with a larger number of digits than permitted in scale, the value will be truncated to match the permitted scale.

`DECIMAL` is often considered to be an alternative to `DOUBLE` or `FLOAT`. As mentioned earlier, `DECIMAL` numbers are an exact representation of `REAL` numbers in mathematics. The only problem with the `DECIMAL` data type is that it occupies much more space, even for small numbers. For example, to store a value of 0.000003, the column declaration should have the data type defined as `DECIMAL(7, 6)`.

If the scale is 0, the column values don't have decimal points or fractional values.

Floating point types

Floating point numbers represent real numbers in computing. Real numbers are useful for measuring continuous values, such as weight, height, or speed.

MySQL has two floating point data types for storing approximate values: `FLOAT` and `DOUBLE`.

For floating point numbers, precision is an important factor. Precision defines the measure of accuracy. MySQL supports single precision and double precision floating point numbers. It consumes four bytes to store a single precision floating point number with the FLOAT data type, whereas it consumes eight bytes to store a double precision floating point number with the DOUBLE data type.

In MySQL, REAL is a synonym for DOUBLE PRECISION. As mentioned earlier, if REAL_AS_FLOAT is enabled, a column defined with the REAL data type will be treated similarly to FLOAT.

The preceding description depicts FLOAT or DOUBLE as similar to DECIMAL. No, it is not. There is a huge difference. As described earlier, fixed point data types such as DECIMAL or NUMERIC can store exact values, up to the maximum digit after the decimal point, whereas floating point data types, such as FLOAT or DOUBLE, store approximate values. The values stored are detailed enough, but not completely accurate. There remains a minor inaccuracy.

Let's understand this through the following code example:

```
mysql> CREATE TABLE typed_numbers(id TINYINT, float_values FLOAT,
decimal_values DECIMAL(3, 2));

mysql> INSERT INTO typed_numbers VALUES(1, 1.1, 1.1), (2, 1.1, 1.1), (3,
1.1, 1.1);

mysql> SELECT * FROM typed_numbers;
+-------+--------------+----------------+
| id    | float_values | decimal_values |
+-------+--------------+----------------+
|    1  |          1.1 |           1.10 |
|    2  |          1.1 |           1.10 |
|    3  |          1.1 |           1.10 |
+-------+--------------+----------------+

mysql> SELECT SUM(float_values), SUM(decimal_values) FROM typed_numbers;
+--------------------+---------------------+
| SUM(float_values)  | SUM(decimal_values) |
+--------------------+---------------------+
| 3.3000000715255737 |                3.30 |
+--------------------+---------------------+
```

In the preceding example:

1. We created a table containing FLOAT and DECIMAL type columns.
2. We inserted the same values in two columns, named float_values and decimal_values.
3. We executed a select query to fetch the sum of stored values.

Though the same values, the output is different. The sum of decimal_values looks more precise compared to that of the float_values. The sum of float_values looks less precise. This is because of internal rounding performed by the MySQL engine for floating point data types, which results in the approximation stored value.

Standard SQL has a provision for specifying precision while defining a FLOAT column. The precision is in bits specified following the keyword FLOAT within parenthesis. MySQL also supports specifying precision values for FLOAT or DOUBLE, but the precision is used to determine the size:

- Precision from 0 to 23 results in a 4 byte single precision FLOAT column
- Precision from 24 to 53 results in an 8 byte double precision DOUBLE column

The following is an example of FLOAT column declaration attributes:

```
FLOAT(M, D)
where,
M - number of digits in total
D - number of digits may be after the decimal point
```

So, the column defined as the following will store a value such as 99.99:

```
FLOAT(4, 2)
```

While storing floating point values, MySQL performs rounding. So, the value inserted as 99.09 into a FLOAT(4, 2) column may be stored as 99.01 as an approximate result.

Though the floating point column definition supports specifying precision, it is advisable to use FLOAT or DOUBLE PRECISION with no precision or number of digits, so as to take advantage of maximum flexibility and portability.

Problems with floating point values

As described earlier, floating point data types store approximate real numbers. Trying to store an exact value and use it in comparison operations considering exact values may lead to various problems. Also, floating point values are interpreted in a platform and implementation-dependent manner. For example, different CPUs or operating systems may evaluate floating point numbers differently. This essentially means that the value intended to be stored in the floating point data type column may not be the same as the actual value stored or represented internally.

The previous point becomes essential when we use floating point numbers in comparison. Consider the following example:

```
mysql> CREATE TABLE temp(id INT, col1 DOUBLE, col2 DOUBLE);

mysql> INSERT INTO temp VALUES (1, 5.30, 2.30), (1, -3.00, 0.00),
    (2, 0.10, -10.00), (2, -15.20, 4.00), (2, 0.00, -7.10),
    (3, 0.00, 2.30), (3, 0.00, 0.00);

mysql> SELECT id, SUM(col1) as v1, SUM(col2) as v2 FROM temp
    GROUP BY id HAVING v1 <> v2;
+------+--------+--------+
| id   | v1     | v2     |
+------+--------+--------+
|    1 |    2.3 |    2.3 |
|    2 |  -15.1 |  -13.1 |
|    3 |    0.0 |    2.3 |
+------+--------+--------+
```

In the preceding example, it seems that the first two rows in the output have similar numbers. It is possible that they might not be, in the case of floating point types. If we want to ensure, in the preceding case, that similar-looking values are considered, we have to compare the difference against a predefined number with precision. For example, in the preceding case, if we modify the HAVING clause to check the condition ABS (v1 - v2) > 0.1, it will return the expected output.

 As interpretation of floating point numbers is platform dependent, if we try to insert a value which is outside of the range of floating point data type supported values, it may insert +- inf or +- 0.

Bit value type

Have you ever come across a requirement to store binary representations of numbers? Can you think of such use cases? One such use case is to store weekly working days information for a year. We will touch base on this example later in the section.

The BIT data type is used to store binary bits or groups of bit values. It is also one of the options to store Boolean, yes/no or 0/1 values.

The BIT type column can be defined as:

```
column_name BIT
or
column_name BIT(m)
where m = number of bits to be stored
```

For a BIT data type, m can vary from 1 to 64. Supplying m is optional. The default value for m is 1.

The following is an example of how a BIT column can be defined:

```
CREATE TABLE working_days (
year INT,
week INT,
days BIT(7),
PRIMARY KEY (year, week));
```

After the BIT data type column declaration, next is storing bit values in a column. The bit values are a combination of zeros (0s) and ones (1s). The b'value' notation is used to specify bit values.

The following are the examples of how to store 11 and 55 in a BIT column:

```
CREATE TABLE bit_values (val BIT(7));

INSERT INTO bit_values VALUES(b'1011');
INSERT INTO bit_values VALUES(b'110111');
```

What happens if the value stored in the BIT column is less than the number of bits (m) specified in the column definition? MySQL will pad the value with 0s on the left of the number. So, for the preceding example, the values stored will be 0001011 and 0110111, respectively.

How do we define a `BIT` column to store `boolean_values`? The following code block shows that:

```
CREATE TABLE boolean_values (value BIT(1));
or
CREATE TABLE boolean_values (value BIT);

INSERT INTO boolean_values VALUES(b'0');
INSERT INTO boolean_values VALUES(b'1');
```

Bit value literals

To store bit values in a table column, we must understand bit literals. As mentioned earlier, bit literals can be written using the `b'val'` notation. There is another notation, which is the `0bval` notation.

 One important note about `b'val'` or `0bval` notations is that the letter case of the leading `b` doesn't matter. We can specify `b` or `B`. A leading `0b` is case-sensitive, and can't be replaced with `0B`.

The following is the list of legal and illegal bit value literals.

Legal bit value literals:

- `b'10'`
- `B'11'`
- `0b10`

Illegal bit value literals:

- `b'3'` (1 and 0 are the only binary digits)
- `0B01` (0B is not valid; it should be 0b)

As a default, a bit literal is a binary string. We can confirm this with the query, as shown in the following code block:

```
mysql> SELECT b'1010110', CHARSET(b'1010110');
+--------------+---------------------+
| b'1010110'   | CHARSET(b'1010110') |
+--------------+---------------------+
|      v       |       binary        |
+--------------+---------------------+
```

```
mysql> SELECT 0b1100100, CHARSET(0b1100100);
+------------+---------------------+
| 0b1100100  |  CHARSET(0b1100100) |
+------------+---------------------+
|     d      |       binary        |
+------------+---------------------+
```

Practical uses of BIT

Let's continue with the working days per week in a year example. Please refer to the `working_days` table schema provided earlier.

How can we specify that the Monday and Friday in the week 4 in the year 2017 are non-working days? The following is the INSERT query for this:

```
INSERT INTO working_days VALUES(2017, 4, 0111011);
```

If we fetch the `working_days` records using the SELECT query, the following is the output:

```
mysql> SELECT year, week, days FROM working_days;
+--------+--------+-------+
|  year  |  week  | days  |
+--------+--------+-------+
|  2017  |     4  |   59  |
+--------+--------+-------+
```

In the preceding output, the days, though being of bit data types, show integer values. How can we show bit values in the output?

The answer is the BIN() MySQL function. The function converts an integer value to its binary representation:

```
mysql> SELECT year, week, BIN(days) FROM working_days;
+--------+--------+----------+
|  year  |  week  |  days    |
+--------+--------+----------+
|  2017  |     4  |  111011  |
+--------+--------+----------+
```

As you can see, the leading zeros are removed from the days' bit value in the output. To accomplish the representation in the output, on top of the BIN function, we can use the LPAD MySQL function:

```
mysql> SELECT year, week, LPAD(BIN(days), 7, '0') FROM working_days;
+--------+--------+----------+
|  year  |  week  |   days   |
+--------+--------+----------+
|   2017 |      4 |  0111011 |
+--------+--------+----------+
```

Type attributes

As shown earlier, while defining integer columns, we can also specify an optional display width attribute. For example, INT(5) indicates an integer number with a display width of 5 digits. When this column is used in the SELECT query, the output will display the number left padded with spaces. So, if the value stored in the INT(5) column is 123, then it will be displayed as __123. The _ will be a space in the actual output.

However, the display width doesn't limit the range of values which can be stored in the INT(5) column. The question then arises: What if we store a value for which the display width is larger than the display width specified? The display width doesn't prevent values wider than the display width of a column from being displayed correctly. So, values wider than the column display width are displayed in full width, using more than the number of digits specified with the display width.

As mentioned earlier, MySQL column definition provides an optional attribute called ZEROFILL. This optional attribute, when specified, replaces left padded spaces with zeros. For example, for a column defined as the following, a value of 82 is retrieved as 00082:

```
INT(5) ZEROFILL
```

This optional attribute is useful where the proper formatting of numbers is important.

The ZEROFILL attribute is ignored when the column value is used in expressions or in a UNION query.

MySQL creates temporary tables when complicated joins are used in a query to store intermediate results. In such a case, we may face issues if we specified a column with display width. In these cases, MySQL considers that the data values fit within the display width.

Another important attribute is UNSIGNED. The UNSIGNED attribute permits only non-negative values to be stored in the column. It is also useful when we need support for a larger range of values to be stored with the same data type.

UNSIGNED is also supported by floating point types and fixed point types.

 If we specify a ZEROFILL attribute for a column, UNSIGNED is automatically added to the column.

Another important attribute for integer and floating point columns is AUTO_INCREMENT. When we insert a NULL value in the column defined with the AUTO_INCREMENT attribute, MySQL stores value+1 instead of NULL. A value of 0 will be treated the same as that of a NULL value, unless the NO_AUTO_VALUE_ON_ZERO mode is enabled. Here, the value is the largest value stored in the column. It is extremely important that the column is defined as NOT NULL. Otherwise, the NULL value will be stored as NULL, even though the AUTO_INCREMENT attribute is provided.

Overflow handling

When an out-of-range value is stored in the numeric type column in MySQL, the value stored depends on the MySQL mode:

- If strict mode is enabled, MySQL will not accept the value and throw an error. The insert operation fails.
- If restrictive modes are enabled, the value is clipped by MySQL to an appropriate value, and that is what is stored in the column.

Date and time data types

DATE, TIME, DATETIME, TIMESTAMP, and YEAR form the group of date and time data types for storing temporal values. Each of these types has a range of permitted values. Apart from the permitted values, a special zero value can also be used to specify an invalid value which MySQL cannot represent. The zero value can be 00-00-0000. MySQL allows this value to be stored in a date column. This is sometimes more convenient than storing NULL values.

The following are the general considerations we must take care of while working with date and time types.

The way MySQL treats storage and retrieval operations for date or time types is different in the context of the format. Basically, for a date or time type value stored in the table, MySQL retrieves values in a standard output format. In the case of inputting a date or time type value, MySQL attempts to apply different formats on the supplied input value. So, it is expected that the supplied value is valid, or unexpected results may occur if used values in unsupported formats.

Though MySQL can interpret input values with several different formats, parts of the date value must be supplied in a year-month-day format. For example, 2017-10-22 or 16-02-14.

Supplying a two-digit year creates ambiguity for MySQL to interpret the year because of the unknown century. The following are the rules that must be followed, using which MySQL interprets two-digit year values:

- Year values between 70-99 are converted to 1970-1999
- Year values between 00-69 are converted to 2000-2069

It is possible to convert a value from one temporal type to another temporal type following certain rules. We will discuss these rules later in the chapter.

If the date or time value is used in a numeric context, MySQL will automatically convert the value to a number.

We have one interesting use case. We want to develop an audit log feature where we store every user-entered value. Suppose that in one of the date fields, the user entered an invalid date, 2017-02-31. Will this be stored in the audit log table? Certainly not. How do we complete the feature, then? MySQL has the `ALLOW_INVALID_DATES` mode. If enabled, it will allow invalid dates to be stored. With this mode enabled, MySQL verifies that the month is in the range of 1-12 and day is in the range of 1-31.

 As ODBC cannot handle zero values for date or time, such values used through Connector/ODBC are converted to `NULL`.

Following table shows zero values for different data types:

Data Type	Zero Value
DATE	0000-00-00
TIME	00:00:00
DATETIME	0000-00-00 00:00:00
TIMESTAMP	0000-00-00 00:00:00
YEAR	0000

Reference: https://dev.mysql.com/doc/refman/8.0/en/date-and-time-types.html

The preceding table shows zero values for different temporal data types. These are special values, as these are allowed by MySQL and are very useful in certain cases. We can also specify zero values using '0' or 0. MySQL has an interesting mode configuration: NO_ZERO_DATE. If this configuration is enabled, MySQL shows a warning if the temporal type has a value with the date as zero.

DATE, DATETIME, and TIMESTAMP types

This section describes the most commonly used MySQL date and time data types: DATE, DATETIME, and TIMESTAMP. This section explains the similarities and differences between these data types.

The DATE data type is suitable when the values we wish to store have a date part, but the time part is missing. The standard MySQL date format is YYYY-MM-DD. The date values are retrieved and displayed in the standard format unless DATE functions are applied. The MySQL supported range of values is 1000-01-01 to 9999-12-31. Supported, here, means the values may work, but there is no guarantee. The same is the case for the DATETIME data type.

The DATETIME data type is suitable for values containing date and time parts. The standard MySQL DATETIME format is YYYY-MM-DD HH:MM:SS. The supported range of values is 1000-01-01 00:00:00 to 9999-12-31 23:59:59.

Similar to DATETIME, the TIMESTAMP data type is also suitable for values containing date and time parts. However, the range of values supported by the TIMESTAMP data type is 1970-01-01 00:00:01 UTC to 2038-01-19 03:14:07 UTC.

Though they look similar, the DATETIME and TIMESTAMP data types differ significantly:

- The TIMESTAMP data type requires 4 bytes to store date and time values. The DATETIME data type requires 5 bytes to store date and time values.
- TIMESTAMP can store values till 2038-01-19 03:14:07 UTC. If we wish to store values beyond 2038, the DATETIME data type should be used.
- TIMESTAMP considers UTC as the time zone while storing values. DATETIME stores values without time zone consideration.

Let's use an example to understand the difference between DATETIME and TIMESTAMP within the context of time_zone.

Suppose the initial time_zone value is set to +00:00:

```
SET time_zone = '+00:00';
```

Let's create a table called datetime_temp. The table has two columns; one is DATETIME and another is of the type TIMESTAMP. We will store the same date and time values in both columns. With the help of the SELECT query, we will try to understand how the representations differ in output:

```
mysql> CREATE TABLE datetime_temp(
  ts TIMESTAMP,
  dt DATETIME);

mysql> INSERT INTO datetime_temp
VALUES(NOW(), NOW());

mysql> SELECT ts, dt FROM datetime_temp;
+-------------------------+-------------------------+
>|           ts            |           dt            |
+-------------------------+-------------------------+
|   2017-10-14 18:10:25   |   2017-10-14 18:10:25   |
+-------------------------+-------------------------+
```

In the preceding example, NOW() is the MySQL function which returns the current date and time values. Looking at the output, it seems that both the TIMESTAMP and DATETIME representations are same. It is because the time_zone value is set to UTC. By default, TIMESTAMP shows the date time value considering the UTC time_zone. On the other part, DATETIME shows date time without a time_zone.

Let's change the `time_zone` and observe the output:

```
mysql> SET time_zone = '+03:00';

mysql> SELECT ts, dt FROM datetime_temp;
+---------------------+---------------------+
|          ts         |          dt         |
+---------------------+---------------------+
| 2017-10-14 21:10:25 | 2017-10-14 18:10:25 |
+---------------------+---------------------+
```

Looking at the output, it is clear that the `TIMESTAMP` considers the `time_zone` value set in MySQL. So, the `TIMESTAMP` value got adjusted when we changed the time zone. `DATETIME` isn't impacted, so the output is not changed, even after changing the time zone.

 If `TIMESTAMP` is used to store date and time values, we must consider it seriously when migrating data to a different server located in a different time zone.

If higher precision for the time value is required, `DATETIME` and `TIMESTAMP` can include trailing fractional seconds as small as microseconds (six digits). So, if we insert a date time value with a microseconds value, it will be stored in the database. The format, including the fractional part, is YYYY-MM-DD HH:MM:SS[.fraction], and the range is from 1000-01-01 00:00:00.000000 to 9999-12-31 23:59:59.999999. The range for `TIMESTAMP`, including the fraction, is 1970-01-01 00:00:01.000000 to 2038-01-19 03:14:07.999999.

The fractional part is separated from the time value by a decimal point because MySQL doesn't recognize any other delimiter for fractional seconds.

Date and time values stored with the `TIMESTAMP` data type are converted from the server's time zone to UTC for storage and from UTC to the server's time zone for retrieval. If we stored a `TIMESTAMP` value and then changed the server's time zone and retrieved the value, the retrieved value would be different from the one we stored.

The following is the list of properties of date value interpretation in MySQL:

- MySQL supports a relaxed format for values specified as string. In a relaxed format, any punctuation character can be used as the delimiter between date parts or time parts. This is a little bit confusing. For example, a value `10:11:12` might look like a time value because of the use of `:`, but is interpreted as a `2010-11-12` date.

- The only recognized delimiter between the rest of the time part and the fractional seconds part is the decimal point.
- It is expected that month and day values are valid. With strict mode disabled, invalid dates are converted to respective zero values and a warning message is shown.
- TIMESTAMP values that include zero in the day or month column are not a valid date. The exception to this rule is the zero value.

If MySQL is run with MAXDB mode enabled, TIMESTAMP is identical to DATETIME. If this mode is enabled at the time of table creation, TIMESTAMP values are converted to DATETIME.

MySQL DATETIME functions

NOW() is the function used to get the current date and time of the system:

```
mysql> SET @dt = NOW();

mysql> SELECT @dt;
+---------------------+
|         @dt         |
+---------------------+
| 2017-10-15 13:43:17 |
+---------------------+
```

The DATE() function is used to extract date information from the DATETIME value:

```
mysql> SELECT DATE(@dt);
+------------------+
|    DATE(@dt)     |
+------------------+
|    2017-10-15    |
+------------------+
```

The TIME() function is used to extract time information from a date time value:

```
mysql> SELECT TIME(@dt);
+------------------+
|    TIME(@dt)     |
+------------------+
|     13:43:17     |
+------------------+
```

The `DATE()` and `TIME()` functions are very useful when you want to display or query a database table based on the date or time value, but the actual value stored in the table contains date and time information.

If we want to extract `YEAR`, `MONTH`, `DAY`, `QUARTER`, `WEEK`, `HOUR`, `MINUTE`, and `SECOND` information from `DATETIME` or `TIMESTAMP` values, respective functions are available:

```
mysql> SELECT
  HOUR(@dt),
  MINUTE(@dt),
  SECOND(@dt),
  DAY(@dt),
  WEEK(@dt),
  MONTH(@dt),
  QUARTER(@dt),
  YEAR(@dt);
+-----------+-------------+-------------+---------+----------+
| HOUR(@dt) | MINUTE(@dt) | SECOND(@dt) | DAY(@dt)| WEEK(@dt)|
+-----------+-------------+-------------+---------+----------+

+-----------+--------------+-----------+
| MONTH(@dt)| QUARTER(@dt) | YEAR(@dt) |
+-----------+--------------+-----------+

+-----------+-------------+-------------+---------+----------+
|        13 |          43 |          17 |      15 |       41 |
+-----------+-------------+-------------+---------+----------+

+-----------+--------------+-----------+
|        10 |            4 |      2017 |
+-----------+--------------+-----------+
```

TIME type

MySQL `DATETIME` or `TIMESTAMP` data types are used to represent specific times at particular dates. How about storing only the time of the day or the time difference between two events? MySQL's `TIME` data type serves the purpose.

The standard MySQL format for storing or displaying `TIME` data type values is `HH:MM:SS`. The time value represents the time of the day, which is less than 24 hours, but the `TIME` data type, as mentioned earlier, can also be used to stored elapsed time or time difference between two events. So, the `TIME` column can store values greater than 24 hours.

The MySQL `TIME` column is defined as follows:

```
column_name TIME;
```

The range of values that can be stored in the `TIME` data type column is -838:59:59 to 838:59:59.

The MySQL `TIME` column can also store the fractional seconds part up to microseconds (six digits), similar to the `DATETIME` column. Considering the fractional second precision, the range of values varies from -838:59:59.000000 to 838:59:59.00000.

The MySQL `TIME` column can also have an optional value:

```
column_name TIME(N);
where N represents number of fractional part, which is up to 6 digits.
```

The `TIME` value usually takes 3 bytes for storage. In the case of the `TIME` value including fractional second precision, it will require additional bytes, based on the number of fractional second precision.

The following table shows the number of additional bytes required to store fractional-second precision:

Fractional Second Precision	Storage (bytes)
0	0
1, 2	1
3, 4	2
5, 6	3

MySQL supports abbreviated values for the `TIME` column. There are two distinct ways for MySQL to interpret abbreviated values:

- If the abbreviated value has a colon(`:`), MySQL interprets it as time of the day. For example, 11:12 is interpreted as 11:12:00 and not as 00:11:12.
- If the abbreviated value doesn't have a colon(`:`), MySQL assumes that the two rightmost digits represent seconds. This means the value is interpreted as elapsed time, rather than time of the day. For example, '1214' and 1214 are interpreted by MySQL as 00:12:14.

The decimal point is the only delimiter accepted by MySQL to separate fractional second precision from the rest of the time value parts.

MySQL, by default, clips the values that lie outside of the permitted range of values to the closest endpoint of the range. For example, -880:00:00 and 880:00:00 are stored as -838:59:59 and 838:59:59. Invalid TIME values are converted to 00:00:00. As 00:00:00 itself is a valid TIME value, it is difficult to know if the value 00:00:00 was stored intentionally, or converted from an invalid TIME value.

MySQL accepts string and numeric values as the TIME values.

Time functions

The CURRENT_TIME() function can be used to find the current time on the server. It is also possible to add or subtract time values using the ADDTIME and SUBTIME functions. For example, the following example adds two hours to the server's current time:

```
mysql> SELECT
  CURRENT_TIME() AS 'CUR_TIME',
  ADDTIME(CURRENT_TIME(), 020000) AS 'ADDTIME',
  SUBTIME(CURRENT_TIME(), 020000) AS 'SUBTIME';

+----------+----------+----------+
| CUR_TIME | ADDTIME  | SUBTIME  |
+----------+----------+----------+
| 10:12:34 | 12:12:34 | 08:12:34 |
+----------+----------+----------+
```

The UTC_TIME() function can be used to fetch the UTC time.

YEAR type

What is the preferred data type for storing manufacturing year? MySQL's answer to this is a YEAR data type. The YEAR data type requires 1 byte to store year information.

A YEAR column can be declared as:

```
manufacturing_year YEAR
or
manufacturing_year YEAR(4)
```

One notable thing is that earlier MySQL versions supported the YEAR(2) type column declaration. The support for YEAR(2) has been discontinued from MySQL 8. It is possible that we might want to upgrade the older MySQL database to the MySQL 8 database. In a later section, we will explain the migration details from YEAR(2) to YEAR(4).

MySQL represents YEAR values in a YYYY format. The range of values is from 1901 to 2155 and 0000.

The following is the list of formats supported for inputting YEAR values:

- Four digit number from 1901 to 2155.
- Four digit string from 1901 to 2155.
- One or two digit number with the range of 0 to 99. YEAR values from 1 to 69 are converted to 2001 to 2069 and from 70 to 99 are converted to 1970 to 1999.
- One or two digit string with the range of 0 to 99. YEAR values from 1 to 69 are converted to 2001 to 2069 and from 70 to 99 are converted to 1970 to 1999.
- Inserting a numeric 0 has a display value of 0000 and an internal value of 0000. If we want to insert 0 and want it to be interpreted as 2000, we should specify it as a string 0 or 00.
- The result of a function that returns an acceptable value YEAR context, for example, NOW().

MySQL converts invalid YEAR values to 0000.

Migrating YEAR(2) to YEAR(4)

As mentioned earlier, MySQL 8 doesn't support the YEAR(2) type. Trying to create a column with YEAR(2) as a data type will give an error as follows:

```
mysql> CREATE TABLE temp(year YEAR(2));
ERROR 1818 (HY000): Supports only YEAR or YEAR(4) column.
```

The ALTER TABLE query, which rebuilds the table, will automatically convert YEAR(2) to YEAR(4). The YEAR(2) column, after upgrading the database to the MySQL 8 database, remains as YEAR(2), but the queries give errors.

There are multiple ways to migrate from YEAR(2) to YEAR(4):

- Using the ALTER TABLE query with FORCE attribute converts the YEAR(2) column to YEAR(4). It doesn't convert the values, though. If the ALTER TABLE query is applied to a replication master, the replication slaves will replicate the ALTER TABLE statement. So, the change will be available on all the replication nodes.
- Using binary upgrade, without dumping or reloading data, is another way of upgrading YEAR(2) to YEAR(4). Running mysql_upgrade subsequently executes REPAIR_TABLE and converts YEAR(2) to YEAR(4) without changing values. Similar to the previous alternative, this will be replicated in replication slaves if it is applied to a replication master.

An important thing to note is that while upgrading, we must not dump the YEAR(2) data with mysqldump and reload the dump file after upgrading. This method has the potential to change the YEAR(2) values significantly.

Before YEAR(2) to YEAR(4) migration, application code must be reviewed for:

- Code that selects the YEAR value in two digits.
- Code that doesn't handle numeric 0 insertions. Inserting 0 into YEAR(2) results in 2000, whereas inserting 0 into YEAR(4) results into 0000.

String data types

Which is the most widely required and used data type for representing values? String or character data types; it's easy, right? MySQL supports a wide range of string data types to fulfill different storage requirements. String data types are categorized into two categories: fixed length and variable length. CHAR, VARCHAR, BINARY, VARBINARY, BLOB, TEXT, ENUM, and SET are the MySQL-supported string data types. The storage requirement for each data type is different and will be explained later in a separate section.

CHAR and VARCHAR data types

The CHAR data type is a fixed-length string data type in MySQL. The CHAR data type is often declared with a maximum number of characters that can be stored as follows:

```
data CHAR(20);
```

In the preceding example, the data column can store string values that are capable of storing maximum characters.

CHAR and VARCHAR are similar in many ways, with certain differences. The CHAR data type is preferred if the string values to be stored are of fixed size. It will give better performance compared to if VARCHAR is used for fixed size strings.

The lengths vary from 0 to 255. The value in the CHAR column cannot exceed the maximum length declared at the time of table creation. If the length of the string is less than the maximum allowed length, MySQL adds padding on the right to the length specified. At the time of retrieval, trailing spaces are removed. The following is an example:

```
mysql> CREATE TABLE char_temp (
    data CHAR(3)
);

mysql> INSERT INTO char_temp(data) VALUES('abc'), (' a ');

mysql> SELECT data, LENGTH(data)
    FROM char_temp;
+--------+--------------+
| data   | LENGTH(data) |
+--------+--------------+
| abc    |      3       |
+--------+--------------+
| a      |      2       |
+--------+--------------+
```

As we can observe in the preceding example, the second record was inserted as ' a ', but in the output, the trailing space is removed. So, the length is displayed to be 2 instead of 3.

Most MySQL collations have a pad attribute. It determines how trailing spaces are treated for comparison of non-binary strings. There are two types of collations: PAD SPACE and NO PAD. In case of PAD SPACE collation, trailing spaces are not considered in comparison. Strings are compared without regard to trailing spaces.

In the case of NO PAD collation, the trailing spaces are treated as any other character. The following is an example:

```
mysql> CREATE TABLE employees (emp_name CHAR(10));

mysql> INSERT INTO employees VALUES ('Jack');

mysql> SELECT emp_name = 'Jack', emp_name = 'Jack ' FROM employees;
+--------------------+---------------------+
| emp_name = 'Jack' | emp_name = 'Jack ' |
+--------------------+---------------------+
|                  1 |                   1 |
+--------------------+---------------------+
mysql> SELECT emp_name LIKE 'Jack', emp_name LIKE 'Jack ' FROM employees;
+---------------------+----------------------+
| emp_name LIKE 'Jack' | emp_name LIKE 'Jack ' |
+---------------------+----------------------+
|                   1 |                    0 |
+---------------------+----------------------+
```

LIKE is a MySQL operator used for comparison in the WHERE clause. It is specifically used for pattern searching in a string. Trailing spaces are significant when comparing string values with the LIKE operator.

 If PAD_CHAR_TO_FULL_LENGTH mode is enabled, at the time of retrieval, the trailing spaces will not be removed.

The MySQL VARCHAR data type is a variable length string data type with a maximum length of up to 65,535 characters. VARCHAR values are stored by MySQL as a one or two byte length prefix, along with actual data. The actual maximum length of a VARCHAR is subject to the maximum row size, which is 65,536 bytes shared among all columns.

If the VARCHAR value requires less than 255 bytes, one byte is used for determining length prefix. If the value requires more than 255 bytes, two bytes are used for determining length prefix.

If MySQL strict mode is enabled and a value to be inserted in the CHAR or VARCHAR column value exceeds the maximum length, an error will be generated. If strict mode is disabled, the value will be truncated to the maximum allowed length with a warning.

Unlike in the CHAR data type, values to be stored in VARCHAR are not padded. Also, trailing spaces are not removed when the values are retrieved.

BINARY and VARBINARY data types

Another set of MySQL string data types is BINARY and VARBINARY. These are similar to CHAR and VARCHAR data types. An important difference between CHAR/VARCHAR and BINARY/VARBINARY is that BINARY/VARBINARY data types contain binary strings than character strings. BINARY/VARBINARY uses binary character sets and collation. BINARY/VARBINARY are different from CHAR BINARY and VARCHAR BINARY data types. The basic difference lies in the character set and collation referred to.

The maximum length for permitted values is similar to that of CHAR and VARCHAR. The only difference is that the length of BINARY and VARBINARY is in bytes, rather than characters.

How would MySQL compare binary values? The answer is that the comparison happens based on the numeric values for the bytes in the values.

Similar to CHAR/VARCHAR data types, the values are truncated if the length of the value exceeds the column length, and a warning is generated. This is if strict mode is not enabled. If strict mode is enabled, an error is generated.

BINARY values are right-padded with the pad value 0x00 (zero bytes) to the specified column length. The pad value is added on insert, but no trailing bytes are removed on retrieval. While comparing BINARY values, all bytes are considered significant. This applies to ORDER BY and DISTINCT operators, as well. Zero bytes and spaces are different when compared with *0x00 < space*. The following is an example of inserting a binary value:

```
mysql> CREATE TABLE temp(
  data BINARY(3));

mysql> INSERT INTO temp(data) VALUES('a ');
```

In this case, 'a ' becomes 'a \0' on insertion. 'a\0' is converted to 'a\0\0'. On retrieval, values remain unchanged.

VARBINARY is a variable length string data type. Unlike BINARY, for VARBINARY, padding is not added on insertion and bytes are not stripped on retrieval. Similar to BINARY, all bytes are significant in comparison for VARBINARY.

If the table has a unique index on columns, insertion of values in the column differing only in number of trailing pad bytes will give a duplicate-key error. For example, if such a column contains 'a ' and we try to insert 'a\0', it will cause a duplicate-key error.

The following example explains the padding of BINARY values in comparison:

```
mysql> CREATE TABLE bin_temp (data BINARY(3));

mysql> INSERT INTO bin_temp(data) VALUES('c');

mysql> SELECT data = 'c', data = 'c\0\0' from bin_temp;
+------------+--------------------+
| data = 'c' |    data = 'c\0\0'  |
+------------+--------------------+
|          0 |                  1 |
+------------+--------------------+
```

In the case that it is required to retrieve the same value as specified without padding, VARBINARY is preferable.

If the value retrieved must be the same as the value specified for storage with no padding, it might be preferable to use VARBINARY or one of the BLOB data types instead.

BLOB and TEXT data types

In what situation could we be required to store data in a **Binary Large Object (BLOB)** column? Any idea? Storing a file or image, you said? It is partially true. Before we make a decision to store the images or files in a database or file system, we need to assess the situation. If the files are stored in a file system and migrated over to another operating system, it is possible that file pointers could get corrupted. It will require additional efforts to fix the file pointers. In such a case, storing files in a database is preferable. However, it might impact performance if we store a large clogged file or image data in the database.

BLOB is MySQL's solution to storing large binary information of variable lengths. MySQL has four BLOB types: TINYBLOB, BLOB, MEDIUMBLOB, and LONGBLOB. The only difference among these data types is the maximum length of values we can store. The storage requirements for these data types are explained in later sections of the chapter.

Similar to BLOB, TEXT data types are TINYTEXT, TEXT, MEDIUMTEXT, and LONGTEXT. These have maximum lengths and storage requirements similar to that of BLOB data types.

Like BINARY data types, BLOB values are stored as byte strings and have binary character sets and collation. Comparisons and sorting are done on the numeric values of the column values. TEXT values are stored as non-binary strings.

In the case of `BLOB` or `TEXT` data types, if the value contains excess trailing spaces, MySQL truncates with a warning, regardless of the MySQL mode. MySQL doesn't pad `BLOB` or `TEXT` column values on insertion and doesn't strip bytes on retrieval.

For a `TEXT` column which is indexed, the index comparisons add trailing spaces as padding at the end of the values. So, a duplicate-key error may occur on insertion if the only difference between an existing `TEXT` value and the `TEXT` value to be inserted is in the trailing spaces. `BLOB` can be regarded as `VARBINARY` and `TEXT` can be regarded as `VARCHAR`, with no restriction on the length of the values.

The following are the differences between `VARBINARY`, `VARCHAR` and `BLOB`, `TEXT`:

- When creating indexes on `BLOB` or `TEXT` columns, we must specify index prefix length
- `BLOB` and `TEXT` cannot have default values

`BLOB` or `TEXT` values are represented internally as objects with separate allocations, unlike other data types, for which the storage is allocated once per column.

ENUM data type

MySQL provides a data type for which lists of permitted values can be predefined when the table is created. The data type is `ENUM`. If we want to restrict the user from inserting values outside a range of values, we should define the column of data type `ENUM`. MySQL encodes the user input string values into numbers for `ENUM` data types.

`ENUM` provides the following mentioned benefits:

- Compact data storage
- Readable queries and output

The following is an example that showcases when `ENUM` is useful:

```
mysql> CREATE TABLE subjects (
 name VARCHAR(40),
 stream ENUM('arts', 'commerce', 'science')
);

mysql> INSERT INTO subjects (name, stream) VALUES ('biology','science'),
('statistics','commerce'), ('history','arts');

mysql> SELECT name, stream FROM subjects WHERE stream = 'commerce';
```

```
+-------------+-----------+
|    name     |  stream   |
+-------------+-----------+
| statistics  | commerce  |
+-------------+-----------+

mysql> UPDATE subjects SET stream = 'science' WHERE stream = 'commerce';
```

ENUM values require one byte of storage. Storing one million such records in this table would require one million bytes of storage, opposed to the six million bytes required by the VARCHAR column.

The following are important limitations to consider:

- ENUM values are stored internally as numbers. So, if the ENUM values look like numbers, literal values may mix up with their internal index numbers.
- Using ENUM columns in ORDER BY clauses requires extra care. ENUM values are assigned index numbers based on the order of listing. ENUM values are sorted based on their index numbers. So, it is important to make sure that the ENUM values list is in alphabetical order. Also, the column should be sorted lexically than by index numbers.
- The ENUM value must be a quoted string literal.
- Each ENUM value has an index beginning with 1. The index of the empty string or error value is 0. We can find invalid ENUM values by querying the table with enum_column_value = 0 in the WHERE clause. The index of NULL value is NULL. Index refers to the position of a value within the ENUM list of values.
- MySQL automatically removes trailing spaces from ENUM member values when a table is created. Upon retrieval, values from an ENUM column are displayed in the case used in the column definition. If a number is to be stored in the ENUM column, the number is treated as an index into the possible values. The value stored is the ENUM value with that index. In the case of a quoted numeric value, it is still interpreted as an index if there is no matching string in the list of enumerated values.
- If an ENUM column is declared to contain NULL values, the NULL value is considered a valid value for the column and NULL becomes the default value. If NULL is not allowed, the first ENUM value becomes the default value.

If ENUM values are used in a numeric context, the index is used. The following is an example query to use ENUM values in a numeric context:

```
mysql> SELECT stream+1 FROM subjects;
+--------------+
|   stream+1   |
+--------------+
|      4       |
|      3       |
|      2       |
+--------------+
```

SET data type

MySQL SET is a data type which can have zero or more values. A permitted list of values is specified at the time of table creation. Each value must be from within the list of permitted values. Multiple set members are specified by a comma (,) separated list of values. A SET can have a maximum of 64 distinct members. If strict mode is enabled, an error is generated if duplicate values are found in the column definition.

It must be taken care that SET member values do not contain commas; otherwise, they are interpreted as SET member separators.

A column specified as SET('yes', 'no') NOT NULL can have any of the following values:

- ''
- 'yes'
- 'no'
- 'yes,no'

Trailing spaces are removed automatically from SET member values. Upon retrieval, SET column values are displayed using the letter case which was used in the column definition.

The following is an example of inserting values in the SET data type:

```
mysql> CREATE TABLE temp(
    hobbies SET('Travel', 'Sports', 'Fine Dining', 'Dancing'));

mysql> INSERT INTO temp(hobbies) VALUES(9);
```

The SET values are stored in the MySQL table as a bitmap in which each element is represented by one bit. In the preceding case, each element in the SET is assigned a bit. If the row has a given element, the associated bit will be one. Because of this approach, each element has an associated decimal value. Also, because of the bitmap, though there are only four values, SET will occupy one byte. The following is the table explaining this:

Element	SET value	Decimal value
Travel	00000001	1
Sports	00000010	2
Fine Dining	00000100	4
Dancing	00001000	8

Multiple SET elements can be represented by adding their decimal values. In the preceding case, the decimal value 9 is interpreted as Travel, Dancing.

The SET data type is not so commonly used. This is because although it is a string data type, it is a bit complex in implementation. The values that can be stored are limited to 64 elements. We cannot add commas as part of SET values, because a comma is a standard SET value separator. From a database design point of view, using SET means the database is not normalized.

JSON data type

JSON stands for JavaScript Object Notation. Suppose that we want to store user preferences for a web application in the database. Usually, we may choose to create a separate table with id, user_id, key, value fields. This may work well for a small number of users, but in the case of thousands of users, the cost of maintenance is unaffordable compared to the value it adds to the web application.

In MySQL, we can utilize the JSON data type for this requirement. MySQL supports the native JSON data type, which enables efficient storage for JSON documents. MySQL supports automatic validation of JSON documents stored in the JSON column. Trying to store invalid JSON documents produces an error. JSON documents stored in JSON columns are converted to an internal format. The format is binary, and structured to enable the server to look up subobjects or nested values directly, by key or array index, without reading other values.

A JSON column cannot have a default value. The JSON data type requires similar storage to that of LONGTEXT or LONGBLOB. JSON columns are not indexed directly, unlike other string data types.

The following is an example of inserting JSON values in a table:

```
mysql> CREATE TABLE users(
    user_id INT UNSIGNED NOT NULL,
    preferences JSON NOT NULL);

mysql> INSERT INTO users(user_id, preferences)
    VALUES(1, '{"page_size": 10, "hobbies": {"sports": 1}}');

mysql> SELECT preferences FROM users;
+--------------------------------------------------------------+
|                          preferences                         |
+--------------------------------------------------------------+
|     {"hobbies": {"sports": 1}, "page_size": 10}              |
+--------------------------------------------------------------+
```

In the preceding example, we have formatted the JSON value. As an alternative, we can also use the built-in JSON_OBJECT function. The function accepts a list of key/value pairs and returns a JSON object. An example follows:

```
mysql> INSERT INTO users(user_id, preferences)
    VALUES(2, JSON_OBJECT("page_size", 1, "network", JSON_ARRAY("GSM",
"CDMA", "WIFI")));
```

The preceding INSERT query will insert the JSON value {"page_size": 1, "network": ["GSM", "CDMA", "WIFI"]}. We can also use nested JSON_OBJECT functions. The JSON_ARRAY function returns a JSON array when passed a set of values.

If the same key is specified multiple times, only the first key/value pair will be retained. In the case of the JSON data type, the object keys are sorted and the trailing space between the key/value pairs is removed. The keys in the JSON object must be strings.

Inserting a JSON value in a JSON column succeeds only if the JSON document is valid. In the case that the JSON document is invalid, MySQL produces an error.

MySQL has one more important and useful function which operates on JSON values. The JSON_MERGE function takes multiple JSON objects and produces a single, aggregate object.

The JSON_TYPE function takes a JSON as an argument and tries to parse it into a JSON value. It returns the value's JSON type if it is valid and produces an error if otherwise.

Partial updates of JSON values

What should we do if we want to update a value in a JSON document stored in a JSON data type? One of the approaches is to remove the old document and insert a new document, with updates. The approach doesn't seem good, right? MySQL 8.0 supports partial, in place update of a JSON document stored in a JSON data type column. The optimizer requires that an update must meet the following conditions:

- The column must be of JSON type.
- One of three functions, JSON_SET(), JSON_REPLACE() or JSON_REMOVE(), can be used to update the column. MySQL doesn't permit direct assignment of the column value as a partial update.
- The input column and target column must be the same. For example, a statement such as UPDATE temp SET col1 = JSON_SET(col2, 'one', 10) cannot be performed as a partial update.
- The changes only update existing arrays or objects, and no new elements are added to the parent object or array.
- The replacement value must not be larger than the value being replaced.

Storage requirements for data types

This section explains storage requirements for different data types in MySQL. The storage requirements depend on different factors. The storage engines represent data types and store raw data differently.

A table has a maximum row size of 65,535 bytes, even if the storage engine is capable of supporting larger rows. BLOB and TEXT data types are excluded.

The following table explains the storage details for numeric data types:

Data Type	Storage required
TINYINT	1 byte
SMALLINT	2 bytes
MEDIUMINT	3 bytes
INT, INTEGER	4 bytes
BIGINT	8 bytes

FLOAT (p)	4 bytes if *0<=p<=24,* 8 bytes if *25<=p<=53*
FLOAT	4 bytes
DOUBLE [precision], REAL	8 bytes
DECIMAL (M, D), NUMERIC (M, D)	Varies
BIT (M)	Approximately *(M+7)/8* bytes

Reference: https://dev.mysql.com/doc/refman/8.0/en/storage-requirements.html

The following table explains the storage requirements for DATE and TIME data types:

Data Type	Storage Required
YEAR	1 byte
DATE	3 bytes
TIME	3 bytes + fractional seconds storage
DATETIME	5 bytes + fractional seconds storage
TIMESTAMP	4 bytes + fractional seconds storage

The following table explains the storage required for fractional seconds precision:

Fractional Seconds Precision	Storage Required
0	0 bytes
1, 2	1 byte
3, 4	2 bytes
5, 6	3 bytes

The following table explains storage requirements for string data types:

Data Type	Storage Required
CHAR (M)	**$M \times w$ bytes, $0 <= M <= 255$, where w is the number of bytes required for the maximum-length character in the character set**
BINARY (M)	M bytes, $0 <= M <= 255$
VARCHAR (M), VARBINARY (M)	$L + 1$ bytes if the column values require $0 - 255$ bytes, $L + 2$ bytes if the values may require more than 255 bytes
TINYBLOB, TINYTEXT	$L + 1$ bytes, where $L < 2^8$
BLOB, TEXT	$L + 2$ bytes, where $L < 2^{16}$
MEDIUMBLOB, MEDIUMTEXT	$L + 3$ bytes, where $L < 2^{24}$
LONGBLOB, LONGTEXT	$L + 4$ bytes, where $L < 2^{32}$
ENUM('value1','value2',...)	1 or 2 bytes, depending on the number of enumeration values (65,535 values maximum)
SET ('value1', 'value2', ...)	1, 2, 3, 4, or 8 bytes, depending on the number of set members (64 members maximum)

Reference: https://dev.mysql.com/doc/refman/8.0/en/storage-requirements.html

In the case of string data types, variable length strings are stored using the length of the value and the length prefix. The length prefix varies from one to four bytes, depending on the data type.

Storage requirements for the JSON data type are similar to that of LONGBLOB and LONGTEXT. However, as the JSON documents are stored in binary representations, it imposes an overhead in storing JSON documents.

Choosing the right data type for column

As a general practice, we should use the most precise type for storing data. For example, a CHAR data type should be used to store a string value that varies in length from 1 to 255 characters. Another example is that MEDIUMINT UNSIGNED should be used to store numbers ranging from 1 to 99999.

Basic operations such as `addition`, `subtraction`, `multiplication`, and division with `DECIMAL` data are performed with the precision of 65 decimal digits.

Based on the importance of accuracy or speed, use of `FLOAT` or `DOUBLE` should be chosen. Fixed point values stored in `BIGINT` can be used for higher precision.

These are general guidelines, but the decision to use the right data type should be made based on the detailed characteristics explained separately for each data type in the earlier sections.

Summary

It was an interesting chapter with important content to learn, right? In this chapter, we understood the significance of data types in MySQL. We saw different categories in which MySQL data types are classified. We learned and understood the characteristics and specifications of each data type in depth. We also learned MySQL data manipulation functions and understood some of the MySQL settings and modes. In the later section of the chapter, we learned storage requirements of data types. Finally, we learned general guidelines for choosing the right data types.

Moving on to next chapter, we will learn MySQL database management. The chapter will focus on server administration, understanding the basic building blocks of the MySQL server, such as the data dictionary, system database, and so on. The chapter will explain how we can run multiple server instances on a single machine and MySQL roles and permissions.

5
MySQL 8 Database Management

In the previous chapter, we learned about MySQL 8 data types, explaining in detail which data types are available and how they are categorized. There are various properties associated with each of these data types, and the storage capacity varies with each type. The previous chapter also provided you with an in-depth understanding of MySQL 8 data types. Now its time to get some practical knowledge on MySQL 8 administrative features. Isn't it interesting to know more about the administrative features of MySQL 8, how configuration will be done for it, and much more? It's extremely important for an administrator to have detailed knowledge on how MySQL 8 works for globalization, how logs are maintained, and how to enhance capability of the server. Now, let's start with some fundamental concepts.

We will cover the follow topics in this chapter:

- MySQL 8 server administration
- Data directory
- The system database
- Running multiple instances on a single machine
- Components and plugin management
- Roles and permissions
- Caching techniques
- Globalization
- MySQL 8 server logs

MySQL 8 server administration

There are many operating parameters that available with MySQL 8, and among them all the required parameters are set by default during the installation process. After installation, you are allowed to change the **option file** by removing or adding a comment sign (#) at the start of the line of a specific parameter setting. The user is also allowed to set parameters at runtime by using command line arguments or the option file.

Server options and different types of variables

In this section, we are going to cover **server options**, **system variable**, and **status variables** available in MySQL 8 on startup.

- **Server option**: As described in the previous chapter MySQL 8 uses the option file and command line arguments to set startup parameters. Refer to https://dev. mysql.com/doc/refman/8.0/en/mysqld-option-tables.html for details on all the available options. mysqld accepts many command options. For a brief summary, execute the following command:

    ```
    mysqld --help
    ```

    To see the full list, use the following command:

    ```
    mysqld -verbose --help
    ```

- **Server System variable**: The MySQL server manages many system variables. MySQL provides the default value for each system variable. System variables can be set using the command line or can be defined in the option file. MySQL 8 has the flexibility to change these variables at runtime without server start or stop. For more details refer to: https://dev.mysql.com/doc/refman/8.0/en/server-system-variables.html.

- **Server status variable**: The MySQL server uses many status variables to provide information about its operation. For more details refer to: https://dev.mysql.com/doc/refman/8.0/en/server-status-variables.html.

Server SQL modes

MySQL 8 provides different modes that will affect MySQL support and data validation checks. This option makes it easier for the user to use MySQL in different environments. To set different modes MySQL provides the `sql_mode` system variable which can be set at either a global or session level. Refer to the following points in detail to understand modes:

Setting the SQL mode

SQL mode can be setup on startup using the `--sql-mode="modes"` option. The user can also define this option in the option file as `sql-mode="modes"`. You can define multiple nodes by adding comma separated values. MySQL 8 uses the following modes as default modes: `ONLY_FULL_GROUP_BY`, `STRICT_TRANS_TABLES`, `NO_ZERO_IN_DATE`, `NO_ZERO_DATE`, `ERROR_FOR_DIVISION_BY_ZERO`, `NO_AUTO_CREATE_USER`, `NO_ENGINE_SUBSTITUTION` To change mode at runtime, execute the following commands:

```
SET GLOBAL sql_mode = 'modes';
SET SESSION sql_mode = 'modes';
```

To retrieve the values of both the variables, execute the following commands:

```
SELECT @@GLOBAL.sql_mode;
SELECT @@SESSION.sql_mode;
```

The available SQL modes

This section describes all the available SQL modes. Out of them, the first three are the most important SQL modes:

- `ANSI`: This mode is used to change syntax and behavior, by making it closer to standard SQL.
- `STRICT_TRANS_TABLES`: As the name implies, this mode is related to transaction and it is mainly used for transactional storage engines. When this mode is enable for nontransactional tables, MySQL 8 will convert invalid values to the closest valid value and insert the adjusted value into the column. If the value is missing, then MySQL 8 will insert an implicit default value related to the column's data type. In this case, MySQL 8 will generate a warning message instead of an error message, and continue with the statement execution without breaking it.In the case of transactional tables, however, MySQL 8 gives an error and will breaks execution.

- TRADITIONAL: This mode generally behaves like traditional SQL database system. It indicates **give error instead of a warning** when an incorrect value inserted into the column.
- ALLOW_INVALID_DATES: This mode checks only the month range and the date range of the date value. In other words, the month range must be between 1 to 12 and date range must be between 1 to 31. This mode is applicable for DATE and DATETIME data types and not for timestamp data type.
- ANSI_QUOTES: Used to consider " as an identifier quote character instead of a string quote character. When this mode is enabled, you cannot use double quotation to quote string literal.
- ERROR_FOR_DIVISION_BY_ZERO: Used to handle the case of division by zero. This mode output also depends on strict SQL mode status:
    - If this mode is not enabled, division by zero inserts NULL and produces no warning.
    - If this mode is enabled, division by zero inserts NULL and produces a warning.
    - If this mode and strict mode are enabled, division by zero produces an error, unless IGNORE is given as well. For INSERT IGNORE and UPDATE IGNORE, division by zero inserts NULL and produces a warning.
- HIGH_NOT_PRECEDENCE: This mode is used to set a high precedence for the NOT operator. For example, when the mode is enabled the expression NOT a BETWEEN b AND c is parsed as NOT (a BETWEEN b AND c) instead of (NOT a) BETWEEN b AND c.
- IGNORE_SPACE: This mode applies to built-in functions rather than user defined functions or stored procedures.
- NO_AUTO_CREATE_USER: This mode is used to prevent GRANT statements by automatically creating new user accounts unless authentication information is specified.
- NO_AUTO_VALUE_ON_ZERO: This mode is used for auto incremental columns. When 0 is found MySQL creates a new sequence number for the field, and that will create problems when you are loading dump. Enable this mode before reloading dump to resolve this problem.
- NO_BACKSLASH_ESCAPES: If this mode is enabled, backslash becomes an ordinary character.

- NO_DIR_IN_CREATE: This option is useful for slave replication servers where the INDEX DIRECTORY and DATA DIRECTORY directives are ignored on table creation.
- NO_ENGINE_SUBSTITUTION: Used to provide substitution of the default storage engine. When this mode is enabled and the desired engine is unavailable, MySQL gives an error and a table is not created.
- NO_FIELD_OPTIONS: This indicates, don't print MySQL specific column options in the output of SHOW_CREATE_TABLE.
- NO_KEY_OPTIONS: This indicates, don't print MySQL specific index options in the output of SHOW_CREATE_TABLE.
- NO_TABLE_OPTIONS: This indicates, don't print MySQL specific table options in the output of SHOW_CREATE_TABLE.
- NO_UNSIGNED_SUBTRACTION: When this mode is enabled, it makes sure that subtraction result must be a signed value even though any of the operand is unsigned.
- NO_ZERO_DATE: The effect of this mode depends on the strict mode as defined below:
    - If it is not enabled, 0000-00-00 is allowed and MySQL produces no warning on insertion
    - If this mode is enabled, 0000-00-00 is allowed and MySQL records a warning
    - If both this mode and strict mode are enabled, 0000-00-00 is not allowed and MySQL produces an error on insertion
- NO_ZERO_IN_DATE: This mode effect is also depending on the strict mode as defined below:
    - If it is not enabled, dates with zero parts are allowed and MySQL produces no warning on insertion
    - If this mode is enabled, dates with zero parts are allowed and produce a warning
    - If this mode and strict mode are enabled, dates with zero parts are not allowed and MySQL produces an error

- ONLY_FULL_GROUP_BY: If this mode is enabled, MySQL will reject queries in which select list, order by list, and the HAVING condition refer to non aggregated columns.

- `PAD_CHAR_TO_FULL_LENGTH`: This mode is applied on the column whose data type is set as `CHAR`. When this mode is enabled, MySQL retrieves column values by padding to their full length.
- `PIPES_AS_CONCAT`: When this mode is set as enabled | | will be considered as a string concatenation operator instead of `OR`.
- `REAL_AS_FLOAT`: By default, MySQL 8 will consider `REAL` as a synonym of `DOUBLE`, but when this flag is enabled MySQL will consider `REAL` as a synonym of `FLOAT`.
- `STRICT_ALL_TABLES`: In this mode invalid data values are rejected.
- `TIME_TRUNCATE_FRACTIONAL`: This mode indicates if truncation is allowed on `TIME`, `DATE`, and `TIMESTAMP` columns or not. The default behavior is to perform rounding on the values instead of truncation.

Combination SQL modes

MySQL 8 also provides some special modes as combinations of mode values:

- `ANSI`: It includes the effects of the `REAL_AS_FLOAT`, `PIPES_AS_CONCAT`, `ANSI_QUOTES`, `IGNORE_SPACE`, and `ONLY_FULL_GROUP_BY` modes.
- `DB2`: It includes the effects of the `PIPES_AS_CONCAT`, `ANSI_QUOTES`, `IGNORE_SPACE`, `NO_KEY_OPTIONS`, `NO_TABLE_OPTIONS`, and `NO_FIELD_OPTIONS` modes.
- `MAXDB`: It includes the effects of `PIPES_AS_CONCAT`, `ANSI_QUOTES`, `IGNORE_SPACE`, `NO_KEY_OPTIONS`, `NO_TABLE_OPTIONS`, `NO_FIELD_OPTIONS`, and `NO_AUTO_CREATE_USER`.
- `MSSQL`: It includes the effects of `PIPES_AS_CONCAT`, `ANSI_QUOTES`, `IGNORE_SPACE`, `NO_KEY_OPTIONS`, `NO_TABLE_OPTIONS`, and `NO_FIELD_OPTIONS`.
- `MYSQL323`: It includes the effects of the `MYSQL323` and `HIGH_NOT_PRECEDENCE` modes.
- `MYSQL40`: It includes the effects of the `MYSQL40` and `HIGH_NOT_PRECEDENCE` modes.
- `ORACLE`: It includes the effects of the `PIPES_AS_CONCAT`, `ANSI_QUOTES`, `IGNORE_SPACE`, `NO_KEY_OPTIONS`, `NO_TABLE_OPTIONS`, `NO_FIELD_OPTIONS`, and `NO_AUTO_CREATE_USER` modes.

- POSTGRESQL: It includes the effect of the PIPES_AS_CONCAT, ANSI_QUOTES, IGNORE_SPACE, NO_KEY_OPTIONS, NO_TABLE_OPTIONS, and NO_FIELD_OPTIONS modes.
- TRADITIONAL: It includes the effects of the STRICT_TRANS_TABLES, STRICT_ALL_TABLES, NO_ZERO_IN_DATE, NO_ZERO_DATE, ERROR_FOR_DIVISION_BY_ZERO, NO_AUTO_CREATE_USER and NO_ENGINE_SUBSTITUTION modes.

Strict SQL mode

The **strict mode** is used to manage *Invalid data* or *missing data*. If strict mode is not enabled, then MySQL will manage the insert and update operations by adjusting values and generating warning messages. We can do the same on strict mode by enabling the INSERT IGNORE or UPDATE IGNORE options. Let's take a key insertion example where a key value exceeds the maximum limit. MySQL produces an error and stops the execution if strict mode is enabled, and on the opposite side it allows key value by truncating if strict mode is disabled. In the same way, in the case of the SELECT statement where the data is not changed, MySQL will still produce an error, generating a warning message in case of invalid values if strict mode is enabled. Strict mode is in effect if either the STRICT_ALL_TABLES or the STRICT_TRANS_TABLES option is enabled. These two options behave similarly in the case of transactional tables and differently in the case of nontransactional tables.

- **For transactional tables**: If either of the modes are enabled, then MySQL will produce an error and aborts the statement execution, in case of invalid or missing values.
- **For nontransactional tables**: The behavior of MySql will depend on the following factors, when the tables are nontransactional:
    - STRICT_ALL_TABLES: In this case, an error will be generated and the execution will be stopped. But still, there is a possibility of error where the partial data gets updated. To avoid this error scenario, use a single-row statement, which will abort execution if the error occurred during first row insertion/updation.
    - STRICT_TRANS_TABLES: This option provide flexibility to convert an invalid value to the closest valid value. In case of missing value, MySQL inserts the data type's default value into the column. Here, MySQL generates a warning message and continues with the execution.

Strict mode affects handling of divisions by zero, zero dates, and zeros in dates as describe in the preceding points with
the `ERROR_FOR_DIVISION_BY_ZERO`, `NO_ZERO_DATE` and `NO_ZERO_IN_DATE` modes.

The SQL mode will be applied on the following SQL statements:

```
ALTER TABLE
CREATE TABLE
CREATE TABLE ... SELECT
DELETE (both single table and multiple table)
INSERT
LOAD DATA
LOAD XML
SELECT SLEEP()
UPDATE (both single table and multiple table)
```

 You can go to : `https://dev.mysql.com/doc/refman/8.0/en/sql-mode.html` for a detailed list of the errors associated with strict SQL mode in MySQL.

The IGNORE keyword

MySQL provides an `IGNORE` keyword which is optional for statement execution. The `IGNORE` keyword is used to downgrade errors to warnings and applicable to several statements. For multiple row statements, the `IGNORE` keyword allows you to skip the particular row, instead of aborting. The following statements support the `IGNORE` keyword:

- `CREATE TABLE ... SELECT`: Individual `CREATE` and `SELECT` statements do not have support on this keyword, but when we insert into the table using `SELECT` statement, rows that duplicate an existing row on a unique key value are discarded.
- `DELETE`: If this statement executes with the `IGNORE` option MySQL avoid errors occurred during execution.
- `INSERT`: Duplicate values in unique key and data conversion issues will be handled by this keyword during row insertion. MySQL will insert the closest possible values into the column and ignore the error.

- `LOAD DATA` and `LOAD XML`: At the time of loading data if duplication is found the statement will discard it and continue insertion for the remaining data if the `IGNORE` keyword is defined.
- `UPDATE`: In cases of duplicate key conflict on unique key during statement execution, MySQL will update the column with the closest identified values.

The `IGNORE` keyword also applies on some specific errors, listed here: `https://dev.mysql.com/doc/refman/8.0/en/sql-mode.html`.

IPv6 support

MySQL 8 provides support for **IPv6**, with the following capabilities:

- MySQL server will accept TCP/IP connections from clients with IPv6 connectivity
- MySQL 8 account names permit IPv6 addresses, which enables DBA to specify privileges for the clients that are connected with server, using IPv6
- The IPv6 functions enable conversions between string and internal IPv6 address formats, and checking whether the values represent a valid IPv6 address or not

Server side help

MySQL 8 provides `HELP` statement, to get information from the MySQL reference manual. To manage this information, MySQL uses several tables of system database. To initialize these tables, MySQL provides the `fill_help_tables.sql` script. This script is available at `http://dev.mysql.com/doc/index-other.html`. After downloading and unzipping the script file, execute the below command, for invoking the `HELP` function:

```
mysql -u root mysql < fill_help_tables.sql
```

At the time of installation process content initialization occurs. In case of upgrading it will be perform so; execute the above command manually.

The server shutdown process

The server shutdown process performs the following steps:

1. **The shutdown process is initiated**: There are several ways to initialize the shutdown process. Execute the `mysqladmin shutdown` command which can be executed on any platform. There are some system specific ways to initialize the shutdown process; for example, Unix based systems will start to shut down when it receives a **SIGTERM** signal. In the same way, Window based systems will start to shut down when the service manager tells them to.

2. **The server creates a shutdown thread if necessary**: Based on the shutdown initialization process, the server will decide to create new thread or not. If it is requested by the client, a new thread will be created. If a signal is received, then the server might create a thread or it might handle it by itself. If the server tries to create a separate thread for the shutdown process and an error occurs, then it produces the following message in the error log:

   ```
   Error: Can't create thread to kill server
   ```

3. **The server stops accepting new connections**: When the shutdown activity is initiated, the server will stop accepting new connection requests, using a handler of network interfaces. The server will be using Windows features such as named pipe, TCP/IP port, the Unix socket file, and shared memory on Windows in order to listen to new connection requests.

4. **The server terminates current activity**: Once the shut down process is initialized, the server will start to break the connection with the client. In the normal scenario, the connection threads will die quickly, but the ones which are working or are in an ongoing activity stage will take a long time to *die*. So if a thread is executing open transactions and if it gets rollback in the middle of execution then the user might get only partially updated data. On the other hand, if the thread is working on a transaction, then the server will wait until the transaction is completed. Also, the user can terminate the ongoing transaction by executing the `KILL QUERY` or `KILL CONNECTION` statements.

5. **The server shuts down or closes storage engines**: In this phase, the server flushes the cache and closes all the open tables. Here, the storage engine performs all the actions necessary for tables. `InnoDB` flushes its buffer pool, writes the current LSN into tablespace and terminates its thread. The `MyISAM` flushes the pending index.

6. **The server exits**: In this phase, the server will provide one of the following values to the management processes:
   - 0 = successful termination (no restart done)
   - 1 = unsuccessful termination (no restart done)
   - 2 = unsuccessful termination (restart done)

Data directory

The data directory is the place where MySQL 8 stores all the information that is managed by itself. Each sub-directory of the data directory represents a database directory and its related data. All the MySQL installations have the following standard databases:

- **The** `sys` **directory**: This represents the sys schema, which contains the objects useful for the Performance Schema information interpretation.
- **The** `performance schema` **directory**: This directory is used to observe the internal execution of the MySQL server at run-time.
- **The** `mysql` **directory**: This directory is related to the MySQL system database, which contains the data dictionary table and the system tables. It contains the information that is required by the MySQL server once it is running.

The system database

The system database mainly contains the data dictionary tables that stores the object's metadata and system tables for other operational purposes. The system database contains a number of system tables. We will learn more about them in the coming sections.

Data dictionary tables

The data dictionary tables contains the metadata about data objects. Tables of this directory are invisible and are not read by general SQL queries such as `SELECT`, `SHOW TABLES`, `INFORMATION_SCHEMA.TABLES`, and so on. MySQL mainly exposes the metadata using the `INFORMATION_SCHEMA` option.

Grant system tables

These tables are used to manage and provide grant information of users, database and relevant privileges. MySQL 8 uses grant tables as transactional tables, not nontransactional (MyISAM, for example) tables, so all the operations on the transaction are either completed or failed; no partial case will be made possible.

Object information system tables

These tables contains information related to the stored programs, components and server-side plugins. The following main tables are used to store information:

- **Component**: Works as a registry for the server. The MySQL 8 server loads all the components listed by this table on server startup.
- **Func**: This table contains information related to all the **user-defined functions (UDF)**. MySQL 8 will load all the UDFs listed in this table during server startup.
- **Plugin**: Contains the information related to the server-side plugins. The MySQL 8 server loads all the available plugins during startup.

Log system tables

These tables are useful for logging and using csv storage engines. For example, the functions general_log and slow_log.

The server-side help system tables

These tables are useful to store help information. The following tables are available in this category :

- help_category: Provides information about the help categories
- help_keyword: Provides keywords associated with help topics
- help_relation: Helps in mappings between help keywords and topics
- help_topic: Help topic contents

Time zone system tables

These tables are useful to store time zone information. The following tables are available in this category:

- `time_zone`: Provides the time zone IDs and whether they use leap seconds
- `time_zone_leap_second`: Will come in handy when leap seconds occur
- `time_zone_name`: Helps in mappings between time zone IDs and names
- `time_zone_transition` and `time_zone_transition_type`: Time zone descriptions

Replication system tables

These tables are useful to support the replication feature. It helps to store replication related information when it is configured to as mentioned in following tables. The following tables are available in this category:

- `gtid_executed`: Used for creating the table for storing GTID values
- `ndb_binlog_index`: Provides the binary log information for MySQL Cluster replication
- `slave_master_info`, `slave_relay_log_info` and `slave_worker_info`: Used to store replication information on slave servers

Optimizer system tables

This tables are useful for optimizer. The following tables are available in this category:

- `innodb_index_stats` and `innodb_table_stats`: Used for getting the InnoDB persistent optimizer statistics
- `server_cost`: Contains the optimizer cost estimates for general server operations.
- `engine_cost`: Contains the estimates for operations specific to particular storage engines

Other miscellaneous system tables

Tables that don't fall into the above-mentioned categories fall under this category. The following tables are available in this category:

- `servers`: Used by the `FEDERATED` storage engine
- `innodb_dynamic_metadata`: Used by the `InnoDB` storage engine to store fast changing table metadata such as auto-increment counter values and index tree corruption flags

> You can learn more about the different system tables at: `https://dev.mysql.com/doc/refman/8.0/en/system-database.html`.

Running multiple instances on a single machine

There might be some situations where you are required to install multiple instances on a single machine. It may be to check the performance of two different versions, or perhaps there is a need to manage two separate databases on different MySQL instances. The reason can be anything, but MySQL allows user to execute multiple instances on the same machine by providing different configuration values. MySQL 8 allows users to configure parameters by making use of the command line, option file, or by setting environment variables. The primary resource used by MySQL 8 for this is the data directory and it must be unique for the two instances. We can define the value for the same using the `--datadir=dir_name` function. Apart from the data directory, we will also configure unique values for the following options as well:

- `--port=port_num`
- `--socket={file_name|pipe_name}`
- `--shared-memory-base-name=name`
- `--pid-file=file_name`
- `--general_log_file=file_name`
- `--log-bin[=file_name]`
- `--slow_query_log_file=file_name`

- `--log-error[=file_name]`
- `--tmpdir=dir_name`

Setting up multiple data directories

As described above, each of the MySQL instances must have a separate data directory. The user is allowed to define separate directories using the following methods:

- **Create a new data directory**: In this method we must follow the same procedure which was defined in `Chapter 2`, *Installing and Upgrading MySQL*. For Microsoft Windows, when we install MySQL 8 from Zip archives, copy its data directory to the location where you want to set up the new instance. In the case of an MSI package along with the data directory, create a pristine `template` data directory named data under the installation directory. Once the installation is complete, copy the data directory to set up additional instances.

- **Copy an existing data directory**: In this method, we will copy an existing instance's data directory to the new instance's data directory. To copy an existing directory, perform the following steps:
    1. Stop the existing MySQL instance. Make sure it's cleanly shut down so that no pending changes are available in the disk.
    2. Copy the data directory to the new location.
    3. Copy the `my.cnf` or `my.ini` option file used by the existing instance to the new location.
    4. Modify the new option as per the new instance. Make sure all the unique configurations are done properly.
    5. Start the new instance with the new option file.

Running multiple MySQL instances on Windows

The user is allowed to run multiple MySQL instances on a single Windows machine either by using the command line and passing values or by the window service.

- **Starting multiple MySQL instances at the Windows command line:** To execute multiple instances using the command line, we can either specify the option at runtime or we can set it in the option file. The option file is a better option to start instances because there is no need to specify arguments every time at startup. To setup or configure the option file, follow the same steps described in `Chapter 2`, *Installing and Upgrading MySQL*.

- **Starting multiple MySQL instances as Windows services:** To start multiple instance on Windows as service, we have to specify different services with unique names. As described in Chapter 2, *Installing and Upgrading MySQL,* use the –install or --install-manual options to define MySQL as a Windows service. The following options are available to define multiple MySQL instances as Windows services:

  - **Approach 1**: Create two separate option files for instances and define the mysqld group inside it. For example, use the function C:\my-opts1.cnf. The code for the same is given below for your reference:

```
[mysqld]
basedir = C:/mysql-5.5.5
port = 3307
enable-named-pipe
socket = mypipe1
```

    We can do the same using C:\my-opts2.cnf function as well. The following code depicts the process:

```
[mysqld]
basedir = C:/mysql-8.0.1
port = 3308
enable-named-pipe
socket = mypipe2
```

    You can install the MySQL8 services using the following commands:

```
C:\> C:\mysql-5.5.5\bin\mysqld --install mysqld1 --
    defaults-file=C:\my-opts1.cnf
C:\> C:\mysql-8.0.1\bin\mysqld --install mysqld2 --
    defaults-file=C:\my-opts2.cnf
```

  - **Approach 2**: Create one common option file as C:\my.cnf for both the services:

```
# options for mysqld1 service
[mysqld1]
basedir = C:/mysql-5.5.5
port = 3307
enable-named-pipe
socket = mypipe1

# options for mysqld2 service
```

```
[mysqld2]
basedir = C:/mysql-8.0.1
port = 3308
enable-named-pipe
socket = mypipe2
```

- Execute the following commands to install MySQL services:

```
C:\> C:\mysql-5.5.9\bin\mysqld --install mysqld1
C:\> C:\mysql-8.0.4\bin\mysqld --install mysqld2
```

- To start MySQL services, execute the following commands:

```
C:\> NET START mysqld1
C:\> NET START mysqld2
```

Components and plugin management

The component based structure is supported by MySQL server, to extend the server capabilities. MySQL 8 uses the INSTALL COMPONENT and UNINSTALL COMPONENT SQL statements to load and unload components at runtime. MySQL 8 manages component details into the mysql.component system table. So, every time a new component is installed, MySQL 8 server performs the following tasks:

- Load components into server to make available instantly
- Load service registered component into the mysql.component system table.

When we uninstall any component, MySQL server will perform the same steps, but in the reverse order. To see which components are available, execute the following query:

```
SELECT * FROM mysql.component;
```

MySQL 8 server plugins

MySQL 8 server has a plugin API that enables the creation of server components. With MySQL 8, you have the flexibility of installing a plugin at runtime or at startup. In the following topics we will learn about the life cycle of the MySQL 8 server plugins.

Installing the plugins

The loading of the plugins varies with their types and characteristics. To get a clearer picture of this, let's go though the following:

- **Built-in plugins**: The server knows about the built-in plugins and loads them automatically, on startup. The user is allowed to change the state of plugins by any of their activation statuses, which will be discussed in the following section.
- **Plugins registered in the** `mysql.plugin` **system table**: On startup MySQL 8 server will load all the plugins which are registered in the `mysql.plugin` table. If the server is started with the `--skip-grant-tables` option, the server will not load the plugins listed there.
- **Plugins named with command-line options**: MySQL 8 provides the `--plugin-load`, `--plugin-load-add`, and `--early-plugin-load` options for loading plugins with the command line. The `--plugin-load` and `--plugin-load-add` options load the plugins on server startup after the built-in plugins are installed. But, we can use the `--early-plugin-load` option to load the plugins, prior to initialization of built-in plugins and storage engines.
- **Plugins installed with the** `INSTALL PLUGIN` **statement**: This is a permanent plugin registration option, which will register the plugin information in the `mysql.plugin` table. It will also load all the plugins available in the plugin library.

Activate plugin

To control the state (like the activation or deactivation) of plugins, MySQL 8 provides the following options:

- `--plugin_name=OFF`: Disables the named plugin. Some of the built-in plugins, such as the `asmysql_native_password` plugin, are not affected by this command.
- `--plugin_name[=ON]`: This command enables the specified plugin. If plugin initialization failed during startup MySQL 8 will start with the plugin disabled.
- `--plugin_name=FORCE`: This is the same as the above command, except the server does not start. This means that it forces the server to start with the plugin if it is mentioned on startup.
- `--plugin_name=FORCE_PLUS_PERMANENT`: The same as the `FORCE` option, but additionally prevents the plugin from being unloaded at runtime.

Uninstall plugin

MySQL 8 uses the `UNINSTALL PLUGIN` statement to uninstall the plugin, without considering whether it was installed during the runtime or at startup. But this statement will not allow us to uninstall the built-in plugins and the plugins that were installed by the `--plugin_name=FORCE_PLUS_PERMANENT` option. This statement just unloads the plugin and removes it from the `mysql.plugin` table, so it requires additional *delete* privileges on the `mysql.plugin` table.

Getting information about the installed plugins

There are multiple ways to get information about the installed plugins. Some of them are listed as follows, for your reference:

- The `INFORMATION_SCHEMA.PLUGINS` table contains plugin details such as `PLUGIN_NAME`, `PLUGIN_VERSION`, `PLUGIN_STATUS`, `PLUGIN_TYPE`, `PLUGIN_LIBRARY`, and many more. Each individual row of this table represents information about the plugin:

  ```
  SELECT * FROM information_schema.PLUGINS;
  ```

- The `SHOW PLUGINS` statement shows the name, status, type, library, and license details for each of the individual plugins. If the library value is `NULL`, it indicates that it is a built-in plugin and hence, it cannot be unloaded.

  ```
  SHOW PLUGINS;
  ```

- The `mysql.plugin` table contains details regarding all the plugins which were registered by the `INSTALL PLUGIN` function.

Roles and permissions

To put it simply, a *role* is a collection of privileges. To create a role in MySQL 8, you must have the global `CREATE ROLE` or `CREATE USER` privilege. MySQL 8 provides various privileges to attach to roles and users. Refer to `https://dev.mysql.com/doc/refman/8.0/en/privileges-provided.html` for more details on the available privileges.

Now, let's take an example to understand the role creation and privileges assignment. Assume we have a `hr_employee` table already created in the current database and we want to give access of this table to the `hrdepartment` role. This dilemma can be resolved by making use of the following code:

```
CREATE ROLE hrdepartment;
grant all on hr_employee to hrdepartment;
```

The above code will help us to create the `hrdepartment` role and grant all the necessary access to it. This topic will be covered in detailed in `Chapter 11`, *Security*.

Caching techniques

Cache is a mechanism used to improve performance. MySQL uses several strategies to cache information in the buffer. MySQL 8 make use of the cache at the storage engine level to handle its operations. It also applies the cache in prepared statements and stored programs to improve performance. MySQL 8 has introduced various system level variables to manage cache, such as `binlog_stmt_cache_size`, `daemon_memcached_enable_binlog`, `daemon_memcached_w_batch_size`, `host_cache_size`, and many more. We will cover caching in detail in `Chapter 12`, *Optimizing MySQL 8*.

Globalization

Globalization is a feature which provides multi-language support for an application, such as enabling the use of native languages. It is much easier to understand messages in our own native language than other languages, right? To achieve this, globalization comes into the picture. Using globalization a user can store, retrieve and update data into many languages. There are certain parameters that are to be considered in globalization. We will discuss them in detail in the following sections.

Character sets

Before going into detail about character sets it is required to understand what a character set actually is, as well as its related terms, right? Let's start with the term itself; the character set is a set of symbols and encoding. Another important term related to character set is **collation**, the set of rules used for comparing characters. Let's take a simple example to understand the character sets and collation. Consider two alphabets, P and Q, and assign a number to each, so that $P=1$ and $Q=2$. Now, assume P is a symbol and 1 is its encoding. Here, the combination of both the letters and their encoding is known as the character set. Now suppose, we want to compare these values; the simplest way is by referring the encoding values. With this as 1 is less than 2 we can say P is less than Q which is known as collation. This is the simplest example to understand character sets and collation, but in real life we have many characters, including special characters, and in the same way collations have many rules.

Character set support

MySQL 8 supports many character sets, with a variety of collations. Character sets can be defined at the column, table, database or server levels. We can use the character set for `InnoDB`, `MyISAM`, and `Memory` storage engines. To check all the available character sets of MySQL 8, execute the following command:

```
mysql> show character set;
+-----------+------------------------------+----------------------+-------
-+
| Charset   | Description                  | Default collation    | Maxlen |
+-----------+------------------------------+----------------------+-------
-+
| armscii8  | ARMSCII-8 Armenian           | armscii8_general_ci  | 1 |
| ascii     | US ASCII                     | ascii_general_ci     | 1 |
| big5      | Big5 Traditional Chinese     | big5_chinese_ci      | 2 | .........
.........
+-----------+------------------------------+----------------------+-------
-+
41 rows in set (0.01 sec)
```

In the same way, to see the collation of characters, execute the following command:

```
mysql> SHOW COLLATION WHERE Charset = 'ascii';
+-------------------+----------+-----+----------+-----------+----------+----------
------+
| Collation | Charset | Id | Default | Compiled | Sortlen | Pad_attribute |
+-------------------+----------+-----+----------+-----------+----------+----------
------+
| ascii_bin | ascii | 65 | | Yes | 1 | PAD SPACE |
| ascii_general_ci | ascii | 11 | Yes | Yes | 1 | PAD SPACE |
+-------------------+----------+-----+----------+-----------+----------+----------
------+
2 rows in set (0.00 sec)
```

The collation will have the following three characteristics:

- Two different character sets cannot have the same collation.
- Each character set has a default collation. As displayed in the above code, the show character set command displays the default collation of the character set.
- Collation follows predefined naming conventions, which will be explained later.
- **Character set repertoire**: A **repertoire** is the collection of characters in the dataset. Any string expression will have a repertoire attribute and will belong to one of the below values:
    - **ASCII**: An expression that contains characters in the Unicode range U+0000 to U+007F.
    - **UNICODE**: An expression that contains characters in the Unicode range U+0000 to U+10FFFF. This includes characters in the **Basic Multilingual Plane** (**BMP**) range (U+0000 to U+FFFF) and supplementary characters outside the BMP range (U+01000 to U+10FFFF).

From the range of both values, we can identify that the ASCII is a subset of the UNICODE range and we can safely convert ASCII values to UNICODE values without any loss in data. The Repertoire is mainly used for the conversion of expressions from one character set to another. In some of the conversion cases MySQL 8 throws an error like illegal mix of collations; to handle these scenarios, repertoire is required. To understand its use, consider the following example:

```
CREATE TABLE employee (
   firstname CHAR(10) CHARACTER SET latin1,
   lastname CHAR(10) CHARACTER SET ascii
);
```

```
INSERT INTO employee VALUES ('Mona',' Singh');

select concat(firstname,lastname) from employee;
+----------------------------+
| concat(firstname,lastname) |
+----------------------------+
| Mona Singh |
+----------------------------+
1 row in set (0.00 sec)
```

- **UTF-8 for metadata**: Metadata means the data about the data. In terms of database we can say that anything that describes database objects is known as **metadata**. For example: column names, usernames, and many more. MySQL follows the below two rules for metadata:
    - Include all characters in all the languages for metadata; this enables a user to use his own language for column name and table name.
    - Manage one common character set for all metadata. Otherwise, the SHOW and SELECT statements for tables in INFORMATION_SCHEMA will not work properly.

To follow the above rules MySQL 8 stores metadata into the Unicode format. Consider that MySQL functions such as USER(), CURRENT_USER(), SESSION_USER(), SYSTEM_USER(), DATABASE(), and VERSION() have the UTF-8 character set by default. MySQL 8 server has defined character_set_system to specify character sets for metadata. Make sure that the storage of metadata in Unicode does not mean that column headers and the DESCRIBE function will return values in the form of the metadata character set. It works as per the character_set_results system variable.

Adding the character set

This section describes how to add character sets in MySQL 8. This method may vary based on the character set type - it might be simple or complex depending on the character type. The following four steps are required for adding character sets into MySQL 8:

1. Add a <charset> element for MYSET to the sql/share/charsets/Index.xml file. For the syntax, refer the already defined file for the other character set.

2. In this step, the process is different for simple and complex character sets. For simple character sets, create a configuration file, `MYSET.xml`, in the `sql/share/charsets` directory to describe the character set properties. In the case of complex character sets, the C source file is required. For example, create the `ctype-MYSET.c` type in the strings directory. For each `<collation>` element, provide `ctype-MYSET.c file`.

3. Modify the configuration information:

   1. Edit `mysys/charset-def.c`, and *register* the collations for the new character set. Add these lines to the **declaration** section:

      ```
      #ifdef HAVE_CHARSET_MYSET
      extern CHARSET_INFO my_charset_MYSET_general_ci;
      extern CHARSET_INFO my_charset_MYSET_bin;
      #endif
      ```

      Add these lines to the **registration** section:

      ```
      #ifdef HAVE_CHARSET_MYSET
      add_compiled_collation(&my_charset_MYSET_general_ci);
      add_compiled_collation(&my_charset_MYSET_bin);
      #endif
      ```

   2. If the character set uses `ctype-MYSET.c`, edit `strings/CMakeLists.txt` and add `ctype-MYSET.c` to the definition of the `STRINGS_SOURCES` variable.

   3. Edit `cmake/character_sets.cmake` with the following changes:
      - Add `MYSET` to the value of with `CHARSETS_AVAILABLE` in alphabetic order.
      - Add `MYSET` to the value of `CHARSETS_COMPLEX` in alphabetic order. This is needed even for simple character sets, or CMake will not recognize `DDEFAULT_CHARSET=MYSET`.

4. Reconfigure, recompile, and test.

Configuring the character sets

MySQL 8 provides the `--character-set-server` and `--collation-server` options to configure the character sets. The default character set has been changed from `latin1` to `UTF8`. `UTF8` is the dominating character set, though it hadn't been a default one in prior versions of MySQL. With these changes globally accepted, character sets and collations are now based on `UTF8`; one of the common reasons is because there are around 21 different languages supported by `UTF8`, which makes systems provide multilingual support. Before configuring collation, refer to the collation list available at `https://dev.mysql.com/doc/refman/8.0/en/show-collation.html`.

Language selection

MySQL 8 uses English languages by default for the error messages, but allows user to choose several other languages. For example, Russian, Spanish, Swedish, and many more. MySQL 8 uses `lc_messages_dir` and `lc_messages`, two system variables that manage the language for error messages, and have the following properties:

- `lc_messages_dir`: It is a system variable and is set up during server startup. It is global variable so is commonly used by all the clients at runtime.
- `lc_messages`: This variable is used at global as well as at session level. Individual users are allowed to use a different language for error messages. For example, if `en_US` is set during server startup but if you want to use French, then execute the following command:

```
SET lc_messages = 'fr_FR';
```

MySQL 8 server follows the below three rules for error message files:

- MySQL 8 will find the file at a location constructed by two system variables, `lc_messages_dir` and `lc_messages`. For example, if you start MySQL 8 with the below command then `mysqld` maps the locale `nl_NL` to the Dutch language and search for the error file in the `/usr/share/mysql/dutch` directory. MySQL 8 stores all language files in the `MySQL8 Base Directory/share/mysql/LANGUAGE` directory. By default, the language files are located in the `share/mysql/LANGUAGE` directory under the MySQL base directory.

```
mysqld --lc_messages_dir=/usr/share/mysql --lc_messages=nl_NL
```

- If the message file does not exist under the directory then MySQL 8 will ignore the value of the `lc_messages` variable and consider the value of the `lc_messages_dir` variable as a location in which to look.
- If the MySQL 8 server does not find the message file, then it shows a message in the error log file and uses English for the messages.

Time zone settings for MySQL8

The MySQL 8 server manages time zones in three different ways:

- **System time zone**: This is managed by the `system_time_zone` system variable, which can be set either by `–timezone=timezone_name` or by the `TZ` environment variable before execution of mysqld.
- **Server's current time zone**: This is managed by the `time_zone` system variable. The default value of the `time_zone` variable is `SYSTEM`, which means the server time zone is the same as the system time zone. MySQL 8 allows users to set the `time_zone` global variable value at startup time by specifying `default-time-zone='timezone'` in the option file, and at runtime by using the following command:

  ```
  mysql> SET GLOBAL time_zone = timezone;
  ```

- **Pre-connection time zone**: This is managed by the `time_zone` variable and specific to the client that connects to the MySQL 8 server. This variable takes its initial value from the global `time_zone` variable but MySQL 8 allows the user to change it at runtime by executing the below command :

  ```
  mysql> SET time_zone = timezone;
  ```

This session variable affects the display and storage of zone specific values. For example, values returned by the `NOW()` and `CURTIME()` functions. On the other hand, this variable does not affects values which are displayed and stored in UTC format, such as with the `UTC_TIMESTAMP()` function.

Locale support

MySQL 8 uses `lc_time_names` system variables to control languages which will impact what day, month name, and abbreviations will be displayed.

The `DATE_FORMAT()`, `DAYNAME()`, and `MONTHNAME()` function outputs depend on the `lc_time_names` variable's value. The first question that comes to mind is, where are these locales defined and how do we get them? Not to worry, refer to `http://www.iana.org/assignments/language-subtag-registry`. All locales are defined with language and region abbreviations by **Internet Assigned Numbers Authority (IANA)**. By default, MySQL 8 sets `en_US` as the locale in the system variable. There is provision for the user to set the value on server startup or to set `GLOBAL` if they have `SYSTEM_VARIABLES_ADMIN` or `SUPER` privileges. MySQL 8 allows a user to check and set the locale for his connection. Execute the following commands to check the locale on your workstation:

```
mysql> SET NAMES 'utf8';
Query OK, 0 rows affected (0.09 sec)

mysql> SELECT @@lc_time_names;
+-----------------+
| @@lc_time_names |
+-----------------+
| en_US |
+-----------------+
1 row in set (0.00 sec)

mysql> SELECT DAYNAME('2010-01-01'), MONTHNAME('2010-01-01');
+-----------------------+-------------------------+
| DAYNAME('2010-01-01') | MONTHNAME('2010-01-01') |
+-----------------------+-------------------------+
| Friday | January |
+-----------------------+-------------------------+
1 row in set (0.00 sec)

mysql> SELECT DATE_FORMAT('2010-01-01','%W %a %M %b');
+----------------------------------------+
| DATE_FORMAT('2010-01-01','%W %a %M %b') |
+----------------------------------------+
| Friday Fri January Jan |
+----------------------------------------+
1 row in set (0.00 sec)

mysql> SET lc_time_names = 'nl_NL';
Query OK, 0 rows affected (0.00 sec)
```

```
mysql> SELECT @@lc_time_names;
+-----------------+
| @@lc_time_names |
+-----------------+
| nl_NL |
+-----------------+
1 row in set (0.00 sec)

mysql> SELECT DAYNAME('2010-01-01'), MONTHNAME('2010-01-01');
+-----------------------+-------------------------+
| DAYNAME('2010-01-01') | MONTHNAME('2010-01-01') |
+-----------------------+-------------------------+
| vrijdag | januari |
+-----------------------+-------------------------+
1 row in set (0.00 sec)

mysql> SELECT DATE_FORMAT('2010-01-01','%W %a %M %b');
+-----------------------------------------+
| DATE_FORMAT('2010-01-01','%W %a %M %b') |
+-----------------------------------------+
| vrijdag vr januari jan |
+-----------------------------------------+
1 row in set (0.00 sec)</strong>
```

MySQL 8 server logs

MySQL 8 server provides the following different type of logs that enable users to track the activity of the server in various situations:

Log type	Information written to log
Error log	Problems encountered starting, running, or stopping `mysqld`
General query log	Established client connections and statements received from clients
Binary log	Statements that change data (also used for replication)
Relay log	Data changes received from a replication master server
Slow query log	Queries that took more than `long_query_time` seconds to execute
DDL log (metadata log)	Metadata operations performed by DDL statements

You can learn more about the different type of logs at `https://dev.mysql.com/doc/refman/8.0/en/server-logs.html`.

MySQL 8 will not generate the logs in MySQL 8, except in error logs in Windows, unless we enable it. By default, MySQL 8 will store all logs into a file under the data directory. When we talk about files, so many questions come into our mind, right? For example; what will be the size of file? How many files will be generated? How do we flush log files? MySQL 8 provides various configurations for managing log files; we will see all these configurations in a later part of this chapter. Another important question is where do we store logs? In tables or in files? Below are some points which describe the benefits of tables compared to files:

- If logs are stored into tables then their contents are accessible through SQL statements. This means that users can execute select queries with required criteria to get a specific output.
- Any remote user can connect to the database and get the details of the log.
- Log entries are managed by standard format. You can check the structure of log tables with the following commands:

The code for a general log:

```
SHOW CREATE TABLE mysql.general_log;
```

The code for a slow query log:

```
SHOW CREATE TABLE mysql.slow_log;
```

The error log

This log is used to record diagnostic messages like error, warnings and notes that occur from the startup of MySQL 8 through till its end. MySQL 8 provides various configurations and components for users to generate log files as per their requirements. When we start writing into files some basics questions come to mind; what do we write? How do we write it? Where do we write it to? Let's start with first question. MySQL 8 uses the `log_error_verbosity` system variable and assigns the below filtering options to decide what type of messages should be written into the error log file:

- Error Only

- `Errors and Warnings`
- `Errors, Warnings and Notes`

To write at the destination place MySQL uses the below format where the time stamp depends on the `log_timestamps` system variable:

```
timestamp thread_id [severity] message
```

After writing log files, the first question that comes to mind is, how do we flush these logs? For that, MySQL 8 provides three ways; `FLUSH ERROR LOGS`, `FLUSH LOGS`, or `mysqladmin flush-logs`. These commands will close and reopen the log file to which it is writing. When we talk about how to write and where to write, there are so many things to understand.

Component configuration

MySQL 8 uses the `log_error_services` system variable to control error log components. It allows users to define multiple components by semicolons, separated for the execution. Here, components will be executed in the order in which they are defined. The user is allowed to change the values of this variable with the following constraints:

- `INSTALL COMPONENT`: To enable any log component we must first install it using this command, and then use the component by listing it in `log_error_services` system variable. Follow the following commands to add the `log_sink_syseventlog` component:

  ```
  INSTALL COMPONENT 'file://component_log_sink_syseventlog';
  SET GLOBAL log_error_services = 'log_filter_internal;
    log_sink_syseventlog';
  ```

  After execution of the installation command MySQL 8 will register the component into the `mysql.component` system table to make it available for loading on each startup.

- `UNINSTALL COMPONENT`: To disable any of the log components, first remove it from the `log_error_services` system variable list and then uninstall it with this command. Execute the below command to uninstall a component:

  ```
  UNINSTALL COMPONENT 'file://component_log_sink_syseventlog';
  ```

To enable error log components on each startup, define it in the `my.cnf` file or use `SET_PERSIST`. When we define it in `my.cnf` it takes effect from the next restart, whereas `SET_PERSIST` will give an immediate effect. Use the following command for `SET_PERSIST`:

```
SET PERSIST log_error_services = 'log_filter_internal;
   log_sink_internal;
   log_sink_json';
```

MySQL 8 also allows users to write error logs into system logs: for Microsoft, consider Event log, and for Unix based systems, consider syslog. To enable error logging into system `logfibf`, configure `log_filter_internal` and the system log writer `log_sink_syseventlog` components and follow the same instructions explain above. Another way is to write a JSON string into the log file configuration `log_sink_json` component. An interesting point about a JSON writer is that it will manage file naming conventions by adding NN (two-digit numbers). For example, consider file names as `file_name.00.json`, `file_name.01.json`, and so forth.

Default error log destination configuration

Error logs can be written into log files or on console. This section describes how to configure the destination of error log on different environments.

Default error log destination on Windows

- `--console`: If this is given then the console will be considered the default destination. `--console` takes precedence over `--log-error` in cases where both are defined. If the default location is console, then MySQL 8 server sets the `log_error` variable's value as `stderror`.
- `--log-error`: If this is not given, or given without naming a file, then the default file name is `host_name.err` and the file will be created in the data directory unless the `--pid-file`option is specified. If the file name is specified in –pid-file option, then the naming convention would be a **PID** file base name with a suffix of `.err` in the data directory.

Default error log destination on Unix and Unix-Like systems

All the above mentioned scenarios in Microsoft Windows will be managed by the –log_error option in Unix systems.

- --log-error: If this is not given then the default destination is the console. If no file name is given, then as with Windows it will create a file in the data directory with the host_name.err name. The user is allowed to specify –log-error in an option file under the mysqld or mysqld_safe sections.

The general query log

The general query log is a general purpose log, used to record all the actions performed by mysqld. In this log, file statements are written in the sequence in which they are received, but the execution sequence may differ from the receiving sequence. It starts logging from the connection of the client and continues until it disconnects. Apart from SQL commands it also logs the connection_type means by which the protocol client is connected, for example TCP/IP, SSL, Socket, and many more. As it logs most of the action performed by mysqld it's very useful when we want to find what error occurred with the client.

By default, this log is disabled. We can enable it by using the --general_log[={0|1}] command. When we do not specify any argument or define 1 as the argument it indicates enable general query log, while 0 indicates disable log. In addition, we can specify log file name with the --general_log_file=file_name command. If no file name is specified by the command, then MySQL 8 will consider the default name as host_name.log. Setting the log file name has no effect on logging if the log destination value does not contain FILE. Server restarts and log flushing do not cause a new general query log file to be generated; you have to use the rename (For Microsoft Windows) or mv (For Linux) commands to create a new file. MySQL 8 provides a second approach for renaming files at runtime by disabling the log using the following command:

```
SET GLOBAL general_log = 'OFF';
```

Once the log is disabled, rename the log file and enable the log again with the ON option. Similarly, to enable or disable the log at runtime for particular connections use the session sql_log_off variable with the ON or OFF option. One more option is aligning with the general log file, that is, --log-output. By using this option, we can specify the destination of log output; it does not mean logs are enabled.

The three following different options are available with this command:

- `TABLE`: Log to tables
- `FILE`: Log to files
- `NONE`: Do not log into tables or files. `NONE`, if present, takes precedence over any other specifiers.

If the `--log-output` option is omitted, then the default value is file.

The binary log

The binary log is a file which contains all the events of a database that describe changes, for example, table creation, data updates, and deletes from the table. It is not used for the `SELECT` and `SHOW` statements as it is not updating any data. Binary log writing will slightly reduce performance of database operations, however it enables users to use replication setup and operation restore. The main purposes of the binary log are:

1. **For replication in master-slave architecture**: For replication based on binary file, master server performs insert and updates operations which are reflected in the binary log file. Now, slaves nodes are configured to read these binary files and same events are executed in the binary file of the slave servers to replicate the data onto the slave servers.
2. **Data recovery operations**: Once backup is restored into database, the events of the binary log are recorded, and these events are in re-executed form, which brings the database up to date from the point of the backup.

The binary log is enabled by default, which indicates that the log_bin system variable is set as ON. To disable this log use `--skip-log-bin` or the `--disable-log-bin` option at startup. To delete all binary log files, use the RESET MASTER statement, or a subset of them with `PURGE BINARY LOGS`. MySQL 8 server uses the following three logging formats to record information into the binary log file:

1. **Statement based logging**: This format is used by starting the server with the `--binlog-format=STATEMENT` command. It is mainly propagation of SQL statements.
2. **Row based logging**: Use `--binlog-format=ROW` on server startup to enable row based logging. This format indicates how rows are affected. This is the default option.

3. **Mixed logging**: Start MySQL 8 with the `--binlog-format=MIXED` option to enabled mixed logging. In this mode statement based logging is available by default and MySQL 8 will automatically switch into row based logging in some of the cases.

MySQL 8 allows users to change format at runtime with global and session scope. Global format is set for all the clients while session is use for the individual client. The following sets the format at runtime with the global and session scope respectively:

```
mysql> SET GLOBAL binlog_format = 'STATEMENT';
mysql> SET SESSION binlog_format = 'STATEMENT';
```

There are two exceptional cases where we cannot change format:

- Within a stored procedure or function
- In cases where the row based format is set and temporary table is open

MySQL 8 has the `--binlog-row-event-max-size` variable to control the size of the binary log file in terms of bytes. Assign as a value to this variable a multiple of 256; the default value of this option is 8192. Individual storage engines of MySQL 8 have their own capabilities for logging. If a storage engine supports row based logging, then it is known as **row-logging** capable, and if a storage engine supports statement based logging then it is known as **statement-logging** capable. Refer to the below table for more information on storage engine logging capabilities.

Storage engine	Row logging supported	Statement logging supported
ARCHIVE	Yes	Yes
BLACKHOLE	Yes	Yes
CSV	Yes	Yes
EXAMPLE	Yes	No
FEDERATED	Yes	Yes
HEAP	Yes	Yes
InnoDB	Yes	Yes when the transaction isolation level is REPEATABLE, READ, or SERIALIZABLE; No otherwise.
MyISAM	Yes	Yes

MERGE	Yes	Yes
NDB	Yes	No

As describe in this section the binary log will work based on types of statement like safe, unsafe, or binary injected, on the logging format such as ROW, STATEMENT, or MIXED, and with the logging capabilities of storage engines like row capable, statement capable, both, or neither. To understand all the possible cases of binary logging refer to the table given in this link: https://dev.mysql.com/doc/refman/8.0/en/binary-log-mixed.html.

The slow query log

Slow query logs are used to record SQL statements that takes long time to execute. MySQL 8 has defined the following two system variables for time configuration of slow query:

- long_query_time: This is used to define the ideal time for query execution. If a SQL statement takes longer than this time, then it is considered a slow query and a statement is recorded into the log file. The default value is 10 seconds.
- min_examined_row_limit: This is the minimum time required for the execution of each query. The default value is 0 seconds.

MySQL 8 will not consider the initial time of acquiring a lock into execution time and will return slow query logs into a file once all locks are released and query execution is completed. When MySQL 8 is started, slow query logging is disabled by default; to start this log use the slow_query_log[={0|1}] command, where 0 indicates slow query log is disabled and 1 or without argument is used to enabled it. To log administrative statements and queries without indexing, use the log_slow_admin_statements and log_queries_not_using_indexes variables. Here, administrative statements include ALTER TABLE, ANALYZE TABLE, CHECK TABLE, CREATE INDEX, DROP INDEX, OPTIMIZE TABLE, and REPAIR TABLE. MySQL 8 allows users to specify the name of the log file using --slow_query_log_file=file_name command. If no file name is specified, then MySQL 8 will create a file with the host_name-slow.log naming convention in the data directory. To write minimal information into this log file use the --log-short-format option.

All the above described parameters are controlled by MySQL 8 in the following sequence:

1. The query must either not be an administrative statement, or `log_slow_admin_statements` must be enabled
2. The query must have taken at least `long_query_timeseconds`, or `log_queries_not_using_indexes` must be enabled and the query must have used no indexes for row lookups
3. The query must have examined at least `min_examined_row_limitrows`
4. The query must not be suppressed according to the `log_throttle_queries_not_using_indexes` setting

> The `--log-output` option is also available for this log file, and has the same implementation and effect as the general purpose log.

The DDL log

As name implies, this log file is used to record all the DDL statement execution related details. MySQL 8 uses this log file to recover from crashes that occur during the metadata operation execution. Let's take one example to understand the scenarios:

- **Drop table t1, t2**: We must be sure that both the t1 and t2 tables are dropped

When we execute any DDL statement, a record of these operations is written into the `ddl_log.log` file under the MySQL 8 data directory. This file is a binary file and not in human readable format. The user is not allowed to update the contents of this log file. Metadata statements recording is not required in normal execution of MySQL server; enable it only if it is required.

Server log maintenance

To maintain log files, we must clean up on a regular basis to manage disk space. For RPM based Linux systems the `mysql-log-rotate` script is available automatically. For other systems no such script is available, so we must install a short script by ourselves to manage log files. MySQL 8 provides the `expire_logs_days` system variable which is used to manage binary log files. Using this variable log Binary log files are automatically removed after a specified period.

The default value of this variable is 30 days; you can change its value by configuration change. Binary log files are remove on server startup or when the log is flushed. In case of replication, you can also use the `binlog_expire_logs_seconds` system variable to manage logs for masters and slaves. Log flushing performs the following tasks:

- If general query logging or slow query logging to a log file is enabled, the server closes and reopens the query log file
- If binary logging is enabled, the server closes the current binary log file and opens a new log file with the next sequence number
- If the server was started with the `--log-error` option to cause the error log to be written to a file, the server closes and reopens the log file

To take backup or rename the old log files before generating a new log file, use the `mv` (move) command for Unix system, and the `rename` function in Windows. In case of general query and slow query log files, you can rename a file by disabling the log using the following command:

```
SET GLOBAL general_log = 'OFF';
```

After renaming log files, enable logs using the following command:

```
SET GLOBAL general_log = 'ON';
```

Summary

This was an interesting chapter for any MySQL 8 user, wasn't it? In this chapter we understood how MySQL 8 manages different log files and which log file to use at what time. At the same time we also covered many of the administrative features, such as globalization, system data database, and component and plugin configuration, and explained how to run multiple instances on a single machine. The later part of the chapter covered log maintenance.

Moving on to the next chapter, we will provide you with information about storage engines, such as what the different types of storage engine are, which one to use for your application, and how to create our own custom storage engine for MySQL 8.

6
MySQL 8 Storage Engines

In the previous chapter, we learned about setting up a new system, data dictionary, and system database. Detailed information was provided on caching techniques, globalization, different types of components, and plugin configuration, along with several types of log files which are very important for administration.

This chapter gives detailed information on MySQL 8 storage engines. It explains the `InnoDB` storage engine and its features in detail and also provides a practical guideline on custom storage engine creation and how to make it pluggable so that it can be installed in MySQL 8. The topics that we will be covering in this chapter are as follows:

- Overview of storage engines
- Several types of storage engines
- The `InnoDB` storage engine
- Creating a custom storage engine

Overview of storage engines

Storage engines are MySQL components for handling the SQL operations used in different types of tables. MySQL storage engines are designed to manage different types of tasks in different types of environments. It is very important to know and choose which storage engine is best suited for the system or application requirements. In following sections, we will get to know in detail about the types of storage engines, the default storage engine, and the creation of custom storage engines.

Let us go through and see why the storage engine is a very important component in databases, including MySQL 8. Storage engines work with database engines to perform various types of tasks in different environments. They execute create, read, update, and delete operations in the form of statements on data from the database. It looks quite simple when you provide the ENGINE parameter with the create table statement but there is configuration for plenty of operations to be done on the data for each of the requests sent via SQL statements. It is much more than just persisting data - the engine takes care of features such as storage limits, transactions, locking granularity/level, multi-version concurrency control, geospatial data types, geospatial indexing, B-tree indexes, T-tree indexes, Hash indexes, full-text search indexes, clustered indexes, data caches, index caches, compressed data, encrypted data, cluster databases, replication, foreign keys, back up, query caches, and updating statistics for the data dictionary.

MySQL storage engine architecture

The MySQL storage engine's pluggable architecture allows a database professional to select any storage engine for the specialization required in any particular application. The MySQL Storage engine architecture provides an easy application model and API with the consistency that isolates the database administrator and the application programmer from all the low-level implementation details underlying at the storage level. Thus, the application always works above different storage engines' different capabilities. It provides standard management and support services that are common for all underlying storage engines.

Storage engines perform activities on the data that is persisted at the physical server level. Such modular and efficient architecture provides solutions to specific needs of any particular application, such as transaction processing, high availability situations, or data warehousing, and at the same time has the advantage of independent interfaces and services from the underlying storage engines.

The database administrator and the application programmer interact with the MySQL database by Connector APIs and services on top of the storage engines. The application is shielded by the MySQL server architecture from the detailed level complexity of the storage engines by providing easy to use APIs that are consistent and applicable on all the storage engines. If the application requires changes in the underlying storage engine, or if one or more storage engines are added to support the needs of the application, no major coding or process changes are required to get things working.

Several types of storage engine

Now we know the importance of storage engines and critical decisions to identify which storage engines to use from plenty of storage engines available for MySQL 8. Let us take a look at what is available and with which specifications. InnoDB is the name that first entered your thoughts when you started thinking of storage engines, right?

InnoDB is the default and most general-purpose storage engine in MySQL 8 and it is recommended by Oracle to use for tables as well as for special use cases. The MySQL server has a pluggable storage engine architecture that enables storage engine loading as well as unloading from the already running MySQL server.

To identify which storage engines your server supports is made very easy in MySQL 8. We only have to go to the MySQL shell or prompt and use the SHOW ENGINES statement. Hit the statement when prompted and result will be the list of engines with a few columns, such as Engine, Support, Transactions, Savepoints, and Comment.

Values in Support column, DEFAULT, YES, and NO, indicate that a storage engine is available and currently set as the default storage.

Overview of the InnoDB storage engine

InnoDB is the default and most general-purpose storage engine in MySQL 8, providing high reliability and high performance.

If you have not configured a different default storage engine, then issuing the SQL statement CREATE TABLE without the ENGINE = clause creates a table with the storage engine InnoDB as the default engine in MySQL 8.

The features and advantages offered by the InnoDB storage engine are explained later in the *The InnoDB storage engine* section.

Custom storage engine

storage engine architecture in MySQL 5.1 and all the later versions and MySQL 8 have taken advantage of the flexible storage engine architecture.

The storage engine pluggable architecture provides the capability to create and add new storage engines without recompilation of the server, adding directly to a running MySQL server. The architecture makes it very easy to develop and deploy new storage engines to MySQL 8.

We will develop a new storage engine by using the pluggable feature of the MySQL storage engine architecture in the upcoming *Creating a custom storage engine* section.

Several types of storage engines

In this section, we will take a closer look at the widely used storage engines that are supported by MySQL 8. But before checking on them, let us see how the storage engine architecture has made it pluggable and provided flexibility to enable using multiple storage engines in the same schema or server.

The following is the list of storage engines supported in MySQL 8:

- `InnoDB`: The default storage engine for MySQL 8. It is an `ACID` compliant (transaction-safe) storage engine that has commit, roll back, and crash-recovery for protecting the user data and `referential-integrity` constraints to maintain data integrity, and much more.
- `MyISAM`: The storage engine with tables having a small footprint. It has table-level locking and so is mostly used in read-only or read-mostly data workloads, such as in data warehousing and web configurations.
- `Memory`: The storage engine previously known as the `HEAP` engine. It keeps data in RAM, which provides faster data access, mostly used in quick lookups of non-critical data environments.
- `CSV`: The storage engine with tables as comma-separated values in text files and tables. They are not indexed and are mostly used for importing and dumping data in `CSV` format.
- `Archive`: The storage engine comprises compact, unindexed tables, intended to store and retrieve a huge amount of historical, archived, or security audit data.
- `Blackhole`: The storage engine with tables that can be used for replication configuration. A query always returns an empty set. `DML` SQL statements are sent to slave servers. It accepts data but data is not stored, such as in a Unix `/dev/null` device use.

- `Merge`: The storage engine provides the capability to logically group a series of similar `MyISAM` tables and refer to them as one object instead of separate table.
- `Federated`: The storage engine that can link many separate physical MySQL servers into one logical database. It is ideal for data marts or distributed environments.
- `Example`: The storage engine that does nothing but works as a `stub`. It is primarily used by the developers who illustrate how to begin writing new storage engines in the MySQL source code.

MySQL does not restrict using the same storage engine for an entire server or schema; instead, specifying the engine at table level makes it flexible based on the type of data and the use case of the application.

Pluggable storage engine architecture

The MySQL server uses the pluggable storage engine architecture, which enables storage engine loading as well as unloading from already running MySQL servers:

- **Plugging in a storage engine**: Before a storage engine can be used in the server, the storage engine plugin shared library has to be loaded into MySQL with the `INSTALL PLUGIN` SQL statement. If you create a `MYEXAMPLE` engine plugin that is named `MyExample` and the shared library is named `MyExample.so`, then you need to load them with the following statement:

    ```
    mysql> INSTALL PLUGIN MyExample SONAME 'MyExample.so';
    ```

    For installing a storage engine, the user issuing the preceding statement must have the `INSERT` privilege for the `mysql.plugin` table and the plugin file must be present in the MySQL plugin directory. The shared library also must be present in the MySQL server plugin directory given in the `plugin_dir` variable.

- **Unplugging a storage engine**: Before unplugging a storage engine, make sure that no tables are using the storage engine. If a storage engine is unplugged and is needed by any existing tables, the tables become inaccessible and will only be present on disk as applicable. If you unplug the `MYEXAMPLE` engine plugin named `MyExample` then execute the following statement for unplugging the storage engine:

    ```
    mysql> UNINSTALL PLUGIN MyExample ;
    ```

The common database server layer

The MySQL pluggable storage engine is responsible for executing I/O operations on the actual data and also to cater to the specific application needs that includes enabling and enforcing the required features whenever required. Using a specific or single storage engine will more likely result in more efficiency and higher database performance because the engine enables the features only needed for a particular application, and resulting in less system overhead on the database.

A storage engine supports the following unique infrastructure components or keys:

- **Concurrency**: Some applications have granular lock levels (such as row-level locks) requirements more than others. Overall performance and overhead due to locking can be affected by choosing the right/wrong locking strategy and this also includes multi-version concurrency control or snapshot read capabilities.
- **Transaction support**: Very well-defined requirements exist, such as ACID compliance and more if the application needs transactions.
- **Referential integrity**: The server can enforce relational database referential integrity using DDL -defined foreign keys if required..
- **Physical storage**: This includes everything from the page size of tables and indexes and also includes the format used for storing data on a physical disk as well.
- **Index support**: This includes indexing strategies based on the application needs, as each of the storage engines have their own indexing methods.
- **Memory caches**: The caching strategies based on the application needs, as each of the storage engines have their own caching methods along with common memory caches across all the storage engines.
- **Performance aids**: This involves bulk insert handing, database check pointing, multiple I/O threads for parallel operations, thread concurrency, and more.
- **Miscellaneous target features**: This may includes support for security restrictions on certain data manipulation operations, geospatial operations, and other similar features.

Each of the preceding infrastructure components are designed to support a specific set of features for a particular application's needs and so it is very important to understand the application requirement very carefully and select the right storage engine, as it may impact on the overall system efficiency and performance.

Setting the storage engine

When you create new table using the CREATE TABLE statement, you can specify which engine to be used for the table with the ENGINE table option. If you do not specify the ENGINE table option then the default storage engine will be used instead. InnoDB is the default engine for MySQL 8.0. You can also convert a table from one storage engine to another storage engine by using the ALTER TABLE statement, as shown in the following example:

```
CREATE TABLE table1 (i1 INT) ENGINE = INNODB;
CREATE TABLE table3 (i3 INT) ENGINE = MEMORY;
ALTER TABLE table3 ENGINE = InnoDB;
```

The default storage engine can be set for the current session by setting the default_storage_engine variable, as shown in the following example:

```
SET default_storage_engine=MEMORY;
```

The default storage engine for TEMPORARY tables using CREATE TEMPORARY TABLE can be set separately by setting the default_tmp_storage_engine variable at either startup or runtime.

The MyISAM storage engine

The MyISAM storage engine uses tables having a small footprint. It has table-level locking implemented and so is mostly used where there are read-only or read-mostly data workloads, such as in data warehousing and web configurations. Each of the MyISAM tables are stored with two files on disk. The filename begins with the table name and its extension type, one with the .MYD extension for the data file and another with the .MYI extension for the index file.

For the MyISAM engine, there are several startup options specified with mysqld that can change the behavior of MyISAM tables; for example:

```
--myisam-recover-options=mode
```

This option will set the mode in the automatic recovery of crashed tables in MyISAM.

Spaces needed for keys in MyISAM, B-Tree indexes are used by MyISAM tables and space compression is used in String indexes. If a string is the first part of the index then prefix compression is also done, which overall makes the index file size smaller. The prefix compression helps if many strings have a similar prefix. By using the table option PACK_KEYS=1 in MyISAM tables, prefix compression can also be applied on the numbers if there are many numbers with a similar prefix.

Partitioning is not supported for MyISAM tables in MySQL 8.0.

Some of the important tables characteristics for MyISAM tables are as follows:

- All data values stored have the low byte first order, which makes the data independent of machine and operating systems
- All numeric key values are stored with high byte first order, which permits better index compression
- MyISAM table is limited with $(2^{32})^2 (1.844E+19)$ rows
- MyISAM table is limited to a maximum number of 64 indexes per table
- MyISAM table columns is limited to a maximum number of 16 columns per index
- Concurrent inserts are supported in MyISAM, if a table does not have any free blocks in the middle of the data files
- TEXT and BLOB type columns can also be indexed in MyISAM
- In indexed columns, NULL values are permitted
- Each of the columns can have a different character set
- It also support for a true VARCHAR type column with a starting length stored of 1 or 2 byte, tables with VARCHAR columns with a fixed or dynamic row length, and UNIQUE constraints with an arbitrary length
- MyISAM table storage formats: The following three different types of storage formats listed are supported in MyISAM:
  - Static **table**: The default format for the tables in the MyISAM storage engine, with fixed-sized columns
  - Dynamic **table**: As the name suggests, the format that contains variable sized columns, including VARCHAR, BLOB , or TEXT
  - Compressed **table**: The table format for keeping read-only data and compressed formats in MyISAM storage engine tables

The first two formats, fixed and dynamic, are chosen automatically based on the column type used. The compressed format can be created by using the `myisampack` utility.

- `MyISAM` **table problems**: The file format has been extensively tested but some circumstances arise that result in corrupted database tables. Let us look at such circumstances and the way to recover those tables.

We could get corrupted tables in the event of any of the following events :

- If the `mysqld` process is killed in the middle of a write
- If there is an unexpected computer shutdown
- If there is any hardware failure
- If a table is being modified at the same time by the MySQL server and an external program, such as `myisamchk`
- The MySQL or `MyISAM` code has a software bug

Check the health of the table with the `CHECK TABLE` statement and attempt to repair any corrupted `MyISAM` table by using the `REPAIR TABLE` statement.

There is also possible issue you get with `MyISAM` tables and that is tables are not being closed properly. In order to identify if the table is closed properly or not, each `MyISAM` index file keeps a counter in the header. The counter can be incorrect under the following circumstances:

- If a table is copied without issuing `LOCK TABLES` and `FLUSH TABLES`
- MySQL crashed before the final close during an update
- `mysqld` is using the table and at the same time it is modified by another program: `myisamcheck --recover` or `myisamchk --update-state`

The MEMORY storage engine

The `MEMORY` storage engine, also previously known as the `HEAP` engine, keeps data in `RAM`, which provides faster data access. It is mostly used in quick lookups of non-critical data environments. It creates special-purpose tables with contents stored in memory but the data is vulnerable to crashes, power outages, and hardware issues. Therefore, these tables are used in temporary work areas or possibly using read only data that is cached after the data is pulled from other tables.

You should choose whether use MEMORY or NDB Cluster. You should check if the application is required for important, highly available, or frequently updated data and consider whether NDB Cluster is the better choice or not. NDB Cluster provides the same features as the MEMORY engine, but with higher performance levels and additional features not provided by MEMORY engine. These include:

- Low contention between clients by multiple thread operations and row-level locking
- Scalability with statements mixes, including writes
- Data durability; it supports optional disk-backed operations
- Shared-nothing architecture, providing multiple-host operations without a single point of failure, enabling 99.999% availability for the application
- Automatic data distributions across nodes
- Support for variable length data types, including BLOB and TEXT

Partitioning is not supported in MEMORY tables.

Performance depends on how busy the server is and the effect of single thread execution with table lock overhead during updates processing. The table locking during updates processing causes a slowdown of concurrent usage from multiple sessions on MEMORY tables.

MEMORY tables characteristics: Table definitions are stored on the MySQL data dictionary and do not create any files on the disk. The following are the table feature highlights:

- 100% dynamic hashing for inserts and space is allocated in small blocks.
- No extra key space or overflow area or extra space for free lists is required. Reuse of deleted rows when new records inserted by putting rows in linked lists.
- Fixed length row-storage format, VARCHAR , is stored with fixed length. Cannot store BLOB or TEXT columns.
- AUTO_INCREMENT columns are supported.

Indexing in HASH and BTREE types are supported by the MEMORY storage engine. MEMORY tables have a maximum of 64 indexes per table, a maximum of 16 columns per index and a maximum key length of 3,072 bytes. MEMORY tables also can have non-unique keys.

User created and temporary tables: Internal temporary tables are created by the server on the fly while processing queries. Two types of tables differ in storage conversion, where the MEMORY tables are not subject to conversion:

- When an internal temporary table becomes too large, it is converted to on-disk storage by the server automatically
- User created MEMORY tables are never converted by the server

Data loading can be performed using the --init-file option, using INSERT INTO ... SELECT or LOAD DATA INFILE statements from any persistence data source if required.

The CSV storage engine

This storage engine stores data in the form of comma-separated values in text files. The engine is always compiled into the MySQL server and the source can be examined from the storage/csv directory of your MySQL distribution.

The data file created by the server begins with the given table and the extension of .CSV. The data file is a plain text file containing data in the comma-separate values format.

The MySQL server creates a corresponding metafile along with a CSV table that stores information about the state of the table and the count for the rows that exists in the table. The metafile is also stored with the table name at the beginning with the .CSM extension.

- **Repairing and checking** CSV **tables**: The storage engine supports CHECK and REPAIR statements to verify and possibly repair a damaged CSV table. You can use the CHECK TABLE statement to verify or validate the table and use the REPAIR TABLE statement to repair a table that copies valid rows from an existing CSV data file and replaces an existing file with newly copied/recovered rows.

> During repair, only rows from the CSV data file to the first damaged row gets copied to the new table or copied data file. The rest of the rows after the damaged row gets removed from the table, including valid rows, so I suggest that you take enough back up of the data file prior to proceeding with the repair.

Indexing or partitioning is not supported in the CSV storage engine and all the tables created with the CSV storage engine must have the NOT NULL attribute on all the columns.

The ARCHIVE storage engine

The ARCHIVE storage engine creates special-purpose tables that are used for storing huge amounts of unindexed data with a very small footprint.

When the ARCHIVE table is created, it begins with the table name and ends with the .ARZ extension. During optimization operations, a file with an .ARN extension may appear.

The AUTO_INCREMENT column attribute is supported by the engine. It also supports INSERT, REPLACE, SELECT, and BLOB columns (all but spatial data types) but it does not support DELETE, UPDATE, ORDER, or BY operations.

Partitioning is not supported by the ARCHIVE storage engine:

- **Storage**: The engine uses lossless data compression with zlib and the rows get compressed as inserted. It supports the CHECK TABLE operation. Several types of insertion are used in the engine:
  - INSERT statement sends rows into a compression buffer, and the buffer gets flushed as necessary. Insertion in the compression buffer is protected by the lock and flush will only occur if SELECT is requested.
  - Once completed a bulk buffer can be seen. It can only be seen if any other inserts occur at the same time. Here flush will not occur upon SELECT, unless while loading any normal insert.
- **Retrieval**: After retrieval, rows gets uncompressed as requested and it does not use any row cache. A complete table scan is performed for the SELECT operation:
  - SELECT checks how many rows are available currently and reads only that number of rows. It is performed as a consistent read operation.
  - The number of rows reported by SHOW TABLE STATUS is always accurate for the ARCHIVE tables.
  - Use OPTIMIZE TABLE or REPAIR TABLE operations to achieve better compression.

The BLACKHOLE storage engine

The BLACKHOLE storage engine acts as a black hole. It accepts data but does not store it and a query always returns an empty result.

The server only adds the table definition in the global data dictionary when you create a BLACKHOLE table and no files are associated with the table.

All kinds of **indexing** is supported in the BLACKHOLE storage engine and so the same can be included in the table definition.

Partitioning is not supported in the BLACKHOLE storage engine.

Insertion to the table does not store any data but if binary logging is enabled for statements, then the statements are logged and replicated to the slave servers. Such a mechanism is useful as a filter or repeater.

The BLACKHOLE storage engine has the following possible uses:

- Dump file syntax verification
- Overhead measurement using binary logging enabled or disabled with a BLACKHOLE performance comparison
- It can also be used for finding any performance bottlenecks, except for the storage engine itself

Auto increment columns: As the engine is a no-op engine, it will not increment any field values but it has implications in the replication, which can be very important. Consider a scenario that has the following conditions:

1. The master server has a BLOCKHOLE table with an auto increment field with a primary key
2. The same table exists on the slave server but uses the MyISAM engine
3. Insertion is performed into the master server's table without setting any auto increment value in the INSERT statement or using the SET INSERT_ID statement

In the preceding scenario, the replication will fail on the primary key column with a duplicate entry.

The MERGE storage engine

The MERGE storage engine, known also as the MRG_MyISAM engine, is collection of similar tables that can be used as one table instead. Here, "similar" means that all the tables have similar column data types and indexing information. It is not possible to merge tables with the columns listed in a different order or to have the same data types in respective columns or have indexing in a different order.

The following is the list of differences in tables that will not restrict a merge:

- Names of respective columns and indexes can be different.
- Comments in between tables, columns, and indexes can be different.
- AVG_ROW_LENGTH, MAX_ROWS , or PACK_KEYS table options can be different.

When a MERGE table is created, MySQL also creates a .MRG file on the disk with the names of underlying MyISAM tables being used as one. The format of the table is stored in the MySQL data dictionary and the underlying tables do not require to be in the same database as the MERGE table.

Having privileges are a must for SELECT, UPDATE, and DELETE on the MyISAM tables that are being mapped with the MERGE table and so SELECT, INSERT, UPDATE, and DELETE statements on the MERGE table can be used.

Executing the DROP TABLE statement on the MERGE table will drop only the specification for the MERGE and nothing is impacted on the underlying tables.

 Using MERGE tables has the following security issues. If the user has access to the MyISAM table t1, then the user can create the MERGE table m1 that can access t1. Now, if the user's privileges on the table t1 are revoked, the user can still continue accessing table t1 by using table m1.

The FEDERATED storage engine

The FEDERATED storage engine can link many separate physical MySQL servers into one logical database and so it can let you access data from a remote MySQL server without using either replication or cluster technology.

When we query to the local FEDERATED table, that automatically pulls the data from the remote federated tables and the data is not required to be stored on local tables.

The FEDERATED storage engine is not supported by default in the MySQL server but starting the server with the --federated option will enable the FEDERATED engine option.

When the FEDERATED table is created the table definition is the same as other tables, but the physical storage of the associated data is handled on the remote server instead. The FEDERATED table consists of the following two elements:

- A **remote server** with a database table consisting of a table definition and the associated table data. This type of table can be any supported by the remote server that includes MyISAM or InnoDB as well.
- A **local server** with a database table consisting of a table definition the same as the respective table on the remote server. The table definition is stored in the data dictionary and no associated data file on the local server is stored. Instead, in addition to the table definition, it keeps a connection string that is pointing to the remote table itself.

The following is the flow of information between the local and remote server when a SQL statement is executed on the FEDERATED table:

1. The engine checks each of the columns the table has and builds an appropriate SQL statement that refers to the remote table.
2. The MySQL client API is used for sending the SQL statement to the remote server.
3. The statement is processed by the remote server and the respective result is retrieved by the local server.

The EXAMPLE storage engine

The EXAMPLE storage engine is only a stub engine and the purpose of the engine is to provide examples in the MySQL source code, which helps developers to write new storage engines.

To work with the EXAMPLE engine source code, look at the storage/example directory of the MySQL source code distribution download.

No files are created if the table is created with the EXAMPLE engine. Data cannot be stored in the EXAMPLE engine and it returns empty results.

Indexing and partitioning is not supported in the EXAMPLE storage engine.

The InnoDB storage engine

InnoDB is the most general-purpose storage engine and is the default engine in MySQL 8, providing high reliability and high performance .

The following are the key advantages offered by the InnoDB storage engine:

- Its DML operations follows the ACID model and transactions have commit, rollback, and crash-recovery features to protect user data
- Oracle-style gives consistent reads and row level locking increases the performance of multi-user concurrency
- Each InnoDB table has a primary key index, known as the clustered index, that arranges data on the disk in order to optimize queries based on primary key and minimizes I/O during primary key lookups
- By supporting foreign keys, inserts, deletes, and updates are checked, ensuring consistency across different tables in order to maintain data integrity

The following are the key benefits of using InnoDB tables:

- If the server crashes due to any hardware or software issue, regardless of what changes were being processed in the server at that time, you're not required to do anything special after restarting the server. It has a crash recovery system that takes care of changes that were committed during the crash of the server. It will go to those changes and start where the processing was left off.
- The engine has it's own buffer pool used for caching table and indexing data to memory based on data accessed. Frequently used data is fetched directly from the cache memory and so it speeds up processing. In dedicated servers, it takes up to 80% of physical memory assigned to be used in the buffer pool.
- Splitting related data to tables using foreign key setup enforces referential integrity which prevents inserting any unrelated data to a secondary table without the respective data in the primary table.
- In case of corrupt data in the memory or disk, the checksum mechanism gives an alert about the corrupt data before we get to use it.
- Change buffering automatically optimizes Insert, Update, and Delete. InnoDB also allows concurrent read and write access to the same table and caching data changes to streamline the disk I/O.

- When the same data rows are accessed from the table repeatedly, the Adaptive Hash Index feature makes the lookups faster and gives performance benefits.
- Compression is allowed on tables and associated indexes.
- Monitoring on internal workings and performance details of the storage engine is easy by querying `INFORMATION_SCHEMA` or `Performance Schema` tables.

Now let us look at each of the areas of the storage engine where `InnoDB` is enhanced or optimized to provide very efficient and enhanced performance.

ACID model

The `ACID` model is a group of database design principles with an emphasis on reliability, which is most important for mission critical applications and business data.

MySQL has components such as the `InnoDB` storage engine that closely adhere to the `ACID` model. Therefore, data is safe and not corrupted, even in exceptional cases of hardware malfunctions or software crashes.

With MySQL 8, `InnoDB` supports atomic `DDL`, ensuring that the `DDL` operations are fully committed or rolled back, even if the server is halted while performing the operation. Now `DDL` logs can be written to the `mysql.innodb_ddl_log` configuration for the data dictionary tables, enabling the `innodb_print_ddl_logs` configuration option to print `DDL` recovery logs to `stderr`.

Multiversioning

InnoDB is a multiversioned storage engine. That means it has the capability to keep old versions of changed row data information and support transnational features, such as concurrency and roll back. The information is stored in the tablespace, data structure, and named rollback segment.

Internally, for each of the rows getting stored in the database, `InnoDB` creates three fields: 6-byte `DB_TRX_ID`, 7-byte `DB_ROLL_PTR` (called a roll pointer) and 6-byte `DB_ROW_ID`. With these fields, `InnoDB` creates clustered indexes to keep the information of changed row data in the database.

Architecture

In this section, we will give a brief introduction to the major components of the `InnoDB` architecture:

- **Buffer pool**: Area of main memory where tables and indexing data are cached to speed up processing
- **Change buffer**: Special data structure where changes to secondary index pages are cached
- **Adaptive Hash Index**: Enables in-memory database, such as lookups, operations on systems with balanced and appropriate combinations of the buffer pool's memory and workload
- **Redo log buffer**: Memory area where data is held to be written on the redo log
- **System tablespace**: Storage area where the `doublewrite` buffer, undo logs, and the change buffer, prior to the MySQL 8 data dictionary information, are stored
- **Doublewrite buffer**: Storage area in the system tablespace where pages are written that are flushed from the buffer pool
- **Undo logs**: Collection of undo log records which are associated with any single transaction
- **File-per-table tablespaces**: Single-table tablespace added to its own data file
- **General tablespaces**: Shared tablespace created by the `CREATE TABLESPACE` syntax
- **Undo tablespace**: One or more files with undo logs
- **Temporary tablespace**: Utilized for non-compressed temporary tables and their related objects
- **Redo log**: Disk-based data structure used for correcting incomplete transaction data during crash recovery

With MySQL 8, the `InnoDB` storage engine utilizes the global MySQL data dictionary and not its own storage engine-specific data dictionary.

Locking and transaction model

This section gives brief information on locking used by InnoDB and the transaction model implemented by InnoDB. InnoDB uses the following different lock types:

- **Shared and exclusive locks**: Two types of standard row-level locking are implemented. A shared lock allows you to read a row to different transactions; an exclusive lock holds to update or delete a row and does not allow you to even read the row to any different transaction.
- **Intention locks**: Table level locks to support multiple granularity locking by which InnoDB practically maintains the coexistence of row-level locks and entire table-level locks.
- **Record locks**: Index record lock that prevents any other transaction to insert, update, or delete the record.
- **Gap locks**: Lock applies on a gap (range) between index records.
- **Next-key locks**: Combination of index record lock plus gap lock on the gap for the preceding index record.
- **Insert intention locks**: Type of gap lock which is set by INSERT operation just before the row insertion.
- **AUTO-INC locks**: Special table-level lock for inserting records with the AUTO_INCREMENT column.
- **Predicate locks for spatial indexes**: Lock on spatial index, enabling support for isolation levels in tables with spatial indexes.

The goal of following the transaction model is to unite traditional two-phase locking with the best of the multiversioning database properties. Row-level locking is performed and queries are run with nonlocking consistent reads. InnoDB takes care of transaction isolation levels, autocommit, rollback and commit, and locking reads. It allows nonlocking consistent reads as applicable. InnoDB also uses a mechanism to avoid phantom rows and a configuration to support automatic deadlock detection.

Configuration

This section provides brief information about the configuration and procedures used in the InnoDB initialization startup for different InnoDB components:

- InnoDB **startup configuration**: This involves specifying startup options, log file configuration, storage considerations, system tablespace data files, undo tablespaces, temporary tablespaces, page sizes, and memory configurations
- InnoDB **for read-only operation**: This enables a MySQL instance for read-only operation, using the `--innodb-read-only=1` option, which is very helpful when using read-only media such as CD or DVD
- InnoDB **buffer pool configuration**: Configures the buffer pool size, multiple instances, flushing, and monitoring
- InnoDB **change buffering**: Configures the change buffer options for secondary index caching
- **Thread concurrency for** InnoDB: Concurrent thread count limit configuration
- **The number of background** InnoDB **I/O threads:** Configures the number of background threads servicing I/O read/write operations on data pages
- **Using asynchronous I/O on Linux**: A configuration to use native asynchronous I/O subsytems on Linux
- **The** InnoDB **master thread I/O rate**: Configures overall I/O capacity for a master thread working in the background, responsible for multiple tasks
- **Spin lock polling**: Configures a spin wait delay period to control the maximum delay for frequent polling between multiple threads requesting to acquire `mutexes` or `rw-locks`
- InnoDB **purge scheduling**: Configures purge threads for applicable scalability
- **Optimizer statistics for** InnoDB: Configures persistent and non-persistent optimizer statistics parameters
- **The merge threshold for index pages**: Configures `MERGE_THRESHOLD` to reduce merge-split behavior
- **Enabling automatic configuration for a dedicated MySQL Server**: Configures the dedicated server option `--innodb_dedicated_server`, which makes automatic configuration for the buffer pool size and log file size

Tablespaces

This section provides brief information on tablespaces and operations related to tablespaces performed in `InnoDB`:

- **Resizing the** `InnoDB` **system tablespace**: Increasing and decreasing the size of the system tablespace with configuration while starting/restarting the MySQL server.
- **Changing the number or size of** `InnoDB` **redo log files**: Configures `innodb_log_files_in_group` and `innodb_log_file_size` values respectively in `my.cnf` prior to starting/restarting the MySQL server.
- **Using raw disk partitions for the system tablespace**: Configures the raw disk partitions to be used as data files in the system tablespace.
- `InnoDB` **File-Per-Table tablespaces**: The feature `innodb_file_per_table` enabled by default which ensures that each of the tables and associated indexes are stored in a separate `.idb` data file.
- **Configuring undo tablespaces**: A configuration to set the number of undo tablespaces where an undo log resides.
- **Truncating undo tablespaces**: Configures `innodb_undo_log_truncate` to enable truncating undo tablespace files exceeding the maximum limit defined in `innodb_max_undo_log_size`.
- `InnoDB` **general tablespaces**: A shared tablespace created using the `CREATE TABLESPACE` statement. It is similar to a system tablespace.
- `InnoDB` **tablespace encryption**: Support for data encryption in tables stored as file-per-table tablespaces which use the `AES` block-based encryption algorithm.

Tables and indexes

This section provides brief information on `InnoDB` tables and indexes and their related operations:

- **Creating** `InnoDB` **tables**: Creates tables using the `CREATE TABLE` statement.
- **The physical row structure of an** `InnoDB` **table**: Depends on the specified row format during the table creation. If not specified, uses the default, `DYNAMIC`.
- **Moving or copying** `InnoDB` **tables**: Different techniques for moving or copying some or all `InnoDB` tables to a different instance or server.

- **Converting tables from** MyISAM **to** InnoDB: Considers guidelines and tips while converting MyISAM tables to InnoDB tables, except a partitioned table, which is not supported with MySQL 8.
- AUTO_INCREMENT **handling in** InnoDB: Configures the mode for AUTO_INCREMENT with the innodb_autoinc_lock_mode parameter as 0,1, and 2 for traditional, consecutive, or interleaved, respectively, where interleaved is the default mode from MySQL 8.
- **Limits on** InnoDB **tables**: A table can contain a maximum of 1,017 columns, a maximum of 64 secondary indexes, and several other limits defined based on the page size, table size, and data-row formats.
- **Clustered and secondary indexes**: InnoDB uses a special index called a clustered index. The rest of the indexes are called secondary indexes.
- **The physical structure of** InnoDB **index**: For spatial indexes, InnoDB uses the R-tree data structure, a specialized data structure. For rest of the indexes, the B-tree data structure is used.
- **Sorted index builds**: Bulk load when creating or rebuilding indexes for inserts. They are known as sorted index builds, and are not supported in spatial indexes.
- InnoDB FULLTEXT **indexes**: Created for text-based columns - char, varchar, or text type. They help to speed up queries and searching operations.

INFORMATION_SCHEMA tables

This section provides usage examples for InnoDB INFORMATION_SCHEMA tables and related information.
It provides metadata, statistics, and status information about the different aspects of the InnoDB storage engine.

The list of InnoDB INFORMATION_SCHEMA tables can be retrieved by executing the SHOW TABLES statement on the INFORMATION_SCHEMA database:

```
mysql> SHOW TABLES FROM INFORMATION_SCHEMA LIKE 'INNODB%';
```

- **Tables about compression**: The number of compression operations and the amount of time spent for compression-related information provided in the INNODB_CMP and INNODB_CMP_RESET tables. Memory allocation during compression is provided in the INNODB_CMPMEM and INNODB_CMPMEM_RESET tables.

- **Transaction and locking information**: INNODB_TRX has information on transactions currently executing and the data_locks and data_lock_waits tables from the Performance Schema table give information about the locks.
- **Schema object tables**: This provides metadata information about the InnoDB schema objects.
- FULLTEXT **index tables**: This provides metadata information about FULLTEXT indexes.
- **Buffer pool tables**: This provides status information and metadata about the pages in the buffer pool.
- **Metrics table**: This provides performance and resource related information.
- **Temporary table information table**: This provides metadata information about all users and system-created temporary tables currently active in an InnoDB instance.
- **Retrieving** InnoDB **tablespace metadata**: This provides metadata information about all the types of tablespaces in an InnoDB instance.

A new view, INNODB_TABLESPACES_BRIEF, has been added to provide the name, path, flag, space, and space type data.

A new table, INNODB_CACHED_INDEXES, has been added to provide the number of index pages cached in the buffer pool for each index.

Memcached plugin

MySQL 8 provides you with the InnoDB memcached plugin named daemon_memcached, which can help us in managing data easily. It will automatically store and retrieve data from InnoDB tables and provide get, set, and incr operations that remove performance overhead by skipping SQL parsing, which speeds up data operations. The memcached plugin uses the integrated memcached daemon that automatically retrieves and stores data from and to the InnoDB table, enabling the MySQL server to send data quickly to the key-value store.

The following are the major benefits of using the InnoDB memcached plugin:

- Accesses the InnoDB storage engine directly, reducing parsing and planning SQL overhead
- memcached uses the same process space as the MySQL server, reducing network overhead

- Data written or requested in the `memcached` protocol is transparently written or queried from `InnoDB` tables, reducing having to go through SQL layer overhead
- Simplifies application logic by automatically transfering between disk and memory
- The MySQL database stores data so that it is protected against corruption, crashes, or outages
- Ensures high availability using the `daemon_memcached` plugin on the master server and MySQL replication in combination
- Repeated data requests are cached using the `InnoDB` buffer pool, providing high speed processing
- As the data is stored in the `InnoDB` tables, the data consistency is enforced automatically

The `InnoDB memcached` plugin supports multiple get operations (fetching multiple key/value pairs in a single `memcached` query) and range queries.

Creating a custom storage engine

MySQL AB introduced pluggable storage engine architecture in MySQL 5.1 and all later versions, including MySQL 8, have taken advantage of the flexible storage engine architecture.

The storage engine pluggable architecture provides the capability to create and add new storage engines without recompiling the server, adding directly to a running MySQL server. The architecture makes it very easy to develop and deploy new storage engines to MySQL 8.

When developing new storage engine, it is required to take care of all the components that work for and with storage engines. These include installation handlers, operations on table such as creating, opening, and closing, `DML`, indexing, and so on.

In this section, we will cover how you can start developing a new storage engine on a high-level basis with reference to the MySQL documentation provided in the development community. The creation of a custom storage engine requires a working knowledge of development with `C` and `CPP`, and compilation with `cmake` and `Visual Studio`.

Creating storage engine source files

The easiest way to implement a new storage engine is to begin by copying and modifying the `EXAMPLE` storage engine. The files `ha_example.cc` and `ha_example.h` can be found in the `storage/example` directory of the MySQL source distribution.

When copying the files, change the names from `ha_example.cc` and `ha_example.h` to something appropriate to your storage engine, such as `ha_foo.cc` and `ha_foo.h`.

After you have copied and renamed the files, you must replace all instances of `EXAMPLE` and `example` with the name of your storage engine.

Adding engine-specific variables and parameters

A plugin can implement status and system variables and in this section we have covered the changes to variables and parameters with appropriate values and data types.

The server plugin interface enables plugins to expose status and system variables using the `status_vars` and `system_vars` members of the general plugin descriptor.

`status_vars` is a member of the general plugin descriptor. If the value is not 0, then it points to an array of the `st_mysql_show_var` structure where each of them describe one status variable followed by a structure with all the members set to 0. The definition for the `st_mysql_show_var` structure is as follows:

```
struct st_mysql_show_var {
  const char *name;
  char *value;
  enum enum_mysql_show_type type;
};
```

When the plugin is installed, the plugin name and the name value are joined with an underscore to form the name displayed by the `SHOW STATUS` statement.

The following list shows the permissible status variable type values and what the corresponding variable should be:

- `SHOW_BOOL`: This is a pointer to the `boolean` variable
- `SHOW_INT`: This is a pointer to the `integer` variable
- `SHOW_LONG`: This is a pointer to the long `integer` variable
- `SHOW_LONGLONG`: This is a pointer to the `longlong integer` variable

- SHOW_CHAR: This is a String index
- SHOW_CHAR_PTR: This is a pointer to String indexes
- SHOW_ARRAY: This is a pointer to another st_mysql_show_var array
- SHOW_FUNC: This is a pointer to a function
- SHOW_DOUBLE: This is a pointer to a double

All session and global system variables have to be published to mysqld before they are used. This is precisely done by constructing a NULL terminated array of the variables and linking to it in the plugin public interface.

All mutable and plugin system variables are stored internally in the HASH structure.

The display of the server command-line help text is generated by compiling DYNAMIC_ARRAY of all the relevant variables, sorting and iterating through them to display each option.

During the plugin installation process, the server processes command-line options, immediately after the plugin has been successfully loaded but the plugin initialization function is yet to be called.

Plugins loaded at runtime do not benefit from any configuration options and must have usable defaults. Once they are installed, they are loaded at mysqld initialization time and configuration options can be set at the command line or within my.cnf.

The thd parameter should be considered as read-only in plugins.

Creating the handlerton

The handlerton (the short form of handler singleton) defines the storage engine. It contains method pointers to methods applied to the storage engine as a whole, instead of methods that work on a per-table basis. Examples of such methods include transaction methods which handle commits and rollbacks operations.

An example from the EXAMPLE storage engine is as follows:

```
handlerton example_hton= {
  "EXAMPLE", /* Name of the storage engine */
  SHOW_OPTION_YES, /* It should be displayed in options or not */
  "Example storage engine", /* Description of the storage engine */
  DB_TYPE_EXAMPLE_DB, /* Type of storage engine it should refer to */
  NULL, /* Initialize handlerton */
```

```
    0, /* slot  available */
    0, /* define savepoint size. */
    NULL, /* handle close_connection */
    NULL, /* handle savepoint */
    NULL, /* handle rollback to savepoint */
    NULL, /* handle release savepoint */
    NULL, /* handle commit */
    NULL, /* handle rollback */
    NULL, /* handle prepare */
    NULL, /* handle recover */
    NULL, /* handle commit_by_xid */
    NULL, /* handle rollback_by_xid */
    NULL, /* handle create_cursor_read_view */
    NULL, /* handle set_cursor_read_view */
    NULL, /* handle close_cursor_read_view */
    example_create_handler, /* Create a new handler instance */
    NULL, /* handle drop database */
    NULL, /* handle panic call */
    NULL, /* handle release temporary latches */
    NULL, /* Update relevant Statistics */
    NULL, /* Start Consistent Snapshot for reference */
    NULL, /* handle flush logs */
    NULL, /* handle show status */
    NULL, /* handle replication Report Sent to Binlog */
    HTON_CAN_RECREATE
};
```

There are 30 `handlerton` elements, only few of which are mandatory.

Handling handler installation

This is the first method call in your storage engine required for creating a new handler instance.

Before the `handlerton` is defined in the source file, there must be the instantiation method defined in method header. The following is an example from the `CSV` engine displaying the instantiation method:

```
static handler* tina_create_handler(TABLE *table);
```

As you can see in the preceding example, the method accepts a pointer to the table. The handler is responsible for managing and returning the handler object. After the method header definition, the method is named with the method pointer in the `create()` `handlerton` element. This identifies the method as being responsible for generating new handler instances when requested.

The instantiation method for the `MyISAM` storage engine is shown in the following example:

```
static handler *myisam_create_handler(TABLE *table)
{
   return new ha_myisam(table);
}
```

Defining filename extensions

Storage engines must provide a list of extensions used by the storage engine associated to a given table, its data, and indexes to the MySQL server.

Extensions should be given in the form of a null-terminated string array and the same is returned when the [custom-engine.html#custom-engine-api-reference-bas_ext bas_ext()] method is called, as shown in the following block:

```
const char **ha_tina::bas_ext() const
{
   return ha_tina_exts;
}
```

By providing extension information, you can also skip implementing DROP TABLE functionality, as the MySQL server will implement the same by closing the table and deleting all files with the extensions specified.

Creating tables

After handler instantiation, the creation of the table method should be followed. The storage engine must implement the [custom-engine.html#custom-engine-api-reference-create create()] method, as shown in the following block:

```
virtual int create(const char *name, TABLE *form, HA_CREATE_INFO *info)=0;
```

The preceding displayed method should create all the necessary files but it does not open the table. The MySQL server will call separately for the table to be opened.

The *name parameter is for passing the name of the table and the *form parameter is for passing the TABLE structure. The table structure defines the table and matches the contents of tablename.frm. Storage engines must not modify the tablename.frm file as that will result in errors or unpredictable issues.

The *info parameter is structure with information on the CREATE TABLE statement. It is used to create the table and the structure is defined in the handler.h file. The following is the structure for reference:

```
typedef struct st_ha_create_information
{
    CHARSET_INFO *table_charset, *default_table_charset; /* charset in
table */
    LEX_STRING connect_string; /* connection string */
    const char *comment,*password; /* storing comments and password values
*/
    const char *data_file_name, *index_file_name; /* data and index file
names */
    const char *alias; /* value pointer for alias */
    ulonglong max_rows,min_rows;
    ulonglong auto_increment_value;
    ulong table_options;
    ulong avg_row_length;
    ulong raid_chunksize;
    ulong used_fields;
    SQL_LIST merge_list;
    enum db_type db_type; /* value for db_type */
    enum row_type row_type; /* value for row_type */
    uint null_bits; /* NULL bits specified at start of record */
    uint options; /* OR of HA_CREATE_ options specification */
    uint raid_type,raid_chunks; /* raid type and chunks info */
    uint merge_insert_method;
    uint extra_size; /* length of extra data segments */
    bool table_existed; /* 1 in create if table existed */
    bool frm_only; /* 1 if no ha_create_table() */
    bool varchar; /* 1 if table has a VARCHAR */
} HA_CREATE_INFO;
```

Storage engines can ignore the contents of *info and *form because the creation and the initialization of the data files is only really required when used by the storage engine.

Opening a table

Prior to any read or write operations performed on any table, the MySQL server calls the [custom-engine.html#custom-engine-api-reference-open `handler::open()`] method to open the table index and data files:

```
int open(const char *name, int mode, int test_if_locked);
```

The first parameter is for the name of the table being opened. The second parameter is for the file operation to take. The values are defined in `handler.h`: `O_RDONLY` – Open read only, `O_RDWR` – Open read/write.

The final option dictates if the handler should check for a lock on the table before opening. The following options are available to choose from:

```
#define HA_OPEN_ABORT_IF_LOCKED 0 /* default */
#define HA_OPEN_WAIT_IF_LOCKED 1 /* wait if table is locked */
#define HA_OPEN_IGNORE_IF_LOCKED 2 /* ignore if locked */
#define HA_OPEN_TMP_TABLE 4 /* Table is a temp table */
#define HA_OPEN_DELAY_KEY_WRITE 8 /* Don't update index */
#define HA_OPEN_ABORT_IF_CRASHED 16
#define HA_OPEN_FOR_REPAIR 32 /* open even if crashed with repair */
```

The typical storage engine will implement some form of shared access control in order to prevent file corruption in a multi-threaded environment. For example, see the `get_share()` and `free_share()` methods of `sql/example/ha_tina.cc` for implementing file locking.

Implementing basic table scanning

The most basic storage engines implement a read-only level of table scanning and they might be used to support SQL queries for requesting information from the logs and other data files that are populated outside of MySQL.

The implementation of the methods is the first step towards the creation of advanced storage engines. The following shows the method calls made during a nine-row table scan of the CSV engine:

```
ha_tina::store_lock
ha_tina::external_lock
ha_tina::info
ha_tina::rnd_init
ha_tina::extra - ENUM HA_EXTRA_CACHE Cache record in HA_rrnd()
```

```
ha_tina::rnd_next
ha_tina::rnd_next
ha_tina::rnd_next
ha_tina::rnd_next
ha_tina::rnd_next
ha_tina::rnd_next
ha_tina::rnd_next
ha_tina::rnd_next
ha_tina::rnd_next
ha_tina::extra - ENUM HA_EXTRA_NO_CACHE End caching of records (def)
ha_tina::external_lock
ha_tina::extra - ENUM HA_EXTRA_RESET Reset database to after open
```

The following methods can be implemented to take care of specific operations:

- **Implementing the** `store_lock()`: This method can modify the lock level, ignoring or adding locks for many tables
- **Implementing the** `external_lock()`: This method is called when the LOCK TABLES statement is issued
- **Implementing the** `rnd_init()`: This method is used in table scanning for resetting counters and pointers at the start of a table
- **Implementing the** `info(uinf flag)`: This method is used to provide extra table information to the optimizer
- **Implementing the** `extra()`: This method is used to provide extra hints information to the storage engine
- **Implementing the** `rnd_next()`: This method is called on each row of scanning until EOF is reached or the search condition is satisfied

Closing a table

When the MySQL server has completed all the requested operations with the table, it will call the `custom-engine.html#custom-engine-api-reference-close` `close()` method. It will close the file pointers and release all the related resources.

Storage engines using the shared access methods are seen in the CSV engine. Other example engines must remove the same from the shared structure, as displayed here:

```
int ha_tina::close(void)
  {
    DBUG_ENTER("ha_tina::close");
    DBUG_RETURN(free_share(share));
  }
```

Storage engines use their own share management systems. They should use the required methods in order to remove the handler instance from the share for the respective table opened in their handler.

 If your storage engine is compiled as a shared object, during loading if you get an error such as `undefined symbol: _ZTI7handler`, then make sure you compile and link your extension using the same flags as the server uses. The usual reason for this error is that LDFLAGS are missing the *-fno-rtti* option.

Reference for advanced custom storage engine

We have gone through the preceding sections in detail, giving high-level information for custom storage engine components and the required changes. For implementing `INSERT`, `UPDATE`, `DELETE`, indexing, and so on, in a custom storage engine, requires a working knowledge of development with `C/CPP` and compilation with `cmake` and `Visual Studio`. For advanced development for the custom storage engines, please refer to the detailed information given at `https://dev.mysql.com/doc/internals/en/custom-engine.html`

Summary

By now, you have learned the different database engines available in MySQL 8 and we learned why we should care about storage engines and available storage engine options in MySQL 8. We covered in detail the `InnoDB` storage engine and related important features already provided within the `InnoDB` storage engine. Now you are practically able to create a custom storage engine as per the system requirement and make it pluggable in MySQL 8. An important aspect was to choose a suitable storage engine for your system, which is covered detail.

In the next chapter, you will learn about how indexing works in MySQL 8, the new features introduced related to indexing, the different types of indexing, and how to use indexing on your tables. Along with that, a comparison will also be provided along with in-depth knowledge of various ways of index implementation.

7
Indexing in MySQL 8

In the previous chapter, we learned about storage engines. Now we are aware what types of storage engines are available and which ones to use for our requirements. The previous chapter also covered the `InnoDB` storage engine in detail, along with other storage engine information. It also described how to define a custom storage engine for use, with a practical example. Now it's time to understand one more important functionality of MySQL 8 and that is, indexing. We will cover different types of indexes with their functionalities, which will encourage you to use indexes and provided you with guidance on how to use them. So, your journey into indexes has started! Let's go.

We will cover the following topics in this chapter:

- An overview on indexing
- Column-level indexing
- B-Tree indexes
- Hash indexes
- Index extensions
- Using an optimizer for indexes
- Invisible and descending indexes

An overview on indexing

To define an index on a table is the best way to improve the performance of the SELECT operation. An index acts like a pointer for the table rows and permits queries to quickly point to matching rows based on the WHERE condition. MySQL 8 allows you to create indexes on all the data types. Although indexing provides good performance on queries, it is recommend to define it in the proper way, because unnecessary indexes waste space and time (for MySQL 8 to find which index is best to use). In addition to that, indexes also add costs to INSERT, UPDATE, and DELETE operations, because during these operations, MySQL 8 will update each index.

As we described previously, an index is a data structure that improves the speed of operations. Based on the structure, an index is bifurcated into two major forms—a clustered index and a non-clustered index:

- **Clustered index**: A clustered index defines the order in which data is physically stored in a table. Therefore, only one clustered index is allowed per table. It greatly increases the speed of retrieval when data is retrieved in a sequential manner, either in the same order or in reverse order. A clustered index also provides better performance when a range of items are selected. A primary key is defined as a clustered index.
- **Non-clustered index**: A non-clustered index doesn't define the order in which data is physically stored. This means a non-clustered index is stored in one place, and data is stored in another place. Therefore, more than one non-clustered index is allowed per table. It refers to non-primary keys.

As we know, the primary key represents the column, or set of columns, which is most widely used for fetching records from the table. The primary key has an index associated with it and is used for fast query performance. It provides comparatively faster performance because a primary key does not allow a NULL value, so no check is required on NULL values. It is recommended that if your table does not have a column or set of columns to define as a primary key, then you define one auto increment field as the primary key for better performance. On the other hand, if your table contains many columns and there is a need to execute a query with a combination of multiple columns, then it is advisable to the less frequently used data and transfer in onto a separate table. Relate all the separate tables with primary and foreign key references, which will help you in managing data, and query retrieval provides you good performance.

Uses of indexes in MySQL 8

Indexes are mainly used to find a row of specific values without iterating a complete table. If an index is not define,d then MySQL 8 will start searching from the first row and then read the entire table, which makes for a costly operation. MySQL 8 uses indexes for the following operations:

- To sort or group tables when it is done on the left-most prefix of an index. This means that if all keys are defined for the DESC clause, then the keys will be considered in reverse order, and if all keys are followed by ASC, then the keys will be considered in forward order.

- To find rows whose values match with the WHERE clause.

- In the case of multiple column indexes, any left-most prefix of the index can be used to find the row. This topic is covered in the later part of this chapter with a detailed example.

- If there is a case where MySQL has to choose one index from multiple options, then it will choose the index which has the smallest set of rows.

- Sometimes, the query is optimized to get the values without referring to rows. For example, if the query uses only columns that are included in indexes, MySQL 8 will get the selected value from the index tree:

```
SELECT key_part3 FROM table_name WHERE key_part1=10;
```

- At the time of performing the join, MySQL 8 will use the index in a more efficient way, if columns are declared with the same type and size. For example, VARCHAR (15) and CHAR(15) will be considered as the same,
but VARCHAR(10) and CHAR(15) will not be considered as the same.

- In the case of MIN () and MAX () functions, if you have used part of the index columns, then the optimizer will check whether all the other parts of the index columns are available in the WHERE condition. If they are mentioned, then MySQL 8 will perform a single lookup for the MIN () and MAX () functions and replace them with constants. For example:

```
SELECT MIN(key_part2), MAX(key_part2) FROM tble_name WHERE
    key_part1=10;
```

SQL commands related to indexes

MySQL 8 provides two main commands related to indexes. We will discuss these commands in the following sections.

Creating an INDEX command

The following command enables the user to add indexes into an existing table. This command is also used with CREATE TABLE and ALTER TABLE to create indexes:

```
CREATE [UNIQUE|FULLTEXT|SPATIAL] INDEX index_name
 [index_type]
 ON tbl_name (index_col_name,...)
 [index_option]
 [algorithm_option | lock_option] ...
index_col_name:
 col_name [(length)] [ASC | DESC]
index_option:
 KEY_BLOCK_SIZE [=] value
 | index_type
 | WITH PARSER parser_name
 | COMMENT 'string'
 | {VISIBLE | INVISIBLE}
index_type:
 USING {BTREE | HASH}
algorithm_option:
 ALGORITHM [=] {DEFAULT|INPLACE|COPY}
lock_option:
 LOCK [=] {DEFAULT|NONE|SHARED|EXCLUSIVE}
```

Using col_name(length) syntax, the user is able to specify an index prefix length, which will consider only a specified number of characters from the string value. At the time of defining, the prefix considers the following points:

- The prefix is optional for CHAR, VARCHAR, BINARY, and VARBINARY column indexes
- The prefix must be specified in the case of BLOB and TEXT column indexes
- MySQL 8 will consider prefixes as a number of characters for non-binary string types (CHAR, VARCHAR, TEXT) and a number of bytes for binary types (BINARY, VARBINARY, BLOB)
- The prefix is not allowed for the spatial columns

A detailed example of the prefix option is described later in this chapter, under the *Column indexes* section. A UNIQUE index is a constraint which indicates that all the values in the index will be unique. If you try to add values which already exist, then MySQL 8 displays an error. All types of storage engines with a UNIQUE index permit multiple null values. In the case of prefixes when you use NULL values, make sure column values are unique within the prefixes. If an index prefix exceeds its size, then MySQL 8 will handle the index as follows:

- **For a non-unique index**: If the strict SQL mode is enabled, then MySQL 8 will throw an error, and if the strict mode is disabled, then the index length is reduced to the maximum column data type size and will produce a warning.
- **For a unique index**: In this case, MySQL 8 produces an error regardless of the SQL mode, because it might break the uniqueness of the column. This means you have defined a column with 25 length and tried to define an index on the same column with a prefix length 27; then MySQL 8 throws an error.

Spatial index characteristics

MySQL 8 follows the following rules for spatial index characteristics:

- It is only available for InnoDB and MyISAM storage engines; if you try to use it for other storage engines, then MySQL 8 gives an error.
- A NULL value is not allowed for indexed columns.
- A prefix attribute is not allowed for this column. Full width will be considered for the index.

Non-spatial index characteristics

MySQL 8 follows the following rules for non-spatial index characteristics:

- A NULL value is allowed for an indexed column in the case of InnoDB, MyISAM, and MEMORY storage engines.
- The column prefix length must be specified in the case of each spatial column, if it exists under a non-spatial index. The prefix length will be considered in terms of bytes.
- Except for ARCHIVE, it is supported for all the storage engines which support spatial columns.

- A NULL value is allowed for this index, unless it is defined as a PRIMARY key.
- For an InnoDB table, run the ANALYZE TABLE statement after creating an index on that table, if the innodb_stats_persistent setting is enabled.
- The index type will depend on the storage engine; currently, B-Tree is used.
- A non-spatial index is allowed on a BLOB or TEXT column only if it is defined using InnoDB and MyISAM tables.

The default value of the index_col_name attribute is in ascending order, and neither an ASC nor DESC value is permitted for HASH indexes with this attribute. MySQL 8 provides any of the following values with the index_option:

- KEY_BLOCK_SIZE [=] value: This parameter defines the size of the index key block in bytes. It is an optional parameter and its value is treated as a hint. MySQL 8 may use a different size if it is required. If this parameter is defined at the individual index level, then it overrides the table-level KEY_BLOCK_SIZE value. The InnoDB engine doesn't support this parameter at the index level; it allows it at the table level only.

- index_type: MySQL 8 permits the user to define the index type at the time of index creation. For example:

```
create table employee (id int(11) not null,name varchar(50));
CREATE INDEX emp_name_index ON employee (name) USING BTREE;
```

Refer to the following table to find the permissible index types related to the storage engine. Consider the first index type as the default type in cases where multiple types are defined. If any storage engine is not mentioned in this table, it means that the index type is not supported by that engine:

Storage Engine	Permissible Index Types
InnoDB	BTREE
MyISAM	BTREE
MEMORY/HEAP	HASH, BTREE
NDB	HASH, BTREE

Reference: https://dev.mysql.com/doc/refman/8.0/en/create-index.html

If you try to define an index type which is not supported by the storage engine, then MySQL 8 will consider it as a supported index type, without affecting the query result. Refer to the following table to learn more about the characteristics of indexes, based on storage types:

Storage Engine	Index Type	Index Class	Stores NULL Values	Permits Multiple NULL Values	IS NULL Scan Type	IS NOT NULL Scan Type
InnoDB	BTREE	Primary key	No	No	N/A	N/A
		Unique	Yes	Yes	Index	Index
		Key	Yes	Yes	Index	Index
	Inapplicable	FULLTEXT	Yes	Yes	Table	Table
	Inapplicable	SPATIAL	No	No	N/A	N/A
MyISAM	BTREE	Primary key	No	No	N/A	N/A
		Unique	Yes	Yes	Index	Index
		Key	Yes	Yes	Index	Index
	Inapplicable	FULLTEXT	Yes	Yes	Table	Table
	Inapplicable	SPATIAL	No	No	N/A	N/A
MEMORY	HASH	Primary key	No	No	N/A	N/A
		Unique	Yes	Yes	Index	Index
		Key	Yes	Yes	Index	Index
	BTREE	Primary	No	No	N/A	N/A
		Unique	Yes	Yes	Index	Index
		Key	Yes	Yes	Index	Index

Reference: https://dev.mysql.com/doc/refman/8.0/en/create-index.html

- WITH PARSER parser_name: This option is valid only for a FULLTEXT index which was supported by a InnoDB and MyISAM storage engine. If FULLTEXT index and searching operations require special handling, then MySQL 8 will use a parser plugin with the index.

- `COMMENT 'string'`: This attribute is optional and allows up to 1024 characters in comments. This option also supports the `MERGE_THRESHOLD` parameter whose default value is 50. Consider the following command to define the `MERGE_THRESHOLD`:

```
CREATE INDEX name_index ON employee(name) COMMENT
  'MERGE_THRESHOLD=40';
```

If the page-full percentage for an index is less than the `MERGE_THRESHOLD` value, then the `InnoDB` storage engine will merge the index page with a neighboring index page.

- `VISIBLE, INVISIBLE`: This parameter defines the index visibility. By default, all indexes are visible. The optimizer will not use an invisible index during the optimization process.

The `ALGORITHM` and `LOCK` attributes will have an impact when you try to use the table for reading or writing, and while simultaneously modifying its indexing.

Drop index command

The following command drops the index from the table. We can also map this statement with `ALTER TABLE` to drop the index from the table:

```
DROP INDEX index_name ON tbl_name
  [algorithm_option | lock_option]...
algorithm_option:
    ALGORITHM [=] {DEFAULT|INPLACE|COPY}
lock_option:
    LOCK [=] {DEFAULT|NONE|SHARED|EXCLUSIVE}
```

In this command, only two options are available: the algorithm and the lock. Both of these options are useful in the case of concurrent access of index and work, similar to the `CREATE INDEX` command. For example, to drop the index of an employee table, execute the following command:

```
DROP INDEX name_index ON employee;
```

SPATIAL index creation and optimization

MySQL 8 allows you to create a spatial index on a `InnoDB` and `MyISAM` storage engine using the same syntax mentioned in the preceding topic. The only change in the standard command is to use the keyword **spatial** at the time of creating the index. When you define a spatial index, make sure that the column is declared as `NOT NULL`. The following code demonstrates the method to create a spatial index on table:

```
CREATE TABLE geom_data (data GEOMETRY NOT NULL, SPATIAL INDEX(data));
```

The spatial index, by default, creates an R-Tree index. From MySQL 8.0.3 onwards, the optimizer checks the **spatial reference identifier** (**SRID**) attribute of the indexed column to find the **Spatial Reference System** (**SRS**) for comparisons and performs calculations according to SRS. For comparison, each column in a spatial index must be SRID-restricted. This means that each column definition must contain an SRID attribute, and all the column values must have the same SRID. The spatial index performs the following two actions based on the SRID:

- If the column is restricted to a **Cartesian SRID**, then it enables Cartesian bounding box computation
- If the column is restricted to a **Geographic SRID**, then it enables geographic bounding box computation

As mentioned above, MySQL 8 will ignore a `SPATIAL INDEX` on a column which does not have an SRID attribute, but MySQL still manages these indexes as follows:

- These types of indexes are updated when the table is modified with the `INSERT`, `UPDATE`, or `DELETE` command.
- These indexes are considered in dump backups and are restored with backward compatibility. As mentioned in the previous point, spatial indexes with no SRID restricted columns are not used by the optimizer, so in that case, all these columns must be modified. To modify them, perform the following steps:
    1. Check all the values of the column that have the same `ST_SRID` with the following command:

        1. `SELECT DISTINCT ST_SRID(column_name) FROM table_name;`

        If the query returns multiple rows, then it indicates that the column contains mixed SRIDs. If so, change the contents of the column for the same SRID value.

2. Define an explicit SRID for the column.
3. Recreate the `SPATIAL INDEX`.

InnoDB and MyISAM index statistics collection

MySQL 8 will consider table statistics based on the value group, which is nothing but a set of rows with the same prefix values. The storage engine collects statistics related to the table, which are used by the optimizer. From the optimization perspective, average value group size is an important statistic. If the average value of the group size increases, then the index is not meaningful. So, it's better to target a small number of rows for each index. This can be achieved by table cardinality, which is nothing but a number of value group. For `InnoDB` and `MyISAM` tables, MySQL 8 provides control on statistics by the `myisam_stats_method` and the `innodb_stats_method` system variables. The following are the possible values for these variables:

- `nulls_ignored`: It indicates that `NULL` values are ignored
- `nulls_equal`: It indicates all `NULL` values are identical
- `nulls_unequal`: It indicates all `NULL` values are not identical

The `innodb_stats_method` system variable has a global value, while the `myisam_stats_method` system variable has both global and session values. When we set a global value of a variable, it will affect statistics collection for tables from the corresponding storage engine. In the case of session value statistics, collection is available only for the current client connection. This means that you have to regenerate a table's statistics for the other client on the same table without affecting other clients, and need to set it in a session value. To regenerate `MyISAM` statistics, use either of these methods:

- Execute the `myisamchk --stats_method=method_name --analyze` command
- Make changes to the table to make its statistics out of date, and then set `myisam_stats_method` and issue an `ANALYZE TABLE` statement

There are some points that must be considered before using these two variables:

- These variables are available only for `InnoDB` and `MyISAM` tables. For other storage engines, only one method is available to collect table statistics, and it is very near to the `nulls_equal` method.

- MySQL 8 provides a way to generate statistics for a table explicitly, but this is not always the case. Sometimes, MySQL 8 may also generate statistics automatically, if it is required. For example, in the case of any operations, if some of the SQL statements modified table data, then MySQL 8 will automatically collect statistics. Consider bulk insert or delete operations.
- We cannot say which method was used to generate statistics for a table.

Column-level indexing

MySQL 8 allows you to create an index on a single column, as well as on multiple columns. The maximum number of indexes per table and maximum index length depend on the storage engine. Mostly, all the storage engines allow at least 16 indexes per table and total index lengths of at least 256 bytes, but most of the storage engines permit higher limits.

Column indexes

This is the most common way to define an index where only a single column is involved. MySQL 8 stores a copy of column values in a data structure so that rows can be accessed quickly. MySQL 8 uses a **B-Tree** data structure to enable values to be accessed quickly. The B-Tree execution will work based on operators, such as =, <, >, BETWEEN, IN, and many more, which were defined in the where condition. You can get details on the B-Tree data structure and its execution in the next topic. We will discuss the characters of column indexes in the coming sections.

Index prefixes

This option allows the user to specify the number of characters for indexing in the case of a string. MySQL 8 has provided the option column_name(N), in index creation to specify a number of characters. Indexing prefers only specified characters, which will make the index file smaller. So, at the time of the BLOB and TEXT column, you must specify the prefix length for better performance. Consider the following example to create indexes with prefix lengths on the BLOB type:

```
CREATE TABLE person (personal_data TEXT, INDEX(personal_data (8)));
```

This command creates an index on the `personal_data` column by considering the first eight characters. The prefix length varies, based on the storage engine. The `InnoDB` storage engine allows up to a 767 byte prefix length for `REDUNDANT` or `COMPACT` row formats, while in the case of `DYNAMIC` or `COMPRESSED` row formats, it allows up to 3072 bytes. In the case of the `MyISAM` storage engine, the prefix can be defined for up to 1,000 bytes.

 Prefix length will be measured in bytes for binary string types, such as `BINARY`, `VARBINARY`, and `BLOB`, while in the case of non-binary string types, it will be considered as a number of characters.

FULLTEXT indexes

As the name implies, `FULLTEXT` indexes allow `CHAR`, `VARCHAR`, and `TEXT` columns only. This index is supported by `InnoDB` and `MyISAM` storage engines. In this type, indexing will take place on an entire column, rather than a prefix length. MySQL 8 evaluates the full text expression during the optimization phase of the query execution. Before making estimations, optimization evaluates the full text expression in the process of developing an execution plan. As a result, the `EXPLAIN` query of full text is slower than non-full text queries. Full text queries are useful in the following scenarios:

- When a `FULLTEXT` query returns either a document ID or a document ID and search rank
- When a `FULLTEXT` query sorts the matching rows by descending order and uses a `LIMIT` clause to fetch *N* number of rows, apply only a single `ORDER BY` clause in descending order, and don't use a `WHERE` clause in it for optimization
- When a `FULLTEXT` query fetches a `COUNT(*)` value from the rows without any additional `WHERE` clauses, apply the `WHERE` clause as `WHERE MATCH(text) AGAINST ('other_text')`, without any > 0 comparison operator

Spatial Indexes

MySQL 8 allows you to create indexes on spatial data types. The `InnoDB` and `MyISAM` storage engines support R-Tree for spatial data, while other storage engines use B-Tree. Since MySQL 5.7, spatial indexes are supported in `MyISAM` and `InnoDB` database engines.

Indexes in the MEMORY storage engine

Memory storage engines support both HASH indexes and B-Tree indexes, but HASH indexes are, by default, set for the MEMORY storage engine.

Multiple-column indexes

MySQL 8 allows you to use multiple columns in a single index creation, which is also known as a **composite index**. It permits up to 16 columns in a composite index. At the time of composite index use, make sure you follow the same order of columns which was mentioned during index creation. A multiple-column index contains values generated by concatenating the values of indexed columns. Consider the following example in order to understand multiple-column indexes:

```
CREATE TABLE Employee (
id INT NOT NULL,
lastname varchar(50) not null,
firstname varchar(50) not null,
PRIMARY KEY (id),
INDEX name (lastname, firstname)
);
```

As described above, we have defined composite indexes using two columns, lastname and firstname. The following queries use the name index:

```
SELECT * FROM Employee WHERE lastname='Shah';
SELECT * FROM Employee WHERE lastname ='Shah' AND firstname ='Mona';
SELECT * FROM Employee WHERE lastname ='Shah' AND (firstname ='Michael' OR
firstname ='Mona');
SELECT * FROM Employee WHERE lastname ='Shah' AND firstname >='M' AND
firstname < 'N';
```

In all the preceding queries, we can see that the orders of columns are maintained in the WHERE condition, similar to that of index declaration. Indexes can also work when we define only the lastname column in the WHERE clause, because it is the left-most column defined in the index. Now, there are some queries in which composite indexes will not work:

```
SELECT * FROM Employee WHERE firstname='Mona';
SELECT * FROM Employee WHERE lastname='Shah' OR firstname='Mona';
```

Remember, in the case of a multiple-column index, any left-most prefix of the index can be used by the optimizer for searching rows. For example, if the index was defined on three columns in sequence, `column1`, `column2`, and `column3`, then you can use indexed capabilities on (`column1`, `column2`, `column3`), (`column1`), (`column1`, `column2`), by defining it in the `WHERE` clause.

B-Tree index

The main purpose of the B-Tree index is to reduce the number of physical read operations. A B-Tree index is created by sorting the data on the search key and maintaining a hierarchical search data structure, which helps to search for the correct page of data entries. `InnoDB` and `MyISAM` storage engines, by default, use the B-Tree index. B-Tree manages to keep an equal distance from all the leaf nodes to the root node. This index speeds up data access because there is no need to scan the whole data to get the desired output. Instead, it starts with the root node. The root node holds a pointer of child nodes, and the storage engine follows these pointers to find the next path. It finds the right path by considering values in the node page. The node page defines the upper and lower bounds of values in the child nodes. At the end of the search process, the storage engine either successfully reaches a leaf page, or concludes that there is no value associated with the search. Remember, the leaf pages point to the indexed data, and not to other pages. Now, let's refer to one diagram to understand B-Tree indexes in more detail:

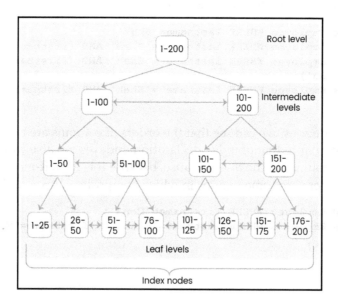

As discussed previously, when the query is executed against an index column, the MySQL 8 query engine starts from the root node, and through the intermediate nodes, it will reach a leaf node. Let's take an example where you want to find the value 89 in an indexed column. In this case, the query engine refers to the root node to get the intermediate page reference. So, it will point to **1-100**. After that, it determines the next intermediate level, and points to the values **51-100**. Then the query engine goes to the third page, which is the next intermediate level, **76-100**. From there, it will find the leaf node for the value 89. The leaf node contains either an entire row or a pointer to that row, depending on whether the index is clustered or non-clustered. Now, let's understand how a B-Tree index works on a select query by considering the following table:

```
CREATE TABLE Employee (
  lastname varchar(50) not null,
  firstname varchar(50) not null,
  dob date not null,
  gender char(1) not null,
  key(lastname, firstname, dob)
);
```

As per the table definition index will contains values in combination of three columns `firstname`, `lastname`, and `dob`. It will sort values as per the order given previously; this means that if some employees have similar names, then they will be sorted by their birth dates. Consider the following types of queries which will benefit from the B-Tree index:

- **Match the range of values**: Finds the employees whose last names are Patel and Gupta.
- **Match the full values**: Finds employee whose name is Mohan Patel and was born on 28/11/1981.
- **Match leftmost prefix**: Finds all employee with a last name. These use only the first column in the index.
- **Match with column prefix**: Finds the employees whose last names begin with M. It uses only the first column in the index.
- **Match one part exactly and with range of another column**: Finds the employee whose last name is Patel and whose first name starts with A.

The following are queries where B-Tree is not useful:

- **Don't use any condition after a range condition**: For example, you have put the `WHERE` condition `lastname='Patel'` and `firstname` like 'A%' and `dob='28/11/1981'`. Here, only the first two columns are considered for the index, because `LIKE` is a range condition.

- **Don't skip any of the columns defined in the index**: This means you are not allowed to use `lastname` and `dob` to find an employee where `firstname` is missing in the `WHERE` condition.
- **Lookup doesn't start with left-most side of indexed columns**: For example, the index will not work if you find the employee whose `firstname` is `Mohan` and whose `dob` is on a certain date. In this query, defined columns are not left-most in the index. In the same way, the index does not work in the case where you find the employee whose `lastname` ends with something.

Hash index

It is very difficult to find a single value from a large database by following complete tree traversals with multiple levels. To overcome this problem, MySQL has provided another index type, which is known as a **hash index**. This index creates a hash table rather than a tree, which is very flat in structure compared to a B-Tree index. Hashing mainly uses hash functions to generate the addresses of data. Two important terms related to hashing are:

- **Hash function**: The mapping function which will be useful to map search-keys with the address where actual records are stored.
- **Bucket**: A bucket is a unit of storage where a hash index stores the data. A bucket indicates a complete disk block, which will store one or more records.

Along with the hashing mechanism, a hash index has some special characteristics, described as follows:

- The whole key is used to search the row. While in the case of a B-Tree, only the left-most prefix of the key is used to find rows.
- The optimizer will not use a hash index to speed up `ORDER BY` operations. In other words, this index is never used to find the next entry.
- Hash indexes are used for equality comparison by using = or <=> operators. It will never use comparison operators which will return a range of values. For example, the < (less than) operator.
- The range optimizer cannot actually gauge how many rows are available between the two values. And, if we use a hash-indexed `MEMORY` table instead of `InnoDB` or `MyISAM`, then it may affect the queries as well.

Index extension

Index extension is the feature by which MySQL 8 extends a secondary index by appending the primary key. The InnoDB engine automatically extends a secondary index if it is required. To control the behavior of index extensions, MySQL 8 has defined a use_index_extensions flag in the optimizer_switch system variable. By default, this option is enabled, but the user is allowed to change it at runtime by using the following command:

```
SET optimizer_switch = 'use_index_extensions=off';
```

Let's look at one example to understand the index extension in detail. Let's create a table and insert the following values:

```
CREATE TABLE table1 (
  c1 INT NOT NULL DEFAULT 0,
  c2 INT NOT NULL DEFAULT 0,
  d1 DATE DEFAULT NULL,
  PRIMARY KEY (c1, c2),
  INDEX key1 (d1)
) ENGINE = InnoDB;

--Insert values into table
INSERT INTO table1 VALUES
(1, 1, '1990-01-01'), (1, 2, '1991-01-01'),
(1, 3, '1992-01-01'), (1, 4, '1993-01-01'),
(1, 5, '1994-01-01'), (2, 1, '1990-01-01'),
(2, 2, '1991-01-01'), (2, 3, '1992-01-01'),
(2, 4, '1993-01-01'), (2, 5, '1994-01-01'),
(3, 1, '1990-01-01'), (3, 2, '1991-01-01'),
(3, 3, '1992-01-01'), (3, 4, '1993-01-01'),
(3, 5, '1994-01-01'), (4, 1, '1990-01-01'),
(4, 2, '1991-01-01'), (4, 3, '1992-01-01'),
(4, 4, '1993-01-01'), (4, 5, '1994-01-01'),
(5, 1, '1990-01-01'), (5, 2, '1991-01-01'),
(5, 3, '1992-01-01'), (5, 4, '1993-01-01'),
(5, 5, '1994-01-01');
```

This table has a primary key on columns `c1`, `c2` and a secondary index `key_d1` on column `d1`. Now, to understand the extension effect, first make it off and then execute following select query with explain command:

```
--Index extension is set as off
SET optimizer_switch = 'use_index_extensions=off';

--Execute select query with explain
EXPLAIN SELECT COUNT(*) FROM table1 WHERE c1 = 3 AND d1 = '1992-01-01';

--Output of explain query
*************************** 1. row ***************************
           id: 1
  select_type: SIMPLE
        table: table1
         type: ref
possible_keys: PRIMARY,key1
          key: PRIMARY
      key_len: 4
          ref: const
         rows: 5
        Extra: Using where
```

In the same way, we will now turn the extension on and execute the explain plan query again to check the effect, using the following code:

```
--Index extension is set as on
SET optimizer_switch = 'use_index_extensions=on';

--Execute select query with explain
EXPLAIN SELECT COUNT(*) FROM table1 WHERE c1 = 3 AND d1 = '1992-01-01';

--Output of explain query
*************************** 1. row ***************************
           id: 1
  select_type: SIMPLE
        table: table1
         type: ref
possible_keys: PRIMARY,key1
          key: key1
      key_len: 8
          ref: const,const
         rows: 1
        Extra: Using index
```

Now, we will check the difference between these two approaches:

- The `key_len` value changes from 4 bytes to 8 bytes, which indicates that key lookups use both the columns d1 and c1, not only d1.
- The `ref` value changes from `(const)` to `(const, const)` which indicates key lookup uses two key parts instead of one.
- The `rows` count changes from 5 to 1, which indicates that `InnoDB` requires fewer rows than the first approach to produce the result.
- The `Extra` value changes from **Using where** to **Using index**. It indicates that the rows can be read by using only the index, without consulting any other columns in the data row.

Using an optimizer for indexes

MySQL 8 allows you to create indexes on generated columns. Generated columns are the columns whose values are computed from an expression included in a column definition. Consider the following example where we have defined one generated column, c2, and created an index on that column:

```
CREATE TABLE t1 (c1 INT, c2 INT AS (c1 + 1) STORED, INDEX (c2));
```

Based on the previous definition of a table, an optimizer will consider an index of a generated column in the execution plan. In addition to that, if we specify the same expression in the query using the `WHERE`, `GROUP BY`, or `ORDER BY` clauses, then the optimizer will use the index of the generated column. For example, if we execute the following query, then the optimizer will use the index defined on the generated column:

```
SELECT * FROM t1 WHERE c1 + 1 > 100;
```

Here, the optimizer will identify that the expression is the same as the definition of column c2. We can check it using the `EXPLAIN` command, as follows:

```
mysql> explain SELECT * FROM t1 WHERE c1 + 1 > 100;
*************************** 1. row ***************************
 id: 1
 select_type: SIMPLE
 table: t1
 partitions: NULL
 type: range
 possible_keys: c2
 key: c2
 key_len: 5
```

```
ref: NULL
rows: 1
filtered: 100.00
Extra: Using index condition
```

There are some limitations on generated column indexes:

- The query expression must be exactly matched with the generated column definition. For example, if we have defined the expression as `c1+1` in a column definition, then use the same in query, instead of applying `1+c1`.
- In the case of JSON string use in a generated column definition, use `JSON_UNQUOTE()` to remove extra quotes from the values. For example, don't use the following column definition:

    ```
    name TEXTAS(JSON_EXTRACT(emp, '$.name')) STORED
    ```

- Instead of the preceding code, we will use the following:

    ```
    name TEXTAS(JSON_UNQUOTE(JSON_EXTRACT(emp, '$.name'))) STORED
    ```

- The optimization applies to these operators: =, <, <=, >, >=, `BETWEEN`, and `IN()`.
- Don't use only references of other columns in generated column expressions. That is, don't use the following code:

    ```
    c2 INT AS (c1) STORED in column definition.
    ```

- Use a index hint if the optimizer tries to use the wrong index, which will disabled it and force the optimizer to use a different choice

Invisible and descending indexes

The **invisible index** is a special feature which will mark an index as unavailable for the optimizer. MySQL 8 will maintain invisible indexes and keep them up-to-date when data is modified. This will apply on indexes other than primary key. As we know, indexes are visible by default; we have to make them invisible explicitly at the time of creation, or by using the `alter` command. MySQL 8 provides the `VISIBLE` and `INVISIBLE` keywords to maintain index visibility. A descending index is the method of storing key values in descending order. A descending index is more efficient, as it can be scanned in the forward order. Let's see these indexes in detail, with examples.

Invisible index

As mention previously, an invisible index is not used by the optimizer. Then what is the use of this index? This question comes into our mind, right? We will explain to you some of the use cases for invisible indexes:

- When many indexes are defined, but you are not sure which index is not in use. In this case, you can make an index invisible and check the performance impact. If it has an impact, then you can make that index visible on an immediate basis.
- Special cases where only one query is using an index. In this case, an invisible index is a good solution.

In the following example, we will create an invisible index using CREATE TABLE, CREATE INDEX, or ALTER TABLE commands:

```
CREATE TABLE `employee` (
 `id` int(11) NOT NULL AUTO_INCREMENT,
 `department_id` int(11),
 `salary` int(11),
 PRIMARY KEY (`id`)
 ) ENGINE=InnoDB;

CREATE INDEX idx1 ON employee (department_id) INVISIBLE;
ALTER TABLE employee ADD INDEX idx2 (salary) INVISIBLE;
```

To change the visibility of the indexes, use the following commands:

```
ALTER TABLE employee ALTER INDEX idx1 VISIBLE;
ALTER TABLE employee ALTER INDEX idx1 INVISIBLE;
```

To get information about an index, execute INFORMATION_SCHEMA.STATISTICStable or SHOW INDEX commands in the following ways:

```
mysql>SELECT * FROM information_schema.statistics WHERE is_visible='NO';
*************************** 1. row ***************************
TABLE_CATALOG: def
TABLE_SCHEMA: db1
TABLE_NAME: employee
NON_UNIQUE: 1
INDEX_SCHEMA: db1
INDEX_NAME: idx1
SEQ_IN_INDEX: 1
COLUMN_NAME: department_id
COLLATION: A
CARDINALITY: 0
SUB_PART: NULL
```

```
PACKED: NULL
NULLABLE: YES
INDEX_TYPE: BTREE
COMMENT:
INDEX_COMMENT:
IS_VISIBLE: NO

mysql>SELECT INDEX_NAME, IS_VISIBLE FROM INFORMATION_SCHEMA.STATISTICS
   -> WHERE TABLE_SCHEMA = 'db1' AND TABLE_NAME = 'employee';
+-------------+------------+
| INDEX_NAME | IS_VISIBLE |
+-------------+------------+
| idx1 | NO |
| idx2 | NO |
| PRIMARY | YES |
+-------------+------------+

mysql> SHOW INDEXES FROM employee;
*************************** 1. row ***************************
Table:employee
Non_unique:1
Key_name:idx1
Seq_in_index:1
Column_name: department_id
Collation:A
Cardinality:0
Sub_part: NULL
Packed: NULL
Null:YES
Index_type: BTREE
Comment:
Index_comment:
Visible: NO
```

MySQL 8 provides a `use_invisible_indexes` flag in the `optimizer_switch` system variable to control invisible indexes used by the query optimizer. If this flag is on, then the optimizer uses invisible indexes in execution plan construction, while if the flag is off, the optimizer ignores invisible indexes. MySQL 8 provides a facility to use an implicit primary key if you have defined a `UNIQUE` index on a `NOT NULL` column. Once you define the index on this field, MySQL 8 does not allow you to make it invisible. In order to understand this scenario, let's take one example with the following table. Let's try to execute the following command to make the `idx1` index invisible:

```
CREATE TABLE table2 (
  field1 INT NOT NULL,
  field2 INT NOT NULL,
```

```
  UNIQUE idx1 (field1)
) ENGINE = InnoDB;
```

The server will now give an error, as shown in the following commands:

```
mysql> ALTER TABLE table2 ALTER INDEX idx1 INVISIBLE;
ERROR 3522 (HY000): A primary key index cannot be invisible
```

Now let's add the primary key into the table, using the following command:

```
ALTER TABLE table2 ADD PRIMARY KEY (field2);
```

Now, we will try to make the idex1 invisible. This time, the server allows it, as shown in the following commands:

```
mysql> ALTER TABLE table2 ALTER INDEX idx1 INVISIBLE;
Query OK, 0 rows affected (0.06 sec)
Records: 0 Duplicates: 0 Warnings: 0
```

Descending index

A descending index is an index which stores key values in descending order. This index is scanned in the forward order, which gives better performance compared to other indexes. Descending indexes allow a user to define multi-column indexes in a combination of ascending and descending orders. Practical knowledge is always easier to understand than theoretical knowledge, right? So, let's take a look at some examples to understand the descending index in detail. First, create a table with the following definition:

```
CREATE TABLE t1 (
 a INT, b INT,
 INDEX idx1 (a ASC, b ASC),
 INDEX idx2 (a ASC, b DESC),
 INDEX idx3 (a DESC, b ASC),
 INDEX idx4 (a DESC, b DESC)
);
```

As per the table definition, MySQL 8 will create four different indexes, and as a result, the optimizer performs a forward index scan for each ORDER BY clause. Consider the following different version of the ORDER BY clause:

```
ORDER BY a ASC, b ASC -- optimizer can use idx1
ORDER BY a DESC, b DESC -- optimizer can use idx4
ORDER BY a ASC, b DESC -- optimizer can use idx2
ORDER BY a DESC, b ASC -- optimizer can use idx3
```

Now, let's take a look at a second scenario for the same table definition, which will describe the performance impact of a descending index compared to the MySQL 5.7.14 version. Consider the following select queries to measure performance:

```
Query 1: SELECT * FROM t1 ORDER BY a DESC;
Query 2: SELECT * FROM t1 ORDER BY a ASC;
Query 3: SELECT * FROM t1 ORDER BY a DESC, b ASC;
Query 4: SELECT * FROM t1 ORDER BY a ASC, b DESC;
Query 5: SELECT * FROM t1 ORDER BY a DESC, b DESC;
Query 6: SELECT * FROM t1 ORDER BY a ASC, b ASC;
```

The following statistical graph is provided by MySQL 8 on 10 million rows, with respect to the previously mentioned queries:

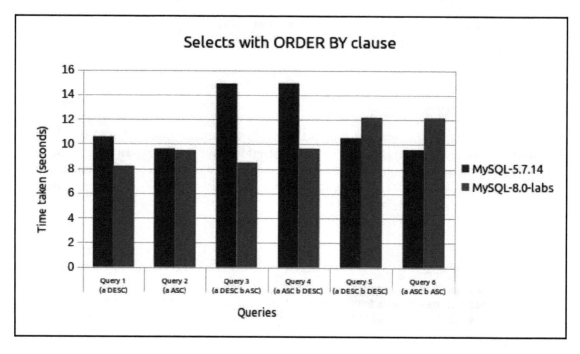

Reference: https://mysqlserverteam.com/mysql-8-0-labs-descending-indexes-in-mysql/

There are some important points that you should remember at the time of using descending indexes, which are as follows:

- All the data types supported by ascending indexes are also supported by descending indexes.
- Descending indexes are supported for `BTREE` but not for `HASH`, `FULLTEXT`, and `SPATIAL` indexes. If you try to use `ASC` and `DESC` keywords explicitly for `HASH`, `FULLTEXT`, and `SPATIAL` indexes, then MySQL 8 will generate an error.
- Descending indexes only support `InnoDB` storage engines, but the `InnoDB` SQL parser does not use descending indexes. Change buffering is not supported for secondary indexes if the primary key includes a descending index.
- `DISTINCT` can use any index, including a descending key, but for `MIN ()`/`MAX ()`, no descending key parts are used.
- Both non-generated and generated columns allow use of descending indexes.

Summary

Everything becomes very interesting when you are aware of how it works, right? We hope you have found the same thing about indexing in this chapter. We have covered very useful information which will help you to define indexes on the right columns to get better performance. In addition to that, we have also described various types of indexing with their storage structures.

In the next chapter, we will provide you with information about replication. We will explain the configuration and implementation of replication in detail.

8

Replication in MySQL 8

In the previous chapter, we dived deep into MySQL 8 indexing. Indexes are an important entity for any database management system. They help improve SQL query performance by limiting the number of records to be visited. Database administrators working on performance improvement must be aware of this important technique. This chapter explains in detail the types of indexes and their advantages. This chapter also explains how indexing works in MySQL 8. It's going to be a pretty informative chapter!

Moving further along the same line, in this chapter, we will discuss database replication. How much are we already aware about database replication? It doesn't actually matter. This chapter covers insightful details about database replication. If you have prior knowledge of database replication, this chapter will add to it. If you have only just heard about it for the first time, you will find every detail that is required to make it work in this chapter. So, are we ready to jump in? The following is a list of topics that we will be covering in this chapter:

- Overview of replication
- Configuring replication
- Implementing replication
- Group replication versus clustering
- Replication solutions

Overview of replication

We will walk through the basics of database replication in this section. We will understand what replication is, the advantages it provides, and the scenarios in which replication can be beneficial.

What is MySQL replication?

It is assumed that you are reading this for two reasons. You're familiar with MySQL replication and are willing to gain more knowledge, and perhaps you're unfamiliar with MySQL replication and want to learn.

MySQL replication is useful for serving lots of different purposes. Usually, people start thinking about MySQL replication when they start having more queries than a single database server can handle. Based on this, do you have any guesses on what MySQL replication is? Replication is the technique to have more than one databases set up to serve single or multiple client applications. A client can be an end user or person who sends a request for any query in terms of read data or write data from different devices, such as computers, mobiles, tablets, and so on. These databases are replicas of the same database. This means all databases participating in database replication are exactly the same as each other. Replication works by frequently copying data from one database to all other replica databases. These databases may be located on the same database server, different database servers, or different machines altogether.

As mentioned earlier, database replication serves various purposes. It depends on the reason why MySQL database replication is set up. MySQL replication is set up to scale up a database or an application that is backed up by the database. It is also useful for maintaining database backups and reporting purposes. We will discuss these in detail a little later in this chapter.

MySQL replication is mostly set up for scaling reads. In any web application, the number of read operations is pretty higher compared to that of write database operations. Most common web applications are always read heavy. Consider an example of a social networking website. If we navigate to a user profile page, we see a lot of information such as the user's personal information, demographic information, social connections, some ratings, and so on. If observed carefully, we will find that the number of SELECT queries executed on a database are much higher than INSERT, UPDATE, or DELETE queries. With MySQL database replication, we can direct read operations to be performed on particular databases so that we can achieve higher performance.

MySQL replication looks pretty easy and can be set up in a couple of hours, but it gets complicated pretty easily. It is very easy to set up on a new database. On the contrary, it is pretty complex to set it up on a production database. We should not confuse MySQL replication with a distributed database system. In a distributed database system, the databases hold different sets of data. Database operations are routed to a particular database based on some key information.

In a traditional MySQL replication, one of the databases acts as a master and the rest of the databases play the role of slaves. It is not always necessary that we have only one master database. We can have multiple master databases in a replication. This technique is called multi-master replication. The slaves copy data from master databases. The process of copying data is asynchronous in traditional MySQL replication. This means slave database servers are not permanently connected with master database servers. MySQL supports replication at different levels. We can replicate all master databases, selected databases, or selected tables from a master database in to slave databases.

MySQL 8 provides different database replication methods. MySQL 8 has a binary log file. The contents of the file are events describing database changes. The event can be of type `statement based` or `row based`. The changes include data definition changes and data manipulation changes or statements that can potentially modify the database such as `DELETE` statements. The binary log also contains information on how much time each SQL statement took to update the database. The traditional MySQL database replication method synchronizes databases from master to slaves based on the binary log file on the master database server. The slaves replicate or copy the contents of binary log file from the master database server based on the positions of log records in the file.

MySQL 8 also supports newer database replication methods along with the one based on the binary log file. Every transaction committed on the MySQL 8 database server is treated as unique. A unique **global transaction identifier** (**GTID**) is associated with every committed transaction on the master database server. As the name suggests, the global identifier is not unique only to the master database server on which it is created, but across all the databases participating in MySQL 8 replication. So, essentially, there is a 1 to 1 mapping between each committed transaction and global transaction identifier. The newer method of MySQL replication is based on the GTID. It greatly simplifies the replication process as it is not dependent on events from binary log files and their positions. GTID is represented as a pair of colon (`:`) separated coordinates, as shown in the following block:

```
GTID = source_id:transaction_id
```

The `source_id` is the identifier for database servers originated from the GTID. Usually, a database server's `server_uuid` is used as the `source_id`. The `transaction_id` is the sequence number in which the transaction was committed on the database server. For example, the following example shows the GTID for the first committed transaction:

```
1A22AF74-17AC-E111-393E-80C49AB653A2:1
```

The sequence number for transactions committed starts with 1. It can never be 0.

A GTID-based MySQL replication method is transactional and so this is why it is more reliable than a binary log file-based replication method. GTID guarantees the replication accuracy and consistency between master and slave databases as long as all the transactions committed on master database servers have also been applied on all of the slave database servers.

As mentioned earlier, MySQL database replication is usually asynchronous. However, MySQL 8 supports different types of synchronization for replication. The usual method of synchronization is asynchronous. It means one server acts as a master database server. It writes all events to a binary log file. Other database servers act as slaves. Slave database servers read and copy position-based event records within binary log files from the master database server. So, it is always from a master database server to a slave database server. MySQL 8 also supports semisynchronous synchronization methods. In semisynchronous methods of replication, any transaction committed on a master database server is blocked until the master database server receives acknowledgement from at least one of the slave database servers that it has received and logged the transaction event. Delayed replication is another replication method supported by MySQL 8. In delayed replication, slave database servers intentionally log the transaction event behind master database servers by some amount of time.

Advantages of MySQL replication

As we are now familiar with what MySQL database replication is, it's time to assess if the added complexity of maintaining multiple database servers is worth it or not.

The advantages of MySQL 8 database replication are as follows:

1. **Scale out solutions**: As described earlier, usually web applications are read-heavy applications. The read operations are much higher in number than the write operations. The applications provide features that require heavy, complex SQL queries to be executed on the database server. These are not the queries that take milliseconds to execute. Such complex queries may take a few seconds to minutes for execution. Execution of such queries put up heavy load on database server. In such cases, it is always better to have such read operations performed on a separate database server than master database servers. Write database operations will always be performed on master database servers. Do you know why? It's because it triggers database modifications. Events of these modifications must be written to binary log files for replication synchronization by slave servers. Also, the synchronization is from master to slaves. So, if we performed write database operations on slaves, those will never be available on master database servers. This approach improves performance of write operations with increased speed for read operations as the read operations are performed across the number of slave servers.

2. **Data Security**: Security, in general, is an important feature that every web application needs. The security can on at an application layer or on a database layer. Data security protects against loss of data. Data security is achieved by backing up a database on a regular basis. If replication is not set up, backing up production databases requires the application to be put on maintenance mode. This is required because simultaneous access to a database by an application and the back up process may corrupt the data. With replication in place, we can use one of the slaves for backup. As the slave database server is always in synchronization with the master database server, we can back up the slave database server. For that, we can make the slave database server stop replicating from a master database server while the back up process is running. This doesn't require the web application to stop using a master database server. In fact, it doesn't impact the master database server in any way. Another data security aspect is to provide role-based access to production or master database servers. We can have only a few roles who can access the master database server from the backend. The rest of the users or roles have access to the slave database server. This reduces the risk of accidental data loss because of human error.

3. **Analytics**: Analytics and reporting are always important features for a database backed application. These features require fetching of information from a database on a frequent basis so that analysis on the data can be performed. If database replication is set up, we can fetch the data required for analytics from the slave database server without affecting the master database server performance.

4. **Long distance data distribution**: It is a common requirement for application developers to replicate production data on local development environments. In a database replication enabled infrastructure, a slave database server can be used to prepare database copy on a development database server without constant access to the master database server.

Configuring replication

In this section, we will learn configuration for different types of MySQL 8 replication methods. It includes step by step instructions for setting up and configuring replication.

Binary log file based replication

One of the most common traditional methods of MySQL database replication is the binary log file position method. This section focuses on configuration of the binary log file position method of replication. Before we jump into the configuration section, it would be good to revise and understand the basics of binary log position based replication.

As described earlier, one of the MySQL database servers acts as master and the rest of the MySQL database servers become slaves. The master database server is the origin for the database changes. The master database server writes events based on updates or changes to the database in the binary log file. The format of the information record being written in the binary log file varies based on the database change being recorded. MySQL REPLICATION SLAVE database servers are configured so that they read the binary log events from the master database server. Slaves execute the events on local database binary log files. This way slaves synchronize the database with the master database. When slave database servers read the binary log file from the master database server, slaves get an entire copy of the binary log file. Once the binary log file is received, it is up to the slaves to decide which statements to execute on the slave binary log file. It is possible to specify that all statements from the master database server binary log file should be executed on the slave database servers binary log file. It is also possible to process events filtered by particular databases or tables.

 Only slave database servers can be configured to filter events from master database server log files. It is not possible to configure the master database server to log only specific events.

MySQL 8 provides a system variable that helps identify the database server uniquely. All the database servers participating in MySQL replication must be configured to have a unique ID. Each of the slave database servers must be configured with the master database server hostname, log file name, and position within the log file. Once set up, it is possible to modify these details from within a MySQL session using the CHANGE MASTER TO statement executed on the slave database server.

When the slave database server reads the information from the master database binary log file, it keeps track of a record of the binary log coordinates. The binary log coordinates consists of the filename and position within the file, which is read and processed from the master database server. The efficiency of slave database servers reading the binary log file from the master database server is very high because multiple slave database servers can be connected to the master database server and process different parts of the binary log file from the master database server. The master database server operations remain unaffected because the connecting and disconnecting of slave database servers from the master database server is controlled by slaves themselves. As mentioned earlier, each slave database server keeps track of the current position within the binary log file. So, it is possible for the slave database server to disconnect and reconnect with the master database server and resume the binary log file processing.

A number of methods for setting up database replication are available in MySQL. The exact method for replication depends on if data already exists in the database and how replication is being set up. Each of the following sections are a step for configuring MySQL replication.

Replication master configuration

Before we set up the replication master database server, it must be ensured that the database server has a unique ID established and binary logging is enabled. It may be required to restart the database server after these configurations are made. The master database server binary log is the basis for MySQL 8 database replication.

To enable binary logging, the `log_bin` system variable should be set to ON. Binary logging is enabled for a MySQL database server by default. If `mysqld` is used to initialize the data directory manually with a `--initialize` or `--initialize-insecure` option, the binary logging is disabled by default. It has to be enabled by specifying the `--log-bin` option. The `--log-bin` option specifies the base name to be used for the binary log files.

If the filename is not specified with the startup option, the binary log filenames will be set based on the database server hostname. It is recommended that the binary log filename is specified with the `--log-bin` option. If the log filename is specified with `--log_bin=old_host_name-bin`, the log filename will be retained even after the database server host is changed.

To set up the master database server, open the MySQL configuration file on the master database server:

```
sudo vim /etc/mysql/my.cnf
```

In the configuration file, make the following changes.

First of all, find the section that binds the server to localhost:

```
bind-address = 127.0.0.1
```

Replace the local IP address with the actual database server IP address. This step is important because the slaves can access the master database server using the public IP address of the master database server:

```
bind-address = 175.100.170.1
```

The following changes are required to configure a unique ID for the master database server. It also includes the configuration required for setting up the master binary log file:

```
[mysqld]
log-bin=/var/log/mysql/mysql-bin.log
server-id=1
```

Now, let's configure the database to be replicated on the slave database servers. If more than one database is required to be replicated on slave database servers, repeat the following line multiple times:

```
binlog_do_db = database_master_one
binlog_do_db = database_master_two
```

Once these changes are done, restart the database server using the following command:

```
sudo service mysql restart
```

Now, we have the master database server set up. The next step is to grant privileges to the slave user as follows:

```
mysql> mysql -u root -p
mysql> CREATE USER 'slaveone'@'%' IDENTIFIED BY 'password';
mysql> GRANT REPLICATION SLAVE ON *.* TO 'slaveone'@'%' IDENTIFIED BY
'password';
```

The preceding commands creates the slave user, grants privileges on the master database server, and flushes database cached privileges.

Now, we have to back up the database that we want to replicate. We will back up the database using the mysqldump command. This database will be used for creating the slave database. The master status output displays the name of the binary log filename, current position, and the name of the database to be replicated:

```
mysql> USE database_master_one;
mysql> FLUSH TABLES WITH READ LOCK;
mysql> SHOW MASTER STATUS;
+-------------------+----------+---------------------+-------------------+
|       File        | Position |     Binlog_Do_DB    | Binlog_Ignore_DB  |
+-------------------+----------+---------------------+-------------------+
| mysql-bin.000001  |   102    | database_master_one |                   |
+-------------------+----------+---------------------+-------------------+
1 row in set (0.00 sec)

mysqldump -u root -p database_master_one > database_master_one_dump.sql
```

Before we take the database backup using the mysqldump command, we have to lock the database to check the current position. This information will be used later to set up the slave database server.

After the database dump is taken, the database should be unlocked using the following commands:

```
mysql> UNLOCK TABLES;
mysql> QUIT;
```

We are done with all the configuration required to set up a replication master database server and make it accessible by the REPLICATION SLAVE database servers.

The following options have an impact on the master database server setup:

1. `innodb_flush_log_at_trx_commit=1` and `sync_binlog=1` options should be set to achieve higher durability and consistency. The options can be set in the `my.cnf` configuration file.
2. The `skip-networking` option must not be enabled. If it is enabled, the slave cannot communicate with the master and database replication fails.

REPLICATION SLAVE configuration

Similar to the master database server, each slave database server must have a unique ID. Once set up, this will require database server restart:

```
[mysqld]
server-id=2
```

For setting up multiple slave database servers, a unique non zero `server-id` must be configured that is different from that of master or any other slave database servers. Binary logging on a slave database server is not required for replication to be set up. If enabled, a binary log file on a slave database server can be used for database backups and crash recovery.

Now, create a new database that will become the replica of the master database and import the database from the database dump prepared from the master database as follows:

```
mysql> CREATE DATABASE database_slave_one;
mysql> QUIT;

# mysql -u root -p database_slave_one &lt;
/path/to/database_master_one_dump.sql
```

Now, we have to configure a few other options in the `my.cnf` file. Like the binary log, a relay log consists of numbered files with database change events as contents of the file. It also contains an index file that has the names of all the used relay log files. The following configurations set the relay log file, binary log file, and name of the slave database, which is a replica of the master database as follows:

```
relay-log = /var/log/mysql/mysql-relay-bin.log
log_bin = /var/log/mysql/mysql-bin.log
binlog_do_db = database_slave_one
```

A database server restart is required after this configuration change. The next step is to enable slave replication from within MySQL shell prompt. Execute the following command to set the `master` database information required by the `slave` database server:

```
mysql> CHANGE MASTER TO MASTER_HOST='12.34.56.789', MASTER_USER='slaveone',
MASTER_PASSWORD='password', MASTER_LOG_FILE='mysql-bin.000001',
MASTER_LOG_POS= 103;
```

As a final step, activate the slave server:

```
mysql> START SLAVE;
```

If the binary logging is enabled on the `slave` database server, a slave can participate in a complex replication strategy. In such a replication setup, database server A acts as a master for database server B. B acts as a slave to the A `master` database server. Now, B in turn can act as a master database server for the C `slave` database server. Something like this can be seen as follows:

```
A -> B -> C
```

Adding slaves to replication

It is possible to add a new slave database server to an existing replication configuration. This doesn't require the master database server to be stopped. The approach should be to make a copy of an existing `slave` database server. Once copied, we have to modify the value for a `server-id` configuration option.

The following instructions set up a new slave database to an existing replication configuration. First, an existing slave database server should be shut down as follows:

```
mysql> mysqladmin shutdown
```

Now, a data directory from the existing slave should be copied to the new slave database server. Along with the data directory, binary logs and relay log files must be copied as well. It is recommended to use the same value for `--relay-log` for the new slave database server as that of the existing slave database server.

If the master info and relay log info repositories use files then those files must be copied from an existing slave database server to a new slave database server. These files hold a master's current binary log coordinates and a slave's relay logs.

Now, start the existing slave server that was stopped earlier.

Now, we should be able to start the new slave database server. We must have the unique `server-id` configured before starting the new slave server, if it is not set up already.

Global transaction identifiers based replication

This section focuses on global transaction identifiers based replication. It explains how GTIDs are defined, created, and represented in MySQL server. It describes the procedure for setting up and starting GTID-based replication.

With GTID-based replication, each transaction is assigned a unique transaction ID as it is committed to the originating database server, known as **GTID**. The unique identifier is global, which means it is unique across all the database servers participating in replication. With GTID, it is easier to track and process each transaction as it is committed on to a `master` database server. With this replication method, it is not necessary to rely on the log files for synchronization between `master` and `slave` databases. It is also easier to identify if the `master` and `slave` databases are consistent as this method of replication is transaction based. Consistency between master and slave databases is guaranteed as long as all the transactions committed on the `master` database are applied on the slave databases as well. Either statement-based or row-based replication can be used with GTID. As mentioned earlier, GTID is represented with a pair of coordinates separated by colons (`:`), as shown in the following example:

```
GTID = source_id:transaction_id
```

The advantages of using the GTID based replication method are:

1. With this method of replication, it is possible to switch the master database server in the event of server failover. The global transaction identifier is unique across all participating database servers. The slaves maintain track of the last executed transaction using GTID. This means if the master database server is switched over to a new database server, it is a little easier for slaves to continue with the new master database server and resume the replication processing.

2. The state of the slave database server is maintained in a crash-safe way. With the newer replication technique, `slave` database server keeps track of the current position in a system table named `mysql.gtid_slave_pos`. Using a transactional storage engine such as `InnoDB`, updates to the state are recorded within the same transaction as that of the database operation. So, if the slave server goes down, on booting up again, the slave server starts the crash recovery and makes sure that the recorded replication position matches the replicated changes. This is not possible with traditional binary log file based replication because the relay log file that is updated independently of the actual database changes can easily go out of synchronization if the slave server crashes.

Before diving into the GTID based replication configuration, let's understand a few more terms.

A `gtid_set` is a set of global transaction identifiers. It is represented in the following example:

```
gtid_set:
    uuid_set [, uuid_set] ...
    | ''

uuid_set:
    uuid:interval[:interval]...

uuid:
    hhhhhhhh-hhhh-hhhh-hhhh-hhhhhhhhhhhh

h:
    [0-9|A-F]

interval:
    n[-n]
    (n >= 1)
```

There are several ways in which GTID sets are used. System variables `gtid_executed` and `gtid_purged` are represented with GTID sets. The MySQL functions `GTID_SUBSET()` and `GTID_SUBTRACT()` require GTID sets as input parameters.

Both master and slave database servers preserve GTIDs. Once a transaction is committed with one GTID on one server, any subsequent transaction with similar GTID is ignored by that server. This means a transaction committed on a `master` database server can only be committed or applied on a `slave` database server only once. This helps to maintain the consistency between `master` and `slave` databases.

The following is a summary of the lifecycle of a GTID:

1. A transaction is executed and committed on the master database server. This transaction is assigned a GTID using the master's UUID. The GTID is written to the binary log file of a master database server.
2. Once the binary log file is received by the slave and recorded in the the slave's relay log, the slave sets the value of the `gtid_next` system variable to the GTID read. This indicates to `slave` that the next transaction to be executed is the one with this GTID.
3. The `slave` database server maintains its set of GTID for already processed transactions in a binary log file. Before applying the transaction with GTID indicated by `gtid_next`, it checks if the GTID is recorded or logged in its binary log file. If the GTID is not found in the binary log file, the slave processes the transaction associated with the GTID and writes the GTID in the binary log file. This way the slave guarantees that the same transaction is not executed more than once.

Let's now move to the master configuration for GTID-based MySQL replication. As a first step, open the `my.cnf` file and make the following changes:

```
[mysqld]
server-id = 1
log-bin = mysql-bin
binlog_format = ROW
gtid_mode = on
enforce_gtid_consistency
log_slave_updates
```

These configuration changes require server restart. The preceding configurations are self-explanatory. The `gtid_mode` option enables the GTID based database replication.

1. Now, create a user for accessing the master database from the slave database server. Also, take a database backup using the `mysqldump` command. The database backup will be used for setting up the slave database server.

```
> CREATE USER 'slaveuser'@'%' IDENTIFIED BY 'password';
> GRANT REPLICATION SLAVE ON *.* TO 'slaveuser'@'%' IDENTIFIED
```

```
BY 'password';
> mysqldump -u root -p databaseName > databaseName.sql
```

This is all for the master database configuration. Let's move onto the slave side of configurations.

2. Using the shell prompt on the `slave` database server, import the database from the `master` database server backup as follows:

```
> mysql -u root -p databaseName &lt; /path/to/databaseName.sql
```

3. Now, add the following configurations in the `my.cnf` file on the slave:

```
[mysqld]
server_id = 2
log_bin = mysql-bin
binlog_format = ROW
skip_slave_start
gtid_mode = on
enforce_gtid_consistency
log_slave_updates
```

4. Once these configurations are made, restart the database server using the following command:

```
sudo service mysql restart
```

5. The next step is to set up master database server information on the `slave` database server using the `CHANGE MASTER TO` command:

```
> CHANGE MASTER TO MASTER_HOST='170.110.117.12', MASTER_PORT=3306,
MASTER_USER='slaveuser', MASTER_PASSWORD='password',
MASTER_AUTO_POSITION=1;
```

6. Now, start the `slave` server:

```
START SLAVE;
```

In this replication method, the master database backup already has GTID information. So, we just need to provide the position from which the slave server should start synchronizing.

7. This is done by setting up the `GTID_PURGED` system variable:

```
-- -- GTID state at the beginning of the backup --
mysql> SET @@GLOBAL.GTID_PURGED='b9b4712a-df64-11e3-
b391-60672090eb04:1-7';
```

MySQL multi-source replication

This section focuses on replicating from multiple immediate masters in parallel. The method is known as **multi-source replication**. With multi-source replication, a `REPLICATION SLAVE` receives transactions from multiple sources at the same time. A channel is created by a `REPLICATION SLAVE` for each `master` from which it should receive transactions.

The multi-source replication configuration requires at least two masters and a slave to be configured. The masters can be configured using binary log position based replication or GTID-based replication. Replication repositories are stored in `FILE` or `TABLE` based repositories. A `TABLE` based repository is crash safe. MySQL multi-source replication requires a `TABLE` based repository. There are two ways to set up a `TABLE` repository.

One is to start `mysqld` with options as follows:

```
mysqld —master-info-repostiory=TABLE && -relay-log-info-repository=TABLE
```

Another preferred way of doing this is to modify the `my.cnf` file as follows:

```
[mysqld]
master-info-repository = TABLE
relay-log-info-repository = TABLE
```

It is possible to modify an existing `REPLICATION SLAVE` that is using a `FILE` repository to use a `TABLE` repository. The following commands convert the existing repositories dynamically:

```
STOP SLAVE;
SET GLOBAL master_info_repository = 'TABLE';
SET GLOBAL relay_log_info_repository = 'TABLE';
```

The following commands can be used to add a new GTID-based replication master to an existing multi-source REPLICATION SLAVE. It adds a master to the existing slave channel:

```
CHANGE MASTER TO MASTER_HOST='newmaster', MASTER_USER='masteruser',
MASTER_PORT=3451, MASTER_PASSWORD='password', MASTER_AUTO_POSITION = 1 FOR
CHANNEL 'master-1';
```

The following commands can be used to add a new binary log file position based replication master to an existing multi-source REPLICATION SLAVE. It adds a master to the existing slave channel:

```
CHANGE MASTER TO MASTER_HOST='newmaster', MASTER_USER='masteruser',
MASTER_PORT=3451, MASTER_PASSWORD='password' MASTER_LOG_FILE='master1-
bin.000006', MASTER_LOG_POS=628 FOR CHANNEL 'master-1';
```

The following commands START/STOP/RESET all the configured replication channels:

```
START SLAVE thread_types; -- To start all channels
STOP SLAVE thread_types; -- To stop all channels
RESET SLAVE thread_types; -- To reset all channels
```

The following commands START/STOP/RESET a named channel using a FOR CHANNEL clause:

```
START SLAVE thread_types FOR CHANNEL channel;
STOP SLAVE thread_types FOR CHANNEL channel;
RESET SLAVE thread_types FOR CHANNEL channel;
```

Replication administration tasks

This section describes a few commonly required MySQL replication administrative tasks. Usually, once set up, MySQL replication doesn't require regular monitoring.

One of the most common tasks is to ensure that replication is taking place without errors between master and slave database servers. A SHOW SLAVE STATUS MySQL statement is used for this as follows:

```
mysql> SHOW SLAVE STATUS\G
*************************** 1. row ***************************
              Slave_IO_State: Waiting for master to send event
                 Master_Host: master1
                 Master_User: root
                 Master_Port: 3306
                 Connect_Retry: 60
              Master_Log_File: mysql-bin.000004
```

```
        Read_Master_Log_Pos: 931
             Relay_Log_File: slave1-relay-bin.000056
              Relay_Log_Pos: 950
     Relay_Master_Log_File: mysql-bin.000004
          Slave_IO_Running: Yes
         Slave_SQL_Running: Yes
           Replicate_Do_DB:
       Replicate_Ignore_DB:
        Replicate_Do_Table:
    Replicate_Ignore_Table:
   Replicate_Wild_Do_Table:
Replicate_Wild_Ignore_Table:
                 Last_Errno: 0
                 Last_Error:
              Skip_Counter: 0
        Exec_Master_Log_Pos: 931
            Relay_Log_Space: 1365
            Until_Condition: None
             Until_Log_File:
              Until_Log_Pos: 0
          Master_SSL_Allowed: No
          Master_SSL_CA_File:
          Master_SSL_CA_Path:
            Master_SSL_Cert:
          Master_SSL_Cipher:
             Master_SSL_Key:
       Seconds_Behind_Master: 0
Master_SSL_Verify_Server_Cert: No
              Last_IO_Errno: 0
              Last_IO_Error:
             Last_SQL_Errno: 0
             Last_SQL_Error:
   Replicate_Ignore_Server_Ids: 0
```

In the preceding output, a few of the key fields are explained as follows:

- `Slave_IO_State`: Current state of the slave
- `Slave_IO_Running`: Indicates if the I/O thread for reading a master's log file is running
- `Slave_SQL_Running`: Indicates if the SQL thread for executing events is running
- `Last_IO_Error`, `Last_SQL_Error`: Last errors reported by I/O or SQL threads processing the relay thread
- `Seconds_Behind_Master`: Indicates the number of seconds the slave SQL thread is running behind the master processing the master binary log

We can check the status of connected slaves using a SHOW_PROCESSLIST statement:

```
mysql> SHOW PROCESSLIST \G;
*************************** 4. row ***************************
     Id: 10
   User: root
   Host: slave1:58371
     db: NULL
Command: Binlog Dump
   Time: 777
  State: Has sent all binlog to slave; waiting for binlog to be updated
   Info: NULL
```

The SHOW_SLAVE_HOSTS statement, when executed on master, provides information about slaves as follows:

```
mysql> SHOW SLAVE HOSTS;
+-----------+---------+------+-------------------+-----------+
| Server_id |  Host   | Port | Rpl_recovery_rank | Master_id |
+-----------+---------+------+-------------------+-----------+
|      10   | slave1  | 3306 |         0         |     1     |
+-----------+---------+------+-------------------+-----------+
1 row in set (0.00 sec)
```

Another important replication administrative task is to be able to start or stop the replication on a slave database server. The following commands are used to do that:

```
mysql> STOP SLAVE;
mysql> START SLAVE;
```

It is also possible to stop and start individual threads by specifying the type of the thread as follows:

```
mysql> STOP SLAVE IO_THREAD;
mysql> STOP SLAVE SQL_THREAD;

mysql> START SLAVE IO_THREAD;
mysql> START SLAVE SQL_THREAD;
```

Implementing replication

The basis for replication is that the master database server keeps track of all the changes taking place on the master database. The changes are tracked in the binary log files in the form of events since the server was started. SELECT operations are not recorded as they modify neither the database nor the contents. Each of the REPLICATION SLAVE pull a copy of the binary log file from master instead of a master database pushing the log file to the slave. The slave in turn executes the events as it is read from the master's binary log file. This maintains the consistency between master and slave servers. In MySQL replication, each slave functions independently from master and other slave servers. So, it is up to the slave to request the master's binary log file at a convenient time without impacting the master or slave functioning.

The focus for this section of the chapter is on MySQL replication details. We have already understood the basics, which will help us understand the in depth details.

Replication formats

As we already know by now, MySQL replication works based on replicating events from the master server generated binary logs. Later, these events are read and processed by the slave. What we do not yet know is the format in which the events are recorded in binary log files. Replication formats is the emphasis of this section.

When the events are recorded in the master's binary log files, the replication format used depends on the binary log format used. Basically, two binary logging formats exist: statement based and row based.

With statement-based binary logging, SQL statements are written in the master's binary log file. Replication on the slave works by executing the SQL statements on the slave database. This approach is called **statement-based** replication. It corresponds with the MySQL statement-based binary logging format. This was the only traditional format that existed until MySQL versions 5.1.4 and earlier.

With row-based binary logging, the events written in the master binary log indicate how individual table rows changed. Replication in this case works by the slave copying the events representing changes to the table rows. This is called row-based replication. Row-based logging is the default MySQL replication method.

MySQL supports configuration to mix statement-based and row-based logging. The decision to use the logging format depends on the change being logged. This is known as mixed-format logging. Statement-based logging is the default format when mixed-format logging is used. Based on the type of statements and storage engine being used, the log automatically switches to row-based format. Replication based on the mixed logging format is known as **mixed-format** replication.

The `binlog_format` system variable controls the logging format used in a running MySQL server. `SYSTEM_VARIABLES_ADMIN` or `SUPER` privileges are required to set the `binlog_format` system variable at a session or global scope.

Statement-based versus row-based replication

In the earlier section, we learned three different logging formats. Each one of these has its own advantages and disadvantages. In usual cases, mixed format should provide the best combination of integrity and performance. However, to achieve the best performance from either statement-based or row-based replication, the advantages and disadvantages described in this section are helpful.

Statement-based replication is a traditional and proven technique in comparison with row-based replication. The number of records or events recorded in the log files is smaller. If a statement impacts many rows, only one statement will be written to the binary log file. In case of row-based replication, a record will be entered for every table row modified though as part of the single statement. In essence, this means statement-based replication requires much less storage space for log files. It also means backing up and restoring or replicating the events is much quicker.

Along with the advantages described previously, statement-based replication has disadvantages as well. As the replication works based on the SQL statements, it is possible that not all the statements that modify data can be replicated with statement-based replication. A few examples are described as follows:

- SQL statements depend on a user-defined function that is non-deterministic when the value returned by such user-defined functions depend on factors other than the parameters supplied to it.
- `UPDATE` and `DELETE` statements with a `LIMIT` clause without an `ORDER BY` clause is non-deterministic as it is possible that the order may have changed while replicating.
- `FOR UPDATE` or `FOR SHARE` locking read statements that use `NOWAIT` or `SKIP LOCKED` options.

- User-defined functions must be applied on the slave databases.
- SQL statements using functions such as `LOAD_FILE()`, `UUID()`, `USER()`, `UUID_SHORT()`, `FOUND_ROWS()`, `SYSDATE()`, `GET_LOCK()`, and so on cannot be replicated properly using statement-based replication.
- `INSERT` or `SELECT` statements require higher number of row level locks.
- `UPDATE` with table scan requires locking a higher number of rows.
- Complex SQL statements must be evaluated and executed on the slave database server before rows are inserted or updated.

Let's see advantages provided by row-based replication. Row-based replication is the safest form of replication because instead of depending on SQL statements, it depends on the values stored in the table rows. So, every change can be replicated. It requires fewer row locks in case `INSERT...SELECT` statements. `UPDATE` and `DELETE` statements with `WHERE` clauses that do not use keys require fewer row level locks.

The major disadvantage with row-based replication is that it generates more data that must be logged. With statement-based replication, one DML SQL statement is sufficient for logging though it modifies many rows. In case of row-based replication, it requires logging for every row that changed. The binary log file grows very quickly with row-based replication. It takes longer time to replicate deterministic user defined functions that generate large `BLOB` values.

Replication implementation details

There are three threads that participate in implementing replication in MySQL. Out of these three threads, one is on the master server and the two others are on the `slave` database server. Let's dive into the details of these threads:

- **Binlog dump thread**: When the slave database server requests the binary log file, the master server is responsible for sending the contents to the slave database server. To accomplish this, the master database server creates a thread when the slave database server connects to the master database server. The `binlog` dump thread sends the binary log contents to the slave database server. In the output of the `SHOW PROCESSLIST` command on the master database server, this thread can be identified as the `Binlog Dump` thread. The `binlog` dump thread locks the binary log file on the master for reading each event that is to be sent to the slave database server. The lock is released as soon as the event is read, even before it is sent to the slave database server.

- **Slave I/O thread:** The primary responsibility of the slave I/O thread is to request binary log updates from the master database server. The slave database server creates the I/O thread when a `START SLAVE` command is executed. The thread connects to the master database server and requests to send updates from the binary logs. Once the contents are sent by the master's `binlog` dump thread, the slave I/O thread reads the contents and copies those to the local files including the slave's relay log. The status of this thread can be obtained in the output of `SHOW SLAVE STATUS` or `SHOW STATUS` commands.

- **Slave SQL thread:** The slave I/O thread writes the events in the slave's relay logs. It is the responsibility of the slave SQL thread to execute those events on the slave database server. The slave SQL thread reads the events in the relay logs written by a slave I/O thread and executes them.

Based on the preceding description, every master-slave connection pair creates three threads. If a master has more than one `slave` databases servers, it creates one dedicated binary log dump thread for each slave connected currently. On the other end, each slave creates its own I/O and SQL threads. Why does the slave database server create two separate threads, one for writing the events and another one for executing the events? The reason is that with this approach, the task of reading the statements is not slowed down by the executing of the statements. Considering the slave server is not running, its I/O thread quickly fetches all the binary logs from a master database when the `slave` server starts regardless of the SQL thread lags behind. Also, if the `slave` database server stops before the SQL thread can execute all of these statements, the statements are recorded in the slave relay logs. So, when the slave starts again, the SQL thread can execute those statements. So, relay logs work as a safe copy of the statements read from the master database server.

The `SHOW PROCESSLIST` statement provides information about what is happening on the `master` or the `slave` database servers. The output of the statement when executed on the `master` database server looks as follows:

```
mysql> SHOW PROCESSLIST\G
*************************** 1. row ***************************
     Id: 2
   User: root
   Host: localhost:32931
     db: NULL
Command: Binlog Dump
   Time: 94
  State: Has sent all binlog to slave; waiting for binlog to be updated
   Info: NULL
```

The preceding output shows that thread 2 is the master's `binlog` dump thread. The state indicates that all the recent updates have been sent to the slave.

When a `SHOW PROCESSLIST` statement is executed on the slave database server, the output looks as follows:

```
mysql> SHOW PROCESSLIST\G
*************************** 1. row ***************************
     Id: 10
   User: system user
   Host:
     db: NULL
Command: Connect
   Time: 11
  State: Waiting for master to send event
   Info: NULL
*************************** 2. row ***************************
     Id: 11
   User: system user
   Host:
     db: NULL
Command: Connect
   Time: 11
  State: Has read all relay log; waiting for the slave I/O thread to update
it
   Info: NULL
```

In the output, thread 10 is the slave's I/O thread and thread 11 is the slave's SQL thread. The I/O thread is waiting for the master's `binlog` dump thread to send binary log contents. The SQL thread has read all the statements logged in the `slave` relay logs. From the `Time` column, it can be determined how slow the `slave` is running behind the `master`.

Replication channels

A replication channel is a path of transaction flow from a master to a slave. This section explains how channels can be used in replication. The MySQL server automatically creates a default channel with the name as " " (empty string) on startup. The default channel is always present and can't be created or destroyed by the user. Replication statements work on the default channel if no other channel is created. This section describes statements that are applied to replication channels when there exists at least one named channel.

In multi-source replication, the `slave` database server opens multiple channels, one for each master. Each channel has its own relay log and SQL threads. The replication channel has a hostname and port association. Multiple channels can be assigned to the same hostname and port combination. A maximum of 256 channels can be added to one slave in a multi-source replication topology in MySQL 8. The channel must have a nonempty unique name.

The `FOR CHANNEL` clause is used with various MySQL statements for the replication operations to be performed on individual channels. The clause can be applied to the following statements:

- `CHANGE MASTER TO`
- `START SLAVE`
- `STOP SLAVE`
- `RESET SLAVE`
- `SHOW RELAYLOG EVENTS`
- `FLUSH RELAY LOGS`
- `SHOW SLAVE STATUS`

Apart from these, the following functions have an additional channel parameter:

- `MASTER_POS_WAIT()`
- `WAIT_UNTIL_SQL_THREAD_AFTER_GTIDS()`

For multi-source replication to work correctly, the following startup options must be configured:

- `--relay-log-info-repository`: As described earlier, this must be set to `TABLE` for multi-source replication. In MySQL 8, the `FILE` option is deprecated and `TABLE` is the default option.
- `--master-info-repository`: This must be set to `TABLE`.
- `--log-slave-updates`: Transactions received from the master are written to the binary logs.
- `--relay-log-purge`: Each channel purges its own relay logs automatically.
- `--slave-transaction-retries`: SQL threads of all channels retry transactions.

- `--skip-slave-start`: No replication threads start on any channels.
- `--slave-skip-errors`: Execution continues and errors are skipped for all channels.
- `--max-relay-log-size=size`: The relay log file is rotated after reaching the maximum size.
- `--relay-log-space-limit=size`: Upper limit for total size of all relay logs for each individual channel.
- `--slave-parallel-workers=value`: Number of slave parallel workers per channel.
- `--slave-checkpoint-group`: Waiting time by I/O thread.
- `--relay-log-index=filename`: Each channel's relay log index filename.
- `--relay-log=filename`: Each channel's relay log filename.
- `--slave-net-timeout=N`: Each channel waits for N seconds to check for broken connection.
- `--slave-skip-counter=N`: Each channel skips N events from the master.

Replication relay and status logs

The `REPLICATION SLAVE` server creates logs that hold the binary log events sent from the master database server to the slave database server. The information is recorded about the current status and location in the relay log. Three types of logs are used in this process:

1. **Relay log**: The relay log has events sent from the master's binary log. The events are written by a slave's I/O thread. Events from the slave's relay log are executed on the slave by the slave's SQL thread.
2. **Master info log**: The master info log has information about status and current configuration for the slave's connection to the master database server. The information held by the master info log includes hostname, login credentials, and coordinates indicating a slave's position on reading the master's binary log. These logs are written to the `mysql.slave_master_info` table.
3. **Relay log info log**: The relay log info log stores information regarding the execution point within the slave's relay log. The relay log info log is written in a `mysql.slave_relay_log_info` table.

No attempt should be made to insert or update rows in the `slave_master_info` or `slave_relay_log_info` tables manually. This may cause unexpected behavior. It is not supported in MySQL replication.

The slave relay log consists of an index file along with a set of numbered log files. The index file contains the names of all relay log files. MySQL data directory is the default location for the relay log files. The relay log file indicates an individually numbered file containing events. Whereas the relay log denotes the set of numbered relay log files and an index file collectively. The format for relay log files is the same as that of the binary log files. The index filename for relay log is `host_name-relay-bin.index` by default for the default channel and `host_name-relay-bin-channel.index` for non-default replication channels. The default locations for the relay log file and relay log index file can be overridden with the `--relay-log` and `--relay-log-index` server startup options. If the slave's hostname is changed after replication has been set up and the slave uses default host-based relay log filenames, it can throw errors such as **Failed to open the relay log** and **Could not find target log** during relay log initialization. This may fail the replication. Such errors may be avoided by using `--relay-log` and `--relay-log-index` options to specify relay log filenames explicitly. Using these options on slave setup will make the names independent of the server's hostname.

Evaluating replication filtering rules

This section focuses on the filtering rules and how servers evaluate these rules. Basically, if the master doesn't log the statement, the slave doesn't replicate the statement. If the master logs the statement in its binary log file, the slave receives the statement. However, it is up to the slave database server if it processes the statement or ignores it. Options are available for the master server to control which databases and tables should be replicated on the slaves. The recommended way is to use filters on the slave to control the events that are to be executed on the slave database server. The decision about whether to execute or ignore the statements received from the master are made based on the `--replicate-*` options used when the slave was started. Once the slave server is started, the `CHANGE REPLICATION FILTER` statement can be used to set the options dynamically.

 All replication filtering options follow the same rules for case sensitivity as names of databases and tables, including the `lower_case_table_names` system variable.

Group replication

This section of the chapter explains what group replication is, setting up group replication, configure and monitor group replication. Basically, MySQL group replication is a plugin that enables us to create elastic, highly-available, fault-tolerant replication topologies.

The purpose of the group replication is to create a fault tolerant system. To create a fault tolerant system, the components should be made redundant. The component should be removed without impacting the way system operates. There are challenges in setting up such a system. The complexity of such a system is of a different level. Replicated databases require maintenance and administration of several servers instead of just one. The servers cooperate together to create a group, which raises the problems related to network partitioning and split-brain scenarios. So, the ultimate challenge is to have agreement from multiple servers on the state of the system and data after every change applied on the system. This means that the servers need to operate as a distributed state machine.

MySQL group replication can provide such a distributed state machine replication with strong coordination between servers. The servers that belong to the same group coordinate themselves automatically. In a group, only one server accepts updates at a time. The election of primary is done automatically. This mode is known as single-primary mode.

MySQL provides a group membership service, which is responsible for keeping the view of the group consistent and available for all servers. The view is kept updated when the servers join or leave the group. In case, any of the servers leaves the group unexpectedly, the failure detection mechanism notifies the group about view change. This behavior is automatic.

The majority of the group members have to agree on the order of the transaction to commit in the global sequence of transactions. It is up to the individual server to decide whether the transaction should be committed or aborted, but all servers make the same decision. The system does not proceed until the members are unable to reach to agreement as a result of split due to network partition. This means the system has built-in, automatic, split-brain protection mechanism. All this is done by **Group Communication System** (**GCS**) protocols. It provides a failure detection mechanism, group membership service, safe and completely ordered message delivery. The implementation of the Paxos algorithm is at the core of this technology, which acts as the group communication engine.

Primary-secondary replication versus group replication

This section focuses on some background details of how replication works. This will be useful in understanding the requirements for group replication and how it is different from the classic asynchronous MySQL replication.

The following figure showcases how traditional asynchronous primary-secondary replication works. The primary is the master and the secondary is one or more slaves connected to the master, as shown in the following figure:

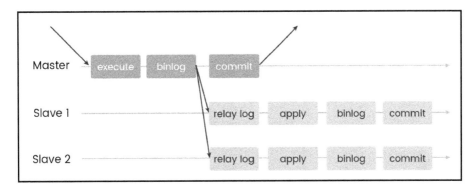

Figure 1. MySQL Asynchronous Replication

MySQL also supports semi synchronous replication in which the **master** waits for at least one of the **slaves** to acknowledge the transaction receipt:

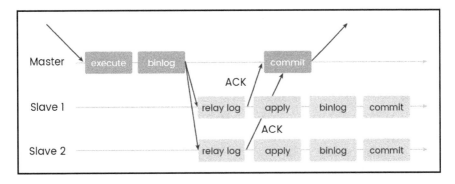

Figure 2. MySQL Semisynchronous Replication

The blue arrows in the figures indicate the messages passed between servers and the client application.

With group replication, a communication layer is provided that guarantees atomic messages and total order message delivery. All read-write transactions are committed only after they are approved by the group. The read only transactions are committed immediately as it does not need coordination. So, in group replication, the decision to commit a transaction or not is not unilateral by the originating server. When the transaction is ready for commit, the originating server broadcasts the write values and corresponding write set. All servers receive the same set of transactions in the same order. So, all servers apply the same transactions in the same order. This way all servers remain consistent within the group:

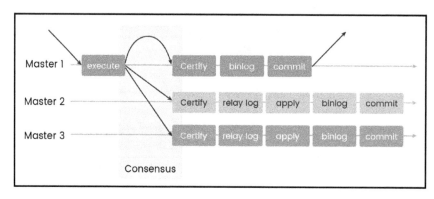

Figure 3. MySQL Group Replication Protocol

Group replication configuration

This section focuses on configuring group replication.

First of all, open the `my.cnf` configuration file and add the following entries in the `mysqld` section as follows:

```
[mysqld]
gtid_mode = ON
enforce_gtid_consistency = ON
master_info_repository = TABLE
relay_log_info_repository = TABLE
binlog_checksum = NONE
log_slave_updates = ON
log_bin = binlog
```

```
binlog_format = ROW
transaction_write_set_extraction = XXHASH64
loose-group_replication_bootstrap_group = OFF
loose-group_replication_start_on_boot = OFF
loose-group_replication_ssl_mode = REQUIRED
loose-group_replication_recovery_use_ssl = 1
```

These are general configurations related to global transaction IDs and binary logging required for group replication.

The next step is to set up group replication configurations. These configurations include group UUID, group members white listing, and indicating seed members:

```
# Shared replication group configuration
loose-group_replication_group_name = "929ce641-538d-415d-8164-ca00181be227"
loose-group_replication_ip_whitelist =
"177.110.117.1,177.110.117.2,177.110.117.3"
loose-group_replication_group_seeds =
"177.110.117.1:33061,177.110.117.2:33061,177.110.117.3:33061"
   . . . Choosing
```

The following configuration is required for deciding whether a single-master group or multi-master group is to be set up. For enabling the multi-master group, uncomment

`loose-group_replication_single_primary_mode` and

`loose-group_replication_enforce_update_everywhere_checks` directives. It will set up a multi-master or multi-primary group:

```
. . .
# Single or Multi-primary mode? Uncomment these two lines
# for multi-primary mode, where any host can accept writes
loose-group_replication_single_primary_mode = OFF
loose-group_replication_enforce_update_everywhere_checks = ON
```

It must be ensured that these configurations are the same on all the servers. Any changes to these configurations require MySQL groups to be restarted.

The following configurations are different on each of the servers in the group:

```
. . .
# Host specific replication configuration
server_id = 1
bind-address = "177.110.117.1"
report_host = "177.110.117.1"
loose-group_replication_local_address = "177.110.117.1:33061"
```

The `server-id` must be unique across all servers in the group. The port 33061 is the one used by members to coordinate for group replication. MySQL server restart is required after these changes are made.

If not already done, we have to allow access to these ports using the following commands:

```
sudo ufw allow 33061
sudo ufw allow 3306
```

The next step is to create a replication user and enable the replication plugin. The replication user is required for each server to establish group replication. We need to turn binary logging off during the replication user creation process as the user will be different for each server, as shown in the following block:

```
SET SQL_LOG_BIN=0;
CREATE USER 'mysql_user'@'%' IDENTIFIED BY 'password' REQUIRE SSL;
GRANT REPLICATION SLAVE ON *.* TO 'mysql_user'@'%';
FLUSH PRIVILEGES;
SET SQL_LOG_BIN=1;
```

Now, use `CHANGE MASTER TO` to configure the server to use the credentials for the `group_replication_recovery` channel:

```
CHANGE MASTER TO MASTER_USER='mysql_user', MASTER_PASSWORD='password' FOR
CHANNEL 'group_replication_recovery';
```

Now, we are all set to install the plugin. Connect to the server and execute the following command:

```
INSTALL PLUGIN group_replication SONAME 'group_replication.so';
```

Use the following statement to verify if the plugin is activated or not:

```
SHOW PLUGINS;
```

The next step is to start up the group. Execute the following statements on one member of the group:

```
SET GLOBAL group_replication_bootstrap_group=ON;
START GROUP_REPLICATION;
SET GLOBAL group_replication_bootstrap_group=OFF;
```

Now, we can start group replication on another server:

```
START GROUP_REPLICATION;
```

We can check the group members list using the following SQL query:

```
mysql> SELECT * FROM performance_schema.replication_group_members;
+------------------------------+------------------------------------------+
|         CHANNEL_NAME         |                MEMBER_ID                 |
+------------------------------+------------------------------------------+
| group_replication_applier    | 13324ab7-1b01-11e7-9dd1-22b78adaa992     |
| group_replication_applier    | 1ae4b211-1b01-11e7-9d89-ceb93e1d5494     |
| group_replication_applier    | 157b597a-1b01-11e7-9d83-566a6de6dfef     |
+------------------------------+------------------------------------------+

+-----------------+-------------+--------------+
|   MEMBER_HOST   | MEMBER_PORT | MEMBER_STATE |
+-----------------+-------------+--------------+
| 177.110.117.1   |    3306     |    ONLINE    |
| 177.110.117.2   |    3306     |    ONLINE    |
| 177.110.117.3   |    3306     |    ONLINE    |
+-----------------+-------------+--------------+
3 rows in set (0.01 sec)
```

Group replication use cases

The MySQL group replication feature provides a way to build fault tolerant systems by replicating the state of the system throughout a set of servers. The group replication system stays available as long as the majority of servers are functioning even if some of the servers fail. Server failures are tracked by a group membership service. The group membership service relies on the distributed failure detector, which signals if any server leaves the group, voluntarily or due to unexpected halt. The distributed recovery procedure ensures that when the servers join the group, they are brought up to date automatically. Therefore, continuous database service is guaranteed with MySQL group replication. There is one problem though. Although the database service is available, the clients connected to it must be redirected to a different server when the server crashes. The group replication does not attempt to resolve it. It should be dealt with by a connector, load balancer, router, or some other middleware.

The following are the typical use cases of MySQL group replication:

1. **Elastic replication**: Group replication is suitable for fluid environments where the number of servers grow or shrink dynamically with minimum side effects. The example is cloud-based database services.
2. **Highly available shards**: MySQL group replication can be used to implement highly available write scale-out shards where each replication group maps to one shard.
3. **Alternative to master-slave replication**: Group replication can be an answer to contention problems arising in certain situations with single master server replication.
4. **Autonomic systems**: MySQL group replication can be deployed for the automation built into the replication protocol.

Replication solutions

MySQL replication is useful in many different scenarios to fulfill a range of purposes. This section focuses on specific use cases and provides general information on how to use the replication.

One of the major use cases is to use replication for backup purposes. The data from the `master` can be replicated on the `slave` database server and then the data on the slave can be backed up. The `slave` database server can be shut down without affecting the operations running on the `master` database server.

Another use case is to handle unexpected halt of the REPLICATION SLAVE. To accomplish this, once the `slave` restarts, the I/O thread must be able to recover information about the transactions received and the transactions that are executed by the SQL thread. This information is stored in the `InnoDB` tables. As the `InnoDB` storage engine is transactional, it is always recoverable. As mentioned earlier, for MySQL 8 replication to use tables, `relay_log_info_repository` and `master_info_repository` must be set to TABLE.

In a row-based replication, it is possible to monitor the current progress of the slave's SQL thread. It is done through performance schema instrument stages. To track the progress of all three row-based replication event types, use the following statement to enable three performance schema stages:

```
mysql> UPDATE performance_schema.setup_instruments SET ENABLED = 'YES'
WHERE NAME LIKE 'stage/sql/Applying batch of row changes%';
```

The MySQL 8 replication process can work even though the source table on the master and the destination table on the slave uses different engine types. The `default_storage_engine` system variable is not replicated. This is a huge advantage in replication wherein different engine types can be used for different replication scenarios. An example is a scale-out scenario where we want all read operations to be performed on the slave database server, whereas all write operations should be performed on the master database server. In such a case, we can use a transactional `InnoDB` engine on the master and a non-transactional `MyISAM` engine type on the slave database server.

Consider an example of an organization that wants to distribute sales data to different departments to spread the load for data analysis. MySQL replication can be used to have a single master replicate different databases to different slaves. This can be achieved by limiting the binary log statements by using the `--replicate-wild-do-table` configuration option on each slave.

Once MySQL replication is set up, as the number of slaves connected to the master increase, the load also increases. The network load on the master also increases as each slave is supposed to receive a full copy of the binary logs. The master database server is also busy processing requests. In this scenario, it becomes necessary to improve the performance. One of the solutions to improve performance is to create a deeper replication structure that enables replication of a master to only one slave. The rest of the slaves connect to the primary slave for their operations.

Summary

In this chapter, we learned insightful details about MySQL 8 replication, what replication is, and how it helps solve specific problems. We also learned how to set up statement-based and row-based replication types. Along the way, we also learned about the system variables and server start up options for replication. In the later part of the chapter, we dived deep into group replication and how it is different from the traditional method of MySQL replication. We also learned logging and replication formats. Last but not least, we learned different replication solutions in brief. We covered a lot of stuff, huh?

It's now time to move on to our next chapter, where we will be setting up several types of partitioning, and exploring the selection of partitioning, and pruning of partitioning. It also explains how to cope with restrictions and limitations while partitioning. The reader will be able to understand which type of partitioning suits a situation as per the requirement.

9
Partitioning in MySQL 8

In the previous chapter, replication in MySQL 8 was explained. This included detailed explanations of replication, configuration, and implementation. The chapter also explained group replication versus clustering, and covered the replication approach as a solution.

In this chapter, we will do partitioning in MySQL 8. Partitioning is the concept of managing and maintaining data with specific operations with several operators, and defining rules to control over partitioning. Basically, it provides a configuration hook for managing the underlying data files in a specified way.

We will cover the following topics on partitioning:

- Overview of partitioning
- Types of partitioning
- Partition management
- Partition selection
- Partition pruning
- Restriction and limitation in partitioning

Overview of partitioning

The concept of partitioning relates to the physical aspects of data storage in the database. If you look at the SQL standards, they do not give much information on the concept, and the SQL language itself intends to work independently of which media or data structure is used for storing information or data specific to different schemas, tables, rows, or columns. Advanced database management systems have added means of specifying the physical location used for data storage as hardware, the file system, or as both. In MySQL, the InnoDB storage engine provides support for these purposes with the notion of tablespace.

Partitioning enables us to distribute parts of individual tables to be stored as separate tables at different locations in the file system. Additionally, the distribution is accomplished with user specified rules provided, such as in the form of modulus, a hashing function, or matching with simple value or range, and the user provided expression acts as a parameter that is commonly known as a partitioning function.

In MySQL 8, currently InnoDB is the only storage engine that supports partitioning. No extra specification is required to enable partitioning in the InnoDB storage engine. Partitioning can not be used with the storage engines MyISAM, CSV, FEDERATED, MERGE. For all examples given in this chapter we assume that the default storage engine is InnoDB.

When a partition table is created, the default storage engine is used, same as creating a table, and can be overridden just as we would do for any table by specifying the STORAGE ENGINE option. The following example demonstrates creating a table partitioned by hash into four partitions, all of which use the InnoDB storage engine:

```
CREATE TABLE tp (tp_id INT, amt DECIMAL(5,2), trx_date DATE)
    ENGINE=INNODB
    PARTITION BY HASH ( MONTH (trx_date) )
    PARTITIONS 4;
```

 Partitioning is applicable on all indexes and all data of the table. It is not applicable on either indexes or data, and vice versa is also not applicable. It can be applicable on both indexes and data together and it cannot be applied on part of the table.

The preceding table `tp` has no unique or primary keys defined but in general practice we usually have primary keys, unique keys, or both as part of the table, and partitioning column choice depends upon these keys if any of them is present. The partitioning column choice is given in detail in the *partitioning keys, primary keys, and unique keys* section. To simplify the concept of partitioning the examples given may not include these keys.

Types of partitioning

Several types of partitioning are supported in MySQL 8, listed as follows :

- RANGE Partitioning: Assigns rows to partitions from the column values that come between the given range of values
- LIST Partitioning: Assigns rows to partitions from the column values that matches with one of the given set of values
- COLUMNS Partitioning: Assigns rows to partitions with multiple column values with either RANGE or LIST partitioning
- HASH Partitioning: Assigns partition based on user specified expressions evaluated on column values
- KEY Partitioning: In addition to HASH partitioning, allows the use of multiple column values
- Subpartitioning: In addition to partitioning, allows further division in partitioned tables, also known as composite partitioning

Different rows of the table can be assigned to different physical partitions; this is known as horizontal partitioning. Different columns of the table can be assigned to different physical partitions; this is known as vertical partitioning. MySQL 8 currently supports horizontal partitioning.

For the LIST, RANGE, and LINEAR HASH types of partitioning, the value of partitioning columns is given to the partitioning function. The partitioning function returns an integer value that is the partition number in which the record should be stored. The partition function must be nonrandom and nonconstant. The partition function cannot contain queries and can use the SQL expression which returns either an integer or NULL, where the integer as intval must follow the expression –MAXVALUE <= intval <= MAXVALUE. Here, –MAXVALUE represents the lower limit and MAXVALUE is the upper limit for the integer type value.

The storage engine must be the same for all partitions of the same table, however there is no restriction on using different storage engines for different partitioned tables in the same database or MySQL server.

Partitioning management

There are different ways to use SQL statements to modify partitioned tables and perform operations such as add, redefine, merge, drop, or split existing partitioned tables. Information about partitioned tables and partitions can also be obtained with SQL statements.

MIN_ROWS and MAX_ROWS can be used to configure the maximum and minimum number of rows and can be stored in the partition table.

Partition selection and pruning

Explicit selection of partition and subpartition is also provided. It enables row matching to the conditions given in the where clause. In partition, the pruning concepts described do not scan partitions where no possible matching values can be present, and are applied using queries, whereas partition selection is applicable for both queries and many of the DML statements.

Restrictions and limitations in partitioning

Stored procedures or functions, user defined functions or plugins, and user variables or declared variables are restricted in partitioning expressions. There are also several restrictions and limitations applicable to partitioning given in the detailed section.

See the following list for some of the advantages of partitioning:

- Partitioning facilitates storing more data in one table than can be held on a file system partition or single disk.
- Data that has become useless can be removed easily by dropping a partition or partitions that only contain the useless data. In some cases where specific data is required to be added separately, this can be done easily with partitioning in single or multiple partitions based on the specified rule.

- Query optimization that occurs automatically based on partitioned data by not searching for data in partitions that are not applicable as per the where condition.
- In addition to partition pruning, partition selection is supported explicitly by which where clause is applied on a specified partition or multiple partitions.
- Greater query throughput is achieved by separating data search into multiple disks.

Types of partitioning

In this section, you will understand different types of partitioning and also the purpose of using specific partitioning. The following is a list of the partitioning types that are available in MySQL 8 :

- RANGE partitioning
- LIST partitioning
- COLUMNS partitioning
- HASH partitioning
- KEY partitioning
- Subpartitioning

In addition to the above list, we will also see NULLhandling in MySQL 8 Partitioning in detailed section.

A very common use case for database partitioning is segregating data by date. MySQL 8 does not support date partitioning, which some database systems provide explicitly, but it is easy to create partitioning schemes with date, time, or datetime columns, or that are based on date/time related expressions that evaluate values from these column types.

You can use the date, time, or datetime types as column values for partition columns without any modifications if using KEY or LINEAR KEY partitioning, whereas in other partitioning types an expression giving back an integer or NULL value is required.

Irrespective of which type of partitioning you use, partitions always get numbered automatically with an integer number in sequence of the partitions created. If, for example, the table uses four partitions, they are numbered as 0,1,2, and 3 for each of the partitions as per creation sequence.

When you specify numbers of partitions, it must be evaluated to a positive, non zero integer without any leading zeros. Decimal fractions are not allowed as partition numbers.

Names of partitions are not case-sensitive and should follow conventions or rules just like other MySQL identifiers such as tables. The options used in partition definition are already provided by the CREATE TABLE syntax.

Now, let's look at partition in detail and examine each of the types to learn how they are different to each other.

RANGE partitioning

In this type of partitioning, as the name states, RANGE is given in an expression that evaluates whether a value lies in the given range or not. Ranges are defined with the VALUES LESS THAN operator and they should not be overlapping and contiguous.

For the next few examples, suppose we are creating a table holding employee personal records for 25 food stores. The stores are numbered from 1 to 25 and is a chain of 25 food stores, as shown in the following block:

```
CREATE TABLE employee (
    employee_id INT NOT NULL,
    first_name VARCHAR(30),
    last_name VARCHAR(30),
    hired_date DATE NOT NULL DEFAULT '1990-01-01',
    termination_date DATE NOT NULL DEFAULT '9999-12-31',
    job_code INT NOT NULL,
    store_id INT NOT NULL
);
```

Now let's do partitioning of the table, so you can partition the table by range as per your need. Suppose you consider using division to split the data five ways with the store_id range for partitioning. For this, the table creation definition will look as follows:

```
CREATE TABLE employee (
    employee_id INT NOT NULL,
    first_name VARCHAR(30),
    last_name VARCHAR(30),
    hired_date DATE NOT NULL DEFAULT '1990-01-01',
    termination_date DATE NOT NULL DEFAULT '9999-12-31',
    job_code INT NOT NULL,
    store_id INT NOT NULL
)
PARTITION BY RANGE (store_id) (
```

```
      PARTITION p0 VALUES LESS THAN (6),
      PARTITION p1 VALUES LESS THAN (11),
      PARTITION p2 VALUES LESS THAN (16),
      PARTITION p3 VALUES LESS THAN (21),
      PARTITION p4 VALUES LESS THAN (26)
);
```

So, as per the above partitioning scheme, all inserted rows that contain the employees working at stores 1 to 5 are stored in the p0 partition, employees working at stores 6 to 10 are stored in the p1 partition, and so on. If you take a look at the partition definition, partitions are ordered from the lowest to highest store_id column values, and the PARTITION BY RANGE syntax looks similar to programming statements if... elseif ... statements, doesn't it?

Well, you are thinking about what will happen if a record comes with store_id 26; this would result in an error as the server does not know where to place the record. There are two ways to keep this error from occurring:

1. By using the IGNORE key word with the INSERT statement.
2. By using MAXVALUE instead of a specified range (26).

And yes, of course, you can extend the limits by using the ALTER TABLE statement to add new partitions for stores 26-30, 30-35, and so on.

Similar to store_id, you could also partition the table based on the job codes - based on the range of column values. Suppose if 5 digit codes are used for management positions, 4 digit codes are used for office and support personnel, and 3 digit codes are used for regular workers, then the partition table creation definition would be as follows:

```
CREATE TABLE employee (
    employee_id INT NOT NULL,
    first_name VARCHAR(30),
    last_name VARCHAR(30),
    hired_date DATE NOT NULL DEFAULT '1990-01-01',
    termination_date DATE NOT NULL DEFAULT '9999-12-31',
    job_code INT NOT NULL,
    store_id INT NOT NULL
)
PARTITION BY RANGE (job_code) (
    PARTITION p0 VALUES LESS THAN (1000),
    PARTITION p1 VALUES LESS THAN (10000),
    PARTITION p2 VALUES LESS THAN (100000)
);
```

You can also specify partitioning with one of the two columns of date type values. Suppose you wish to partition based on the year each of the employee joined - so by the value of YEAR(hired_date). Now the table definition will be as follows:

```
CREATE TABLE employee (
    employee_id INT NOT NULL,
    first_name VARCHAR(30),
    last_name VARCHAR(30),
    hired_date DATE NOT NULL DEFAULT '1990-01-01',
    termination_date DATE NOT NULL DEFAULT '9999-12-31',
    job_code INT NOT NULL,
    store_id INT NOT NULL
)
PARTITION BY RANGE (YEAR(hired_date)) (
    PARTITION p0 VALUES LESS THAN (1996),
    PARTITION p1 VALUES LESS THAN (2001),
    PARTITION p2 VALUES LESS THAN (2006),
    PARTITION p3 VALUES LESS THAN MAXVALUE
);
```

According to this scheme, all employees recorded hired before 1996 will be stored in the partition p0, then records with a hire date before 2001 will be stored in the partition p1, records between 2001 and 2006 in p2, and the rest of the records will be stored in partition p3.

Partition schemes based on time intervals can be implemented using the following two options:

1. Partition the table by RANGE and use a function operating on the date, time or datetime column values to return an integer value for the partitioning expression
2. Partition the table by RANGE COLUMN and use the date, time, or datetime columns as the partition column

RANGE COLUMN is supported in MySQL 8 and is described in detail in the COLUMN PARTITIONING section.

LIST partitioning

As the name states, LIST partitioning uses lists for table partitioning. The list is comma separated integer values defined while partitioning with VALUES IN (value_list); here, value_list refers to comma separated integer literals.

LIST partitioning is similar to RANGE partitioning in many ways, but there are differences. The operator used in each partitioning is different. The operator uses a list of comma separated values to be matched with the column value or the partition expression evaluating to integer value.

Considering the employee table as an example, the basic definition for the table using the create table syntax will be as follows:

```
CREATE TABLE employee (
    employee_id INT NOT NULL,
    first_name VARCHAR(30),
    last_name VARCHAR(30),
    hired_date DATE NOT NULL DEFAULT '1990-01-01',
    termination_date DATE NOT NULL DEFAULT '9999-12-31',
    job_code INT NOT NULL,
    store_id INT NOT NULL
);
```

Suppose you wish to distribute these 25 food stores among five zones—North, South, East, West, and Central, with the store ID numbers (1,2,11,12,21,22), (3,4,13,14,23,24), (5,6,15,16,25), (7,8,17,18), and (9,10,19,20) respectively for the zones.

Partitioning the table with the zones list will provide the following definition for table partition:

```
CREATE TABLE employee (
    employee_id INT NOT NULL,
    first_name VARCHAR(30),
    last_name VARCHAR(30),
    hired_date DATE NOT NULL DEFAULT '1990-01-01',
    termination_date DATE NOT NULL DEFAULT '9999-12-31',
    job_code INT NOT NULL,
    store_id INT NOT NULL
)
PARTITION BY LIST (store_id) (
    PARTITION pNorth VALUES IN (1,2,11,12,21,22),
    PARTITION pSouth VALUES IN (3,4,13,14,23,24),
    PARTITION pEast VALUES IN (5,6,15,16,25),
    PARTITION pWest VALUES IN (7,8,17,18),
    PARTITION pCentral VALUES IN (9,10,19,20)
);
```

As you can see in the preceding statement, partitioning per zones means it will be easy to update records for stores based on zones within particular partitions. Suppose the organization sold the west zone to another company; then you might need to remove all employee records from the west zone using the pWest partition in query. Executing ALTER TABLE employee TRUNCATE PARTITION pWest would be much easier and efficient than the DELETE statement DELETE from employee where store_id IN (7,8,17,18); also, you can use the DROP statement for employee records removal - ALTER TABLE employee DROP PARTITION pWest. Along with the previous statement execution you will also remove the pWest PARTITION from the table partition definition, and will need to use the ALTER statement again to add the pWest PARTITION and restore the partition table scheme you had earlier.

Similar to RANGE partitioning, you can also use LIST partitioning using hash or key to produce composite partitioning, which is also known as subpartitioning. You will get to know more details on subpartitioning as a dedicated section for subpartitioning follows.

In LIST partitioning there is no catch-all mechanism such as MAXVALUE that can contain all possible values. Instead, you have to manage the expected values list in the values_list itself, otherwise the INSERT statement will result in an error where the table has no partition for value 9, as in the following example:

```
CREATE TABLE tpl (
    cl1 INT,
    cl2 INT
)
PARTITION BY LIST (cl1) (
    PARTITION p0 VALUES IN (1,3,4,5),
    PARTITION p1 VALUES IN (2,6,7,8)
);

INSERT INTO tpl VALUES (9,5) ;
```

As you can see in the preceding INSERT statement, value 9 is not part of the list given during partition schema and so there is an error. If you use multiple value insert statements, the same error can result in failure for all inserts and no records will be inserted; instead use the IGNORE keyword to avoid such errors, as in the following INSERT statement example:

```
INSERT IGNORE INTO tpl VALUES (1,2), (3,4), (5,6), (7,8), (9,11);
```

COLUMNS partitioning

As the name suggests, this type of partitioning uses columns themselves. We can use two versions of column partitioning. One is RANGE COLUMN and the other is LIST COLUMN. In addition to both RANGE COLUMN and LIST COLUMN partitioning, MySQL 8 supports using non-integer types of column that can be used to define value ranges or list values. The list of permitted data types are as follows:

- All column types of INT, BIGINT, MEDIUMINT, SMALLINT, and TINYINT are supported for the RANGE and LIST partitioning columns, but other numeric column types such as FLOAT or DECIMAL are not supported
- DATE and DATETIME are supported but other column types relating to date and time are not supported as partitioning columns
- The string column types BINARY, VARBINARY, CHAR and VARCHAR are supported but the TEXT and BLOB column types are not supported as partitioning columns

Now, let's see RANGE COLUMN partitioning and LIST COLUMN partitioning in detail one by one.

RANGE COLUMN partitioning

As the name suggests, you can define range using columns with RANGE partitioning and RANGE COLUMN partitioning, but the difference is that you can define multiple columns providing range, and additionally you are able to select column types other than integer.

Thus, RANGE COLUMN partitioning is different to RANGE partitioning in the following listed ways :

- RANGE COLUMNS can use one or multiple columns and the comparison occurs between list of column values and not between scalar values
- RANGE COLUMNS can use only names of columns and not any expressions
- RANGE COLUMNS partitioning column types are not restricted to INTEGER column types only but can use the string, date, and datetime column types as partitioning columns

Table partitioning by RANGE COLUMNS has the following basic syntax:

```
CREATE TABLE table_name
PARTITION BY RANGE COLUMNS (column_list) (
    PARTITION partition_name VALUES LESS THAN (value_list) [,
    PARTITION partition_name VALUES LESS THAN (value_list) ] [,
...]
)
column_list:
    column_name[, column_name] [, ...]
value_list :
    value[, value][, ...]
```

In the preceding syntax, column_list stands for partitioning column list and value_list stands for partition definition value list, and value_list must be given for each of the partition definitions, along with the same number of values defined in column_list. To say it straight, the number of columns (column_list) in the COLUMNS clause must be the same as the number of values (value_list) in the VALUES LESS THAN clause.

The following example makes clear what it is and how it goes with the table definition:

```
CREATE TABLE trc (
    p INT,
    q INT,
    r CHAR(3),
    s INT
)
PARTITION BY RANGE COLUMNS (p,s,r) (
    PARTITION p0 VALUES LESS THAN (5,10,'ppp'),
    PARTITION p1 VALUES LESS THAN (10,20,'sss'),
    PARTITION p2 VALUES LESS THAN (15,30,'rrr'),
    PARTITION p3 VALUES LESS THAN (MAXVALUE,MAXVALUE,MAXVALUE)
);
```

Now you go and insert records into the table trc with the following statement :

```
INSERT INTO trc VALUES (5,9,'aaa',2) , (5,10,'bbb',4) , (5,12,'ccc',6) ;
```

LIST COLUMN partitioning

In this type of partitioning, lists of columns are used in the table partitioning definition, and similar to the RANGE COLUMN the value list for the respective columns must be provided. Similar to RANGE COLUMN, column types other than integer types can be used—that is, the string, date, and datetime column types.

Suppose you have the requirement that a business has spread over 12 cities, and for marketing purposes you manage them with four zones of three cities as follows:

- **Zone 1 with cities**: Ahmedabad, Surat, Mumbai
- **Zone 2 with cities**: Delhi, Gurgaon, Punjab
- **Zone 3 with cities**: Kolkata, Mizoram, Hyderabad
- **Zone 4 with cities**: Bangalore, Chennai, Kochi

Now, create a table for the customer data that has four partitions of the corresponding zones, and list them with the name of the city where the customer resides. The table partition definition will look as follows:

```
CREATE TABLE customer_z (
    first_name VARCHAR(30),
    last_name VARCHAR(30),
    street_1 VARCHAR(35),
    street_2 VARCHAR(35),
    city VARCHAR(15),
    renewal DATE
)
PARTITION BY LIST COLUMNS (city) (
    PARTITION pZone_1 VALUES IN ('Ahmedabad', 'Surat', 'Mumbai'),
    PARTITION pZone_2 VALUES IN ('Delhi', 'Gurgaon', 'Punjab'),
    PARTITION pZone_3 VALUES IN ('Kolkata', 'Mizoram', 'Hyderabad'),
    PARTITION pZone_4 VALUES IN ('Bangalore', 'Chennai', 'Kochi')

);
```

Similar to RANGE COLUMN partitioning, it is not required to provide any expression in the COLUMNS() clause that converts the column value to an integer literal, and nothing other than the list of column names itself is permitted.

HASH partitioning

The primary intention behind introducing HASH partitioning is to ensure an even distribution of date among the number of partitions defined. So, with HASH partitioning you need to specify the column value or the expression evaluating the column value being hashed, and the number of partitions into which the partitioned table is to be divided.

For defining HASH partitioning in table you need to specify the PARTITION BY HASH (expr) clause in the table definition, where expr is the expression that will return the integer, and additionally you need to specify the number of partitions with PARTITIONS n, where n is a positive integer number that stands for the number of partitions.

The following definition creates a table with HASH partitioning on the store_id column, dividing into five partitions:

```
CREATE TABLE employee (
    employee_id INT NOT NULL,
    first_name VARCHAR(30),
    last_name VARCHAR(30),
    hired_date DATE NOT NULL DEFAULT '1990-01-01',
    termination_date DATE NOT NULL DEFAULT '9999-12-31',
    job_code INT NOT NULL,
    store_id INT NOT NULL
)
PARTITION BY HASH (store_id)
PARTITIONS 4;
```

In the above statement, if you exclude the PARTITIONS clause, the number of partitions automatically defaults to one.

LINEAR HASH partitioning

MySQL 8 supports linear hashing, which is based on a linear power-of-two algorithm instead of regular hashing, which is based on the modulus of the hashing function's value. LINEAR HASH partitioning requires the LINEAR keyword in the PARTITION BY clause, shown as follows:

```
CREATE TABLE employee (
    employee_id INT NOT NULL,
    first_name VARCHAR(30),
    last_name VARCHAR(30),
    hired_date DATE NOT NULL DEFAULT '1990-01-01',
    termination_date DATE NOT NULL DEFAULT '9999-12-31',
    job_code INT NOT NULL,
```

```
    store_id INT NOT NULL
)
PARTITION BY LINEAR HASH ( YEAR(hired_date))
PARTITIONS 4;
```

An advantage of using linear hashing is faster partitioning operations, and a disadvantage is less even data distribution compared to regular hashing partitioning.

KEY partitioning

This type of partitioning is similar to HASH partitioning, with the change of the use of a user-defined expression instead of the hashing function. KEY PARTITIONING uses the PARTITION BY KEY clause in the CREATE TABLE statement for the partitioning definition. The syntax rules for KEY partitioning are similar to that of HASH partitioning, so let's list out the differences so as to understand:

- Instead of HASH, KEY is used for partitioning

One or more column names list is taken in KEY(), and if there is no column defined in KEY but the table has a defined primary key or unique key with the NOT NULL constrain, the column is automatically taken as partitioning column for KEY:

```
CREATE TABLE tk1 (
    tk1_id INT NOT NULL PRIMARY KEY,
    note VARCHAR(50)
)
PARTITION BY KEY ()
PARTITIONS 2;
```

Unlike other partitioning types, the column type is not only limited to NULL or integer values:

```
CREATE TABLE tk2 (
    cl1 INT NOT NULL,
    cl2 CHAR(10),
    cl3 DATE
)
PARTITION BY LINEAR KEY (cl1)
PARTITIONS 3;
```

As you can see in the preceding example statement, similar to HASH partitioning, KEY partitioning also supports LINEAR KEY partitioning and has the same effect as LINEAR HASH partitioning.

Subpartitioning

Subpartitioning is also known as composite partitioning, and as the name suggests it is only a division of each partition into a partitioned table itself. See the following statement:

```
CREATE TABLE trs (trs_id INT, sold DATE)
PARTITION BY RANGE ( YEAR(sold) )
    SUBPARTITION BY HASH ( TO_DAYS(sold) )
    SUBPARTITIONS 2 (
        PARTITION p0 VALUES LESS THAN (1991),
        PARTITION p1 VALUES LESS THAN (2001),
        PARTITION p2 VALUES LESS THAN MAXVALUE
);
```

As you can see in the preceding example statement, table `trs` has three RANGE partitions and each of the partitions `p0`, `p1`, `p2` is further divided into two more subpartitions. Effectively, the entire table is divided into six partitions.

Subpartitioning is possible on tables partitioned using RANGE or LIST partitioning, and subpartitioning can use the KEY or HASH partitioning types. The syntax rules for subpartitioning are the same as in regular partitioning, with the exception to specify the default column in KEY partitioning as it does not take the column automatically for subpartitioning.

The following is a list of points to consider when using subpartitioning:

- Number of partitions must be same for each of the partitions defined
- Name must be specified with the SUBPARTITIONING clause or specify a default option instead
- Names specified for subpartitioning must be unique across the table

Handling NULL in partitioning

There is nothing specific to MySQL 8 that disallows NULL in partitioning as a column value, partitioning expression, or the value from the user-defined expression. Even if NULL is permitted as a value ,the value returned from the expression must be an integer and so MySQL 8 has implementation for partitioning such that it treats NULL as less than any non-NULL value as done in the ORDER BY clause.

Behavior for NULL handling varies among different types of partitioning:

- **Handling NULL in RANGE partitioning**: If a NULL value contained in the column is inserted, the row will be inserted in the lowest partition specified in range
- **Handling NULL with LIST partitioning**: If the table has a partitioning definition with LIST partitioning and its partitions are defined with a value list that explicitly specifies NULL as a value in value_list, then insertion will be successful; otherwise, it will give an error table that has no partition specified for NULL
- **Handling NULL with HASH and KEY partitioning**: NULL is handled differently when table partitioning is defined with HASH or KEY partitioning, and if a partition expression returns NULL it is wrapped with zero value. So that based on partitioning the insertion operation will successfully insert the record to partition being zero.

Partition management

There are plenty of ways to use SQL statements in order to modify partitioned tables—you can drop, add, merge, split, or redefine partitions with the ALTER TABLE statement. There are also ways to retrieve partitioned tables and partition information. We will see each of these in the following sections:

- RANGE and LIST partition management
- HASH and KEY partition management
- Partition maintenance
- Obtain partition information

RANGE and LIST partition management

Partition adding and dropping is handled in a similar way for the RANGE and LIST partition types. A table partitioned by RANGE or LIST partitioning can be dropped using the ALTER TABLE statement with the DROP PARTITION option available.

Make sure you have the DROP privilege before executing the ALTER TABLE ... DROP PARTITION statement. DROP PARTITION will delete all the data and also remove the partition from the table partition definition.

The following example illustrates the DROP PARTITION option with the ALTER TABLE statement:

```
SET @@SQL_MODE = '';
CREATE TABLE employee (
 id INT NOT NULL AUTO_INCREMENT PRIMARY KEY,
 first_name VARCHAR(25) NOT NULL,
 last_name VARCHAR(25) NOT NULL,
 store_id INT NOT NULL,
 department_id INT NOT NULL
)
 PARTITION BY RANGE(id) (
 PARTITION p0 VALUES LESS THAN (5),
 PARTITION p1 VALUES LESS THAN (10),
 PARTITION p2 VALUES LESS THAN (15),
 PARTITION p3 VALUES LESS THAN MAXVALUE
);
INSERT INTO employee VALUES
 ('', 'Chintan', 'Mehta', 3, 2), ('', 'Bhumil', 'Raval', 1, 2),
 ('', 'Subhash', 'Shah', 3, 4), ('', 'Siva', 'Stark', 2, 4),
 ('', 'Chintan', 'Gajjar', 1, 1), ('', 'Mansi', 'Panchal', 2, 3),
 ('', 'Hetal', 'Oza', 2, 1), ('', 'Parag', 'Patel', 3, 1),
 ('', 'Pooja', 'Shah', 1, 3), ('', 'Samir', 'Bhatt', 2, 4),
 ('', 'Pritesh', 'Shah', 1, 4), ('', 'Jaymin', 'Patel', 3, 2),
 ('', 'Ruchek', 'Shah', 1, 2), ('', 'Chandni', 'Patel', 3, 3),
 ('', 'Mittal', 'Patel', 2, 3), ('', 'Shailesh', 'Patel', 2, 2),
 ('', 'Krutika', 'Dave', 3, 3), ('', 'Dinesh', 'Patel', 3, 2);

ALTER TABLE employee DROP PARTITION p2;
```

In the preceding statement, after executing the ALTER TABLE employee DROP PARTITION p2; statement, you can see that all data is removed from partition p2. In case you want to remove all the data but also need to keep the table definition and the partitioning scheme, you can use the TRUNCATE PARTITION option to achieve a similar result.

In order to add new LIST or RANGE partitions to existing partitioned tables you can use the ALTER TABLE ... ADD PARTITION statement.

By using the SHOW CREATE TABLE statement you can verify and see if the ALTER TABLE statement has the desired effect on the table definition and the partitioning schema.

HASH and KEY partition management

Table partitions of the HASH or KEY types are similar compared to table partitioning by the RANGE or LIST types of partitioning. Dropping a partition is not applicable if a table is partitioned by the HASH or KEY type of partitioning, but there is option for merging HASH or KEY partitions, using ALTER TABLE ... COALESCE PARTITION.

Consider if you have client table data partitioned by HASH partitioning, divided in twelve partitions as follows:

```
CREATE TABLE client (
    client_id INT,
    first_name VARCHAR(25),
    last_name VARCHAR(25),
    signed DATE
)
PARTITION BY HASH (MONTH (signed))
PARTITIONS 12;
```

In the preceding table partitioning schema, if you want to reduce the number of partitions to eight instead of twelve, use the following ALTER TABLE statement:

```
ALTER TABLE client COALESCE PARTITION 8;
```

In the preceding statement the number 8 represents the number of partitions to be removed from the table. You cannot remove more partitions than already exist in the table partitioning schema. Similarly, you can add more partitions using the ALTER TABLE... ADD PARTITION statement.

Partition maintenance

There are many maintenance tasks that can be done with several statements on a number of tables and partitions. They can be done using statements such as ANALYSE TABLE, CHECK TABLE, REPAIR TABLE, and OPTIMIZE TABLE , which are supported specifically for partitioned tables.

There are a number of extensions of ALTER TABLE available for such operations on single or multiple partitioned tables, listed as follows:

- **Rebuilding partitions**: This option drops all records from the partitions and reinserts them, so this is considered helpful in the defragmentation process. The following is an example:

  ```
  ALTER TABLE trp REBUILD  PARTITION p0, p1, p2;
  ```

- **Optimizing partitions**: If many rows are deleted from a partition or partitions of the table, or there are many row changes in a huge amount of data in variable length column types such as VARCHAR, BLOB, TEXT, and so on, you can perform OPTIMIZE PARTITION to reclaim unused space in the partition data file. The following is an example:

  ```
  ALTER TABLE top OPTIMIZE PARTITION p0, p1, p2;
  ```

 ALTER TABLE ... OPTIMIZE PARTITION does not work correctly with the InnoDB storage engine, so instead use ALTER TABLE ... REBUILD PARTITION and ALTER TABLE ... ANALYZE PARTITION for such tables.

- **Analyzing partitions**: In this option key distributions of the partitions are read and stored. The following is an example:

  ```
  ALTER TABLE tap ANALYZE  PARTITION p1, p2;
  ```

- **Repairing partitions**: This option is only used when there are corrupt partitions found to be repaired. The following is an example:

  ```
  ALTER TABLE trp REPAIR PARTITION p3;
  ```

- **Checking partitions**: This option is used to check for any errors in partitions such as the CHECK TABLE option used in nonpartitioned tables. The following is an example:

  ```
  ALTER TABLE tcp CHECK PARTITION p0;
  ```

There is an option to use ALL instead of a specific partition, specified in all above options, in order to perform the operation on all the partitions.

Obtain partition information

Information about partitions can be obtained in a number of ways, as follows:

- The SHOW CREATE TABLE statement can be used to view the partition's schema information containing all partitioning clauses in the partitioned tables
- The SHOW TABLE STATUS statement can be used to check if the table is partitioned or not by viewing its status
- The EXPLAIN SELECT statement can be used to see partitions used by given SELECT option
- Using the INFORMATION_SCHEMA.PARTITIONS table for querying partition table information.

The following is an example with the SHOW CREATE TABLE statement option to see partition information:

```
SHOW CREATE TABLE employee;
```

The output from the preceding statement has separate information for partitioning schema, including common information for the table schema.

Similarly, you can retrieve information about partitioning from the INFORMATION_SCHEMA.PARTITIONS table.

The EXPLAIN option gives a lot of information on partitioning with column. For example it gives number of rows obtained from the query specific to partitions. The partition would be searched as per the query statement. It also gives information about keys.

EXPLAIN is also used to get information from nonpartitioned tables. It does not give any error if there are no partitions, but gives a NULL value in the partitions column.

Partition selection and pruning

In this section, you will see how partitioning can optimize SQL statements clause execution with the optimizer known as partition pruning, and the use of SQL statements to effectively use partition data for selection and perform modification operations on the partitioning.

Partition pruning

Partition pruning is related to the optimization concept in partition. In partition pruning the concept described as *Do not scan partitions where no possible matching values can be present* is applied based on the query statements.

Suppose there is a partitioned table, tp1, created with the following statement:

```
CREATE TABLE tp1 (
    first_name VARCHAR (30) NOT NULL,
    last_name VARCHAR (30) NOT NULL,
    zone_code TINYINT UNSIGNED NOT NULL,
    doj DATE NOT NULL
)
PARTITION BY RANGE (zone_code) (
    PARTITION p0 VALUES LESS THAN (65),
    PARTITION p1 VALUES LESS THAN (129),
    PARTITION p2 VALUES LESS THAN (193),
    PARTITION p3 VALUES LESS THAN MAXVALUE
);
```

In the preceding example table tp1, suppose you want to retrieve a result from the following SELECT statement:

```
SELECT first_name, last_name , doj from tp1 where zone_code > 126 AND
zone_code < 131;
```

Now, you can see from the preceding statement that there are no rows that have data in partitions p0 or p3 as per the statement, so we only need to search the data in p1 or p2 for matching criteria. So, by limiting the search, it is possible to spend less time and effort matching and searching for the data through all the partitions in the table. This cutting away of the unmatched partitions is known as pruning.

The optimizer can make use of partition pruning for performing the query execution much faster compared to nonpartitioned tables that have the same schema, data, and query statements.

The optimizer can do pruning in the following cases based on the WHERE condition reduction:

- partition_column IN (constant1, constant2, ..., contantN)
- partition_column = constant

In the first case, the optimizer evaluates the partitioning expression for each of the values in the list and creates a list of partitions that are matched during evaluation, and then scanning or searching is performed only on the partitions in this partition list.

In the second case, the optimizer only evaluates the partitioning expression based on the given constant or specific value and determines which partition contains the value, and searching or scanning is performed only on this partition. There can be use of another arithmetic comparison instead of equals for this type of case.

Currently, pruning is not supported on INSERT statements but is supported in SELECT, UPDATE, and DELETE statements.

Pruning is also applicable to short ranges where the optimizer can convert the ranges into an equivalent list of values. The optimizer can be applied when the partitioning expression consists of equality or range that can be reduced to equalities set or if an increasing or decreasing relationship is represented by the partitioning expression.

Pruning can also applicable to the column types of DATE or DATETIME if the partitioning uses the TO_DAYS() or YEAR() function, and also applicable if such tables use the TO_SECONDS() function in their partitioning expression.

Suppose you have a table, tp2, as per the following statement :

```
CREATE TABLE tp2 (
    first_name VARCHAR (30) NOT NULL,
    last_name VARCHAR (30) NOT NULL,
    zone_code TINYINT UNSIGNED NOT NULL,
    doj DATE NOT NULL
)
PARTITION BY RANGE (YEAR(doj)) (
    PARTITION p0 VALUES LESS THAN (1971),
    PARTITION p1 VALUES LESS THAN (1976),
    PARTITION p2 VALUES LESS THAN (1981),
    PARTITION p3 VALUES LESS THAN (1986),
    PARTITION p4 VALUES LESS THAN (1991),
    PARTITION p5 VALUES LESS THAN (1996),
    PARTITION p6 VALUES LESS THAN (2001),
    PARTITION p7 VALUES LESS THAN (2006),
    PARTITION p8 VALUES LESS THAN MAXVALUE
);
```

Now, in the preceding statement the following statements can benefit from partition pruning:

```
SELECT * FROM tp2  WHERE doj = '1982-06-24';
UPDATE tp2  SET region_code = 8 WHERE doj BETWEEN '1991-02-16' AND
'1997-04-26';
DELETE FROM tp2  WHERE doj >= '1984-06-22' AND doj <= '1999-06-22';
```

For the last statement, the optimizer can act as follows:

1. Finding the partition that has the low end of the range as YEAR('1984-06-22') gives the value 1984, found in the p3 partition.
2. Finding the partition that has the high end of the range as YEAR('1999-06-22') gives the value 1999, found in the p5 partition.
3. Scan only the above two identified partitions and any partitions that lie between them.

So, in the above mentioned case the partitions to be scanned are p3, p4, and p5 only, and the rest of the partitions can be ignored while matching.

The preceding examples use RANGE partitioning but partition pruning is also applicable on other types of partitioning as well. Suppose you have the table tp3 schema as per the following statement:

```
CREATE TABLE tp3 (
 first_name VARCHAR (30) NOT NULL,
 last_name VARCHAR (30) NOT NULL,
 zone_code TINYINT UNSIGNED NOT NULL,
 description VARCHAR (250),
 doj DATE NOT NULL
)
PARTITION BY LIST(zone_code) (
 PARTITION p0 VALUES IN (1, 3),
 PARTITION p1 VALUES IN (2, 5, 8),
 PARTITION p2 VALUES IN (4, 9),
 PARTITION p3 VALUES IN (6, 7, 10)
);
```

For the preceding table schema, consider if this statement SELECT * FROM tp3 WHERE zone_code BETWEEN 1 AND 3 is to be executed. The optimizer determines which of the partitions can have the values 1, 2, and 3 and finds p1 and p0, so it skips the rest of the partitions p3 and p2.

Column values with a constant can be pruned, as in the following example statement :

```
UPDATE tp3 set description = 'This is description for Zone 5' WHERE
zone_code = 5;
```

 The optimization is performed only when the size of the range is smaller than the number of partitions.

Partition selection

Explicit selection of partition and subpartition is also supported and this enables row matching to conditions given in the where clause - this is known as partition selection. It is very similar to partition pruning as only specific partitions are scanned for matching, but differs in the following two key aspects:

- The partitions to be scanned are specified by the issuer of the statement and are not automatic such as with partition pruning
- The partition pruning is limited to queries, whereas partition selection supports both queries and a number of DML statements

SQL statements supported for explicit partition selection are listed as follows:

- INSERT
- SELECT
- UPDATE
- REPLACE
- LOAD DATA
- LOAD XML
- DELETE

The following syntax with the PARTITION option is used for explicit partition selection:

```
PARTITION (partition_names)
partition_names :
    partition_name, ...
```

The preceding option is always followed by the table structure or table schema it belongs to. `partition_names` stands for the list of comma separated names of partitions or subpartitions that will be used in partitioning. Partition and subpartition names in `partition_names` can be in any order or even overlap but each name from the list must be the existing partition or subpartition name of the specific table, otherwise the statement will fail with the error message `partition_name` doesn't exist.

If the `PARTITION` option is used, only listed partitions and subpartitions are checked for matching rows. `PARTITION` option can also be used in the `SELECT` statement to retrieve rows belonging to any given partition.

Suppose you have the table `employee` created with the following statements:

```
SET @@SQL_MODE = '';
CREATE TABLE employee (
 id INT NOT NULL AUTO_INCREMENT PRIMARY KEY,
 first_name VARCHAR(25) NOT NULL,
 last_name VARCHAR(25) NOT NULL,
 store_id INT NOT NULL,
 department_id INT NOT NULL
)
 PARTITION BY RANGE(id) (
 PARTITION p0 VALUES LESS THAN (5),
 PARTITION p1 VALUES LESS THAN (10),
 PARTITION p2 VALUES LESS THAN (15),
 PARTITION p3 VALUES LESS THAN MAXVALUE
);
INSERT INTO employee VALUES
 ('', 'Chintan', 'Mehta', 3, 2), ('', 'Bhumil', 'Raval', 1, 2),
 ('', 'Subhash', 'Shah', 3, 4), ('', 'Siva', 'Stark', 2, 4),
 ('', 'Chintan', 'Gajjar', 1, 1), ('', 'Mansi', 'Panchal', 2, 3),
 ('', 'Hetal', 'Oza', 2, 1), ('', 'Parag', 'Patel', 3, 1),
 ('', 'Pooja', 'Shah', 1, 3), ('', 'Samir', 'Bhatt', 2, 4),
 ('', 'Pritesh', 'Shah', 1, 4), ('', 'Jaymin', 'Patel', 3, 2),
 ('', 'Ruchek', 'Shah', 1, 2), ('', 'Chandni', 'Patel', 3, 3),
 ('', 'Mittal', 'Patel', 2, 3), ('', 'Shailesh', 'Patel', 2, 2),
 ('', 'Krutika', 'Dave', 3, 3), ('', 'Dinesh', 'Patel', 3, 2);
```

Now, if you check with partition p1, you see the following output as rows added in partition p1:

```
mysql> SELECT * FROM employee PARTITION (p1);
+----+------------+------------+----------+---------------+
| id | last_name  | last_name  | store_id | department_id |
+----+------------+------------+----------+---------------+
| 5  | Chintan    | Gajjar     | 1        | 1             |
```

```
| 6 | Mansi | Panchal | 2 | 3 |
| 7 | Hetal | Oza | 2 | 1 |
| 8 | Parag | Patel | 3 | 1 |
| 9 | Pooja | Shah | 1 | 3 |
+----+-----------+------------+----------+----------------+
5 rows in set (0.00 sec)
```

If you use this statement `SELECT * FROM employee WHERE id BETWEEN 5 AND 9;`, it will give the same output.

In order to retrieve rows from multiple partitions you can use a comma separated list of partition names. For example, `SELECT * FROM employee PARTITION (p1,p2)`, will result in all the rows from partitions `p1` and `p2` and exclude the remaining partitions.

Any supported partitioning types can be used using partitioning selection statements. MySQL 8 automatically adds partition names when a table is created with the `LINEAR HASH` or `LINEAR KEY` partitioning types specified without any names, and this is also applicable to subpartitions as well. While executing the `SELECT` statement on this table you can specify partition names generated by MySQL 8 for partition specific data retrieval.

The `PARTITION` option is also applicable on the `SELECT` statement for the `INSERT ...` `SELECT` statement, by which we can insert data retrieved from specific partitions or subpartitions as well.

The `PARTITION` option is also applicable on the `SELECT` statement with join queries on tables with specific partition or subpartition data.

Restrictions and limitations in partitioning

In this section, you will see the restrictions and limitations in MySQL 8 partitioning, covering prohibited constructs, performance considerations, and limitation aspects related to storage engines and functions in detail, to gain optimum benefits from the table partitioning.

Partitioning keys, primary keys, and unique keys

The relationship between partitioning keys with primary keys and unique keys is very important for partition schema structure design. To say the rule in one line it will be that All the columns used in the partitioning in the partition table must include every unique key of the table. So every unique key, including the primary key column on the table, must be part of the partitioning expression. Take a look at the following example for the CREATE TABLE statement using a unique key that does not adhere to the rule:

```
CREATE TABLE tk1 (
    cl1 INT NOT NULL,
    cl2 DATE NOT NULL,
    cl3 INT NOT NULL,
    cl4 INT NOT NULL,
    UNIQUE KEY (cl1, cl2)
)
PARTITION BY HASH(cl3)
PARTITIONS 4;

CREATE TABLE tk2 (
    cl1 INT NOT NULL,
    cl2 DATE NOT NULL,
    cl3 INT NOT NULL,
    cl4 INT NOT NULL,
    UNIQUE KEY (cl1),
    UNIQUE KEY (cl3)
)
PARTITION BY HASH(cl1 + cl3)
PARTITIONS 4;
```

In each of the preceding statements for the creation of table tk1 and tk2 the proposed table can have at least one unique key that does not include all columns in the partition expression.

Now look at the following modified table creation statements, which are made to work and are turned from invalid to valid statements:

```
CREATE TABLE tk1 (
  cl1 INT NOT NULL,
  cl2 DATE NOT NULL,
  cl3 INT NOT NULL,
  cl4 INT NOT NULL,
  UNIQUE KEY (cl1, cl2, cl3)
)
PARTITION BY HASH(cl3)
PARTITIONS 4;
```

```
CREATE TABLE tk2 (
 c11 INT NOT NULL,
 c12 DATE NOT NULL,
 c13 INT NOT NULL,
 c14 INT NOT NULL,
 UNIQUE KEY (c11, c13)
)
PARTITION BY HASH(c11 + c13)
PARTITIONS 4;
```

If you take a look at the following table structure, it cannot be partitioned at all because there is no way to include both the unique key columns that can be part of partitioning key columns:

```
CREATE TABLE tk4 (
 c11 INT NOT NULL,
 c12 INT NOT NULL,
 c13 INT NOT NULL,
 c14 INT NOT NULL,
 UNIQUE KEY (c11, c13),
 UNIQUE KEY (c12, c14)
);
```

As per the definition, every primary key is a unique key. The restriction is also applicable on a table's primary key, if any. The following are two examples for table tk5 and tk6 that are invalid statements:

```
CREATE TABLE tk5 (
 c11 INT NOT NULL,
 c12 DATE NOT NULL,
 c13 INT NOT NULL,
 c14 INT NOT NULL,
 PRIMARY KEY(c11, c12)
)
PARTITION BY HASH(c13)
PARTITIONS 4;

CREATE TABLE tk6 (
 c11 INT NOT NULL,
 c12 DATE NOT NULL,
 c13 INT NOT NULL,
 c14 INT NOT NULL,
 PRIMARY KEY(c11, c13),
 UNIQUE KEY(c12)
)
PARTITION BY HASH( YEAR(c12) )
PARTITIONS 4;
```

In both the preceding statements, the corresponding primary key is not included in all the columns referenced as in the partitioning expression. The following statements are valid:

```
CREATE TABLE tk7 (
 cl1 INT NOT NULL,
 cl2 DATE NOT NULL,
 cl3 INT NOT NULL,
 cl4 INT NOT NULL,
 PRIMARY KEY(cl1, cl2)
)
PARTITION BY HASH(cl1 + YEAR(cl2))
PARTITIONS 4;

CREATE TABLE tk8 (
 cl1 INT NOT NULL,
 cl2 DATE NOT NULL,
 cl3 INT NOT NULL,
 cl4 INT NOT NULL,
 PRIMARY KEY(cl1, cl2, cl4),
 UNIQUE KEY(cl2, cl1)
)
PARTITION BY HASH(cl1 + YEAR(cl2))
PARTITIONS 4;
```

If the table does not have a unique key or primary key then the restriction is not applicable, and any column or columns can be used in the partitioning expression as per compatible column types for the partitioning type. All above restrictions are also applicable to the ALTER TABLE statements as well.

Partitioning limitations relating to storage engines

Partitioning support is not provided by MySQL server but from the storage engine's own or native partitioning handler in MySQL 8. In MySQL 8, the InnoDB storage engine only provides a native partitioning handler and so the partitioned table creation is not applicable with any other storage engine.

ALTER TABLE ... OPTIMIZE PARTITION does not work correctly with the InnoDB storage engine, so instead use the ALTER TABLE ... REBUILD PARTITION and ALTER TABLE ... ANALYZE PARTITION operations for such tables.

Partitioning limitations relating to functions

In partitioning expressions only the following listed MySQL functions are allowed in MySQL 8:

- `ABS()`: It provides an absolute value for the given argument
- `CEILING()`: It provides the smallest integer number possible for the given argument
- `DAY()`: It provides the day of the month for the given date
- `DAYOFMONTH()`: It provides the day of the month for the given date same as `DAY()`
- `DAYOFWEEK()`: It provides the weekday number for the given date
- `DAYOFYEAR()`: It provides the day of the year for the given date
- `DATEDIFF()`: It provides the number of days between two given dates
- `EXTRACT()`: It provides part of the given argument
- `FLOOR()`: It provides the largest integer value possible for the given argument
- `HOUR()`: It provides the hour from the given argument
- `MICROSECOND()`: It provides the microseconds from the given argument
- `MINUTE()`: It provides the minute from the given argument
- `MOD()`: It performs the Modulo operation and provides the remainder of `N` divided by `M` where `MOD(N,M)`
- `MONTH()`: It provides the month from the given argument
- `QUARTER()`: It provides the quarter from the given argument
- `SECOND()`: It provides the second from the given argument
- `TIME_TO_SEC()`: It provides the second from the given time value argument
- `TO_DAYS()`: It provides the number of days from year 0 for the given argument
- `TO_SECONDS()`: It provides the number of seconds from the year 0 for the given argument
- `UNIX_TIMESTAMP() (with TIMESTAMP columns)`: It provides the seconds since '1970-01-01 00:00:00' UTC for the given argument
- `WEEKDAY()`: It provides the weekday index for the given argument
- `YEAR()`: It provides the year for the given argument
- `YEARWEEK()`: It provides the year and week for the given argument

Partition pruning supports the `TO_DAYS()`, `TO_SECONDS()`, `TO_YEAR()`, and `UNIX_TIMESTAMP()` functions in MySQL 8.

Summary

In this chapter, we learned about different types of partitioning and the need for partitions. We also covered detailed information on managing all types of partitions. We learned about partition pruning and selection of partitions which is used by the optimizer. We also discussed applicable limitations and restrictions to consider while using partitioning.

In the next chapter, you will learn how to do scaling in MySQL 8, and discover common challenges faced when providing scalability in MySQL 8. You will also learn how to make the MySQL server highly available and achieve high availability.

10
MySQL 8 – Scalability and High Availability

In this chapter, we will cover the following important topics for MySQL 8 scalability and high availability:

- Overview of scalability and high availability in MySQL 8
- Scaling MySQL 8
- Challenges in scaling MySQL 8
- Achieving high availability

Before we move on to the details, let's have an overview of scalability and high availability in MySQL 8

Overview of scalability and high availability in MySQL 8

In any type of application, be it mobile, web portals, websites, social, e-commerce, enterprise or cloud applications, data is the core portion of the business. Data availability is considered an utmost concern for any business or organization. Data loss or any downtime of an application can result in a heavy loss in terms of money and also impact the credit of the company in the market.

If we consider an example of an online shopping site which has a nicely covered market in a specific area, with customers and good business credit. If this business faced an issue with data loss or any application server or database server downtime, it would impact the whole business. Many customers would lose faith in the business and also the business would suffer a loss both in terms of finance and credit.

There is no single formula that can provide a solution. Different businesses have their own application requirements, business needs, distinct processes, different infrastructure in different locations, and operational competencies. In these circumstances, technology plays a major role in achieving high availability.

As per the requirements of scalability and high availability, MySQL can be used for various applications, and as per need it is capable of overcoming failures, including failures of MySQL, failures from the operating system, or any planned maintenance activity that may impact availability. Scalability in simple terms, that has the capability to distribute database load and application queries between MySQL servers.

The attributes that matter when choosing the right solution for high availability depend on to what extent the system can be called highly available, as such requirements vary from system to system. For smaller applications, where the user load is not expected to be very high, setting up the replication or cluster environment can result in very high cost. In such cases, providing the correct configuration of the MySQL can also be enough to reduce application load.

The following sections briefly describe the primary solutions supported by MySQL 8 for high availability.

MySQL replication

MySQL replication allows data from one server to be replicated onto the multiple MySQL servers. MySQL replication provides master-slave design, so that one of the servers from the group acts as a master where write operations are performed from the application and then the master server copies the data to the multiple slave servers. Replication is a well established solution for high availability and is used by the social giants such as Facebook, Twitter, and so on.

MySQL cluster

This is another popular high availability solution for MySQL. Clustering enables data to be replicated to multiple MySQL servers with automated sharing. It is designed for better availability and throughput.

Oracle MySQL cloud service

Oracle MySQL cloud service provides an efficient means to help build a secure, cost-effective MySQL database as a service for applications used in modern world. It proves to be scalable and cost-efficient with less resource utilization for managing the service when compared to on-premises.

MySQL with the Solaris cluster

The sun Solaris cluster provided by the MySQL data service provides a mechanism for orderly startup and shutdown, fault monitoring, and automatic failover of the MySQL service. The following MySQL components are protected by the sun cluster HA for the MySQL data service.

There are some further options available using third-party solutions. Each architecture that is used to achieve highly available database services is differentiated by the levels of uptime that each offers. These architectures can be grouped into three main categories:

- Data replication
- Clustered and virtualized systems
- Geographically-replicated clusters

Based on the best answer to the question, you can select the right option for your application with optimal cost and a highly available solution. This discussion gives us a fair overview of MySQL 8's high availability.

Scaling MySQL 8

Scalability is the ability to distribute the load of any application queries across various MySQL instances. For some cases, it is unpredictable that data cannot exceed up to some limit or the number of users will not go out of bounds. Scalable databases would be a preferable solution so that, at any point, we can meet unexpected demands of scale. MySQL is a rewarding database system for its scalability, which can scale horizontally and vertically; in terms of data, distribution of client queries across various MySQL instances is quite feasible. It is pretty easy to add horsepower to the MySQL cluster to handle the load.

The requirements for achieving **High Availability (HA)** and scalability may vary from system to system. Each system requires a different configuration in order to achieve these abilities. There are many questions that come to mind when we think about scaling in MySQL, and while we perform scaling operations in MySQL:

- Why is scaling required?
- What are the advantages of scaling in MySQL?
- What points need to put across in our minds when we perform scaling in MySQL?
- How will scaling work?
- Is it secure for data - does it provide surety of data security?
- Plus many more...

Let's take a real time example to understand why we need scaling in MySQL. We have an online e-commerce website that has covered a small market, with limited users and limited hits on the website, with a single database server. The business is growing up nicely; the performance of the business is continuously increasing and the user count is increasing, and with our single database server all requests and performance cannot be scaled at all time. This may possibly result in a server crash and the business might face loss in terms of profit and credit in the market. To avoid such a situation, scalability will perform a major part. If any request from a customer fails due to any reason, or if the node goes down, the other node will take care of it quickly and give the appropriate response to the customer.

Scaling is required for the continuous increase in performance of database response time and to improve the productivity of the product. It will help the end product in terms of data scalability, performance, and better results. Cluster and replication are both key features in MySQL that can be leveraged for scaling.

Scaling using cluster

Basic cluster architecture is divided into four different layers:

- Client node
- Application node
- Management node
- Data node

These are shown in the following image:

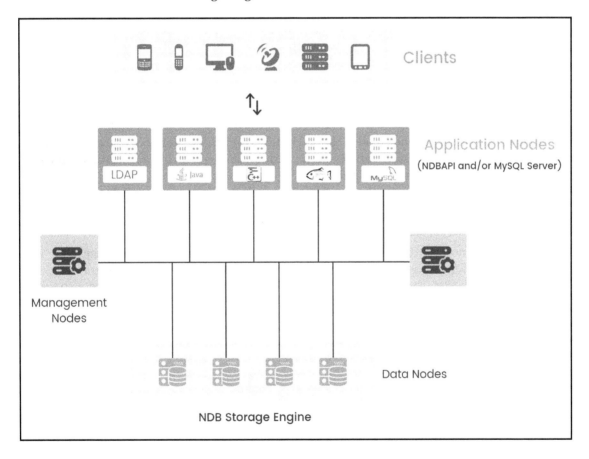

Client node

The client node is an end user or application that sends a request for any query in terms of read data or write data from a different device, such as a computer, mobile, tablet, and so on.

Application node

The application node is meant to provide the bridge between the logic of the application and the nodes containing the data in MySQL. Applications can access the data, which is stored in the MySQL cluster, by SQL, with one or many MySQL servers using the function of SQL. In the application we have multiple technologies from where we connect to the MySQL server. We connect MySQL server with standard the MySQL connectors, which gives us the ability to connect with a wide range of access technologies.

As another option, we have NDB API; a high performance interface that can be used to control real-time user experiences and provide better throughput. In MySQL we have NDB API, which adds a layer additionally to NoSQL interfaces that consist capability to access the cluster directly. Application nodes can fetch data from all the data nodes, so the only cause of failure can be the unavailability of application services, as the application can use all data nodes to perform data manipulation.

Management node

The management node performs the important role of publishing relevant cluster information across the nodes in its cluster, along with node management. Nodes for management work at startup when all nodes want to join the MySQL cluster and also when reconfiguration of the system is required. The management node can be stopped and restart all services without damaging or impacting an ongoing operation, execution, or processing of data and the application node.

Data node

The data nodes stores the data. Tables get shared across the data nodes, which also helps to handle load balancing, replication, and high availability failover.

Data nodes are the main nodes of a MySQL cluster solution. It provides the following functionality and benefits:

Data storage and management of disk-based and in-memory data

In a shared-nothing scenario, data is stored in at least one replica without the use of shared-disk space. MySQL create one replica of the database which does a synchronous replication process. If any data node fails due to any specific reason, the replicated data will take care of it and provide the respective output. It does a synchronous copy of the node so it consists of the same data as the main node data.

We can store the data either in memory or partially on disk based on the requirement. Data that frequently change are suggested to be stored in-memory. In-memory data is routinely checked with the local disk and coordinates to update the data to the rest of the data nodes.

Automatic and user-defined partitioning of tables or sharding of tables

MySQL cluster provides low latency, high throughput, scalability, and high availability. This adopts horizontal scaling and auto sharding to serve heavy load read/write operations through the different NoSQL queries. An NDB cluster is a set of different nodes where each task is running on its own processor.

Synchronous data replication between data nodes

When we have data replication for the data node it follows synchronous replication, so at any time all node data will be in-sync. If any node fails for any reason, the other nodes have the same data and so will be able to provide the data for a query. So, without any downtime for data response, MySQL provides a perfect solution.

Data retrieval and transactions

MySQL supports each of the transactions that can be mapped, as it is committed on the master server and applied on the slave server. This method is not referring to `binlog` files or the relevant position in the `binlog` file. `GTID` replication is solely working based on transactions; it becomes very easy to identify whether the master and the slave servers are in sync or not.

Automatic fail over

If any data node fails for any reason, the other nodes take responsibility and gives the response to the request. Replication of the database is very helpful in critical conditions of downtime or a failure in any of the nodes.

Automatic re-synchronization for self-healing after failure

If any node is failed it will start automatically and again perform the synchronization of data to the rest of the nodes, which are active nodes, and copy all recent data in the node. In that case it does self-healing of the failures.

Scaling using memcached in MySQL 8

In MySQL 8, using memcached is one of the ways to achieve scalability. Memcached is a simple and highly scalable solution for storing data in key and value form in cache whenever memory is available. Memcached is commonly used for quick access of data. Data stored in memory doesn't have I/O operations performed for fetching the data.

As all the information is stored in memory, the access speed for data is much faster than compared to loading every time from disk and results in a better query execution time on the database server. This plugin also has the feature of serialization, which converts binary files, code blocks, or any other objects to strings that can be stored, and provides a simple means to retrieve such objects. While specifying a memory allocation it should not be larger than the available physical memory of the server.

If you specify too large of a value then some of the memory allocated for memcached will use swap space and not physical memory. This may lead to delays when storing and retrieving values because data is swapped to disk instead of storing the data directly in memory:

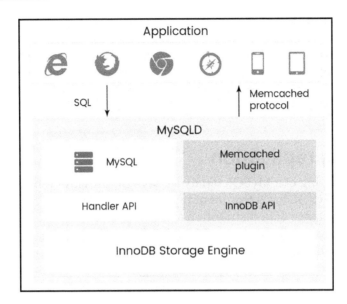

The preceding image depicts memcached architecture, which displays the flow of the data from memcached to a client or an end user, or a request of the data from an application.

The data in memcached never gets stored in the database. It's always available in memory itself. If either of the memcached servers fail, data will be fetched from the database, so it will not impact end-users for data retrieval or have a major performance impact on the application. The only thing need to keep in mind while we use a memcached server is that data related to any important information, for instance a financial transaction, should not be placed in memcached. In that case if there is a failure in memcached, the data might not be retrieved. In a memcached server data integrity is not healthy as it stores in memory, so during failure it would be good to have data that is important not saved in memcached. When configuring a memcached server, memory size is the key factor. If there is improper configuration, then you can expect a bad situation.

This way we can use memcached to scale the MySQL server for an increased data response time, and to provide faster performance. It will reduce the load on MySQL server and multiple servers as a part of cache group and also provides an interface for multiple languages. It is suggested to be used ideally when there are heavy read operations.

NoSQL APIs

MySQL cluster provides numerous ways to help access the data store. One of most generic way is leveraging SQL; however, in real-world use cases we can also depend on native APIs, which allow the fetching of the data from within the database without affecting performance or adding further complexity by developing an application to convert SQL.

Scaling using replication

Replication is the copying of a MySQL database. MySQL provides replication with a different approach. MySQL has a feature of replication that provides scale-out solutions, data security, long distance data distribution and many more benefits. We have discussed this at length in Chapter 8, *Replication in MySQL 8*. The following image explains the basic architecture of replication in MySQL:

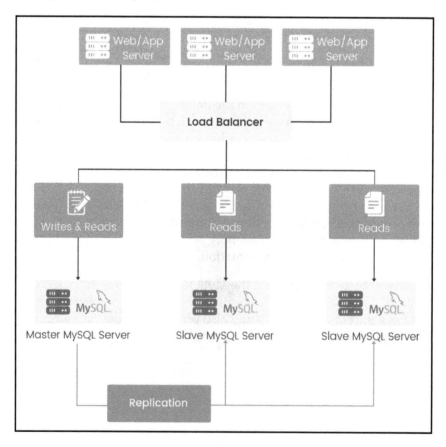

Replication is one of the best features of MySQL. It simply creates a copy of the data to the new server or another physical machine, which will import the data from the master server. Whenever the data is required it will populate the accurate results. It follows the master and slave approach for the replication. The master database is the actual database of the application and the slave database is created by MySQL in the database server of another physical server, which contains replicated data from the master server. We can configure the slave database for the specific operation, such as when the query relates to reading the data from the database; we can execute this on the slave server. In this case the master data will have less load than earlier. Suppose we have a ratio of the 40% write data query and 60% read data query; in this case if we have a single server it will handle all operations related to the read and write operation. But, as defined in the preceding image we have replicated the database in two different servers and read operations are performed on the slave servers, so we can make use of one of the slave server to perform complex read queries. This makes it possible to generate reports for doing data analysis on MySQL 8, as performing complex read queries will not impact the overall application performance.

In standard MySQL replication the master server creates binary log files and maintains the index of the log files to maintain and keep track of log rotation. The binary log files serve the records updates and are sent to the slave server. When the slave server connects to the master database server it considers the last position it has read in the log files, after which the slave server then receives any updates that have taken place since that time. The slave subsequently blocks and waits for the master to notify it for further updates.

The question in mind is why do we need replication? Or, what is the purpose of the replication? If replication requires another database server, complexity, and additional configuration, it increases the maintenance and monitoring time. Still, we have many additional benefits for business and database admin.

Single server dependancy

In any case, if the master database server fails we can easily switch our database connection to the replicated slave server to provide stability in critical situations. This includes if there is network failure, server failure, hardware issues, and many more reasons for failure.

Performance

Performance is the main part in the database. When we have a distributed database over multiple servers we can connect different applications to different database servers to increase performance. This feature reduces the response time of the query.

Backup and recovery

Replication helps back up the master database. It is more efficient than storing the database on disk. Users can store the database in the master using the replicated database as a backup instead of digging up the backup files. When required to restore the data of the master server a user can easily get it from the slave server, with no need to work on the backup files and go about finding the last updates and other operations.

Load distribution

By using the replication load of the database, query execution can be reduced; we can split read and write operations over the databases. If we execute write operations in the master database and read operations in the slave database that will improve the response time of the application. We can create load balanced environments in MySQL, which share the load of all requests to the database server. The load balancer then further sends requests to the database that can handle each transaction with much better throughput.

Asynchronous data replication

Asynchronous data replication means that data is copied from one machine to another, with a resultant delay. This delay is based on networking bandwidth, resource availability, or a time interval set by the administrator in configuration. The correct configuration and time setting provides an accurate result in response. It's based on the network administrator's configuration. Synchronous data replication implies that data is committed to one or more machines at the same time.

Geographical data distribution

Group replication makes it possible to copy the master's data to the slave server that resides at a remote location and perform the read operations for a separate group of client without impacting the master's operations.

GTID replication

Global transaction identifiers (GTID) uses transaction based replication of data instead of binary log file based replication. Until and unless transactions that have been operated and committed on the master servers are present on all the slave servers, GTID will not consider replication in a consistent state.

In MySQL 8 replication can be done either in asynchronous mode or in semi-synchronous mode. In asynchronous mode, write operations are performed on the master server immediately, while replication in slaves is done periodically as per the configuration.

In the semi-synchronous mode of replication, if semi-synchronous configuration is enabled on the master and at least one slave server, a transaction on the master node waits before getting a transaction time out until the semi-synchronous enabled node confirms that required data or update has been received. And on time-out, the master node again looks for the semi-synchronous slave and performs the replication.

MySQL 8 provides a new replication method, GTID, where a unique identifier is created and connected with each transaction saved or committed on the master server. The uniqueness of these identifiers is in all servers that are in the server where it's created, and also in the replicated servers. GTID have one to one mapping between all transactions. The concept of the log file referencing a position within files is not required when starting a new slave creation or failover to a new MySQL master. You can use either row-based or statement-based replication with GTIDs.

Using a global transaction ID primarily provides two major benefits:

- **It's easy to change a master server to connect with a slave server during failover**: GTID is unique out of all servers in the replication group. The slave server remembers the global transaction ID of the last event from the old master. This means it becomes easy to identify where to reinitialize replication on the new MySQL master, as the global transaction IDs are known throughout the entire replication hierarchy.
- **The status of the slave provides a crash-safe method**: The slave holds current position information in the `mysql.gtid_slave_pos` system table. If this table is using a transactional storage engine (such as `InnoDB`, which is the default), then further updates are done in the same transaction.

A GTIDs is a unique key created and associated with each transaction (insert and update operations) committed on the master server. The key is not only unique to the master server, but it's unique across all servers in replication.

ZFS replication

The ZFS file system has the ability to provision a snapshot of the server files, such as file system contents, transfer the snapshot to another machine, and extract the snapshot to recreate the file system on a different server. Users can create a snapshot at any time and can create as many snapshots as required. By continually creating, transferring, and restoring snapshots, it can provide synchronization between one or more machines in a fashion similar to DRBD.

We have seen all the possible ways to scale a database in MySQL, using different techniques. As per business need and flexibility we can perform scaling with database backup. Scaling is not an easy task but its possible in MySQL 8, with the proper knowledge and understanding of the requirements of the business and a configuration provided by MySQL 8. For database scaling, we must have proper understanding of the entire workflow of the database and communication approach.

Challenges in scaling MySQL 8

We have seen how scaling works and the advantages and purpose of scaling in the previous topic. When we start working with scaling in MySQL 8, what type of challenges will we face, and what steps need to be kept in mind while we work towards scaling? We have to account for if we are doing scaling and the master server fails, limits are reached, read and write operations are not able to handle the requests of the application, or while re-platforming the database. Scaling is not an easy task; it needs to ensure it is able to handle increasing transactions without any difficulty. At the time of performing the scaling we need to keep in mind many points, such as the write and read operation limits in the master and slave servers. Database load balancing is one of the approaches that help reduce the traffic of the transaction, but again it needs perfection, and needs to understand the load balancing configuration properly. The following are the major challenges faced when we perform scaling.

Business type and flexibility

This is the first point that needs to kept in mind while we perform the scaling. Business type or business behavior is the core part; if the business is an e-commerce, we already know e-commerce businesses have a number of functionalities and very critical data about clients, such as product details, monopoly of the business for offers and discounts. The main thing is customer details and payment information such as credit card details, debit card details, and customer feedback.

In this case, while we are doing scaling in MySQL 8, all parameters need to kept in mind, such as database back up, security, roles/privileges of the database and backward compatibility of the scaling. While doing scaling by clustering all data nodes need to be on the same page. If the application is developed using multiple technologies and we perform the scaling for each of the stack, we can have different data nodes available; in this case the database sync is one of the most important things that need to be sure in configuration while scaling. Which type of data should reside in cached memory in memcached and in disk should also be clear before we design scaling.

The behavior of the application accesses data from the shared data nodes. If we have an e-commerce site and we perform the sharding for the same and at a certain level the data are not available for the client who uses the data of the other shard server for any reason, at that time the cross-node transaction would be required. It's completely based on the business behavior, and depends on how flexible the business is when it comes to accepting changes regarding database scaling.

Understand server workload

For the setup of flexibility, scale, and performance improvement many options and actions are available in MySQL 8. Many people face issues while performing such activities because they do not have enough understanding or knowledge to handle various technology stacks and configuration option selections that can improve scalability, performance, security, and the flexibility of the application and deployment activity. These configuration options including clustering, replication, sharding, memcached, storage engine, and many more, which can be well designed to handle the whole workload of the application. The database workload and business behavior helps to decide the MySQL configuration.

Read-write operation limit

What happen if the read and write limit is reached and the transaction increases on the master database server. MySQL has limitations to the capacity; for instance if a number of customers are visiting the site at the same time that a read-write operation is running and the server or node are not synced, then at that time it will create confusion or misunderstanding for the end user. Or, in an e-commerce site, if one customer is purchasing the product, which is last item left in stock, and at same time another customer searches for the same product and it's still available, in this case both operations are not in sync in terms of the read and write operation of the database.

In the end, the other customer might purchase the same product, which we don't have in the warehouse. This impacts inventory calculation, and customers have doubts about the process of the purchase cycle. In that case we would loose the faith of the customer in the business and the credit of the business would also be impacted.

Another approach is to have database sharding. Sharding can be simply stated as partitioning the database in multiple servers. Sharding helps to reduce the load on a single database or the master database. If we have databases sharding geographically, and for different country or region we have different servers for the database, we can solve the issue of the limit of read and write operations on the MySQL server. But again, the technique which we use for the sharding also determines the performance of the database. We have already learned about this in detail in Chapter 9, *Partitioning in MySQL 8*.

Maintenance

While we have performed scaling in MySQL 8, we must know how to manage master and slave servers, and which configuration is required while performing scaling. What are the steps that need to be taken care of at the time when the server is in a critical stage? What steps needs to be performed at time of sharding, clustering, or replication of the database server?

Scaling is possible but its not an easy operation. If we want to perform scaling we should know that the database can handle more transactions without any issue. We should know the appropriate configuration to be done to overcome the default limits on the master server for the write and read operation. Once it's completed, we need to perform similarly steps to configure the slave database server, which should only have read operations available for the end user and should always be in sync with the master database.

If we have multiple servers, then the maintenance of the server also becomes a costly overhead. All the server needs to be on same page, configuration should be in proper manner, and the cost of the server will also affect the business. If the number of data constantly increases at that time, server space also needs to be managed in an appropriate manner.

Master server failure

If the master server fails and data is not available to the customer at that time, the end user will get frustrated and the business will be hampered in terms of credit in market and in losing the customer also. The business will have to suffer from the loss.

Synchronization

Whether we perform the scaling with clustering or replication, in both cases we need to secure synchronization. All slave servers should have the same database as the master server. If write operations are performed on the master server and read operations are performed on the slave server, at that time all data needs to be synced up. All results should be same, and if any server goes down at a time when data was not synced, it will create issues regarding the loss of data.

Database security

How do we secure the database if we have different servers and sharding is performed? If we have different database servers at different locations and access to the database is not restricted to the user specific at that time then the issue of a data leak is a strong possibility. We have to completely understand access points of the data in terms of IP configuration of the database server, with appropriate roles and privileges for the database users who perform various activities. Which IPs have access and which IPs need to restrict the data transaction from the server? While we are performing the cross node transaction on the database, accurate data should be available; it should not give the permission to access restricted data from the server.

Cross node transaction

Cross node transaction is required when we have multiple nodes after doing scaling and one node requires the other node data as a part of input. For instance, if we have different nodes at different locations and we have a single inventory for all the locations at that time, one user request for any product that is not available in that data node at that time will have to communicate with other data nodes for the information of the product, based on the user's request.

Growing team for development

While the application may have a positive response and its continuous success increase the business team, the expansion of the database administrators will also be required. When we performing sharing and scaling or replication in MySQL 8, we require appropriate team members with the proper knowledge and experience to handle continuous expansion and the management of database servers. It's not only limited to the setup of database servers; we also need to keep an eye on maintenance of the server and keep watching the server activity also.

Manage change request

When we have a change in any database structure and we have already performed the scaling or replication than a few things need to be taken care of as part of a change request, or if we add a new feature or an enhancement of the functionality. This includes things such as updating sharing keys, modifying the data distribution with replication of the nodes, updating the queries to take replication latency into account to avoid stale data with on-going managing shards, data balancing, and ensuring that data is available with new updates.

Scale-up and scale-out

Scale-up describes the process of maximizing the capacity that a single MySQL node can handle. The process of scaling-up can involve optimally tuning your database software and choosing the right storage engine, as previously discussed in `Chapter 6`, *MySQL 8 Storage Engines,* and selecting appropriate hardware. There are limits on how far you can scale-up a node and these are determined by some combination of data size, schema complexity, CPU cycles, system memory, and disk IO operations. While scale-out has been garnering much attention because of the need to handle increasingly massive data sets, it is very important to remember that the better we scale-up, the fewer scale-out nodes that we will require and so the less we need to spend on hardware.

Scale-out can be used to deliver solutions that cover several different use cases. Some of most common ones are to increase read capacity by using replication or to use database sharding to increase total database size and overall transaction throughput.

All of these are the key challenges faced while scaling MySQL 8. These challenges need to be considered while we are performing scaling of the database in MySQL 8. A single mistake can put a business into an situation which none of us would like to be in. Scaling is the the better way to improve the performance of the database.

Achieving high availability

High availability refers to systems that are durable and can perform operations without any hindrance on the data that is required for the response or any request from any mobile, web portals, websites, social, e-commerce, enterprise, and cloud applications. Data availability is considered an utmost concern for any business or organization. Any issues with downtime may have an impact on the business credit, and in some cases businesses have to suffer financial loss.

For instance, if we have an e-commerce application with a single database server, if that server goes down for reasons such as hardware failure, network issue, virus, or operating system issues, it impacts the data also. An e-commerce application may have a large number of customer hits at same time, and any server failures to serve the response to user requests will impact the user; they will search for other options for the purchase commodity.

MySQL 8 has capabilities to provide backend for the application to help achieve high availability and prepare a fully scalable system. An ability of the system to keep the connection persistent, in case a part of the infrastructure fails, and the ability of the system to recover from such failures is considered high availability. A failure of the system can be caused by either a maintenance activity on one part of the system, such as a hardware or software upgrade, or by the failure of the installed software.

Purpose of high availability

The requirements for achieving HA and scalability may vary from system to system. Each system requires a different configuration in order to achieve these abilities. MySQL 8 also supports different approaches, such as the replication of data across multiple MySQL servers, or preparing multiple data centers based on geographical locations and serving the client requests from the data centers closest to the location of the client. Such solutions can be used to achieve the highest uptime of MySQL.

Today, in the world of competitive marketing, an organization's key point is to have their system up and running. Any failure or downtime directly impacts business and revenue. Hence, high availability is a factor that cannot be overlooked. MySQL is quite reliable and has constant availability using cluster and replication configurations. Cluster servers instantly handle failures and manage the failover part to keep your system available almost all the time. If one server gets down, it will redirect the user's request to another node and perform the requested operation.

Data availability

Data is always available in any situation. In any application, data is the core part, which is actually the wealth of the application owner. If we have a health care system and at the time of medical check up of any patient their data is not available, due to server downtime or any other reason, it might block further process of the doctor and in this case impacts the life of the patient.

Security of data

The first thing that comes to mind is securing data, because nowadays data has become precious and it can impact business continuity if legal obligations are not met; in fact, it can be so bad that it can close down your business in no time. MySQL is the most secure and reliable database management system, used by many well-known enterprises such as Facebook, Twitter, and Wikipedia. It really provides a good security layer that protects sensitive information from intruders. MySQL gives access control management so that granting and revoking required access on the user is easy. Roles can also be defined with a list of permissions that can be granted or revoked for the user. All user passwords are stored in an encrypted format using plugin-specific algorithms.

Synchronization of data

While we have a single database server, if it goes down for any reason we would lose the whole database, and if we have database backup available up to the current day, we can restore the database till that day, but all current transactions would also be lost in this case. The last transaction data would not be available at that time.

Backup of the data

Database backup till the last transaction should be in the plan when a business has any server base application where a single database server is performing all the tasks. When doing high availability, include all scenarios of the backup and restore operation in the architecture.

Competitive market

In the market many competitors are available with the same nature of business. In this case, if a business is having issues with data availability to end users, customers might not continue with that business and instead move to another provider. Its an integral part of business continuity.

Performance

High availability is also important in terms of the performance of the data operation. If we have a single server and all operations are performed on that server only, it will reach its limit at some stage, where the server capacity is exhausted. So, in that case, if we have high availability architecture implemented it would provide a means to load the balance of a transaction and the performance of the data manipulation operation. Replication and clustering enables for better concurrency and manages the workload.

Updates in the system

While any online site or application requires updates or any new production release is planned it directly impacts the end users. If an application has only limited users at that time, we can manage the update regarding all end-users via emails or messages within the application before the release. But in cases where there are a large number of user in a single application, at that time it will impact the business. It will stop all users at the same time, and due to this running transactions would be impacted.

Choosing the solution

Again, we have to think about selecting the right solution for the availability. Many things need to be kept in mind while we plan high availability in MySQL. The requirements for achieving HA and scalability may vary from system to system. Each system requires a different configuration in order to achieve these abilities.

Such solutions can be used to achieve the highest uptime of MySQL with regard to the following:

- The level of availability required
- The type of application being deployed
- Accepted best practices within your own environment

In MySQL, replication and clustering are the best options for achieving high availability. All applications have their own architecture, and nature of their business needs to be considered when we are selecting any technique to achieve high availability of MySQL 8.

Advantages of high availability

The following are the advantages that we have when we perform high availability in MySQL:

- MySQL is quite reliable and has constant availability using cluster and replication configurations.
- Cluster servers instantly handle failures and manage the failover part to keep your system available almost all the time. If one server goes down, it will redirect the user's request to another node and perform the requested operation.
- An ability of the system to keep the connection persistent, in case a part of infrastructure fails, and the ability of the system to recover from such failure is considered as high availability.
- MySQL 8 also supports different approaches such as replication of data across multiple MySQL servers or preparing multiple data centers based on geographical locations and serving the client requests from the data centers closest to the location of the client.
- MySQL gives high speed transaction processing with optimal speed. It can cache the results, which boosts read performance.
- Replication and clustering enables better concurrency and manages the workload. Group replication basically takes care of committing transactions once most of the members in group replication have acknowledged the transaction has been received concurrently. This helps create better throughput if the overall number of writes does not exceed the capacity of the members in the group replication.
- Clustering enables data to be replicated to multiple MySQL servers with automated sharing. It is designed for better availability and throughput.

- Memcached removes the SQL layer and directly accesses the InnoDB database tables. Hence, overhead operations like SQL parsing will no longer be executed, which really impacts the performance.
- Memcached with MySQL also provides you with a way to make in-memory data persistent so that we can use it for various data types without losing it.
- Memcached APIs are available in different programming languages such as Perl, Python, Java, PHP, C, and Ruby. With the help of a Memcached API, an application can interact with the Memcached interface to store and retrieve information.

Summary

In this chapter, we started with an overview of scalability and high availability in MySQL 8, which covered the various scalability needs, advantages, methods, and key points to be noted when we make scalable designs of MySQL 8. We also discussed the shortcomings that we generally come across when we perform scalability and how to overcome challenges with appropriate solutions. We have learned about scaling in MySQL 8 and troubleshooting challenges in scaling MySQL 8. We also learned about many diverse ways to achieve high availability in MySQL 8.

In the following chapter, we will learn how to take care of MySQL 8 security. We will learn about general factors that affect security, the security of core MySQL 8 files, access control, and securing the database system itself. We will also learn the details of security plugins and gain an in-depth understanding of database security in general for relational databases.

11
MySQL 8 – Security

In previous chapters, we learned about the scalability of MySQL 8 and how to troubleshoot challenges when scaling MySQL 8. Apart from that, we also learned how to make MySQL 8 highly available for use. Nowadays, security is important for any application, right? When we talk about security, it includes account management, roles, privileges, and more. Considering these aspects, we will cover all of these topics in this chapter. This chapter mainly focuses on MySQL 8 database security and its related features. The following topics are covered in this chapter:

- Overview of security for MySQL 8
- Common security issues
- Access control in MySQL 8
- Account management in MySQL 8
- Encryption in MySQL 8
- Security plugins

Overview of security for MySQL 8

The term security is not bound to a specific topic; it covers a wide range of topics related to MySQL 8. Before starting a detailed discussion on it, let's mention some important points related to security:

- Consider security within a database where users and their privileges related to various database objects need to manage.
- Password security for users.

- Security configuration during the installation process, which includes various types of files, such as log files, data files, and many more. These files must be protected for their read/write operations.
- To handle system level failure scenarios, you must have a backup and recovery plan. This includes all the required files, such as database files, configuration files, and many more.
- Manage network security of the system where MySQL 8 was installed, which permits a limited number of hosts for the connection.

Now your ride begins with another important and very interesting topic. Here we go.

Common security issues

Before going into detail on complex issues, you must first understand some basic points that will help you prevent misuse or attacks.

General guidelines

In MySQL 8, all connections, queries, and operations performed by the user are based on the **Access Control Lists** (**ACLs**) security. The following are some general guidelines related to security:

- Don't allow access to the user table to any user except the root account. Manage user privileges with GRANT and REVOKE statements.
- Use encrypted protocol, such as SSH or SSL, in the case of data transfer over the internet. MySQL 8 supports SSL connections for that.
- Use proper defensive programming techniques at the time when the client is entering data into MySQL using an application.
- Use a hashing function to store passwords into the MySQL 8 database; don't store plain text as a password. As the same way for password recovery consider some string as salt and use hash(hash(password)+salt) values.
- Use a proper password policy to protect it from break down. This means your system should accept only those passwords which follow your rules/conventions.
- Use of a firewall reduces the chance of failure by 50% and provides more protection to your system. Define MySQL under a demilitarized zone or behind a firewall to protect from distrusted hosts.

- The Linux based system provides the `tcpdump` command to perform tasks of transferring in a more secure way. This command works on the network layer to provide security. For example, using the following command, you can check whether MySQL data streams are encrypted or not:

```
shell> tcpdump -l -i eth0 -w - src or dst port 3306 | strings
```

Guidelines for a secure password

In this section, we describe guidelines for securing passwords with respect to different users and cover how to manage it during the logging process. MySQL 8 provides the `validate_password` plugin to define the policy for acceptable passwords.

Guidelines for end users

This section describes various methods to define your password, as an end user, in the safest way. It explains how to make your password more secure. The safest way is to define the password in a protected option file or prompt for the password in a client program. See the following different ways to define your password:

- Provide the password using the command line with the following options:

```
cmd>mysql -u root --password=your_pwd
--OR
cmd>
```

- In the preceding two commands, you have to specify your password in the command line itself, which is not preferable. MySQL 8 provides another secure way to connect with the command line for that. Execute the following command, which will prompt you for the password. Once you enter the password, MySQL shows the asterisk (*) sign for each password character:

```
cmd>mysql -u root -p
Enter password: ********
```

This is a more secure way than the previous two, where you define the password in the command-line argument:

- Use the MYSQL_PWD environment variable to define your password. This method is insecure as compared to other methods because there is a possibility that the environment variable is accessible by the other users.
- Define the password using the mysql_config_editor utility, which is a provided option to store the password into an encrypted login path file, named named.mylogin.cnf. MySQL 8 will use this file later to connect with the MySQL server.
- Use the option file to store your password. When you define your credentials into the file, make sure this file is not accessible by any other user. For example, in a UNIX-based system, you define the password in the option file under the client section as follows:

```
[client]
password=your_pass
```

To make your file safe or to set an access mode on it, execute the following command:

```
shell> chmod 600 .my.cnf
```

Guidelines for administrators

For a database administrator, the following guidelines should be followed to secure passwords:

- Use validate_password to apply the policy on accepted passwords
- MySQL 8 uses the mysql.user table to store user passwords, so configure the system in a way that only administrative users can access this table
- Users should be allowed to reset account passwords in the case of expired passwords
- Apply protection on the log file if it contains passwords
- Manage access to the plugin directory and the my.cnf file, because it can modify capabilities provided by the plugins

Password and logging

MySQL 8 allows you to write passwords as plain text in SQL statements, such as CREATE USER, SET PASSWORD, and GRANT. If we execute these statements, MySQL 8 will write passwords as text in log files, and they are visible to all the users that have access to the log files. To overcome this problem, avoid direct updates on grant tables using the mentioned SQL statements.

Secure MYSQL 8 against attackers

To secure MySQL 8 against attackers, strongly consider the following points:

- Set a password for all MySQL accounts. Never define an account with no password, because this permits access to your account by any user.
- To make a connection with MySQL 8, use secure protocols/channels, such as compressed protocols, MySQL 8 internal SSL connections, or SSH for encrypted TCP/IP connections.
- For a Unix-based system, set read/write privileges on the data directory for the Unix account which is used for running mysqld. Don't use the root user to start the MySQL 8 server.
- Use the secure_file_priv variable to specify the directory for read and write permission. Using this variable, you can restrict non-administrative users from accessing important directories. Use this variable to set permissions on plugin_dir; it is very important. In the same way, do not provide FILE privileges to all the users, because it permits users to write files anywhere in the system.
- Use the max_user_connections variable to restrict the number of connections per account.
- At the time of creating grant table entries, use wildcards properly. It is preferable to use IPs instead of DNS.
- Follow security guidelines during stored program and view creation.

Security options and variables provided by MySQL 8

The following `mysqld` options and variables are provided by MySQL 8 for security:

Name	Cmd-Line	Option File	System Var	Status Var	Var Scope	Dynamic
allow-suspicious-udfs	Yes	Yes				
automatic_sp_privileges			Yes		Global	Yes
chroot	Yes	Yes				
des-key-file	Yes	Yes				
local_infile			Yes		Global	Yes
old_passwords			Yes		Both	Yes
safe-user-create	Yes	Yes				
secure-auth	Yes	Yes			Global	Yes
- Variable: secure_auth			Yes		Global	Yes
secure-file-priv	Yes	Yes			Global	No
- Variable: secure_file_priv			Yes		Global	No
skip-grant-tables	Yes	Yes				
skip-name-resolve	Yes	Yes			Global	No
- Variable: skip_name_resolve			Yes		Global	No
skip-networking	Yes	Yes			Global	No
- Variable: skip_networking			Yes		Global	No
skip-show-database	Yes	Yes			Global	No
- Variable: skip_show_database			Yes		Global	No

Reference: `https://dev.mysql.com/doc/refman/8.0/en/security-options.html`

Security guidelines for client programming

Don't trust any data entered by the application user, because there is the possibility that the user has entered a `drop` or `delete` statement for the MySQL database. So, there is always the risk of security leaks and data loss. As an administrator of a MySQL database, the following checklist should be followed:

- The size of the data must be checked before passing it to MySQL 8.
- To make MySQL 8 more restrictive, enable the strict MySQL mode.

- For numeric fields, enter characters, special characters, and spaces instead of numeric itself. Change field values to their original forms by your application before sending them to the MySQL 8 server.
- Use two different users for application connection to the database and for database administration.
- Modify datatypes from numeric to character types by adding quotes in the case of dynamic URLs and web forms. Also add %22 ("), %23 (#), and %27 (') in dynamic URLs.

Previously defined functionalities are available built in to all of the programming interfaces. For example, Java JDBC provides prepared statements with placeholders, and Ruby DBI provides the `quote()` method.

Access control in MySQL 8

Privileges are mainly used to authenticate users and will verify user credentials and check if a user is allowed for the requested operation or not. When we connect with the MySQL 8 server, it will first check the identity of the user by the provided host and user name. After connection, when a request comes in, the system will grant privileges according to the user's identity. Based on this understanding, we can say that access control contains two stages when we try to connect with the MySQL 8 server using the client program:

- **Stage 1**: The MySQL server will either accept or reject the connection, based on the provided identity
- **Stage 2**: After getting a connection from the MySQL server, when the user sends a request for performing any operation, the server will check whether sufficient privileges are available for the user or not

There are some limitations of the MySQL 8 privilege system:

- User is not allowed to set a password on specific objects, such as a table or a routine. MySQL 8 allows it globally at the account level.
- As an admin user, we cannot specify privileges in a way that create/drop table is allowed but create/drop database of that table is not allowed.

You are not allowed to restrict user access explicitly, which means that explicitly matching the user and refusing its connection is not possible. MySQL 8 manages the content of grant tables in memory, so in the case of INSERT, UPDATE, and DELETE statements, execution on grant tables requires the server to restart for effect. To avoid server restarts, MySQL has provided a command for flushing privileges. We can execute this command in three different ways:

1. By issuing FLUSH PRIVILEGES.
2. Using mysqladmin reload.
3. Using mysqladmin flush-privileges.

When we reload grant tables, it will work as per the following mentioned points:

- **Table and column privileges**: Changes of these privileges will be available from the next client's request
- **Database privileges**: Changes of these privileges will be available the next time the client executes a USE dbname statement
- **Global privileges and passwords**: Changes of these privileges are unaffected for a connected client; it will be applicable from the subsequent connections

Privileges provided by MySQL 8

Privileges define which operations are permissible to the user accounts. Based on the level of operation and the context in which it is applied, it will work. It is mainly classified as follows:

- **Database privileges**: Applied on the database, and all objects of the database within it. It can be granted to a single database or defined globally to apply on all databases.
- **Administrative privileges**: It is defined at the global level, so not restricted to a single database. It enables users to manage operation of the MySQL 8 server.
- **Database object's privileges**: It is used to define privileges on the database objects, such as tables, views, indexes, and stored routines. It can be applied on a specific object of the database, can be applied on all objects of a given type in a database, or can be applied globally for all the objects of a given type in all databases.

MySQL 8 will store account privilege related information into grant tables and store the contents of these tables into memory upon server start-up for better performance. Privileges are further classified in terms of static and dynamic privileges:

- **Static privileges**: These are available built in with the server and cannot be unregistered. These privileges are always available for the user to be granted.
- **Dynamic privileges**: These privileges can be registered or unregistered at runtime. If privileges are not registered, then they are not available to be granted for user accounts.

Grant tables

Grant tables contain information related to user accounts and granted privileges for that user. MySQL 8 automatically inserts data into these tables when we execute any account management statements in the database, such as CREATE USER, GRANT, and REVOKE. MySQL allows insert, update, or delete options on grant tables to the admin user, but it's not a preferable approach. The following tables of the MySQL 8 database contain grant information:

- `user`: It contains details related to user accounts, global privileges, and other non-privilege columns
- `password_history`: It contains history of password changes
- `columns_priv`: It contains column level privileges
- `procs_priv`: It contains privileges related to stored procedures and functions
- `proxies_priv`: It contains privileges for proxy users
- `tables_priv`: It contains table level privileges
- `global_grants`: It contains details related to dynamic global privileges assignments
- `role_edges`: It contains edges for role subgraphs
- `db`: It contains privileges at the database level
- `default_roles`: It contains details related to default user roles

Grant tables contain scope and privilege columns:

- **Scope column:** This column defines the scope of rows in the tables, which means the context under which the row applies.
- **Privilege column:** This column indicates which operation is permitted to the user. The MySQL server combines information from the various grant tables to build a complete detail of a user's privileges.

From MySQL 8.0 onward, grant tables use the `InnoDB` storage engine by managing transactional states, but before that, MySQL used the `MyISAM` engine by managing nontransactional states. This change enables users to manage all account management statements in the transactional mode, so in the case of multiple statements, either all of them are successfully executed or none of them are executed.

Verification of access control stages

MySQL 8 performs access control checks in two different stages.

Stage 1 - Connection verification

This is the connection verification stage, so after verification, MySQL 8 will either accept or reject your connection request. Verification will be performed with the following conditions:

1. Based on a user's identity, with its password.
2. Whether a user's account is locked or not.

The server will deny access if either of these cases fails. Here, the identity contains the username and hostname from which the request is coming. MySQL performs a locking check on the `account_locked` column of the user table and a credential check on the three columns of the user table scope: `Host`, `User`, and `authentication_string`.

Stage 2 - Request verification

Once a connection is established with the MySQL server, stage 2 comes into the picture, where the MySQL server checks which operation you want to perform and whether that is permissible to you or not. For this verification, MySQL uses the privilege columns of the grant tables; it might be coming from `user`, `db`, `tables_priv`, `columns_priv`, or `procs_priv` tables.

Account management in MySQL 8

As the name implies, this topic describes how to manage user accounts in MySQL 8. We will describe how to add new accounts, how to remove accounts, how to define usernames and passwords for the accounts, and more.

Add and remove user accounts

MySQL 8 provides two different ways to create accounts:

- **Using account management statements**: These statements are used to create users and set their privileges; for example, with CREATE USER and GRANT statements, which inform the server to perform modifications on the grant table

- **Using manipulation of grant tables**: Using INSERT, UPDATE, and DELETE statements, we can manipulate the grant table

Out of these two approaches, account management statements are preferable, because they are more concise and less error-prone. Now, let's see an example of using the commands:

```
#1 mysql> CREATE USER 'user1'@'localhost' IDENTIFIED BY 'user1_password';
#2 mysql> GRANT ALL PRIVILEGES ON *.* TO 'user1'@'localhost' WITH GRANT
OPTION;

#3 mysql> CREATE USER 'user2'@'%' IDENTIFIED BY 'user2_password';
#4 mysql> GRANT ALL PRIVILEGES ON *.* TO 'user2'@'%' WITH GRANT OPTION;

#5 mysql> CREATE USER 'adminuser'@'localhost' IDENTIFIED BY 'password';
#6 mysql> GRANT RELOAD,PROCESS ON *.* TO 'adminuser'@'localhost';

#7 mysql> CREATE USER 'tempuser'@'localhost';

#8 mysql> CREATE USER 'user4'@'host4.mycompany.com' IDENTIFIED BY
'password';
#9 mysql> GRANT SELECT,INSERT,UPDATE,DELETE,CREATE,DROP ON db1.* TO
'user4'@'host4. mycompany.com';
```

The preceding commands perform the following actions:

- #1 command creates 'user1' and command #2 assigns full privileges to 'user1'. But 'user1'@'localhost' indicates that 'user1' is allowed to connect with localhost only.
- #3 command creates 'user2' and command #4 assigns full privileges to 'user2', the same as 'user1'. But in #4, 'user2'@'%' is mentioned, which indicates that 'user2' is allowed to connect with any host.
- #5 creates 'adminuser' and allows it to connect with localhost only. In #6, we can see that only RELOAD and PROCESS privileges are provided to the 'adminuser'. It allows 'adminuser' to execute the mysqladmin reload, mysqladmin refresh, mysqladmin flush-xxx commands, and the mysqladmin processlist command, but it has no access on any database.
- #7 creates the 'tempuser' account without a password and allows the user to connect with localhost only. But no grant is specified for 'tempuser', so this user is not able to access the database nor perform any administrative commands.
- #8 creates 'user4' and allows the user to access the database using 'host4' only. #10 indicates 'user4' has grant on 'db1' for all the mention operations.

To remove a user account, execute the DROP USER command as follows:

```
mysql> DROP USER 'user1'@'localhost';
```

This command will drop the 'user1' account from the system.

Security using roles

The same as a user account role having privileges, we can also say that a role is a collection of privileges. As an admin user, we can grant and revoke privileges from the roles. MySQL 8 provides the following commands, functions, and variables related to role configuration.

SET ROLE

SET ROLE changes the active roles within the current session. Refer to the following commands related to SET ROLE:

```
mysql> SET ROLE NONE; SELECT CURRENT_ROLE();
+-----------------+
| CURRENT_ROLE() |
+-----------------+
| NONE |
+-----------------+
mysql> SET ROLE 'developer_read'; SELECT CURRENT_ROLE();
+-----------------+
| CURRENT_ROLE() |
+-----------------+
| `developer_read`@`%` |
+-----------------+
```

The first command will deactivate all roles for the user in the current session. You can see the effect with the CURRENT_ROLE(); function. In the second command, we are setting the 'developer_read' role as default, and then checking the current role using the predefined function again.

CREATE ROLE

CREATE ROLE is used to create a role; refer to the following command, which will create a role with the name 'developer_role':

```
CREATE ROLE 'developer_role';
```

DROP ROLE

DROP ROLE is used to remove a role. Refer to the following command, which will remove the 'developer_role' role:

```
DROP ROLE 'developer_role';
```

GRANT

GRANT assigns privileges to roles and assigns roles to accounts. For example, the following command assigns all privileges to the developer role:

```
GRANT ALL ON my_db.* TO 'developer_role';
```

In the same way, to assign roles to the user account, execute the following command:

```
GRANT 'developer_role' TO 'developer1'@'localhost';
```

This command assigns the `'developer_role'` role to the `developer1` account. MySQL 8 also provides a feature to assign GRANT from user to user and role to role. Consider the following example:

```
CREATE USER 'user1';
CREATE ROLE 'role1';
GRANT SELECT ON mydb.* TO 'user1';
GRANT SELECT ON mydb.* TO 'role1';
CREATE USER 'user2';
CREATE ROLE 'role2';
GRANT 'user1', 'role1'TO 'user2';
GRANT 'user1', 'role1'TO 'role2';
```

In this example, `user1` and `role1` is created and GRANT is applied on them in a simple way by using the GRANT command. Now, for `user2` and `role2`, we have applied GRANT from the `user1` and `role1`, respectively.

REVOKE

REVOKE is used to remove privileges from the role and remove a role assignment from the user account. Refer to the following commands:

```
REVOKE developer_role FROM user1;
REVOKE INSERT, UPDATE ON app_db.* FROM 'role1';
```

The first command is used to remove `'developer_role'` for `user1`, and the second command is used to remove insert and update privileges from the `'role1'` on `'app_db'`.

SET DEFAULT ROLE

SET DEFAULT ROLE indicates which roles are active by default, whenever user login default roles are available to the user. To set a default root, execute the following command:

```
mysql>SET DEFAULT ROLE app_developer TO root@localhost;

mysql> SELECT CURRENT_ROLE();
+----------------------+
| CURRENT_ROLE()  |
+----------------------+
| `app_developer`@`%` |
+----------------------+
1 row in set (0.04 sec)
```

After setting the default role, restart the server and execute the current_role() function to check whether a role is assigned or not.

SHOW GRANTS

SHOW GRANTS lists down privileges and role assignments related to accounts and roles. For a role, execute the following command:

```
mysql> show grants for app_developer;
+------------------------------------------------+
| Grants for app_developer@% |
+------------------------------------------------+
| GRANT USAGE ON *.* TO `app_developer`@`%` |
+------------------------------------------------+
1 row in set (0.05 sec)
```

This command shows the grant available on the 'app_developer' role. In the same way, to check grants on a user, execute the following command:

```
mysql> show grants for root@localhost;
```

The preceding command lists down all the access available with the user root:

- CURRENT_ROLE (): This function is used to list current roles within the current session. As described in the default role command, it shows currently assigned roles of the user.
- activate_all_roles_on_login: This is a system variable used to automatically activate all granted roles at the time of user login. By default, automatic activation of roles is disabled.

- `mandatory_roles`: This is a system variable used to define mandatory roles. Remember that roles which are defined as mandatory can't be deleted using the `drop` command. Define your mandatory roles in the server file `my.cnf` as follows:

```
[mysqld]
mandatory_roles='app_developer'
```

To persist and set these roles at runtime, use the following statement:

```
SET PERSIST mandatory_roles = 'app_developer';
```

This statement applies changes on the running MySQL 8 instance and also saves it for subsequent restarts. If you want to apply changes for the running instance and not for other restarts, then use the keyword `GLOBAL` instead of `PERSIST`.

Password management

MySQL 8 provides the following password management related capabilities:

- **Password expiration**: Used to define periods for password expiration so that users can change it periodically. MySQL 8 allows for setting password expiration manually for accounts, along with an expiration policy. For an expiration policy, the `mysql_native_password`, `sha256_password`, or `caching_sha2_password` plugins can be used. To set a password manually, execute the following command:

```
ALTER USER 'testuser'@'localhost' PASSWORD EXPIRE;
```

This will mark a password as expired for the mentioned user. For password policies, you have to define the duration in terms of the number of days. MySQL uses the system variable `default_password_lifetime`, which contains a positive integer number to define the number of days. We can define it in the `my.cnf` file or can define it at runtime using the `PERSIST` option:

- **Password reuse restrictions**: Used to prevent the use of old passwords again. MySQL 8 defines this restriction based on two parameters - the number of changes and time elapsed; they can be used separately or in combination. MySQL 8 defines `password_history` and `password_reuse_interval` system variables, respectively, to apply restrictions. We can define these variables in the `my.cnf` file, or can persist them.

- `password_history`: This variable indicates that new passwords cannot be set/duplicated from the old passwords. Here, consider the most recent old passwords as per the specified number.
- `password_reuse_interval`: This variable indicates that the password cannot be set/duplicated from the old password. Here, interval defines the specific period and MySQL 8 will check new password with all the passwords which were falls under that period for a user. For example, if the interval is set as 20 days, then the new password should not have existed in the last 20 days of changed data.
- **Password strength assessment**: Used to define strong passwords. It is implemented using the `validate_password` plugin.

Encryption in MySQL 8

When there is a need to transfer data over the network, it is a must to use encryption for the connection. If you are using unencrypted data, then someone who has access to the network can easily watch all of your traffic and can see what data is transferred between the client and server. To protect your data over the network, use encryption. Make sure the encryption algorithm used contains security elements to protect your connection from known attacks, like changing the order of a message or replay twice on data. Based on your application requirements, you can choose either an encrypted or unencrypted type connection. MySQL 8 performs encryption per connection using **Transport Layer Security (TLS)** protocol.

Configuring MySQL 8 to use encrypted connections

This section describes how to configure the server and client for the encrypted connection.

Server-side configuration for encrypted connections

On the server side, MySQL 8 uses the –ssl option to specify properties related to encryption. The following options are used at the server side to configure encryption:

- `--ssl-ca`: This option specifies the path name of the **Certificate Authority (CA)** certificate file

- `--ssl-cert`: This option specifies the path name of the server public key certificate file
- `--ssl-key`: This option specifies the path name of the server private key file

You can use the above options by specifying them in the `my.cnf` file as follows:

```
[mysqld]
ssl-ca=ca.pem
ssl-cert=server-cert.pem
ssl-key=server-key.pem
```

The `--ssl` option is enabled by default, so on server startup, MySQL 8 will try to find the certificate and key file under the data directory, even though you have not defined it in the `my.cnf` file. If those files are found, then MySQL 8 will provide an encrypted connection, or else continue without an encrypted connection.

Client-side configuration for encrypted connections

At the client side, MySQL uses the same `–ssl` options used at the server side to specify the certificate and key file, but apart from that, it has `–ssl-mode` options. By default, the client is allowed to set up an encrypted connection with the server if the server permits it. For further control, the client program uses the following `–ssl-mode` options:

- `--ssl-mode=REQUIRED`: This option indicates that an encrypted connection must be established, and fails if it is not established
- `--ssl-mode=PREFFERED`: This option indicates the client program can establish an encrypted connection if the server permits it, or else establish an unencrypted connection without a fail
- `--ssl-mode=DISABLED`: This option indicates the client program is unable to use an encrypted connection, and only an unencrypted connection is allowed
- `--ssl-mode=VERIFY_CA`: This option is the same as `REQUIRED`, but in addition to that, it verifies the CA certificate against the configured CA certificate and returns a fail if no matches are found
- `--ssl-mode=VERIFY_IDENTITY`: It is the same as the `VERIFY_CA` option, but in addition to that, it will perform the hostname identity

Command options for encrypted connections

The following options are available in MySQL 8 for an encrypted connection. You can use these options on the command line, or you can define them in an option file:

Format	Description
--skip-ssl	Do not use encrypted connection
--ssl	Enable encrypted connection
--ssl-ca	File that contains a list of trusted SSL Certificate Authorities
--ssl-capath	Directory that contains trusted SSL Certificate Authority certificate files
--ssl-cert	File that contains X509 certificate
--ssl-cipher	List of permitted ciphers for connection encryption
--ssl-crl	File that contains certificate revocation lists
--ssl-crlpath	Directory that contains certificate revocation list files
--ssl-key	File that contains X509 key
--ssl-mode	Security state of connection to server
--tls-version	Protocols permitted for encrypted connections

Reference: `https://dev.mysql.com/doc/refman/8.0/en/encrypted-connection-options.html`

Connect with MySQL 8 remotely from Windows with SSH

To connect remotely with MYSQL 8 by using SSH from the Microsoft Windows system, perform the following steps:

1. Install the SSH client on your local system.
2. After starting the SSH client, set the hostname and user ID by which you want to connect with the server.

3. Configure port forwarding as follows and save the information:
   - **For remote forwarding configure**: `local_port:3306`, `remote_host:mysqlservername_or_ip, remote_port:3306`
   - **For local forwarding configure**: `local_port:3306`, `remote_host:localhost, remote_port:3306`

4. Log in to the server with the created SSH session.
5. In your local Microsoft Windows machine, start any ODBC application, such as Microsoft Access.
6. In your local system, create new file and try to link with MySQL server using the ODBC driver. Make sure you have defined `localhost` in the connection instead of `mysqlservername`.

Security plugins

MySQL 8 provides several plugins to implement security. These plugins provide various features related to authentication protocols, password validation, secure storage, and much more. Let's discuss the various types of plugins in detail.

Authentication plugins

The following list of authentication plugins, with their details:

- **Native pluggable authentication**: To implement native authentication, MySQL 8 uses the `mysql_native_password` plugin. This plugin uses a common name in server and client both the side and inbuilt provided by MySQL 8 for both the server and client program.

- SHA-256 pluggable authentication

To implement SHA-256 hashing MySQL 8 provides two different plugins:

1. `sha256_password`: This plugin is used to implement basic SHA-256 authentication.
2. `caching_sha2_password`: This plugin implements SHA-256 authentication along with caching for better performance, and has some additional features as compared to the basic plugin.

This plugin is inbuilt available with MySQL 8 server and client program with the same name as `sha256_password`. In the client, it is located under the `libmysqlclient` library. To use this plugin for an account, execute the following command:

```
CREATE USER 'testsha256user'@'localhost'
IDENTIFIED WITH sha256_password BY 'userpassword';
```

SHA-2 pluggable authentication

SHA-2 pluggable authentication is the same as the SHA-256 pluggable plugin, except its plugin name is `caching_sha2_password`. When compare to `sha256_password`, this plugin has the following advantages:

1. If you are using Unix socket-file and shared-memory protocols, then support is provided for client connections.
2. In-memory caching is available in SHA-2 plugins, which provides faster re-authentication for users who have connected previously.
3. This plugin provides RSA-based password exchange, which works regardless of the SSL library provided by MySQL 8.

Client-side cleartext pluggable authentication

This plugin is used to send passwords to the server without hashing or encryption. It is available at the client side with the name `mysql_clear_password`. MySQL 8 provides it built-in within the client library.

No-login pluggable authentication

This is a server-side plugin used to prevent all client connections to any account that uses it. The plugin name is `'mysql_no_login'`, and it's not a built-in MySQL plugin, so we must use the `mysql_no_login.so` library. To make it usable, put the library file under the plugin directory first, then perform either of these steps:

1. Load the plugin on server startup by adding the `--plugin-load-add` parameter in the `my.cnf` file:

```
[mysqld]
plugin-load-add=mysql_no_login.so
```

2. To register the plugin at runtime, execute the following command:

```
INSTALL PLUGIN mysql_no_login SONAME 'mysql_no_login.so';
```

To uninstall this plugin, execute the following commands:

1. If the plugin was installed on the server startup by using `--plugin-load-adoption`, then restart the server by removing the option.
2. If the plugin was installed using the `INSTALL PLUGIN` command, then use the uninstall command to remove it:

```
UNINSTALL PLUGIN mysql_no_login;
```

Socket peer-credential pluggable authentication

The server-side plugin named `auth_socket` is used to authenticate clients which are connected from the local host using the Unix socket file. It is only used for a system that supports the `SO_PEERCRED` option. `SO_PEERCRED` is used to obtain information about the user running the client program. This is not a built-in plugin; we must use the `auth_socket.so` library with this plugin. To make it usable, put the library file under the plugin directory first, and then perform either of these steps:

1. Load the plugin on server startup by adding the `--plugin-load-add` parameter in the `my.cnf` file:

```
[mysqld]
plugin-load-add=auth_socket.so
```

2. Register the plugin at runtime by executing the following command:

```
INSTALL PLUGIN auth_socket SONAME 'auth_socket.so';
```

To uninstall this plugin, execute the following commands:

1. If the plugin was installed on server startup using `--plugin-load-addoption`, then restart the server by removing the option.
2. If the plugin was installed using the `INSTALL PLUGIN` command, then use the `UNINSTALL` command to remove it:

```
UNINSTALL PLUGIN auth_socket;
```

Test pluggable authentication

A test plugin is provided by MySQL 8 to check account credentials and log successes or failures on the server logs. It is not a built-in plugin and needs to be installed before use. This is available for both the server and client side, and is named `test_plugin_server` and `auth_test_plugin`, respectively. MySQL 8 uses the `auth_test_plugin.so` library for this plugin. To install and uninstall this plugin, perform the same steps mentioned in the preceding plugin.

The connection-control plugins

MySQL 8 uses these plugins to introduce an increasing delay in the server response to the client after some specific number of failed connection attempts. MySQL has provided two plugins for connection control.

CONNECTION_CONTROL

This plugin will check all the incoming requests of connections and, based on that, add a delay in the server response if required. This plugin uses some system variables for configuration, and status variables for monitoring purposes. It also uses some other plugins, event classes, and processes, like audit plugin, `MYSQL_AUDIT_CONNECTION_CLASSMASK` event class, `MYSQL_AUDIT_CONNECTION_CONNECT`, and `MYSQL_AUDIT_CONNECTION_CHANGE_USER` processes for checking whether the server should have added a delay before attending any client connection:

    CONNECTION_CONTROL_FAILED_LOGIN_ATTEMPTS

This plugin implements uses of the `INFORMATION_SCHEMA` table to provide details on monitoring of the failed connections.

Plugin installation

We must use the `connection_control.so` library with this plugin. To make it usable, put the library file under the plugin directory first, and then perform either of the steps:

1. Load the plugin on server startup by adding the `--plugin-load-add` parameter in the `my.cnf` file:

```
[mysqld]
plugin-load-add= connection_control.so
```

2. Register the plugin at runtime by executing the following command:

```
INSTALL PLUGIN CONNECTION_CONTROL SONAME
   'connection_control.so';
INSTALL PLUGIN CONNECTION_CONTROL_FAILED_LOGIN_ATTEMPTS SONAME
   'connection_control.so';
```

Variables related to CONNECTION-CONTROL

The following variables are provided by CONNECTION-CONTROL plugins:

- Connection_control_delay_generated: This is a status variable, mainly used to manage the counter. It indicates how many times the server added a delay in its response on failed connection attempts. It also depends on the connection_control_failed_connections_threshold system variable, because this status variable does not increment the count unless the number of attempts reaches the limit defined by the threshold variable.
- connection_control_failed_connections_threshold: This is a system variable which indicates how many consecutive failed attempts are allowed to clients before the server adds a delay on each attempt.
- connection_control_max_connection_delay: This is a system variable which defines the maximum delay time in milliseconds for the server response on failed connections attempts. MySQL 8 will consider this variable once the threshold variable contains a value higher than zero.
- connection_control_min_connection_delay: This system variable defines the minimum delay time in milliseconds for the server to failed connection attempt. MySQL 8 will consider this variable once the threshold variable contains a value higher than zero.

The password validation plugin

For password validation, MySQL provides a plugin named validate_password. It is mainly used to test passwords and improve security. The following are the two major capabilities of this plugin:

- VALIDATE_PASSWORD_STRENGTH(): An SQL function used to find the strength of a password. It takes a password as an argument and returns an integer value between 0 and 100. Here, 0 indicates a weak password and 100 indicates a strong password.

- **Check password as per policy in SQL statements**: For all the SQL statements which use a password as a clear text value, the plugin will check the provided password against the policy of the password and, based on that, return a response. In the case of a weak password, the plugin will return an `ER_NOT_VALID_PASSWORD` error. `ALTER USER`, `CREATE USER`, `GRANT`, `SET PASSWORD` statements, and the `PASSWORD()` function are always checked by this plugin if the password is defined as clear text in an argument.

Install password validation plugin

We must use the `validate_password.so` library with this plugin. To make it usable, put the library file under the plugin directory first, and then perform either of these steps:

1. Load the plugin on server startup by adding the `--plugin-load-add` parameter in the `my.cnf` file:

   ```
   [mysqld]
   plugin-load-add=validate_password.so
   ```

2. Register the plugin at runtime by executing the following command:

   ```
   INSTALL PLUGIN validate_password SONAME 'validate_password.so';
   ```

Variables and options related to the password validation plugin

MySQL 8 provides following system variables, status variables and options related to password validation plugin.

- `validate_password_check_user_name`: This is a system variable, and is enabled by default in MySQL 8. As the name implies, it is used to compare a password with the username of the currently effective user. If the password matches with the username or its reverse, MySQL 8 will reject the password, irrespective of the `VALIDATE_PASSWORD_STRENGTH()` function value.
- `validate_password_dictionary_file`: This system variable contains the pathname of the directory which is used by the `validate_password` plugin. You can set it at runtime without a server restart, and it is available once the plugin is installed. Set the password policy value as 2(strong), if you define the directory for the password check. Possible values for password policy is describe under `validate_password_policy` system variable.

- `validate_password_length`: This system variable is available once a plugin is installed and is used to define the minimum number of characters for a password to check with the `validate_password` plugin.
- `validate_password_mixed_case_count`: This system variable is available once a plugin is installed and is used to define the minimum number of lowercase and uppercase characters for a password check.
- `validate_password_number_count`: This system variable is available once the plugin is installed and is used to define the minimum number of digits for the password check.
- `validate_password_special_char_count`: This system variable is available once a plugin is installed and is used to define the minimum number of non-alphanumeric characters in a password check.
- `validate_password_policy`: This system variable is available once a plugin is installed, and it indicates how a plugin should behave in the case of other system variables. The following values of this variable describe the behavior of the `validate_password` plugin:

Policy	Tests Performed
0 or LOW	Length
1 or MEDIUM	Length; numeric, lowercase/uppercase, and special characters
2 or STRONG	Length; numeric, lowercase/uppercase, and special characters; dictionary file

Reference:`https://dev.mysql.com/doc/refman/8.0/en/validate-password-options-variables.html`

- `validate_password_dictionary_file_last_parsed`: This is a status variable used to indicate the time when a directory file was last parsed.
- `validate_password_dictionary_file_words_count`: This is a status variable used to indicate the number of words read from the directory file.
- `--validate-password[=value]`: This option is used to define how a server loads the `validate_password` plugin on startup. This option is available only if the plugin was registered with `INSTALL PLUGIN` or if it is loaded with the `--plugin-load-add` feature.

MySQL 8 keyring

MySQL 8 provides a keyring service, which allows the MySQL server's internal components and plugins to store their sensitive information for later use. For this feature, MySQL 8 uses the `keyring_file` plugin, which will store data into the file located on the server host. This plugin is available in all distributions of MySQL, such as the Community Edition and Enterprise Edition.

Install keyring plugin

We must use the `keyring_file.so` library with this plugin. To make it usable, put the library file under the plugin directory first, and then perform either of these steps:

- Load the plugin on server startup by adding the `--plugin-load-add` parameter in the `my.cnf` file:

      ```
      mysqld]
      plugin-load-add=keyring_file.so
      ```

- Register the plugin at runtime by executing the following command:

      ```
      INSTALL PLUGIN keyring_file SONAME 'keyring_file.so';
      ```

System variables related to keyring plugin

MySQL 8 provides below system variable related to keyring plugin:

- `keyring_file_data`: This system variable is available once a plugin is installed and is used to define a pathname of the data file which is used by the `keyring_file` plugin to store secure data. Keyring operations are transactional, so this plugin uses a backup file during write operation to handle a rollback scenario. In this case, the backfile is also named with the same naming convention as defined in the `keyring_file_data` system variable, with the suffix as `.backup`.

Summary

In this chapter, we started with an overview of security, and then the ride began with the MySQL 8 security related features. First we discussed some common security issues, then we showed how to assign privileges and how to manage access control in MySQL 8. Encryption was also covered in this chapter, to secure your sensitive data. And finally, we covered some important security plugins, which are useful to implement security in MySQL 8.

It's now time to move on to our next chapter, where we will be configuring MySQL 8 for optimization. For optimization, we will cover different areas of the database, such as optimizing queries, optimizing tables, optimizing buffering and caching, and much more. Apart from server configuration, it also covers how to configure a client for optimization.

12
Optimizing MySQL 8

In the previous chapter, we learned about security, which is an important aspect of any production-grade application. The chapter started with an introduction to security and identifying common security issues. Moving on, the chapter covered access control mechanisms, account management, and encryption in MySQL 8. We learned various MySQL 8 security plugins in the later part of the chapter. Security is an important benchmark for every production-grade application. That's why the previous chapter is an important one.

Moving along a similar line, with the objective of developing highly optimized databases, this chapter focuses on optimization methods. It starts with an overview of what optimization means in MySQL 8. It takes the reader through MySQL 8 server and client optimization, optimizing database structure, and optimizing common queries and database tables. Later in the chapter, emphasis is given to buffering and caching techniques.

The following is a list of topics to be covered:

- Overview of MySQL 8 optimization
- Optimizing MySQL 8 servers and clients
- Optimizing database structure
- Optimizing queries
- Optimizing tables
- Leveraging buffering and caching

Overview of MySQL 8 optimization

Let's start with understanding MySQL 8 optimization. Optimization is the process of identifying performance bottlenecks and implementing optimized solutions to overcome these issues. Optimization in MySQL 8 involves performance measurement, configuration, and tuning at several different levels. It is an important task for an administrator to optimize the performance at different levels, like individual SQL queries, entire database applications, database servers, or distributed database servers. Performance optimization at the CPU and memory levels improves scalability. It also allows the database to handle more complex queries without slowing down the database server.

The performance of a database depends on multiple factors. At the database level, these factors can be tables, queries, and configurations. Database server startups and database query executions are a couple of the events when these constructs impact the CPU or perform I/O (Input/Output) operations at the hardware level. This is a responsibility of the MySQL 8 database administrator: to make sure that the hardware performance stands at an optimum level. It is required that the hardware is used with the maximum efficiency possible. At the software level, performance optimization starts by learning generic rules and guidelines and measuring performance with clock time. Gradually, we understand the internals of various database operations. We can measure the performance in terms of CPU cycles and I/O operations. To attain the best database performance, we can optimize the software and hardware configurations at a basic level. At an advanced level, we can improve MySQL itself by developing custom storage engines and hardware appliances, which expand the MySQL ecosystem.

Optimizing the database

What is the most important factor in making the database perform at the optimum speed? The answer is, basic database design. The following is a checklist to keep an eye on for database design:

- The database columns have to be of the right data types. Tables must have appropriate columns for the purposes to be served. Applications that have frequent operations to be performed on the database have many tables with fewer columns, whereas applications that analyze large amounts of data have limited tables with many columns.

- As we learned in one of the previous chapters, database indexing plays an important role in enhancing query performance. So, it is important to have correct indexes in place for query execution efficiency.
- We discussed database storage engines, such as MyISAM or InnoDB, in earlier chapters. Use of an appropriate storage engine for each individual table is important. InnoDB is preferable for transactional database tables, whereas MyISAM is preferable for defining non-trasactional database tables. The choice of storage engine plays a vital role in defining the performance and scalability of the database.
- In the chapter on MySQL 8 data types, we learned about row formats in detail. It is again important for each to have an appropriate row format. The choice of row format depends on the storage engine chosen. Compressed tables occupy less disk space and require fewer disk I/O operations. For InnoDB tables, compression is available for all read and write operations. On the contrary, compression is available for read-only MyISAM tables.
- The MySQL database supports multiple locking strategies. The locking can be at a table-level or a row-level. The application must use an appropriate locking strategy. By granting shared access wherever appropriate, it becomes possible to run database operations concurrently. Also, it should be possible to request exclusive access, so that critical database operations can be executed with data integrity issues and priority can be maintained. In this case, the choice of storage engine is again significant. The InnoDB storage engine handles most locking issues without user involvement. It allows for better concurrency and reduces the amount of experimentation and tuning for the code.
- The memory areas must use the correct caching size. It should be large enough to hold frequently accessed data, and at the same time, not so large that they overload physical memory and cause paging. The InnoDB buffer pool and MyISAM key cache are the main memory areas to be configured.

 For newly created tables, MyISAM is the default storage engine. In practical use, InnoDB advanced performance features mean that tables with InnoDB storage engines outperform the MyISAM tables for an operations-heavy database.

Optimizing the hardware

Growth is the nature of every software application. As the application grows, so does the database. The database becomes more and more busy in performing operations. At a certain point, the database application eventually hits the hardware limits. An administrator must evaluate the possibility of tuning the application or re-configuring the server to avoid these issues. It should also be evaluated whether deploying more hardware resources would help. System bottlenecks usually arise from the following sources:

- **Disk seeks**: As part of the disk read operation, finding a piece of data takes time for the disk. The mean time for finding a piece of data is usually lower than 10 milliseconds with modern disks. So, in theory, it should be 100 seeks per second. With technological evolution, the new disks have improvements on the disk time, but it is very hard to optimize for single tables. To optimize the seek time, it is necessary to distribute data across more than one disk.
- **Disk reading and writing**: To read or write data from a disk, it is required for the disk to be at the correct position. One disk delivers at least 10 to 20 MB of throughput per second (throughput is the amount of data read or written per second). So, the read and write throughput is more easily optimized than the seek time, as we can read in parallel from multiple disks.
- **CPU cycles**: We must process the data when it is in the main memory to get the desired result. With large tables, the amount of memory is the most common limiting factor. With small tables, however, speed is usually not an issue.
- **Memory bandwidth**: In an uncommon scenario, the main memory bandwidth becomes a bottleneck when the CPU needs more data than can be fit in the CPU cache memory.

Optimizing MySQL 8 servers and clients

This section focuses on optimization for MySQL 8 database servers and clients, starting with optimizing the server and followed by optimizing MySQL 8 client-side entities. This section is more relevant to database administrators, to ensure performance and scalability across multiple servers. It would also help developers preparing scripts (which includes setting up the database) and users running MySQL for development and testing to maximize the productivity.

Optimizing disk I/O

In this section, we will learn ways to configure storage devices to devote more and faster storage hardware to the database server. A major performance bottleneck is disk seeking (finding the correct place on the disk to read or write content). When the amount of data grows large enough to make caching impossible, the problem with disk seeds becomes apparent. We need at least one disk seek operation to read, and several disk seek operations to write things in large databases where the data access is done more or less randomly. We should regulate or minimize the disk seek times using appropriate disks.

In order to resolve the disk seek performance issue, increasing the number of available disk spindles, symlinking the files to different disks, or stripping disks can be done. The following are the details:

- **Using symbolic links**: When using symbolic links, we can create a Unix symbolic links for index and data files. The symlink points from default locations in the data directory to another disk in the case of MyISAM tables. These links may also be striped. This improves the seek and read times. The assumption is that the disk is not used concurrently for other purposes. Symbolic links are not supported for InnoDB tables. However, we can place InnoDB data and log files on different physical disks.

- **Striping**: In striping, we have many disks. We put the first block on the first disk, the second block on the second disk, and so on. The N block on the (N % number-of-disks) disk. If the stripe size is perfectly aligned, the normal data size will be less than the stripe size. This will help to improve the performance. Striping is dependent on the stripe size and the operating system. In an ideal case, we would benchmark the application with different stripe sizes. The speed difference while striping depends on the parameters we have used, like stripe size. The difference in performance also depends on the number of disks. We have to choose if we want to optimize for random access or sequential access. To gain reliability, we may decide to set up with striping and mirroring (RAID 0+1). **RAID** stands for **Redundant Array of Independent Drives**. This approach needs 2 x N drives to hold N drives of data. With a good volume management software, we can manage this setup efficiently.

- There is another approach to it, as well. Depending on how critical the type of data is, we may vary the RAID level. For example, we can store really important data, such as host information and logs, on a RAID 0+1 or RAID N disk, whereas we can store semi-important data on a RAID 0 disk. In the case of RAID, parity bits are used to ensure the integrity of the data stored on each drive. So, RAID N becomes a problem if we have too many write operations to be performed. The time required to update the parity bits in this case is high.

- If it is not important to maintain when the file was last accessed, we can mount the file system with the -o noatime option. This option skips the updates on the file system, which reduces the disk seek time. We can also make the file system update asynchronously. Depending upon whether the file system supports it, we can set the -o async option.

Using NFS with MySQL

While using a **Network File System** (**NFS**), varying issues may occur, depending on the operating system and the NFS version. The following are the details:

- Data inconsistency is one issue with an NFS system. It may occur because of messages received out of order or lost network traffic. We can use TCP with hard and intr mount options to avoid these issues.
- MySQL data and log files may get locked and become unavailable for use if placed on NFS drives. If multiple instances of MySQL access the same data directory, it may result in locking issues. Improper shut down of MySQL or power outage are other reasons for filesystem locking issues. The latest version of NFS supports advisory and lease-based locking, which helps in addressing the locking issues. Still, it is not recommended to share a data directory among multiple MySQL instances.
- Maximum file size limitations must be understood to avoid any issues. With NFS 2, only the lower 2 GB of a file is accessible by clients. NFS 3 clients support larger files. The maximum file size depends on the local file system of the NFS server.

Optimizing the use of memory

In order to improve the performance of database operations, MySQL allocates buffers and caches memory. As a default, the MySQL server starts on a **virtual machine** (**VM**) with 512 MB of RAM. We can modify the default configuration for MySQL to run on limited memory systems.

The following list describes the ways to optimize MySQL memory:

- The memory area which holds cached `InnoDB` data for tables, indexes, and other auxiliary buffers is known as the `InnoDB` buffer pool. The buffer pool is divided into pages. The pages hold multiple rows. The buffer pool is implemented as a linked list of pages for efficient cache management. Rarely used data is removed from the cache using an algorithm. Buffer pool size is an important factor for system performance. The `innodb__buffer_pool_size` system variable defines the buffer pool size. `InnoDB` allocates the entire buffer pool size at server startup. 50 to 75 percent of system memory is recommended for the buffer pool size.
- With `MyISAM`, all threads share the key buffer. The `key_buffer_size` system variable defines the size of the key buffer. The index file is opened once for each `MyISAM` table opened by the server. For each concurrent thread that accesses the table, the data file is opened once. A table structure, column structures for each column, and a 3 x *N* sized buffer are allocated for each concurrent thread. The `MyISAM` storage engine maintains an extra row buffer for internal use.
- The optimizer estimates the reading of multiple rows by scanning. The storage engine interface enables the optimizer to provide information about the recorded buffer size. The size of the buffer can vary depending on the size of the estimate. In order to take advantage of row pre-fetching, `InnoDB` uses a variable size buffering capability. It reduces the overhead of latching and B-tree navigation.
- Memory mapping can be enabled for all `MyISAM` tables by setting the `myisam_use_mmap` system variable to 1.
- The size of an in-memory temporary table can be defined by the `tmp_table_size` system variable. The maximum size of the heap table can be defined using the `max_heap_table_size` system variable. If the in-memory table becomes too large, MySQL automatically converts the table from in-memory to on-disk. The storage engine for an on-disk temporary table is defined by the `internal_tmp_disk_storage_engine` system variable.
- MySQL comes with the MySQL performance schema. It is a feature to monitor MySQL execution at low levels. The performance schema dynamically allocates memory by scaling its memory use to the actual server load, instead of allocating memory upon server startup. The memory, once allocated, is not freed until the server is restarted.

- Thread specific space is required for each thread that the server uses to manage client connections. The stack size is governed by the `thread_stack` system variable. The connection buffer is governed by the `net_buffer_length` system variable. A result buffer is governed by `net_buffer_length`. The connection buffer and result buffer starts with `net_buffer_length` bytes, but enlarges up to `max_allowed_packets` bytes, as needed.
- All threads share the same base memory.
- All join clauses are executed in a single pass. Most of the joins can be executed without a temporary table. Temporary tables are memory-based hash tables. Temporary tables that contain `BLOB` data and tables with large row lengths are stored on disk.
- A read buffer is allocated for each request, which performs a sequential scan on a table. The size of the read buffer is determined by the `read_buffer_size` system variable.
- A random read buffer is allocated when reading rows in an arbitrary manner to avoid disk seeks. The buffer size is determined by the `read_rnd_buffer_size` system variable.
- The memory allocated to a thread is released as soon as the thread is no longer needed. The released memory is returned to the system unless the thread is put into the thread cache.
- MySQL closes all tables that are not in use at once when `FLUSH TABLES` or `mysqladmin` flush-table commands are executed. It marks all in-use tables to be closed when the current thread execution finishes. This frees in-use memory. `FLUSH TABLES` returns only after all tables have been closed.

It is possible to monitor the MySQL performance schema and sys schema for memory usage. Before we can execute commands for this, we have to enable memory instruments on the MySQL performance schema. It can be done by updating the `ENABLED` column of the performance schema `setup_instruments` table. The following is the query to view available memory instruments in MySQL:

```
mysql> SELECT * FROM performance_schema.setup_instruments WHERE NAME LIKE
'%memory%';
```

 If memory instruments are enabled on startup, it ensures memory allocations on startup are counted.

This query will return hundreds of memory instruments. We can narrow it down by specifying a code area. The following is an example to limit results to `InnoDB` memory instruments:

```
mysql> SELECT * FROM performance_schema.setup_instruments WHERE NAME LIKE
'%memory/innodb%';
+------------------------------------------+---------+-------+
|                   NAME                   | ENABLED | TIMED |
+------------------------------------------+---------+-------+
|      memory/innodb/adaptive hash index   |   NO    |  NO   |
|      memory/innodb/buf_buf_pool          |   NO    |  NO   |
| memory/innodb/dict_stats_bg_recalc_pool_t |  NO    |  NO   |
|   memory/innodb/dict_stats_index_map_t   |   NO    |  NO   |
| memory/innodb/dict_stats_n_diff_on_level |   NO    |  NO   |
|         memory/innodb/other              |   NO    |  NO   |
|         memory/innodb/row_log_buf        |   NO    |  NO   |
|        memory/innodb/row_merge_sort      |   NO    |  NO   |
|           memory/innodb/std              |   NO    |  NO   |
|      memory/innodb/trx_sys_t::rw_trx_ids |   NO    |  NO   |
+------------------------------------------+---------+-------+
```

The following is the configuration to enable memory instruments:

```
performance-schema-instrument='memory/%=COUNTED'
```

The following is an example to query memory instrument data in the `memory_summary_global_by_event_name` table in the performance schema:

```
mysql> SELECT * FROM performance_schema.memory_summary_global_by_event_name
WHERE EVENT_NAME LIKE 'memory/innodb/buf_buf_pool'\G;

EVENT_NAME: memory/innodb/buf_buf_pool
COUNT_ALLOC: 1
COUNT_FREE: 0
SUM_NUMBER_OF_BYTES_ALLOC: 137428992
SUM_NUMBER_OF_BYTES_FREE: 0
LOW_COUNT_USED: 0
CURRENT_COUNT_USED: 1
HIGH_COUNT_USED: 1
LOW_NUMBER_OF_BYTES_USED: 0
CURRENT_NUMBER_OF_BYTES_USED: 137428992
HIGH_NUMBER_OF_BYTES_USED: 137428992
```

It summarizes data by `EVENT_NAME`.

The following is an example of querying the sys schema to aggregate currently allocated memory by code area:

```
mysql> SELECT SUBSTRING_INDEX(event_name,'/',2) AS
  code_area, sys.format_bytes(SUM(current_alloc))
  AS current_alloc
  FROM sys.x$memory_global_by_current_bytes
  GROUP BY SUBSTRING_INDEX(event_name,'/',2)
  ORDER BY SUM(current_alloc) DESC;
+----------------------------+---------------+
| code_area                  | current_alloc |
+----------------------------+---------------+
| memory/innodb              | 843.24 MiB    |
| memory/performance_schema  | 81.29 MiB     |
| memory/mysys               | 8.20 MiB      |
| memory/sql                 | 2.47 MiB      |
| memory/memory              | 174.01 KiB    |
| memory/myisam              | 46.53 KiB     |
| memory/blackhole           | 512 bytes     |
| memory/federated           | 512 bytes     |
| memory/csv                 | 512 bytes     |
| memory/vio                 | 496 bytes     |
+----------------------------+---------------+
```

Optimizing use of the network

The MySQL database server opens up network interfaces to connect with the clients and starts listening to these interfaces. The connection manager threads are responsible for handling client connection requests. The connection manager threads additionally handle socket files on the Unix platform. The connection manager thread takes care of shared-memory connection requests, and one other thread handles named-pipe connection requests on the Windows system. Threads are not created for the interfaces that the server does not listen to.

The connection manager thread allocates a thread to each client connection. The thread authenticates and takes care of request processing for that client connection. The manager threads check within the thread cache for a thread first, which can be used for the client connection. If no thread is available in the cache, it creates a new thread. Once the client request is processed and the connection ends, the thread which was created to serve the client connection is returned to the thread cache unless the cache is full.

There are as many threads as the number of clients currently connected in this thread connection model. It has disadvantages, as well. When the server is required to be scaled to handle a higher number of connections than it is handling right now, thread creation and disposal becomes expensive. In this thread connection model, server and kernel resources are required for each thread.

Few server variables can be used to set up the server for optimized network usage. The `thread_cache_size` is the system variable which defines the size of the thread cache. The default value for thread cache size is 0. This means that for each new connection, a thread is to be set up and disposed when the connection terminates. If we set `thread_cache_size` to 10, it enables 10 inactive connection threads to be cached. The thread connection becomes inactive when the connection with the client it was associated with terminates.

The complexity of the SQL statements a server can handle is limited by the size of the thread stack. The MySQL 8 server can be started with `--thread_stack=N` to set N bytes of stack size for each thread.

After setting the thread cache size, it becomes critical to monitor the impact. `Threads_cached` and `Threads_created` are the status variables to find out the number of threads in the thread cache, and the number of threads created because it could not be taken from the cache. The following is an example command to find out server status variable values:

```
mysql> show global status;
+-------------------------------+---------+
| Variable_name                 | Value   |
+-------------------------------+---------+
| Aborted_clients               |    0    |
| Aborted_connects              |    1    |
| Acl_cache_items_count         |    0    |
| Binlog_cache_disk_use         |    0    |
| Binlog_cache_use              |    0    |
| Binlog_stmt_cache_disk_use    |    0    |
| Binlog_stmt_cache_use         |    0    |
| Bytes_received                |  443    |
| Bytes_sent                    |  346    |
| Threads_cached                |    0    |
| Threads_connected             |    1    |
| Threads_created               |    1    |
| Threads_running               |    2    |
+-------------------------------+---------+
```

The following is an example of filtering the `status` variables:

```
mysql> show status like '%Thread%';
+------------------------------------------------+--------+
| Variable_name                                  | Value  |
+------------------------------------------------+--------+
| Delayed_insert_threads                         |     0  |
| Performance_schema_thread_classes_lost         |     0  |
| Performance_schema_thread_instances_lost       |     0  |
| Slow_launch_threads                            |     0  |
| Threads_cached                                 |     0  |
| Threads_connected                              |     1  |
| Threads_created                                |     1  |
| Threads_running                                |     2  |
+------------------------------------------------+--------+
```

Optimizing locking operations

As discussed in one of the earlier chapters, MySQL 8 uses locking mechanisms to manage contention. Contention occurs when concurrently executing queries in multiple threads try to get ahold of one table at the same time. If these queries are performed on the table concurrently, the table data is left in an inconsistent state. MySQL 8 supports two types of locking: internal locking and external locking.

Internal locking is performed by multiple threads within the MySQL server to manage contention for table contents. This type of locking is performed entirely by the MySQL server, without involving any other programs. So, why it is called internal locking? In the case of external locking, the MySQL server and other programs lock table files to decide which programs can access the table at a time.

The following are the two methods for internal locking:

- Row-level locking.
- Table-level locking.

Row-level locking in MySQL supports simultaneous write access to multiple sessions. This enables multi-user and highly concurrent applications. While performing multiple concurrent write operations on a single table, it is highly possible that a deadlock may occur.

In order to avoid such a deadlock situation, a locking mechanism acquires locks at the beginning of the transaction using the SELECT ... FOR UPDATE statement for each set of rows to be modified. MySQL applies the statements in the same order within each transaction if transactions lock more than one table. The InnoDB database engine automatically detects deadlock conditions and rolls back the affected transactions. Considering this, deadlocks affect performance.

The deadlock detection may cause slowdown if many threads wait for the same lock in highly concurrent systems. In such cases, it becomes more efficient to disable deadlock detection. We can rely on the innodb_lock_wait_timeout setting for transaction rollback when deadlock occurs. Using the innodb_deadlock_detect configuration option, we can disable the deadlock detection.

The following are the advantages of row-level locking:

- When different sessions access different rows in a table, the number of lock conflicts is fewer
- The number of changes to be rolled back is fewer
- It becomes possible to lock a single table row for a long time

Table-level locking is used by MySQL for MyISAM, MEMORY, and MERGE tables. In the case of table-level locking, MySQL permits only one session to update these tables at a time. With table-level locking, these storage engines become suitable for read-only or single-user applications. These storage engines request all the required locks at once, when the query begins, to avoid any deadlocks. It always locks the tables in the same order. The major drawback with table-level locking is that it affects concurrency. If other sessions need to modify the table, they must wait until the concurrent data change statement finishes.

The following are the advantages of table-level locking:

- It requires less memory compared to row-level locking
- When used on a large part of the table, it is fast, because only one lock is required
- If GROUP BY operations are performed frequently, it is fast

The following is the strategy for MySQL to grant write locks on tables:

1. Put a write lock on the table if there are no write locks on the table
2. Put a lock request in the write lock queue if the table already has a write lock

The following is the strategy for MySQL to grant read locks on tables:

1. Put a read lock on the table if there are no read locks on the table
2. Put a lock request in the read lock queue if the table already has a read lock

More priority is given to table updates than table retrievals. The lock is available to the write lock requests first, and then to the read lock requests when a lock is released.

The following is an example to analyze table lock contention:

```
mysql> SHOW STATUS LIKE 'Table_locks%';
+-----------------------+-------+
| Variable_name         | Value |
+-----------------------+-------+
| Table_locks_immediate |     5 |
| Table_locks_waited    |     0 |
+-----------------------+-------+
```

The MyISAM storage engine inherently supports multiple concurrent inserts in order to reduce contention between readers and writers for a table. It allows the MyISAM table to insert rows in the middle of a data file. If the table does not have any free blocks in the middle of the data file, the rows are inserted at the end of the file. This enables MySQL to execute INSERT and SELECT queries on the same table, concurrently. concurrent_insert is the global system variable which controls the behavior of the MyISAM storage engine to allow execution of concurrent INSERT and SELECT statements. If this system variable is set to AUTO, concurrent INSERT and SELECT are allowed.

If concurrent inserts are not possible and we want to perform multiple INSERT and SELECT operations on a table tab1, we can use the temporary table temp_tab1 to hold the tab1 table data and update the tab1 table with the rows from the temp_tab1 table. The following is an example which demonstrates this scenario:

```
mysql> LOCK TABLES tab1 WRITE, temp_tab1 WRITE;
mysql> INSERT INTO tab1 SELECT * FROM temp_tab1;
mysql> DELETE FROM temp_tab1;
mysql> UNLOCK TABLES;
```

Performance benchmarking

We must consider the following factors when measuring performance:

- While measuring the speed of a single operation or a set of operations, it is important to simulate a scenario in the case of a heavy database workload for benchmarking
- In different environments, the test results may be different
- Depending on the workload, certain MySQL features may not help with performance

MySQL 8 supports measuring the performance of individual statements. If we want to measure the speed of any SQL expression or function, the BENCHMARK() function is used. The following is the syntax for the function:

```
BENCHMARK(loop_count, expression)
```

The output of the BENCHMARK function is always zero. The speed can be measured by the line printed by MySQL in the output. The following is an example:

```
mysql> select benchmark(1000000, 1+1);
+-------------------------+
| benchmark(1000000, 1+1) |
+-------------------------+
|                       0 |
+-------------------------+
1 row in set (0.15 sec)
```

From the preceding example, we can find that the time taken to calculate 1+1 for 1000000 times is 0.15 seconds.

Examining thread information

At times, we may need to figure out what the MySQL server is doing. So, it becomes necessary to find out the process list. The process list is the set of threads currently being executed within the MySQL server.

The following are the sources for getting process list information:

- The SHOW [FULL] PROCESSLIST statement. The following is an example of process list information:

```
mysql> show processlist;
+----+------------------+-----------------+------+---------+--------+
| Id |      User        |      Host       |  db  | Command |  Time  |
+----+------------------+-----------------+------+---------+--------+
```

```
+----------------------+--------------------------+
|         State        |          Info            |
+----------------------+--------------------------+
```

```
+----+------------------+-----------------+------+---------+--------+
| 4  | event_scheduler  |    localhost    | NULL | Daemon  | 214901 |
+----+------------------+-----------------+------+---------+--------+
| 8  | root             | localhost:58629 | NULL | Query   |   0    |
+----+------------------+-----------------+------+---------+--------+
```

```
+----------------------+--------------------------+
| Waiting on empty queue |        NULL            |
+----------------------+--------------------------+
| starting             | show full processlist    |
+----------------------+--------------------------+
```

- The SHOW PROFILE statement.
- The INFORMATION_SCHEMA PROCESSLIST table:

```
mysql> select * from information_schema.processlist;
+----+------------------+-----------------+------+---------+--------+
| ID |      USER        |      HOST       |  DB  | COMMAND |  TIME  |
+----+------------------+-----------------+------+---------+--------+
```

```
+----------------------+----------------------------------------------+
|         STATE        |                   INFO                       |
+----------------------+----------------------------------------------+
```

```
+----+------------------+-----------------+------+---------+--------+
| 8  | root             | localhost:58629 | NULL | Query   |   0    |
+----+------------------+-----------------+------+---------+--------+
| 4  | event_scheduler  | localhost       | NULL | Daemon  | 215640 |
+----+------------------+-----------------+------+---------+--------+
```

```
+----------------------+----------------------------------------------+
| executing            | select * from information_schema.processlist  |
+----------------------+----------------------------------------------+
| Waiting on empty queue | NULL                                       |
+----------------------+----------------------------------------------+
```

- The `mysqladmin processlist` command.
- The performance schema threads table, stage tables, and lock tables.

We must be able to view the information of user threads. The `PROCESS` privilege is required to view the information about threads being executed. To access threads, a Mutex access is not required. It has less impact on the MySQL server performance. Accessing `INFORMATION_SCHEMA.PROCESSLIST` and `SHOW PROCESSLIST` requires a Mutex and has an impact on performance. Threads also provide details of background threads. `INFORMATION_SCHEMA.PROCESSLIST` and `SHOW PROCESSLIST` do not provide information about background threads.

The following table shows the information contained in each process list entry:

Information	Details
Id	Client connection identifier for the client that the thread is associated with.
User, Host	Account associated with the thread.
db	Default database for the thread or `NULL`.
Command, State	It indicates what the thread is currently doing.
Time	It indicates how long the thread has been in the current state.
Info	It contains the information of the statement being executed by the thread.

The following is the thread state values associated with general query processing:

- `After create`: It occurs when the thread creates a table, including internal temporary tables
- `Analyzing`: It occurs when the thread is calculating `MyISAM` key distribution
- `Checking permissions`: It occurs when checking if the server has the required privileges to execute the SQL statement
- `Checking table`: It occurs when the thread is performing a table check operation
- `Cleaning up`: It occurs when the thread has processed one command and frees the memory

- `Closing tables`: It occurs when the thread is flushing the changed table data to disk and closing the used tables
- `Altering table`: It occurs when the server is processing the ALTER TABLE statement
- `Creating index`: It occurs when the thread is processing ALTER TABLE ... ENABLE KEYS for the MyISAM table
- `Creating table`: It occurs when the thread is creating a table
- `end`: It occurs at the end, but before the clean up of ALTER TABLE, CREATE VIEW, DELETE, INSERT, SELECT, or UPDATE statements
- `executing`: It occurs when the thread has begun executing a statement
- `init`: It occurs before the initialization of ALTER TABLE, DELETE, INSERT, SELECT, and UPDATE statements

The following is the list of common states in the master's `binlog` dump thread for replication master threads:

- Finished reading one `binlog`; switching to next `binlog`
- Master has sent all `binlog` to slave; waiting for more updates
- Sending `binlog` event to slave
- Waiting to finalize termination

The following is a list of common states for a slave server I/O thread:

- Checking master version
- Connecting to master
- Queueing master event to the relay log
- Reconnecting after a failed `binlog` dump request
- Reconnecting after a failed master event read
- Registering slave on master
- Requesting `binlog` dump
- Waiting for its turn to commit
- Waiting for master to send event
- Waiting for master update
- Waiting for slave Mutex on exit
- Waiting for the slave SQL thread to free enough relay log space
- Waiting to reconnect after a failed `binlog` dump request
- Waiting to reconnect after a failed master event read

The following is a list of common states for a slave server SQL thread:

- Killing slave
- Making temporary file (append) before replaying `LOAD DATA INFILE`
- Making temporary file (create) before replaying `LOAD DATA INFILE`
- Reading event from the relay log
- Slave has read all relay log; waiting for more updates
- Waiting for an event from coordinator
- Waiting for slave Mutex on exit
- Waiting for slave workers to free pending events
- Waiting for the next event in relay log
- Waiting until `MASTER_DELAY` seconds after master executed event

Optimizing database structure

As a database administrator, we must look for efficient ways to organize table schema, tables, and columns. We minimize I/O, plan ahead, and keep related items together to tune the application code in order to keep performance high with an increase in data volume. It usually starts with efficient database design, which makes it easier for team members to write high-performance application code. It also makes the database likely to sustain itself as applications evolve or are rewritten.

Optimizing data size

In order to minimize the space on the disk, we should start designing the database tables. This results in huge performance improvements, as it reduces the amount of data to be written to and read from the disk. Smaller tables usually need less main memory, while the contents are actively processed during query execution. Any reduction in table data space results in a need for smaller indexes that can be processed faster.

As discussed in the chapter on MySQL 8 data types, MySQL supports many different storage engines and row formats. We can decide the storage and indexing method to be used for each table. It is a big performance gain to choose the proper table format.

Table columns

We should use the smallest feasible data type for a table column. This results in the most efficient approach. MySQL supports specialized data types to save memory and disk space. For example, we should use integer types wherever possible to get smaller tables. Comparing MEDIUMINT and INT, MEDIUMINT is a better choice, as it uses 25% less space compared to INT.

We must declare columns to be NOT NULL wherever possible. This enables better use of indexes and eliminates the overhead of testing whether each value is NULL or not. It results in faster SQL operations. We can also save one bit per column of storage space. We should use NULL if we really require it. NULL values should not be allowed as a result of default settings for every column.

We can attain huge performance gain for a table and minimize storage space requirement by using following techniques:

Row format

As a default, the DYNAMIC row format is used when creating InnoDB tables. We can configure innodb_default_row_format to use row formats other than DYNAMIC. We can also specify the ROW_FORMAT option explicitly in a CREATE TABLE or ALTER TABLE statement.

The row formats include COMPACT, DYNAMIC, and COMPRESSED. They decrease row storage space at the cost of increased CPU use for some operations. For the average workload, which is limited by the cache hit rates and disk speed, it will be faster. If it is limited by the CPU speed, it will be slower.

The row formats also optimize the CHAR data type column storage when it uses a variable length character set. With the REDUNDANT row format, the CHAR(N) column value occupies N times the maximum byte length in the character set. The InnoDB storage engine allocates variable amounts of storage within the range of N to N times the maximum byte length in the character set.

A fixed-size row format is used if we do not have variable-length columns, such as VARCHAR, TEXT, or BLOB, in the case of MyISAM tables.

Indexes

A table's primary index must be as short as feasible. This enables easy identification of each row. It is efficient, too. In the case of `InnoDB` tables, the primary key column is duplicated in each secondary index entry. If we have a short primary key, it saves space in the case of many secondary indexes.

We should create only those indexes which improve query performance. The indexes improve information retrieval, but they slow down the insert and update operations. Indexes must be created with proper attention to the performance impact. If it is required to access a table by searching on a combination of columns, it is preferred to have a composite index on the combination of columns, rather than a separate index on each of the columns. The most used column should be the first part of the index. If it is a common requirement to use many columns in selected operations on the table, it is advisable to have the column with the most duplicates as the first column in the index. This gives better compression of the index.

If a long string column is supposed to have a unique prefix as the first few characters, it is advisable to index only the prefix, using MySQL's support for indexing on the leftmost part of the column. Shorter indexes are preferred, not only for the less space they require, but also because they provide more hits in the index cache and require fewer disk seeks.

Joins

If a table is scanned very often, it is beneficial to split the table into two tables, if feasible. This holds true especially if it is a dynamic-format table. It is also possible to use smaller static format tables, which can be used to search for relevant rows while scanning the tables.

The columns with identical information should be declared in different tables with identical data types. This speeds up joins based on matching columns.

Column names must be kept simple, so as to use the same name across tables. It simplifies join queries. For example, in a customer table, we should use the column name of `name`, rather than using `customer_name`. In order to make the names portable to other SQL servers, we should keep the column names shorter than 18 characters.

Normalization

The data in the table columns must be kept non-redundant, considering the third normal form in the normalization theory. If the column holds repeating lengthy values, such as names or addresses, it is preferable to assign unique IDs and repeat these IDs across multiple smaller tables. In the event of searching, join queries should be used by referencing IDs in the join clauses.

In an application, if the preference is speed and not disk space or the maintenance costs of using multiple copies of data, it is advisable to duplicate the information or create summary tables to gain more speed. An example scenario could be a business intelligence system, where data is analyzed from large tables. In this case, normalization rules are not strictly followed.

Optimizing MySQL data types

The following are the guidelines for optimizing numeric data types:

- Numeric columns must be preferred over string columns to store unique IDs or other values that can be represented as either strings or numbers. It is faster and occupies less memory to transfer and compare, because large numeric values are stored in fewer bytes compared to strings.
- It is faster to access information from a database than from a text file. This is especially true when numeric data is used. Information in the database is stored in a more compact format than in the text file. So, it requires fewer disk accesses.

The following are the guidelines for optimizing character and string data types:

- The binary collation order (logical sequence) should be used for faster comparisons and sort operations. The binary operator can also be used within a query to use binary collation order.
- With an InnoDB table, when we use a randomly generated value as a primary key, it should be prefixed with an ascending value, such as the date and time, if feasible. In this case, primary key values are stored nearer to each other, physically. InnoDB can insert or retrieve such values faster.
- The binary VARCHAR data type should be used instead of BLOB for column values that are expected to hold less than 8 KB of data. If the original table does not have any BLOB columns, the GROUP BY and ORDER BY clauses generate temporary tables. These temporary tables can use the MEMORY storage engine.

- In order to avoid string conversions while running a query, the columns should be declared with the same character set and order wherever possible when comparing the values from different columns.
- If the table holds string columns which are not frequently used in retrieval operations, splitting the string columns into a separate table should be considered. In the retrieval operations, join queries should be used with a foreign key wherever necessary. MySQL reads a data block containing all the columns of a row when it retrieves any value from a row. It allows more rows to fit within each data block when we keep the rows small, with only frequently used columns. These compact tables reduce memory usage and disk I/O.

The following are the guidelines for optimizing `BLOB` data types:

- The performance requirements for a `BLOB` column may be different when retrieving and displaying information. So, storing the `BLOB` specific table in a different storage device or a separate database instance should be considered. For example, it is required to retrieve a `BLOB` in a large sequential disk read. So, a traditional hard drive or an SSD device might better suit needs.
- In order to reduce the memory requirements for a query which does not use a `BLOB` column, for a table with several columns, splitting the `BLOB` into separate tables and referencing with join queries should be considered, as needed.
- If a table column is a large blob with textual data, compressing should be considered first. If the entire table is compressed by the storage engine, such as `InnoDB` or `MyISAM`, this technique should not be used.

Optimizing for many tables

We learned the technique of splitting a table into many tables for faster execution of queries in certain situations. This technique cannot be applied in all of the scenarios, as if the number of tables runs into thousands, the overhead of managing all these tables becomes another performance nightmare.

In this section, we will see how MySQL opens and closes tables. The following shows how to discover open files on the MySQL server:

```
> mysqladmin status
Uptime: 262200 Threads: 2 Questions: 16 Slow queries: 0 Opens: 111 Flush
tables: 2 Open tables: 87 Queries per second avg: 0.000
```

The MySQL 8 server is multi-threaded. It is possible that many clients issue queries for a table simultaneously. MySQL opens the table independently for each concurrent session, in order to minimize the problem of multiple client sessions with different states on the same table. This improves performance, though it requires additional memory. One extra file descriptor is required in the data file for each client that opens the `MyISAM` table.

The `table_open_cache` system variable determines the number of open tables for all the threads. The number of file descriptors `mysqld` requires can be increased by increasing this value. The `max_connections` system variable determines the maximum permitted number of simultaneous client connections. In a way, these two system variables affect the maximum number of files that the MySQL server can keep open. If we increase both values, we may run against a limit imposed by the operating system on the per process number of open files.

The following are the circumstances under which MySQL closes unused tables:

- A thread tries to open a table which is not in the table cache when the table cache is full.
- When the table cache contains more entries than specified in the `table_open_cache` system variable and a table in the cache is no longer used by any threads.
- When someone issues the `FLUSH TABLES` statement or executes a `mysqladmin flush-tables` or `mysqladmin refresh` command, the table flushing operation occurs. MySQL closes the table on this event.

The MySQL 8 server uses the following process to locate a cache entry when the table cache is full:

- Unused tables are released, starting with the table used the least recently.
- If it is required to open a new table and the table cache is full and no tables can be released, the cache is temporarily extended, as needed. If a table transitions from a used to unused state when the table cache is in a temporarily extended state, the table is closed and released from the table cache.

The following is an example of finding the number of open tables:

```
mysql> SHOW GLOBAL STATUS LIKE '%Opened_Tables%';
+---------------+-------+
| Variable_name | Value |
+---------------+-------+
| Opened_tables | 112   |
+---------------+-------+
```

Use of an internal temporary table in MySQL

The MySQL 8 server creates temporary internal tables while processing SQL statements, in some cases. The following are the conditions under which the server creates temporary tables:

- UNION statements
- Views which uses the TEMPTABLE algorithm, UNION, or aggregation
- Derived tables
- Common table expressions
- Tables created for subquery or semi join materialization
- Statements that contain ORDER BY and GROUP BY clauses
- Statements with DISTINCT combined with ORDER BY
- Queries that use the SQL_SMALL_RESULT modifier
- INSERT ... SELECT statements that select from and insert into the same table
- Multiple table UPDATE statements
- GROUP_CONCAT() or COUNT(DISTINCT) expressions

The EXPLAIN statement can be used to determine whether the statement requires a temporary table. The EXPLAIN statement has limitations. It will not indicate if the statement requires a temporary table for derived or materialized temporary tables.

The Created_tmp_tables status variable keeps track of the number of temporary tables created in internal memory. When the MySQL server creates a temporary table, it increments the value in the Created_tmp_tables status variable. Created_tmp_disk_tables is another status variable that keeps track of the number of tables created on the disk.

Based on the query conditions, the server prevents the use of temporary tables in memory. In such cases, the server creates a table on the disk. The following are some instances:

- If the table has a BLOB or TEXT column
- If the statement has a string column with a maximum length larger than 512 bytes in the SELECT list, if UNION or UNION ALL is used
- If the SHOW COLUMNS and DESCRIBE statements use BLOB as the type of the column

The following are the conditions in which a UNION is evaluated without creating temporary tables:

- The union is UNION ALL and not UNION or UNION DISTINCT
- There is no global ORDER BY clause
- In a SELECT query, the union is not at the top-level query block

Optimizing queries

Similar to tables, database queries are the most crucial element of any database. Applications interact with the databases using queries. Queries are also called executable SQL statements. This section focuses on techniques to improve the performance of query execution.

Optimizing SQL statements

SQL statements are used to perform the core logic of any database application. It does not matter whether the statements are issued directly through an interpreter or submitted behind the scenes by an API. This section outlines guidelines to improve the performance of SQL operations that read and write data in the database.

SELECT statements perform all of the lookup operations in the database. Considering the frequency of SELECT statements, it becomes important to tune these statements at the top priority. The tuning techniques must be applied to constructs like CREATE TABLE...AS SELECT, INSERT INTO...SELECT, and WHERE clauses in DELETE statements.

The following are the main considerations for optimizing queries:

- In order to optimize the SELECT ... WHERE query, the first thing to check is if an index can be added. We should add indexes on the columns used in the WHERE clause of the SELECT query. This will speed up the evaluation, filtering, and the retrieval of results. The strategy should be to construct a small set of indexes that can speed up many related queries used in the application. It also avoids the wasted disk space.
- The indexes are important for queries which reference different tables using joins and foreign keys. The EXPLAIN statement can be used to determine which indexes are used in a SELECT statement execution.

- The next step should be to isolate and tune parts of the query; for example, a function call which takes excessive time. Depending upon the structure of the query, a function call can be done for every row in the table or for every row in the result set.

- The number of full table scans in the query must be minimized, specifically for big tables.

- The `ANALYZE TABLE` statement should be used periodically to keep the table statistics up-to-date. The optimizer provides the information required to build an efficient query execution plan.

- If the basic guidelines do not solve the performance issues, queries should be investigated for internal details by reading the `EXPLAIN` plan and adjusting your indexes, `WHERE` clauses, join clauses, and so on.

- Transforming queries in a way that makes them hard to understand should be avoided, especially when the optimizer does some of the same transformations automatically.

- The `InnoDB` buffer pool, `MyISAM` key cache, and the MySQL query cache must be used efficiently for repeated queries to run faster as the results are retrieved from memory after the first time. The size and properties of the memory area must be adjusted, as MySQL uses it for caching.

- If the query runs faster using the cache memory area, we should still optimize it further, so that it requires less cache memory. It makes the application more scalable, which makes the application capable of handling more simultaneous users, larger requests, and so on, without experiencing performance drop.

- Where the speed of the query is affected by other sessions accessing the table at the same time, we should deal with locking issues.

The following are the guidelines to optimize the `WHERE` clause. These optimizations are applicable to `WHERE` clauses in `SELECT`, `DELETE`, or `UPDATE` queries, equally:

- Unnecessary parentheses should be removed. The following is an example of parentheses removal:

```
((a AND b) AND c OR (((a AND b) AND (c AND d))))
-> (a AND b AND c) OR (a AND b AND c AND d)
```

- Constant folding is the process of evaluating values at compile time instead of runtime. If we have assigned a constant value to a variable and then use that variable in an expression, we should use the constant value instead. The following is an example of constant folding:

```
(a<b AND b=c) AND a=5
-> b>5 AND b=c AND a=5
```

- Because of constant folding, we should remove constant conditions. The following is an example of constant condition removal:

```
(B>=5 AND B=5) OR (B=6 AND 5=5) OR (B=7 AND 5=6)
-> B=5 OR B=6
```

Optimizing indexes

The basic use of indexes is to quickly find the rows with specific column values. If the index is not present, MySQL begins with the first row and reads through the entire table to find all the matching rows. It takes more time, depending on how large a table is. If the index is present for the appropriate columns, MySQL is able to quickly determine the position to seek to in the middle of the data file, without looking at the whole table data.

The following is a list of operations for which MySQL uses indexes:

- To find matching rows, based on a WHERE clause, quickly.
- MySQL uses the index with the smallest number of rows (most selective index) in the case of choosing from multiple indexes to eliminate rows from consideration.
- The optimizer uses the leftmost prefix of the index to look up rows if the table has a composite index. For example, in a table with three columns indexed (on col1, col2, col3), the optimizer can look for rows with indexed search capabilities on (col1), (col1, col2), and (col1, col2, col3).
- MySQL uses indexes while it fetches rows from other tables using joins. If the indexes are declared as the same type and size, MySQL can use them efficiently on the column. The VARCHAR and CHAR are considered the same when declared as the same size.
- MySQL also uses indexes to find the minimum (MIN ()) or maximum (MAX ()) value for an indexed column key_col. The preprocessor checks whether it is using WHERE key_part_N = constant on all key parts to optimize it.

- It is also possible to optimize the query to retrieve values without consulting the data rows. (A covering index is an index that provides all the results for a query.) If the query uses only those columns from a table which are included in some index, the selected values will be fetched from the index tree. This will have a higher speed in retrieving values.

Query execution plan

The MySQL optimizer considers optimization techniques to efficiently perform the lookups involved in the query, depending on the details of the tables, columns, and indexes, and the conditions in the WHERE clause. A query can also be performed without reading all the rows on a huge table. An SQL join can also be performed without comparing every combination of rows. A query execution plan is a set of operations that the MySQL optimizer chooses to perform the most efficient query. It is also known as the EXPLAIN plan. As an administrator, the goal is to recognize the aspects of the query execution plan which indicate if a query is optimized.

The EXPLAIN statement is used to determine the query execution plan. The following is the set of information provided by the EXPLAIN statement:

- The EXPLAIN statement works with SELECT, DELETE, INSERT, UPDATE, and REPLACE statements.
- MySQL displays information from the MySQL optimizer about the query execution plan when EXPLAIN is used with the SQL statement. This means MySQL explains the process with which the statement is executed. It includes information about how tables are joined, and in which order.
- If EXPLAIN displays the execution plan for the statement execution in the named connection if it is used with FOR CONNECTION connection_id instead of explainable SQL statement.
- EXPLAIN displays additional execution plan information for SELECT statements.
- EXPLAIN is also useful in examining queries which involve partitioned tables.
- EXPLAIN supports a FORMAT option, which can be used to select the output format. The TRADITIONAL format displays the output in a tabular format. This is the default format option. The **JavaScript Object Notation** (**JSON**) format option produces information in the JSON format.

Based on the output from the EXPLAIN statement, it can be figured out where indexes can be added to the tables, so that the statement executes faster. It can also be found whether the optimizer joins the tables in the optimized order. Begin the statement with SELECT STRAIGHT_JOIN, instead of just SELECT, to give a hint to the optimizer to use the join order corresponding to the order the tables are named in the SELECT statement. As STRAIGHT_JOIN disables semi-join transformations, it may prevent the use of indexes.

The optimizer trace is another tool to find the information on the query execution. It is possible that the optimizer trace may provide information differing from that of EXPLAIN. The format and content of the optimizer trace are subject to variation, based on the versions.

The following table shows the output format of the EXPLAIN statement:

Column	JSON Name	Details
id	select_id	The SELECT identifier
select_type	None	The SELECT type
table	table_name	The table for the output row
partitions	partitions	The matching partitions
type	access_type	The join type
possible_keys	possible_keys	The possible indexes to choose
key	key	The index actually chosen
key_len	key_length	The length of the chosen key
ref	ref	The columns compared to the index
rows	rows	Estimate of rows to be examined
filtered	filtered	Percentage of rows filtered by table condition
Extra	None	Additional Information

Reference: https://dev.mysql.com/doc/refman/8.0/en/explain-output.html#explain-output-column-table

Optimizing tables

Database tables are the most basic building blocks for any database. In this section of the chapter, we will focus on optimizing tables. The section provides detailed guidelines for improving performance through table optimization techniques.

Optimization for InnoDB tables

The InnoDB storage engine is preferred in production environments in situations where reliability and concurrency are important. It is the default storage engine for MySQL tables. This section focuses on optimizing database operations for InnoDB tables.

The following are the guidelines to optimize InnoDB tables:

- Use of the OPTIMIZE TABLE statement should be considered to reorganize the table and compact the wasted space once the data reaches a stable size or the table has increased by tens of megabytes. It requires less disk I/O to perform full table scans for reorganized tables.
- The OPTIMIZE TABLE statement copies the data in the table and rebuilds the indexes. It is beneficial because of improved packing of the data within indexes, and fragmentation reduction within the table spaces on the disk. The benefits may vary, depending on the data in each table. It may be noticeable that the gains are significant in some cases, and not for others. The gains may also decrease over time until the next table optimization is done. The operation can be slow if the table is large or the indexes being rebuilt do not fit in the buffer pool.
- A long primary key in a InnoDB table wastes a lot of disk space. It should be avoided.
- In InnoDB tables, preference should be given to the VARCHAR data type instead of the CHAR data type to store variable length strings, or for columns which are expected to contain NULL values. A CHAR(N) column always occupies *N* characters to store data, even if the value is NULL. Smaller tables are more suitable to fit in the buffer pool and reduced disk I/O.
- Consider using a COMPRESSED row format for big tables, or tables containing lots of repetitive text or numeric data.

Optimization for MyISAM tables

For read-only or read-mostly data, or for low concurrency operations, the `MyISAM` storage engine fits the best. This is because table locks limit the ability to perform simultaneous updates. In this section, the focus will be on optimizing queries to be executed on `MyISAM` tables.

The following are the guidelines for speeding up queries on `MyISAM` tables:

- Avoid executing complex `SELECT` queries on frequently updated `MyISAM` tables. It prevents problems with table locking that occur because of contention between writers and readers.
- The `MyISAM` storage engine supports concurrent inserts. If the table data file does not have free blocks in the middle, we can `INSERT` new rows in it at the same time that other threads are reading from the table. Consider using the table to avoid deleting rows if it is important to be able to do concurrent read-write operations. Another option is to execute `OPTIMIZE TABLE` to defragment the table after deletion of the rows. This behavior can be controlled or modified by setting the `concurrent_insert` system variable.
- Avoid all variable-length columns for frequently changing `MyISAM` tables. The dynamic row format is used by the table if it includes even a single variable length column.
- The `myisamchk --sort-index --sort-records=1` command can be used to sort an index. It also sorts data according to the index. This makes the queries run faster if we have unique indexes, based on which we want to read all rows in the order according to the index. It takes a long time when we sort a large table this way for the first time.
- If we usually retrieve rows in the order of `expression1`, `expression2`, and so on, use `ALTER TABLE ... ORDER BY expression1, expression2,..`, and so on. This will give higher performance, if this option is used after extensive changes to the table.

Optimization for MEMORY tables

MySQL `MEMORY` tables should be considered for use only for noncritical data that is accessed often and is read-only and rarely updated. The application should be benchmarked against equivalent `InnoDB` or `MyISAM` tables under realistic workloads to confirm that additional performance is worth the risk of losing data.

We should examine the kinds of queries against each table for best performance with
MEMORY tables. We should also specify the type of use for each associated index. It can be a
B-tree index or a hash index. Use the USING BTREE or USING HASH clause on the CREATE
INDEX statement.

Leveraging buffering and caching

This section focuses on using buffering and caching techniques to increase the performance.

InnoDB buffer pool optimization

The InnoDB storage engine maintains a storage area known as the buffer pool. It is used for
caching data and indexes in the memory. It is important to know how the InnoDB buffer
pool works, so as to take advantage of it to keep frequently accessed data in memory. It is
an important aspect of MySQL tuning.

The following are the general guidelines for improving performance with the InnoDB buffer
pool:

- In an ideal case, the size of the buffer pool should be set large enough, while
  leaving enough memory for other processes on the server to run without
  excessive paging. With larger buffer pools, more InnoDB functions, like an in-
  memory database. In this case, it reads data from the disk once, and then accesses
  the data from memory in subsequent reads.
- We can consider splitting the buffer pool into many parts for 64-bit systems with
  large memory sizes. This minimizes contention for memory during concurrent
  operations.
- The frequently accessed data should be kept in memory.
- It is possible to control when and how InnoDB performs read-ahead requests to
  prefetch pages into the buffer pool asynchronously. InnoDB uses two read-ahead
  algorithms to improve I/O performance. Linear read ahead predicts what pages
  might be needed soon, based on the pages being accessed in the buffer pool
  sequentially. Random read ahead predicts when pages might be needed based on
  the pages in the buffer pool, regardless of the order in which pages are read. The
  innodb_read_ahead_threshold configuration parameter controls the
  sensitivity of linear read ahead. We can enable random read a heads by setting
  innodb_random_read_ahead to ON.

- `innodb_buffer_pool_read_ahead` determines the number of pages read into the `InnoDB` buffer pool. `innodb_buffer_pool_read_ahead_evicted` determines the number of pages read into the buffer pool by the read-ahead background thread that was subsequently evicted without having been accessed by queries. The `innodb_buffer_pool_read_ahead_rnd` determines the number of random read aheads initiated by `InnoDB`.

MyISAM key cache

The `MyISAM` storage engine incorporates a strategy that is supported by many database management systems to minimize the disk I/O. The cache mechanism is employed by `MyISAM` to keep the most frequently accessed table blocks in memory as follows:

- A special structure known as a key cache is maintained for index blocks. The most used index blocks are placed in the structure containing a number of block buffers.
- MySQL relies on the native operating system filesystem cache for data blocks.

The `key_buffer_size` system variable determines the size of the key cache. If it is set to zero, no key cache is used. The key cache is also not used if the `key_buffer_size` value is too small to allocate the minimum order of block buffers. All the block buffers in the key cache structure are of the same size. This size can be equal to, greater than, or less than the size of the table index block. In usual cases, one of these two values is a multiple of the other.

When it is required to access data from any table index block, the server first checks if it is available in some block buffer of the key cache. If the data is available, the server accesses data from the key cache rather than on the disk. If the data is not available, the server selects a cache block buffer that contains a different table index block and replaces the data in it by copying the required table index block. The index data can be accessed as soon as the new index block is available in the cache.

The MySQL server follows the **Least Recently Used** (**LRU**) strategy. According to it, it selects the least recently used index block while choosing a block for replacement. The key cache module contains all used blocks in the LRU chain (a special list). The list is ordered by the time of use. It is the most recently used when the block is accessed. The block is placed at the end of the list. Blocks at the beginning of the list are the least recently used when the blocks need to be replaced. So, the block at the top becomes the first candidate for eviction.

The block is considered dirty if the block selected for replacement has been modified. The block contents are flushed to the table index from which they came prior to replacement.

Based on the following conditions, the threads can access key cache buffers simultaneously:

- The buffer which is not being updated can be accessed by multiple sessions
- The buffer which is being updated causes sessions that require waiting until the update is complete to use it
- As long as the sessions are independent and do not interfere with each other, multiple sessions can initiate requests resulting in cache block replacements

In this way, shared access to the key cache improves performance significantly.

Summary

In this chapter, we learned, in detail, the techniques to optimize MySQL 8 components. The chapter started with the basics of optimization, including hardware and software optimization guidelines. We also discussed optimization guidelines for the MySQL 8 server and client, database structure, queries, and tables. We also covered optimization for tables belonging to different storage engines, such as MyISAM, InnoDB, and MEMORY. We learned the tools, such as EXPLAIN and EXPLAIN ANALYZE, needed to understand the query execution plan. In the later part of the chapter, we learned buffering and caching techniques to improve performance.

It's time to move on to the next chapter now. The next chapter focuses on techniques to extend MySQL 8. The chapter will cover in-depth details of MySQL 8 plugins, which help to extend the default MySQL 8 features. It will also explain the services to call these plugins. The chapter will discuss adding new functions, debugging, and porting methods. It is going to be an important chapter for database administrators.

13
Extending MySQL 8

In the previous chapter, we learned how to optimize MySQL 8. We also learned what configurations need to be done to achieve optimization, and also how to leverage caching and buffering for optimization. We went through the use case study step by step for achieving optimization in the following components:

- Optimizing MySQL 8 server and client
- Optimizing data structures
- Optimizing queries
- Optimizing tables

In this chapter, we will learn about extending MySQL 8. We will check what MySQL 8 components are allowed to extend, and we will look at how to customize MySQL 8 for specific business needs. You will learn about the fundamental components prior to extending MySQL 8 and the features of the MySQL plugin API that will be used to extend MySQL 8. The following is the list of topics covered in this chapter:

- An overview of extending MySQL 8
- Extending plugins and using services to call them
- Adding new functions
- Debugging and porting

An overview of extending MySQL 8

In this section, you will learn about one of the most exciting topics on how to extend MySQL 8 as per your needs. There are several components of MySQL 8 that you should understand well prior attempting to extend MySQL 8. Here is a list of the components that are important for extending MySQL 8:

- MySQL 8 internals
- MySQL 8 plugin API
- MySQL 8 services for components and plugins
- Adding new functions to MySQL 8
- Debugging and porting MySQL 8

MySQL 8 internals

There are few things you should know before you start working on the MySQL code. To contribute or track MySQL development you should follow the instructions for the installation of source code distribution as per your system or operating system platform. The source code includes internal documentation, which is very important to understand how MySQL internally works from developer's perspective. You can also subscribe to the internals mailing list from `https://lists.mysql.com/internals`, which includes people who work on MySQL code, and you can also discuss topics related to MySQL development or posting patches:

- **MySQL 8 threads**: MySQL server creates threads such as connection manager threads, signal threads, read and write threads if using `InnoDB` storage engine, scheduler threads to handle connection, and replication and event processing.
- **MySQL 8 test suite**: MySQL 8 provides the test systems included with Unix source distribution to help users and developers performing regression testing with MySQL code. You can also write your own test cases using the test framework.

MySQL 8 plugin API

MySQL 8 provides support for plugin API by which server components themselves can be created. The plugins can be loaded during server startup and can also be loaded and unloaded during runtime; there is no need to restart the server. The API is very generic in that it does not specify what plugins can do in terms of limitation but instead they are allowed to do more than build-in components. The API supports interfaces for components such as storage engines plugins, full-text parser plugins, server extensions and so on.

The plugin interface makes use of the `plugin` table in the MySQL 8 database to store the information about installed plugins permanently by using the `INSTALL PLUGIN` statement. During the MySQL 8 installation process the `plugin` table is created. For single server invocation the plugins can also be installed using the `--plugin--load` option, but using this option does not record the installed plugin to the `plugin` table.

MySQL 8 also provides support API for client plugins to be used for specific purposes such as enabling the server connection by client through different authentication methods.

MySQL 8 services for components and plugins

The MySQL 8 server plugins can access and initiate server plugin services; similarly, the server components can also access and request component services. The MySQL 8 plugin Services interface complements the API plugin by exposing server functionality, which can be called by plugins. The following are the plugin service characteristics:

- The services enable plugins to access the server code using ordinary function calls and can also call user-defined functions
- The services are portable and can work on multiple platforms
- The services provide versioning support that protects against incompatibilities between plugins and services
- The services also provide support for testing plugin services

MySQL provides two services types for plugins and components, listed as follows:

1. **The locking service**: The locking service interface is provided at two levels—that is, at C level and at SQL level. The interface works on lock namespace, lock name, and lock mode attributes.
2. **The keyring service**: The keyring service provides an interface for securely storing sensitive information for internal server components and plugins to retrieve later.

Adding new functions to MySQL 8

You can add your own functions to MySQL 8, and this can be done with any one of the three supported types of function. The new function can be called the same way we invoke the built-in functions such as ABS(), and that is true irrespective of which function type you have newly added. The following list is of the supported three types of new function in MySQL 8:

1. Adding a function through the **user-defined function** (**UDF**) interface.
2. Adding a function as native (built-in) MySQL function.
3. Adding a function by creating a stored function.

Debugging and porting MySQL 8

Porting MySQL 8 to other operating systems is currently supported by many operating systems; the list of supported operating systems is provided at http://www.mysql.com/support/supportedplatforms/database.html. In case you have added a new port and are running into problems with the new port, you might use debugging of MySQL 8.

There are different possible ways to start debugging based on where you are running into the problems—they could be in MySQL server or in MySQL client. Depending on the problem's location, you can start debugging in MySQL server or client respectively and also get help from the DBUG package to trace the program's activities.

Extending plugins and using services to call them

In this section, you will gain an understanding of how the plugin API, its interface, and the MySQL services interact with one another and provide extensions in MySQL 8. The plugins are also considered as components in the MySQL 8 architecture, and therefore you can use them to provide pluggable features. The plugin API and the plugin services interfaces have the following differences:

- The plugin API enables plugins that will be used by the server. The calling and invoking of plugins is initiated by the server, so the plugins can extend the server's functionality or can register themselves in order to receive server processing notifications.

- The plugin services interface allows plugins to call the server code. The calling and invoking of service functions is initiated by the plugins so that the same server functionality can be leveraged by many plugins without requiring individual implementation for the functionality.

Writing plugins

To create a plugin library, providing the required descriptor information is a must, as it specifies which plugins the library file contains. Writing the interface function for each of the plugins specified is also necessary.

Every server plugin must have a general descriptor providing information to the plugin APIs, and a type specific descriptor providing information about the interface for specified plugin types. The structure for specifying a general descriptor is the same for all the plugin types, and the type specific descriptor can vary based on the requirements of the plugin's behavior or function. The server plugin interface allows plugins to expose system variables and status.

Client-side plugins have a slightly different architecture than that of server side plugins. For example, each plugin must have descriptor information, but there is no separate division between general and type specific descriptors.

Plugins can be written in C or C++ or any other language that can use C calling conventions. Plugins are loaded and unloaded dynamically, hence the operating system must dynamically support where you have dynamically compiled the calling application. Specifically, for server plugins this means that `mysqld` must be linked dynamically.

As we cannot be sure of what application will use the plugin, the dependencies on the symbols of the calling application should be avoided by the client plugin writers.

The following are the types of supported plugin creations that can implement several capabilities:

- Authentication
- Password validation and strength checking
- Protocol tracing
- Query rewriting

- Secure keyring storage and retrieval
- Storage engines
- Full-text parsers
- Daemons
- INFORMATION_SCHEMA tables
- Semisynchronous replication
- Auditing

Component and plugin services

You can identify the component services and functions provided by MySQL by looking into the include/mysql/components and respective services directories of the MySQL 8 source distribution.

Similarly, you can identify the plugin services and functions provided by MySQL by looking into the include/mysql directory of the MySQL 8 source distribution and the relevant files as follows:

- The plugin.h file includes the services.h file, which services.h file contains all the available service-specific header files within it
- Service-specific header files will have names in the form of service_xxx.h

The following is a list of available component services in MySQL 8:

- component_sys_variable_register, component_sys_variable_unregister: For registering and unregistering system variables
- log_builtins, log_builtins_string: For log components services
- mysql_service_udf_registration, mysql_service_udf_registration_aggregate: For enabling registration and unregistration of scalar and aggregate user-defined functions in components and plugins
- mysql_string: For string service APIs
- pfs_plugin_table: For dynamic Performance Schema table manipulation

The following is list of available plugins services in MySQL 8:

- `get_sysvar_source`: For retrieving system variable settings
- `locking_service`: For lock implementation with C language and SQL level interfaces, having the attributes namespace, name, and mode
- `my_plugin_log_service`: For writing errors messages to logs
- `my_snprintf`: For string formatting to keep the output consistent across platforms
- `status_variable_registration`: For registering the status variable
- `my_thd_scheduler`: For thread scheduler selection
- `mysql_keyring`: For keyring storage service
- `mysql_password_policy`: For password strength and validation checking
- `plugin_registry_service`: For accessing the component registry and related services
- `security_context`: For managing thread security contexts
- `thd_alloc`: For memory allocation
- `thd_wait`: For reporting to sleep or stall

Now, you have a clear understanding of plugin services and component services. MySQL 8 provides the following types of services to support plugins and components services:

1. The locking service
2. The keyring service

The following sections give detailed information on both types of services.

The locking service

The locking service interface is provided at two levels: C level and at SQL level. The interface works on the lock namespace, lock name, and lock mode attributes. The C language interface is callable as a plugin service from user-defined functions or server plugins, and the SQL level interface is used as set of user-defined functions, being mapped to call the service routines.

The following are the characteristics of the locking interface:

- Lock namespace, lock name, and lock mode are three three attributes of locks.
- Locks are identified by forming a lock namespace and lock name combination.
- Lock mode can be either read or write. Read locks are shared whereas write locks are exclusive.
- Lock names and namespaces can have a maximum of 64 characters and must be non-NULL and non-empty strings.
- Lock names and namespace are treated as binary strings so comparison will be case-sensitive.
- Functions are provided to acquire and release locks and do not require any special privileges to call the functions.
- Detects deadlock during lock acquisition calls in different sessions; a caller is chosen and terminated for its lock acquisition request and caller sessions holding read locks are preferred over the sessions holding write locks.
- A typical session can request for multiple locks acquisition with a single lock acquisition call. It provides atomic behavior for the request and succeeds if all locks are acquired or fails if any of the lock acquisitions fail.
- Multiple locks for the same lock identifier can be acquired by the session where the lock instances can be write locks, read locks, or a mix of both read and write locks.
- Acquired locks are released from the session by explicitly calling the release-lock function, or implicitly if the session gets terminated.
- All locks in the given namespace when released are released together within the session.

The keyring service

The keyring service provides an interface for securely storing sensitive information for internal server components and plugins to retrieve later. In the keyring service, the record from the keystore itself consists of data—the key and unique identifier by which the key can be accessed. The identifier consists of the following two parts:

1. `key_id`: The name. `key_id` or key ID values beginning with `mysql_` are reserved by the MySQL server.
2. `user_id`: The `user_id` stands for an effective `user_id` per session. It can be `NULL` if there is no user context and the value does not necessarily need to be an actual `user` but depends upon the application.

The following are the common characteristics of the keyring service functions:

- Each of the functions returns 1 for failure and 0 for success
- A unique combination is formed by the `user_id` and `key_id` arguments, indicating which key is to be used in the keyring
- Additional information about the key is provided with the `key_type` argument value as its intended use, its encryption method, or other such information
- User names, key IDs, types, and values are treated as binary strings in keyring service functions so the comparisons are case sensitive

The following is the list of keyring service functions that are available:

- `my_key_generate()`: As the name suggests, it generates a new random key of given type and length and is stored in the keyring. The function consists of the arguments `key_id`, `user_id`, `key_type`, and `key_len`, as well as the following function syntax:

```
bool my_key_generate(const char *key_id, const char*key_type,
    const char *user_id, size_t key_len)
```

- `my_key_fetch()`: Deobfuscates the argument value and retrieves a key from the keyring and its type. The function consists of the arguments `key_id`, `user_id`, `key_type`, `key`, and `key_len`, as well as the following function syntax:

```
bool my_key_fetch(const char *key_id, const char **key_type,
    const char* user_id, void **key, size_t *key_len)
```

- `my_key_remove()`: Removes an associated key from the keyring. The function consists of the arguments `key_id` and `user_id`, as well as the following function syntax:

```
bool my_key_remove(const char *key_id, const char* user_id)
```

- `my_key_store()`: Obfuscates the argument value and stores a key in the keyring. The function consists of the arguments `key_id`, `user_id`, `key_type`, `key`, and `key_len`, as well as the following function syntax:

```
bool my_key_store(const char *key_id, const char *key_type,
    const char* user_id, void *key, size_t key_len)
```

Adding new functions

New functions can be added with any of the three supported types in MySQL 8. Each of the types have their own advantages and disadvantages. Where and which type of function should be added or implemented depends on the requirements of the function.

The following is the list of the supported three types of new function in MySQL 8, which we will look at in the following section:

1. Adding a function through the user-defined function interface.
2. Adding a function as a native (built-in) MySQL function.
3. Adding a function by creating a stored function.

Features of a user-defined function interface

A user-defined function interface provides independent capabilities to a user purpose function.

The following features and capabilities are provided by the MySQL interface for user-defined functions:

- Functions can accept arguments of integer, string, or real values and can return values for the same types
- Simple functions can be defined to operate on a single row at a time or it can be aggregate functions to operate on groups of rows
- Functions are given information to enable them so that they can check the types, names, and numbers of arguments passed
- Before passing arguments to the given function, you can also ask MySQL to coerce arguments
- Indications can be made if the function results in any error or returns NULL

Adding a new user-defined function

The UDF functions must be written in C or C++ and the underlying operating system must support dynamic loading behavior. There is a file, `sql/udf_example.cc`, that defines five UDF functions and it's included in the MySQL source distributions. Analyzing the file will let you know how calling conventions work for UDFs. User-defined function related symbols and data structures are defined in the `include/mysql_com.h` file and the file is included in the `mysql.h` header file.

Typical code contained in the UDFs gets executed in the running server, so all constraints are applicable when writing UDF code—server code. Currently applicable constraints may get revised when a server is upgraded, and this can possibly result into the need to rewrite UDF code, so it is essential to be careful when writing code for the UDF.

In order to use UDF, linking `mysqld` dynamically is a must. For any function to be used in SQL statements there must be underlying C or C++ functions. The convention for separating SQL and C/C++ code is followed where `xxx()` in uppercase indicates an SQL function call whereas `xxx()` with lowercase indicates a C/C++ function call.

> Encapsulate your C function as shown in following sentence when you are using C++: `extern "C" { ... }` This way it is ensured that your C++ function names are readable in the completed user-defined function.

To write and implement the interface function name `XXX()`, the main function `xxx()` is a must and additionally requires one or more function to be implemented from the following:

- `xxx()`: The main function where the function result is being produced
- `xxx_init()`: The initialization function for the main function `xxx()`, it can be used for any of the following purposes:
    - Checking number of arguments to be passed on to `XXX()`
    - Verifying argument types with a declaration when calling the main function
    - Allocating memory to the main function whenever required
    - Result's maximum length verification
    - Setting a decimal number limit for maximum in the result
    - Specifying whether the result can be `NULL` or not
- `xxx_deinit()`: Represents deinitialization for the main function and deallocates memory if any is allocated by the initialization function for the main function

Aggregate UDFs are handled as in the following sequence in MySQL 8:

1. Call xxx_init() so that it allocates the required memory to store result information.
2. Sort the table/result as specified by the GROUP BY function.
3. Call xxx_clear() so that it reset the current aggregate value for the first row in each new group.
4. Call xxx_add() that adds the argument to the current aggregate value.
5. Call xxx() to get the result of aggregate data on group by changes or after processing the last row.
6. Repeat steps 3-5 until all specified/resulted rows are processed.
7. Call xxx_deinit() to free any allocated memory for the UDF.

All the functions must be thread-safe, including the main function as well as other additional functions as required, along with the initialization and deinitialization functions.

Similar to the above sequence, the following are important aspects that need to be taken care of while adding new user-defined functions:

- UDF argument processing
- UDF return values and error handling
- UDF compiling and installing
- UDF security precautions

Adding a new native function

For adding a new native function, source distribution is required in order to compile using modified source that consists of the new native function. It is also required to repeat this when you migrate to another MySQL version.

In a case where a new native function is to be referred in the statements and also replicated to slave servers, ensure that each of the slave servers has the new native function available, otherwise replication on the slave server will fail when the new native function invocation is attempted.

The followings are the steps for adding a new native function in the source distribution files of the `sql` directory:

1. A subclass for the function needs to be added in `item_create.cc`:
   - In case of a fixed number of arguments, the subclass is to be created from `Create_func_arg0`, `Create_func_arg1`, `Create_func_arg2`, or `Create_func_arg3` depending upon the number of arguments required in your native function. You can refer to the `Create_func_abs`, `Create_func_uuid`, and `Create_func_pow` classes.
   - In case of a variable number of arguments, the subclass is to be created from `Create_native_func`. You can refer to the `Creat_func_concat` class.

2. The function name to be referred to in SQL statements needs to be registered in `item_create.cc` by adding the following line to the array: `static Native_func_registry func_array[]`:
   - If required, several names can be registered for the same function. You can refer to lines for LOWER and LCASE which are aliases stands for `Create_func_lcase`.

3. Declaring the class inherited from `Item_str_func` or `Item_num_func` is necessary, depending upon if your function return type is a string or a number in the `item_func.h` file.

4. Adding one of the following declarations is necessary, depending upon if your function defines as a string or numeric function in the `item_func.cc` file:

```
double Item_func_newname::val()
longlong Item_func_newname::val_int()
String *Item_func_newname::Str(String *str)
```

   - If your object is inherited from any of the standard items then you probably need to define only one of the preceding functions, as the parent object will take care other of the function. You can refer to the `Item_str_func` class that has defined the `val()` function that executes the `atof()` function on the returned value of the `::str()` function.

5. If the function is nondeterministic—that is, if the returned result varies at different invocations for fixed given arguments - then the following statement needs to be included in the item constructor, indicating that the function results should not be cached: `current_thd->lex->safe_to_cache_query=0;`.

6. You probably also need to define the following object function for your native function:
   - `void Item_func_newname::fix_length_and_dec()`
   - The function should at least include the `max_length` calculation on the given arguments
   - You should also set `maybenull = 0` if your main function cannot return any `NULL` values
   - You can refer to `Item_func_mod::fix_length_and_dec` for the same

Thread safety is a must for all functions. You should not be using any static or global variables in the functions without being protected by mutexes.

Debugging and porting

Porting MySQL 8 to other operating systems is currently supported by many operating systems. The list of the latest supported operating systems is provided at `http://www.mysql.com/support/supportedplatforms/database.html`. If you have added or attempted to add new ports (supported platforms) and are running into problems, you might use debugging of MySQL 8 to find and fix the problems.

First, you should get the test program `mysys/thr_lock` to work before debugging `mysqld`. This makes sure that your thread installation can have a remote chance to work!

There are different possibilities for starting debugging, based on where you are running into the problems - it could be in MySQL server or in MySQL client. Depending on the problem's location you can start debugging in MySQL server or MySQL client respectively, and for tracing the program's activities you will get help from the `DEBUG` package.

The MySQL source code includes internal documentation written using Doxygen, which is very helpful in understanding the developer perspective on how MySQL works.

In this section, you will see detailed information on the following topics:

- Debugging MySQL server
- Debugging MySQL client
- The DBUG package

Debugging MySQL server

If you are using some of very new functionality in MySQL and facing some issues—let's say the server is crashing—you can try running mysqld with the --skip-new option. This option tells the MySQL server to disable all new and potentially unsafe functionality.

In cases where mysqld is not getting started, verify the my.cnf files, as they can interfere with the setup! You can check the arguments in my.cnf with the mysqld --print-defaults option and then start mysqld with the --no-defaults option to avoid using them.

In cases where mysqld starts to eat up memory or CPU or hangs, you can check mysqladmin processlist status and find out if a query executed by someone is taking a long time. In cases where you are facing performance issues or problems and new clients are not able to connect, you can use mysqladmin -i10 process list status.

You can also use the debug command mysqladmin, which dumps information about query usage, memory usage, and locks in use to the MySQL log file and can solve some problems for you. This command also works in case you have not compiled MySQL for debugging, providing some useful information.

In cases where you are facing any issue with the table getting slower, you should try to optimize the table using myisamchk or OPTIMIZE_TABLE. You should probably check the slow queries, if there are any, using EXPLAIN to find and fix the problem with queries.

The following are the important areas to consider when debugging in MySQL 8:

- **Compiling MySQL for debugging**: In case of very specific problems you can always try to debug MySQL. To do that you must configure MySQL with the –DWITH_DEBUG=1 option. The debugging configuration automatically enables lots of extra safety check functions that monitor the health of mysqld.
- **Creating trace files**: You can attempt to find the problem by creating a trace file. To do that you must have mysqld compiled with debugging support. You can then use the --debug option, which will add trace logs in /tmp/mysqld.trace on Unix and \mysqld.trace on Windows.
- **Using WER with PDB to create a Windows crashdump**: Program database files are included in the ZIP archive debug binaries and test suite as a separate distribution of MySQL. These files provide information on debugging for a MySQL installation problem. They can be used with WinDbg or Visual Studio to debug mysqld.
- **Debugging mysqld under gdb**: You can use this option when you are facing issues with threads or when the mysqld server hangs prior to ready for connections.
- **Using a stack trace**: You can also use this option when mysqld dies unexpectedly and find out the problem.
- **Using server logs to find causes of errors in** mysqld: You can use this option by enabling the general query log - prior to that, you should check all your tables using the myisamchk utility and verify if there are any problems from the logs.
- **Making a test case if you experience table corruption**: This option is used when you are facing an issue with table corruption and is applicable only to MyISAM tables.

Debugging MySQL client

In cases where you are facing an issue in MySQL client you can also debug within MySQL client as well, but in order to do so you must have the integrated debug package. You need to configure MySQL with –DWITH_DEBUG=1 to enable debugging in MySQL client.

Prior to running MySQL client, you should set the environment variable MYSQL_DEBUG as follows:

```
shell> MYSQL_DEBUG=d:t:O,/tmp/client.trace
shell> export MYSQL_DEBUG
```

This makes MySQL client generate a trace file in `/tmp/client.trace` for Unix or `\client.trace` for Windows.

In cases where you have problems with your own client code, you can attempt to connect to the server by running your query using the client that is known to work. For doing this you should run `mysqld` in debugging mode:

```
shell> mysql --debug=d:t:O,/tmp/client.trace
```

This trace will provide useful information if you want to mail a bug report for the problem.

In cases where your client crashes at some `legal` looking code, you can check that your `mysql.h` header file includes file matches with your MySQL library file. This is one of the very common mistakes, using an older `mysql.h` file from an old MySQL installation with a new MySQL library, resulting in this issue.

The DBUG package

Fred Fish originally created the DBUG package with MySQL server and most of the MySQL clients. If MySQL is configured for debugging, this package makes it possible to generate a trace file that has information about what the program is doing.

There are debug options available to be specified in order to get specific information to the trace files using the DBUG package. It can be used in program invocation with the `-#
[debug_options]` option or the `--debug[=debug_options]` option.

Most MySQL programs will use a default value if the `--debug` or `-#` option is specified without specifying a `debug_options` value. The server default value is `d:t:i:O,\mysqld.trace` on Windows and `d:t:i:o,/tmp/mysqld.trace` on Unix. The effect of this default is listed as follows:

- `d`: Enables output for all debug macros
- `t`: Traces function calls and exits
- `i`: Adds `PID` to output lines in trace file
- `o,/tmp/mysqld.trace, O,\mysqld.trace`: Sets the debug output file in Unix and Windows respectively

In most of the cases, use the default `debug_options` value
of `d:t:o,/tmp/myprogram_name.trace` for most of the client programs irrespective of
platform works. For Windows, use `\myprogram_name.trace`.

The following are some examples of debug control strings to be specified on the shell
command line:

```
--debug=d:t
--debug=d:f,main,subr1:F:L:t,20
--debug=d,input,output,files:n
--debug=d:t:i:O,\\mysqld.trace
```

Summary

In this chapter, you learned how to extend MySQL 8 through custom functions and APIs.
You also got to know about writing functions and the associated characteristics of the
plugin services and APIs. You can now create your own function or plugin, cater to specific
business requirements, and also debug if a function does not work as per expectations, and
test whether it does.

In next chapter, you will learn about MySQL 8 best practices and benchmarking in MySQL
8. You will learn about benchmarking and tools used for benchmarking. You will also learn
best practices for some of very important features of MySQL 8, such as memcached,
replication, data partitioning, and indexing.

14
MySQL 8 Best Practices and Benchmarking

In the previous chapter, you learned how to extend MySQL 8. It covered a lot of interesting aspects, such as extending plugins and calling them by using services in MySQL 8, adding and debugging new functions to MySQL 8, and so on. In this chapter, we will go through the best practices of MySQL 8, which is a much-awaited version that promises to address many of the shortfalls of the prior versions and has exciting new features. MySQL 8 promises not to be just a standalone database, but it will also play a significant role in various areas, including big data solutions. We will learn how best practices can be implemented for optimal use of features in MySQL 8. Benchmarking will enhance our understanding further.

We will cover the following topics in this chapter:

- MySQL benchmarking and tools
- Best practices for the memcached
- Best practices for replication
- Best practices for data partitioning
- Best practices for queries and indexing

Due to prominent optimizations and changes, MySQL 8 advanced its version directly from the release of MySQL 5.7. MySQL 8 will not have the limitation of files, which was previously restricting the number of databases that you could have. There are many more exciting features, which we have covered in Chapter 1, *Introduction to MySQL 8*. MySQL 8 can now store millions of tables in a database. It will also make modifications to tables swiftly.

I am excited to go through this chapter, as MySQL 8 best practices not only impact your database performance, scalability, security, and availability, but will also, on the whole, expose how your system performs for the end user. This is our end goal, isn't it? Let's look at some benchmarks that have been derived in our test lab, which will raise your eyebrows for sure:

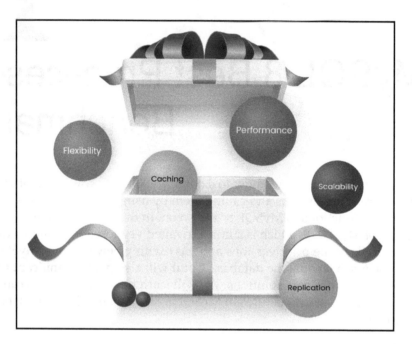

MySQL benchmarking and tools

We have gone through various new features and improvements in MySQL 8. It makes us more excited, as performance is always what we crave. With MySQL 8 not being generally available yet, Oracle hasn't published its benchmark results. We didn't wait for it to do so and carried out our own analysis in a few areas.

Configuration best practices of MySQL is the cherry on the cake; without the cherry, the cake seems incomplete. In addition to configurations, benchmarking helps us validate and find bottlenecks and address them. Let's look at a few specific areas that will help us understand the best practices for configuration and performance benchmarking.

Resource utilization

IO activity, CPU, and memory usage is something that you should not miss out. These metrics help us know how the system is performing while doing benchmarking and at the time of scaling. It also helps us derive impacts per transaction.

Stretching your benchmarking timelines

We may often like to have a quick glance at performance metrics; however, ensuring that MySQL behaves in the same way for a longer duration of testing is also a key element. There is some basic stuff that might impact on performance when you stretch your benchmark timelines, such as memory fragmentation, degradation of IO, impact after data accumulation, cache management, and so on.

We don't want our database to get restarted just to clean up junk items, correct? Therefore, it is suggested to run benchmarking for a long duration for stability and performance validation.

Replicating production settings

Let's benchmark in a production-replicated environment. Wait! Let's disable database replication in a replica environment until we are done with benchmarking. Gotcha! We have got some good numbers!

It often happens that we don't simulate everything completely that we are going to configure in the production environment. It could prove to be costly, as we might unintentionally be benchmarking something in an environment that might have an adverse impact when it's in production. Replicate production settings, data, workload, and so on in your replicated environment while you do benchmarking.

Consistency of throughput and latency

Throughput and latency go hand in hand. It is important to keep your eyes primarily focused on throughput; however, latency over time might be something to look out for. Performance dips, slowness, or stalls were noticed in `InnoDB` in its earlier days. It has improved a lot since then, but as there might be other cases depending on your workload, it is always good to keep an eye on throughput along with latency.

Sysbench can do more

Sysbench is a wonderful tool to simulate your workloads, whether it be thousands of tables, transaction intensive, data in-memory, and so on. It is a splendid tool to simulate and gives you nice representation.

Virtualization world

I would like to keep this simple; bare metal as compared to virtualization isn't the same. Hence, while doing benchmarking, measure your resources according to your environment. You might be surprised to see the difference in results if you compare both.

Concurrency

Big data is seated on heavy data workload; high concurrency is important. MySQL 8 is extending its maximum CPU core support in every new release, optimizing concurrency based on your requirements and hardware resources should be taken care of.

Hidden workloads

Do not miss out factors that run in the background, such as reporting for big data analytics, backups, and on-the-fly operations while you are benchmarking. The impact of such hidden workloads or obsolete benchmarking workloads can make your days (and nights) miserable.

Nerves of your query

Oops! Did we miss the optimizer? Not yet. An optimizer is a powerful tool that will read the nerves of your query and provide recommendations. It's a tool that I use before making changes to a query in production. It's a savior when you have complex queries to be optimized.

These are a few areas that we should look out for. Let's now look at a few benchmarks that we did on MySQL 8 and compare them with the ones on MySQL 5.7.

Benchmarks

To start with, let's fetch all the column names from all the `InnoDB` tables. The following is the query that we executed:

```
SELECT t.table_schema, t.table_name, c.column_name
FROM information_schema.tables t,
information_schema.columns c
WHERE t.table_schema = c.table_schema
AND t.table_name = c.table_name
AND t.engine='InnoDB';
```

The following figure shows how MySQL 8 performed a thousand times faster when having four instances:

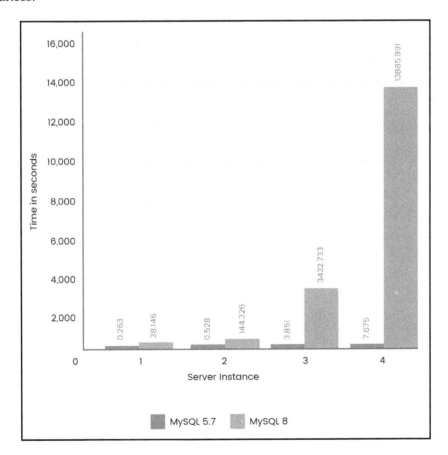

Following this, we also performed a benchmark to find static table metadata. The following is the query that we executed:

```
SELECT TABLE_SCHEMA, TABLE_NAME, TABLE_TYPE, ENGINE, ROW_FORMAT
FROM INFORMATION_SCHEMA.TABLES
WHERE TABLE_SCHEMA LIKE 'chintan%';
```

The following figure shows how MySQL 8 performed around 30 times faster than MySQL 5.7:

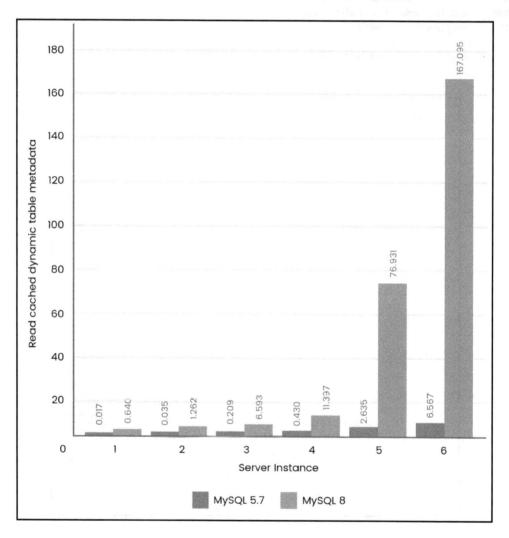

It made us eager to go into a bit more detail. So, we thought of doing one last test to find dynamic table metadata.

The following is the query that we executed:

```
SELECT TABLE_ROWS
FROM INFORMATION_SCHEMA.TABLES
WHERE TABLE_SCHEMA LIKE 'chintan%';
```

The following figure shows how MySQL 8 performed around 30 times faster than MySQL 5.7:

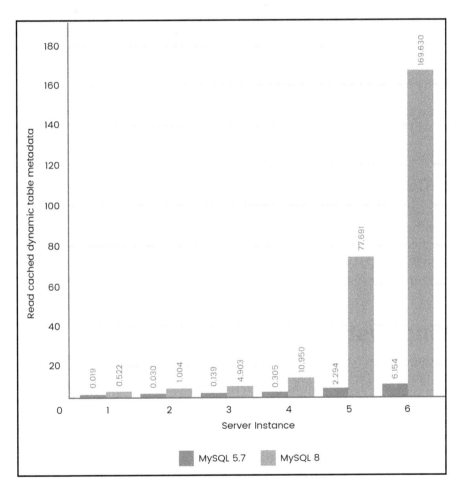

MySQL 8.0 brings enormous performance improvements to the table. Scaling to one million tables, which is a need for many big data requirements, is now achievable. We look forward to many more benchmarks being officially released once MySQL 8 is available for general purposes.

Let's now look at our next topic, which will make your life easier. It's all about taking things into consideration for best practices of memcached.

Best practices for memcached

Multiple `get` operations are now possible with the `InnoDB` memcached plugin, which will really help in improving the read performance. Now, multiple key value pairs can be fetched in a single memcached query. Frequent communication traffic has also been minimized, as we can get multiple data in a single shot.

The key takeaways that you should consider for memcached configuration best practices are what we will be going through now.

Resource allocation

Memory allocation for memcached shouldn't be allocated over the available physical memory or without considering other resources that would be utilizing memory. If we over-allocate memory, there is a high chance that memcached would have memory allocated from the swap space. This may lead to delays while inserting or fetching values because the swap space is stored on the disk, which is slower than in-memory.

Operating system architecture

As the operating system architecture has 32-bits, one needs to be cautious. As we know, there are limitations to provision resources in a 32-bit operating system architecture.

Similarly, memcached with 4 GB RAM with a 32-bit operating system architecture shouldn't be set more than 3.5 GB RAM, as it can behave strangely in performance and can also result in crashes.

Default configurations

Some key default configuration parameters should always be fine-tuned based on your needs:

- **Memory allocation**: By default, this is 64 MB; instead it should be reconfigured based on your requirements and testing
- **Connections**: By default, this is 1,024 concurrent connections; instead it should be reconfigured based on your requirements and testing
- **Port**: By default, this listens on port `11211`; instead it should listen to another port for security purposes
- **Network interface**: By default, this accepts connections from all network interfaces; instead it should be limited for security purposes

Max object size

You should look at configuring the maximum object size, which by default is 1 MB. However, it can be bumped up to 128 MB. It is purely based on what type of data you are going to store and, accordingly, its maximum object size should be allowed. Allowing overhead data to be stored in memcached can have an adverse impact, as there may be much more data to retrieve, which can cause failures.

Backlog queue limit

The backlog queue limit is all about the number of connections to memcached that should be kept in queue if it reaches the limit of allowed connections. Ideally, your number of connections allowed should be configured in a way that should suffice for most of your needs. The backlog queue limit can be helpful when there is an unexpected peak load on memcached. Ideally, it should not go beyond 20% of the total connections or it could impact the experience of system fetching information from memcached because of heavy delays.

Large pages support

On systems that support large memory pages, you should enable memcached to leverage them. Large pages support helps allocate a large data chunk to store data and also reduces the number of caches missed calls using this.

Sensitive data

Storing sensitive data in memcached could be a security threat, as somebody with access to memcached could view the sensitive information. You should obviously take precautions to limit the exposure of memcached. You can also have sensitive information encrypted before storing it on memcached.

Restricting exposure

Memcached doesn't have many security features built in. One measure involves exposing memcached access within the required boundaries. If your application server needs to talk to memcached, it only allows memcached to be accessed from that server with the help of system firewall rules, such as IP Tables or similar techniques.

Failover

Memcached doesn't have good failover techniques. It is suggested that you have your application configured in a way to failover to an unavailable node and regenerate data into another instance. It is good to have at least two memcached configured to avoid failure owing to the unavailability of the instance.

Namespaces

You can leverage namespaces provided by memcached, which basically adds prefixes to the data before storing it in memcached. It can help when you have multiple applications talking to memcached. This is helpful and, using some basic principles of naming conventions, you can derive a solution. If there is data that is storing first names and last names, you can use prefixes, such as FN and LN, respectively. This would help you easily identify and retrieve data from the application.

Caching mechanism

One of the easiest ways to start leveraging caching in memcached is to use a two-column table; you can leverage namespaces provided by memcached, which basically adds prefixes. The first columns would be a primary key, and database schema should be the address requirement of a unique identifier with the help of primary key mapping along with unique constraints. In case you want to have a single item value by combining multiple column values, you should make sure you choose appropriate data types.

Queries with a single WHERE clause can be mapped easily into memcached lookups while using = or IN operators in the queries themselves. In cases where multiple WHERE clauses are used or complex operations are parsed, such as <, >, LIKE, and BETWEEN, memcached would get you through challenges. It is suggested that you have such complex operations using traditional SQL queries added to your database.

It would be beneficial to cache entire objects in memcached instead of opting to cache individual rows from MySQL 8. For instance, for a blogging website, you should cache the entire object of the blog port in memcached.

Memcached general statistics

To help you understand the statistics of memcached better, we will provide an overview of health and performance. Statistics returned by memcached and their meaning are shown in the following table:

Terms used to define the value for each of the statistics are:

- **32u**: 32-bit unsigned integer
- **64u**: 64-bit unsigned integer
- **32u:32u**: Two 32-bit unsigned integers separated by a colon
- **String**: Character string

Statistic	Datatype	Description
pid	32u	Process ID of the memcached instance.
uptime	32u	Uptime (in seconds) for this memcached instance.
time	32u	Current time (as epoch).
version	string	Version string of this instance.

Statistic	Datatype	Description
`pointer_size`	string	Size of pointers for this host specified in bits (32 or 64).
`rusage_user`	32u:32u	Total user time for this instance (seconds:microseconds).
`rusage_system`	32u:32u	Total system time for this instance (seconds:microseconds).
`curr_items`	32u	Current number of items stored by this instance.
`total_items`	32u	Total number of items stored during the life of this instance.
`bytes`	64u	Current number of bytes used by this server to store items.
`curr_connections`	32u	Current number of open connections.
`total_connections`	32u	Total number of connections opened since the server started running.
`connection_structures`	32u	Number of connection structures allocated by the server.
`cmd_get`	64u	Total number of retrieval requests (`get` operations).
`cmd_set`	64u	Total number of storage requests (`set` operations).
`get_hits`	64u	Number of keys that have been requested and found present.
`get_misses`	64u	Number of items that have been requested and not found.
`delete_hits`	64u	Number of keys that have been deleted and found present.
`delete_misses`	64u	Number of items that have been delete and not found.
`incr_hits`	64u	Number of keys that have been incremented and found present.

Statistic	Datatype	Description
incr_misses	64u	Number of items that have been incremented and not found.
decr_hits	64u	Number of keys that have been decremented and found present.
decr_misses	64u	Number of items that have been decremented and not found.
cas_hits	64u	Number of keys that have been compared and swapped and found present.
cas_misses	64u	Number of items that have been compared and swapped and not found.
cas_badvalue	64u	Number of keys that have been compared and swapped, but the comparison (original) value did not match the supplied value.
evictions	64u	Number of valid items removed from cache to free memory for new items.
bytes_read	64u	Total number of bytes read by this server from network.
bytes_written	64u	Total number of bytes sent by this server to network.
limit_maxbytes	32u	Number of bytes this server is permitted to use for storage.
threads	32u	Number of worker threads requested.
conn_yields	64u	Number of yields for connections (related to the -R option).

Reference: https://dev.mysql.com/doc/refman/8.0/en/ha-memcached-stats-general.html

These are a few useful items that should be kept handy for best practices of memcached. It's now time for us to move ahead and look at best practices for replication.

Best practices for replication

MySQL 8 has made some great improvements on the replication side. MySQL 8 is all about scalability, performance, and security with the utmost integrity of data, which is expected to be a game-changer in big data too.

Throughput in group replication

Group replication basically takes care of committing transactions once most of the members in group replication have acknowledged the transaction received concurrently. This results in a better throughput if the overall number of writes doesn't exceeding the capacity of the members in group replication. If there is a case where capacity is not planned appropriately, you would notice lags on affected members as compared to other members in the group.

Infrastructure sizing

Infrastructure sizing is a common success factor for performance and the best practices checklist. If infrastructure sizing is not proper or uneven across the nodes in group replication, it could adversely impact the replication fundamentals topology. Each component should be considered while considering the throughput required from the components.

Constant throughput

To achieve constant throughput is a good success factor. What if you start experiencing a workload that starts affecting the rest of the members in group replication? It might be a case where your master keeps on accepting additional workload and is lagging behind, after which it might return to an acceptable level before burning out all the resources. Additionally, you can implement a queuing methodology that can prevent you from burning down resources and only allows you to pass on workloads to the members that are predefined based on capacity.

While considering a queuing methodology, you mustn't allow queues grow exponentially. This would impact the end user, as there would be a lag in the data being updated. However, you needs to decide based on your needs and the business requirement to achieve constant throughput across the system.

Contradictory workloads

Fundamentally, group replication is designed to allow updates from any of the members in the group. Rollback of transactions based on overlap of rows is checked for each of the transactions; the rest are committed and sent to be updated to other members in the group. If several updates on the same row happen frequently, it can result in multiple rollbacks. You might come across cyclic situations where one server updates, requests others to update, and, in parallel, another has already updated for the same row. This would result in rollback.

To prevent such a scenario, you can have the last member of the group apply the update, after which you proceed to another one. You can have similar updates routed only from the same node where the earlier one had been executed to prevent the chances of cyclic rollback conditions.

Write scalability

Distribute your write workload by sharing out write operations, which might result in better throughput and better scalability on write performance. It would be dependent on contradictory workloads that you would be expecting in the system. This is helpful when your peak workload is being executed is one that can share the load. In common cases, if you have good capacity planning done with write scalability, you would see trivial improvement.

Refer to the following diagram that depicts this:

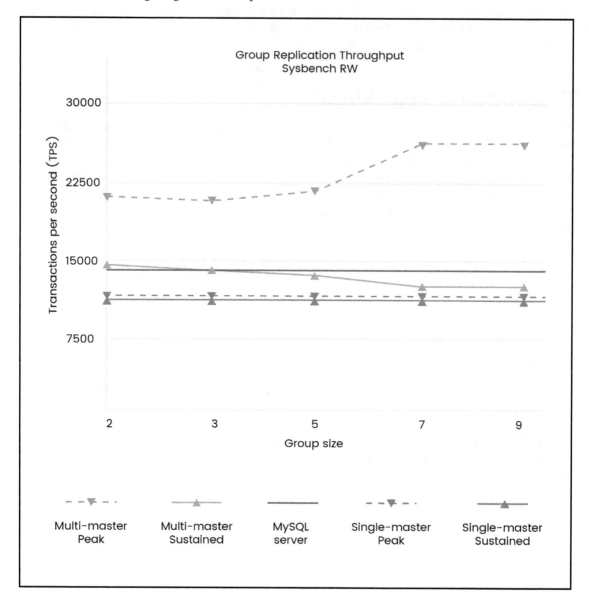

You will notice that with the help of multi-masters to distribute, your load has better throughput. It also considers the group size in multi-master configuration.

Best practices for data partitioning

In general terms, partitioning is logically dividing anything into multiple subgroups so that each subgroup can be identified independently and can be combined into a single partition.

Let's now learn different partitioning methods and how partitioning can help where there are large data tables.

For any organization, it is very important to store data in such a way that the database provides scalability, performance, availability, and security. For instance, in a highly accessed e-commerce store, there are thousands, or more, of orders placed frequently. So to maintain day-to-day order delivery showing a dashboard of current orders, what is required is to query a table showing orders from the past five years; the process will take a long time to execute with the current data. Here, historical order data is needed for the analytical purpose of finding user behavior or trends, but this will be required to be performed on limited datasets.

There are various ways to achieve the best suitable solution for high availability, scalability, and highly performing architecture; the key ingredient is partitioning. In a database, data in each table is stored in physical file groups. So by dividing this data table from a single file group to a multiple file group can reduce the file size and help us create a scalable and high-performing database.

The following are the key benefits of using partitioning in a database:

- **Scalability**: As data will be shared among more than one partition, servers can be configured to use multiple nodes and partitions can be configured among multiple nodes. Doing so will eliminate any hardware limits and allow the database to scale up to a large extent to accommodate high volume data.
- **High performance**: As data is stored among multiple partitions, each query will be executed on a small portion of the data. For example, in an e-commerce store with an order history of more than two years, to get a list of orders placed in the current month will require checking only a single partition and not the entire order history, thus reducing the query execution time. To fetch the query on more than one partition, we can also run this in parallel, thus reducing the overall time to fetch data from the database.

- **High availability**: In partitioning, data is divided across multiple file groups. Each file group is logically connected but can be accessed and worked on independently. So if one of the file groups or partitions gets corrupted or one of the nodes in the server fails, then we will not lose access to the entire table, but only a section of the database will not be available, thus eliminating the chances of system failure and making your system highly available.
- **Security**: It may be that some of the data in tables requires high security measurements to avoid data theft or data leaks. By partitioning, you can provide additional security to one or more partitions to avoid any security issues, thus improving data accessibility with data security.

In general terms, partitioning is logically dividing anything into multiple subgroups so that each subgroup can be identified independently and can be combined into a single partition. Let's understand what partitioning means in terms of RDBMS.

Partitioning is generally used to divide data into multiple logical file groups for the purpose of performance, availability, and manageability. When dealing with big data, the normal tendency of data is to be in terms of billions of records. So to improve performance of the database, it is better to divide data among multiple file groups. These file groups can be on a single machine or shared across multiple machines and identified by a key. These file groups are known as partitioned data.

Data in the table can be partitioned in two ways:

- Horizontal partitioning
- Vertical partitioning

Horizontal partitioning

When the number of rows in the table is very large, the table can be divided into multiple partitions; this is known as **horizontal partitioning**. When horizontal partitioning is used, each partition of the table contains the same number of columns. It is possible to access all partitions at once, or you can access each partition individually.

Vertical partitioning

In vertical partitioning, the columns of the tables are partitioned to achieve performance and better management of the database. Vertical partitioning can be achieved in two ways. The first one is by normalizing tables. Instead of having too many columns in the table, columns can be divided into multiple tables by dividing the data. The second one is by creating separate physical file groups for defined columns in the table. Vertical partitioning is currently not supported in MySQL 8.

Let's look at a few of the benefits associated with partitioning:

- If a table contains historical data, such as logs of an application, data older than six months does not provide any significance to the application to be active. If partitioning is created based on months, you can easily remove one of the partitions.
- In the same preceding case of logs, if we want to filter data between two dates, the MySQL optimizer can identify the specific partitions, where it can find the filtered records, which can result in much faster query results, as the number of rows to check is reduced drastically.
- MySQL 8 also supports querying data on particular partitions. It can reduce the number of records to check when you know the partition that needs to be queried for the data required.

Pruning partitions in MySQL

Pruning is the selective extraction of data. As we have multiple partitions, it will go through each partition during retrieval, which is time consuming and impacts on performance. Some of the partitions will also be included in searching while the requested data is not available inside that partition, which is an overhead process. Pruning helps here to search for only those partitions that have the relevant data, which will avoid the unnecessary inclusion of those partitions during retrieval.

This optimization that avoids the scanning of partitions where there can be no matching values is known as the **pruning of partitions**. In partition pruning, the optimizer analyzes FROM and WHERE clauses in SQL statements to eliminate unneeded partitions, and scans those database partitions that are relevant to the SQL statement.

Best practices for queries and indexing

It would be difficult to write the best queries for reference and reuse. It will always vary based on the nature of your application, architecture, design, table structure, and so on. However, precautions can be taken while writing MySQL queries for better performance, scalability, and integrity.

Let's go through a few of the best practices that we should keep in mind while designing or writing MySQL queries.

Data types

A database table could consist of multiple columns with data types, such as numerics or strings. MySQL 8 provides various data types rather than just limiting to numerics or strings:

- Small is good. As MySQL loads data in memory, a large data size would have an adverse impact on its performance. Smaller sets can accommodate more data in memory and reduce overheads of resource utilization.
- Fix your length. If you don't fix the data type length, it would have to go and fetch the required information each time it needs to. So, wherever it's possible, you can limit the data length by using the char data type.

Not null

Not null data is something that MySQL doesn't like much. Not null columns use more storage, impact the performance, and require additional processing within MySQL.

Optimizing such queries referring to null data is difficult as well. When a null data column is indexed, it uses additional bytes for each entry.

Indexing

Indexing is important, as it can improve the performance of your badly designed query and table structure or it can even turn a well-designed query into a bad one, which can impact performance too.

Search fields index

Generally, we do indexing on fields that are used as filters in MySQL queries. It obviously helps reading faster but can adversely impact writes/updates so indexing only what you need would be a smart decision.

Data types and joins

MySQL can do joins for data types that are different but the performance can be impacted if MySQL is asked to use different data types for join fields, as it would have to convert from one to another for each row.

Compound index

If a query is supposed to refer to multiple columns of a table, a composite index for such columns might be helpful. A compound index refers the columns from the results set by the first column, second column, and so on.

The order of columns plays a significant role in the performance of the query, so while designing the table structure and index, you need to use it effectively.

Shortening up primary keys

Small is good for primary keys too. Shortening up primary keys would benefit analogously to how we discussed datatypes. Because of smaller primary keys, your index size would be smaller and hence the usage of cache would be less, so it can accommodate more data in memory.

It is preferred to use numeric types, as these would be much smaller than characters to achieve the goal of shortening up primary keys. It can be helpful while doing joins, as generally, primary keys are referred for the joining.

Indexing everything

Indexing everything is a good idea; however, MySQL won't do this. Do you know that MySQL will do a full table scan if it is supposed to scan an index higher than 30%? Do not index values that don't need to be indexed.

We need to keep in mind that indexing helps—if done correctly—in fetching data; however, while writing/updating data, it is an overhead.

Fetching all data

`select *...` - Arrghh! Do not use this unless it is really needed. So far, my experience hasn't needed this. Fetching all data will slow down the execution time and impact heavily on resource utilization of the MySQL server. You need to provide a specific column name or appropriate conditions.

Letting the application do the job

Let the application also do the job for MySQL. You can avoid having clauses such as `order by` by letting applications do the ordering. Doing ordering in MySQL is much slower than in applications. You can identify queries that should be planned to be taken care of by the application.

Existence of data

Checking the existence of data with the help of the `EXISTS` clause is much faster. The `EXISTS` clause will return the output as soon as it fetches the first row from the fetched data.

Limiting yourself

Limit yourself to the data that you need to fetch. Always ensure that you use appropriate limits while fetching the data, as unwanted data being fetched wouldn't be useful and would impact performance. Use the `LIMIT` clause in your SQL queries.

Analyzing slow queries

This is a good practice to follow. We might miss out queries to either optimize or realize having adverse impact as data grows. You might have changes in the requirement of the data to be fetched where we might miss seeing the impact of the queries. It is good to always keep a watch on slow queries that can be configured in MySQL and optimize them.

Query cost

What is the cost of your query? Explain is the right answer to this. Use the `explain` query parameter to know what is impacting your query—whether it is a full table scan, index scans, range access, and so on. Use the information provided by explain wisely, to optimize the query further. It is a wonderful, quick handy tool of MySQL. If you know that you have done your best, indexing comes as a savior to optimize it further based on your needs.

Best practices while writing a query start with requirements, designs, implementations, and ongoing maintenance. It's a complete life cycle that we can't diversify. Understanding schemas, indexes, and analyses plays a significant role. What matters to us is the response time and optimum resource utilization.

I personally love to deep dive into this much more than we can mention here—it's a world of relations! Your query will meet a row or column of a table or get joined with another table. On top of this, if you haven't done it right, you are trying to find a relation from a subset that is not required. How do we forget indexes that are saviors if used appropriately? All these together would show our relations and would promptly respond to a requested query.

Summary

I am sure that while reading the chapter, you have kept in mind the things to be taken care of or recollecting them, if there's anything missing in your MySQL 8 implementation. In these chapter, we discussed best practices for MySQL 8 which would be helpful at various stages, such as implementation, usage, management, and troubleshooting and would act as pointers for best practices of MySQL 8; these might vary based on different use cases. Proper testing and verification would help affirm the benefits of having best practices implemented.

We have broadly covered some exciting topics about MySQL 8 benchmarks and a few configuration parameters along with best practices of memcached. We discussed MySQL replication best practices, in which we went through a few critical pointers. Lastly, MySQL queries and indexing pointers were also discussed with best practices for data partitioning. Anything written in this chapter would be less, but the pointers provided are necessary.

By now, we should have a good understanding of MySQL 8; it's now time to solve problems.

Let's now move on to the next chapter and look at how we could come across many common issues, identifying error codes along with real-world scenarios for troubleshooting MySQL 8.

15
Troubleshooting MySQL 8

In the previous chapter, we learned an important aspect of the MySQL 8 database, benchmarking, and best practices. Benchmarking helps in comparing the current database performance against the expected performance matrices. We learned what benchmarking is and the tools that can be used to find the benchmark performance of a MySQL 8 server. In a later part of the chapter, we learned about the best practices to be followed for memcached, replication, partitioning, and indexing. Best practices help ensure the optimum configuration of the MySQL 8 database.

In this chapter, the focus will be on understanding the common errors that we may encounter while working with the MySQL 8 database. The errors may be server errors or client errors. We will look at a way to determine that the problem has occurred. We will also learn troubleshooting and resolution techniques for errors. In a later part of the chapter, we will look into real-world scenarios where these techniques are applicable. The following is the list of topics to be covered:

- MySQL 8 common problems
- MySQL 8 server errors
- MySQL 8 client errors
- MySQL 8 troubleshooting approach
- Real-world scenario

MySQL 8 common problems

When troubleshooting is an issue, the first thing to be done is to find out the program or piece of equipment that is causing it when we run into a problem.

The following are symptoms that indicate a hardware or kernel problem:

- The keyboard is not functioning. It can be checked by pressing the *Caps Lock* key. If the light on the *Caps Lock* key does not light up, it is an issue with the keyboard. Similarly, the mouse not moving indicates an issue with the mouse.
- `ping` is an operating system command to check the accessibility of one machine from another machine. The machine from which the ping command is executed is called the **local machine**, whereas the machine pinged is called the **remote machine**. If the remote machine does not respond to the local machine's pings, it indicates a hardware or network related issue.
- It may indicate an issue with the operating system kernel program if the programs other than MySQL are not working correctly.
- It may indicate an issue with the operating system or hardware if the system restarts unexpectedly. In a typical case, a user-level program should never be able to take the system down.

To troubleshoot the issue, one or more of the following can be done:

- Run a diagnostic tool to check hardware
- Ensure the relevant library files are up to date
- Check for the availability of updates, patches, or service packs for the operating system
- Check all connections

`ECC memory` is an error correcting code memory. It can detect and correct most common internal data corruption issues. It is advisable to use ECC memory in order to detect the memory issues at an early stage.

The following instructions may help further identify the issue:

- Examining the system log files may help to discover the reason for the problem. MySQL log files must also be checked in case there appears to be an issue with MySQL.
- Operating system specific commands can be used to check issues with memory, file descriptors, disk space, or other critical resources.

- A bug can be identified in the operating system kernel if a problematic runaway process does not die even though we have executed a command to kill it.
- If there appears not to be a problem with the hardware, attempts should be made to identify the program that may be causing the problem. Using operating system specific commands, such as Task manager on Windows, `ps` and `top` on Linux, or similar programs, we can identify programs that eat up CPU or block system processes.
- It is possible to recover the access to the machine even though the keyboard is locked up. This can be done by logging on to the system from another machine. Execute the `kbd_mode -a` command upon successful login.

MySQL users can report issues by using one of the multiple channels provided by MySQL. After having examined all the possible alternatives, if it can be decided that either the MySQL server or the MySQL client causes the problem, a user can either create a bug report for the mailing list or contact the MySQL support team. The bug reporter must provide detailed information about the bug, system information, and behavior and the expected behavior. The reporter must describe the reason based on why it seems to be a MySQL bug. It is useful to know the following information if the program fails:

- With the help of the `top` command, check if the program in question has taken up all the CPU time. In such cases, we should allow a program to run for a while because it is possible that the program may be executing intensive computational instructions.
- Observe the response from the MySQL server when a client program tries to connect to it. Has it stopped responding? Did the server provide any output?
- If it is found that the MySQL server is causing problems in the `mysqld` program, try to connect using the `mysqladmin` program to check whether `mysqld` responds. The `mysqladmin -u root ping` or `mysqladmin -u root processlist` commands can be used.
- Did the failed program make a segmentation fault?

Most common MySQL errors

This section provides a list of the most common MySQL errors that users encounter very frequently.

Access denied

MySQL provides a privilege system that authenticates the user who connects from a host, and associates the user with access privileges on a database. The privileges include SELECT, INSERT, UPDATE, and DELETE and are able to identify anonymous users and grant privileges for MySQL specific functions, such as LOAD DATA INFILE and administrative operations.

The access denied error may occur because of many causes. In many cases, the problem is caused because of MySQL accounts that the client programs use to connect with the MySQL server with permission from the server.

Can't connect to [local] MySQL server

In this section, we will focus on the circumstances in which **Can't connect to MySQL server error** is encountered. But before we jump onto error-specific details, it is necessary to understand how the MySQL client connects to the MySQL server.

On a Unix system, two different ways are available for the MySQL client to connect to the mysqld server process. The following are the details of these two methods:

- **TCP/IP connection**: The mysqld server process listens for client connections on a specific port. The MySQL clients connects to the server using the specified TCP/IP port.
- **Unix socket file**: In this mode of connection, a Unix socket file is used to connect through a file in the filesystem (/tmp/mysql.sock).

The socket file connection is faster compared to TCP/IP but it can be used when connecting to a server on the same machine. To use the Unix socket file, we do not specify a hostname or a special hostname localhost should be specified.

The following are the ways for the MySQL client to connect to the MySQL server on Windows:

- **TCP/IP connection**: As described previously for the Unix systems, the TCP/IP connection runs on a specified port number. The MySQL client connects to the port on which the MySQL server is listening.

- **Named pipe connection**: The MySQL server can be started with the `--enable-named-pipe` option. If the client is running on the host on which the server is running, the client can connect with named pipes. **MySQL** is the default name of the named pipe. If no hostname is provided while connecting to the `mysqld` server process, MySQL first tries to connect to the default named pipe. If it is unable to connect to the named pipe, it tries to connect to the TCP/IP port. The use of named pipes can be forced on Windows by using `.` as the hostname.

MySQL errors are identified by predefined unique error codes. The same error can have different error codes associated with it. The **Can't connect to MySQL server error** with the error code `2002` indicates one of three problems. It can be that the MySQL server is not running on the system, or the Unix socket filename provided is incorrect, or the TCP/IP port number provided to connect to the server is incorrect. The TCP/IP port may be blocked by the firewall or the port blocking service.

The error code `2003` also associates with can't connect to MySQL server. It indicates refusal of the network connection by the server. It should be checked if the MySQL server has network connections enabled, the MySQL server is running, and the specified network port is configured on the server.

The following command can be used to ensure that the `mysqld` server process is running:

```
> ps xa | grep mysqld
```

If the `mysqld` server process is not running, we should start the server. If the server is already running, the following commands should be used:

```
> mysqladmin version
> mysqladmin variables
> mysqladmin -h `hostname` version variables
> mysqladmin -h `hostname` --port=3306 version
> mysqladmin -h host_ip version
> mysqladmin --protocol=SOCKET --socket=/tmp/mysql.sock version
```

In the preceding commands, `hostname` is the hostname of the machine on which the MySQL server is running. `host_ip` is the IP address of the server machine.

Lost connection to MySQL server

The lost connection to MySQL server error can occur because of one of the three likely causes explained in this section.

One of the potential reasons for the error is that the network connectivity is troublesome. Network conditions should be checked if this is a frequent error. If the **during query** message is part of the error message, it is certain that the error has occurred because of network connection issues.

The `connection_timeout` system variable defines the number of seconds that the `mysqld` server waits for a connection packet before connection timeout response. Infrequently, this error may occur when a client is trying for the initial connection to the server and the `connection_timeout` value is set to a few seconds. In this case, the problem can be resolved by increasing the `connection_timeout` value based on the the distance and connection speed. `SHOW GLOBAL STATUS LIKE` and `Aborted_connects` can be used to determine if we are experiencing this more frequently. It can be certainly said that increasing the `connection_timeout` value is the solution if the error message contains **reading authorization packet**.

It is possible that the problem may be faced because of larger **Binary Large OBject (BLOB)** values than `max_allowed_packet`. This can cause a lost connection to the MySQL server error with clients. If the `ER_NET_PACKET_TOO_LARGE` error is observed, it confirms that the `max_allowed_packet` value should be increased.

Password fails when entered incorrectly

MySQL clients ask for a password when the client program is invoked with the `--password` or `-p` option without the password value. The following is the command:

```
> mysql -u user_name -p
Enter password:
```

On a few systems, it may happen that the password works fine when specified in an option file or on the command line. But it does not work when entered interactively on the Command Prompt at the `Enter password:` prompt. It occurs because the system-provided library to read the passwords limits the password values to a small number of characters (usually eight). It is an issue with the system library and not with MySQL. As a workaround to this, change the MySQL password to a value that is eight or fewer characters or store the password in the option file.

Host host_name is blocked

If the `mysqld` server receives too many connection requests from the host that is interrupted in the middle, the following error occurs:

```
Host 'host_name' is blocked because of many connection errors.
Unblock with 'mysqladmin flush-hosts'
```

The `max_connect_errors` system variable determines the number of successive interrupted connection requests that are allowed. Once there are `max_connect_errors` failed requests without a successful connection, `mysqld` assumes that something is wrong and blocks the host from further connections until the `FLUSH HOSTS` statement or `mysqladmin flush-hosts` command is issued.

`mysqld` blocks a host after 100 connection errors as a default. It can be adjusted by setting the `max_connect_errors` value on the server startup, as follows:

```
> mysqld_safe --max_connect_errors=10000
```

This value can also be set up at runtime, as follows:

```
mysql> SET GLOBAL max_connect_errors=10000;
```

It should be checked first that there is nothing wrong with TCP/IP connections from the host if the `host_name` is blocked error is received for a particular host. Increasing the value of the `max_connect_errors` variable does not help if the network has problems.

Too many connections

This error indicates that all available connection are in use for other client connections. The `max_connections` is the system variable that controls the number of connections to the server. The default value for the maximum number of connections is 151. We can set a larger value than 151 for the `max_connections` system variable to support more connections than 151.

The `mysqld` server process actually allows one more than `max_connections` (`max_connections + 1`) value clients to connect. The additional one connection is kept reserved for accounts with `CONNECTION_ADMIN` or the `SUPER` privilege. The privilege can be granted to the administrators with access to the `PROCESS` privilege. With this access, the administrator can connect to the server using the reserved connection. They can execute the `SHOW PROCESSLIST` command to diagnose the problems even though the maximum number of client connections is exhausted.

Out of memory

If the `mysql` does not have enough memory to store the entire request of the query issued by the MySQL client program, the server throws the following error:

```
mysql: Out of memory at line 42, 'malloc.c'
mysql: needed 8136 byte (8k), memory in use: 12481367 bytes (12189k)
ERROR 2008: MySQL client ran out of memory
```

In order to fix the problem, we must first check if the query is correct. Do we expect the query to return so many rows? If not, we should correct the query and execute it again. If the query is correct and needs no correction, we can connect `mysql` with the `--quick` option. Using the `--quick` option results in the `mysql_use_result()` C API function for fetching the result set. The function adds more load on the server and less load on the client.

Packet too large

The communication packet is one of the following:

- A single SQL statement that the MySQL client sends to the MySQL server
- A single row that is sent to the MySQL client from the MySQL server
- A binary log event that is sent from a replication master server to the replication slave

A 1 GB packet size is the largest possible packet size that can be transmitted to or from the MySQL 8 server or client. The MySQL server or client issues an `ER_NET_PACKET_TOO_LARGE` error and closes the connection if it receives a packet bigger than `max_allowed_packet` bytes.

The default `max_allowed_packet` size is 16 MB for the MySQL client program. The following command can be used to set a larger value:

```
> mysql --max_allowed_packet=32M
```

The default value for the MySQL server is 64 MB. It should be noted that there is no harm in setting a larger value for this system variable, as the additional memory is allocated as needed.

The table is full

The table-full error occurs in one of the following conditions:

- The disk is full
- The table has reached the maximum size

The actual maximum table size in the MySQL database can be determined by the constraints imposed by the operating system on the file sizes.

Can't create/write to file

This indicates that MySQL is unable to create a temporary file in the temporary directory for the result set if we get the following error while executing a query:

```
Can't create/write to file '\\sqla3fe_0.ism'.
```

The possible workaround for the error is to start the `mysqld` server with the `--tmpdir` option. The following is the command:

```
> mysqld --tmpdir C:/temp
```

As an alternative, it can be specified in the `[mysqld]` section of the MySQL configuration file, as follows:

```
[mysqld]
tmpdir=C:/temp
```

Commands out of sync

If the client functions are called in the wrong order, the commands out of sync error is received. It means that the command cannot be executed in the client code. As an example, if we execute `mysql_use_result()` and try to execute another query before executing `mysql_free_result()`, this error may occur. It may also happen if we execute two queries that return a result set without calling the `mysql_use_result()` or `mysql_store_result()` functions in between.

Ignoring user

The following error is received when an account in the user table is found with an invalid password upon the `mysqld` server startup or when the server reloads the grant tables:

```
Found wrong password for user 'some_user'@'some_host'; ignoring user
```

The account is ignored by the MySQL permission system as a result. To fix the problem, we should assign a new valid password for the account.

Table tbl_name doesn't exist

The following error indicates that a specified table does not exist in the default database:

```
Table 'tbl_name' doesn't exist
Can't find file: 'tbl_name' (errno: 2)
```

In some cases, the user may be referring to the table incorrectly. It is possible because the MySQL server uses directories and files for storing database tables. Depending upon the operating system file management, the database and table names can be case sensitive.

For non case-sensitive filesystems, such as Windows, the references to a specified table used within a query must use the same letter case.

MySQL 8 server errors

This section focuses on MySQL 8 server errors. The section describes the errors related to MySQL server administration, table definitions, and known issues in the MySQL 8 server.

Issues with file permissions

If the UMASK or UMASK_DIR environment variables are set incorrectly upon server startup, we may have problems with file permissions. The MySQL server may issue following error message upon table creation:

```
ERROR: Can't find file: 'path/with/file_name' (Errcode: 13)
```

The default values for UMASK and UMASK_DIR system variables are 0640 and 0750, respectively. If the value of these environment variables starts with zero, it indicates to the MySQL server that the values are in octal. For example, the default values 0640 and 0750 in octal are equivalent to 415 and 488, respectively, in decimal.

In order to change the default UMASK value, we should start mysqld_safe, as follows:

```
> UMASK=384 # = 600 in octal
> export UMASK
> mysqld_safe
```

The MySQL server creates database directories with a default access permission value of 0750. We can set the UMASK_DIR variable to modify this behavior. If this value is set, new directories are created with access permission values as a combination of the UMASK and UMASK_DIR values.

The following is an example of providing group access to all new directories:

```
> UMASK_DIR=504 # = 770 in octal
> export UMASK_DIR
> mysqld_safe &
```

Resetting the root password

The MySQL server does not need a password for connecting as a root user if the root password is never set in MySQL. If the password was assigned earlier has been forgotten, it can be reset.

The following are the instructions to reset the root @ localhost account password on the Windows system:

1. Log in to the system using system administrator credentials.
2. If the MySQL server is already running, stop the server. If the MySQL server is running as a Windows service, go to **Services** by following **Start menu** | **Control panel** | **Administrative tools** | **Services**. In the services, find the MySQL service and stop it. If the MySQL server is not running as a Windows service, kill the MySQL server process by using Windows Task Manager.
3. Once the MySQL server is stopped, create a text file that has a single line of the password assignment statement, as follows:

```
ALTER USER 'root'@'localhost' IDENTIFIED BY 'NewPassword';
```

4. Save the file. For example, the file is saved as `C:\mysql-root-reset.txt`.

5. Open the Windows Command Prompt by following **Start menu | Run | cmd**.

6. In the Command Prompt, start the MySQL server with the `--init-file` option, as follows:

```
C:\> cd "C:\Program Files\MySQL\MySQL Server 8.0\bin"
C:\> mysqld --init-file=C:\\mysql-root-reset.txt
```

7. Once the MySQL server is restarted, delete the `C:\mysql-root-reset.txt` file.

The following are the instructions to reset the root user password on Unix-like systems:

1. Log on to the system with the same user the the MySQL server runs by. Usually, it is `mysql` user.

2. If the MySQL server is already running, stop the server. To accomplish this, find the `.pid` file containing the process ID of the MySQL server. Depending on the Unix distribution, the actual location and name of the file may differ. The usual locations are `/var/lib/mysql/`, `/var/run/mysqld/`, and `/usr/local/mysql/data/`. Usually, the filename begins with either `mysqld` or the hostname of the system and has an extension of `.pid`. The MySQL server can be stopped by sending a normal kill command to the `mysqld` server process. The following command can be used with actual path name of the `.pid` file:

```
> kill 'cat /mysql-data-directory/host_name.pid'
```

3. Once the MySQL server is stopped, create a text file that has a single line of the password assignment statement, as follows:

```
ALTER USER 'root'@'localhost' IDENTIFIED BY 'NewPassword';
```

4. Save the file. It is assumed that the file is stored at `/home/me/mysql-reset-root`. As the file contains the password for the root user, it should be ensured that other users are not able to read it. If we are not logged in with the appropriate user, we should make sure that the user has permission to read the file.

5. Start the MySQL server with the `--init-file` option, as follows:

```
> mysqld --init-file=/home/me/mysql-reset-root &
```

6. Once the server is started, delete the file at `/home/me/mysql-reset-root`.

The following are the generic instructions to reset the root user password:

1. If the MySQL server is running, stop the server. Once it is stopped, restart the MySQL server with the `--skip-grant-tables` privilege. Along with `--skip-grant-tables`, the `--skip-networking` option is automatically enabled so as to prevent remote connections.

2. Connect to the MySQL server using the `mysql` client program. As the server is started with `--skip-grant-tables`, no password is necessary:

   ```
   > mysql
   ```

3. In the MySQL client itself, ask the server to reload the grant tables. This will enable account management statements:

   ```
   mysql> FLUSH PRIVILEGES;
   ```

4. Change the `root @ localhost` account password by using following command:

   ```
   mysql> ALTER USER 'root'@'localhost' IDENTIFIED BY
     'NewPassword';
   ```

5. Restart the server and log in with the root user and newly set password.

MySQL crashes prevention

As a standard release practice, every MySQL version is verified on different platforms before its release. It is assumed that MySQL may have a few hard to find bugs. As we encounter an issue with MySQL, it is helpful if we try to find out the cause for the system crash. The first thing to identify is if the `mysqld` server process crashes or the issue is with the MySQL client program. It can be checked how long the MySQL server was up for by executing the `mysqladmin version` command. The following is an example output:

```
C:\Program Files\MySQL\MySQL Server 8.0\bin>mysqladmin version -u root -p
Enter password: *****
mysqladmin Ver 8.0.3-rc for Win64 on x86_64 (MySQL Community Server (GPL))
Copyright (c) 2000, 2017, Oracle and/or its affiliates. All rights
reserved.

Oracle is a registered trademark of Oracle Corporation and/or its
affiliates. Other names may be trademarks of their respective
owners.
```

```
Server version 8.0.3-rc-log
Protocol version 10
Connection localhost via TCP/IP
TCP port 3306
Uptime: 9 days 4 hours 4 min 52 sec

Threads: 2 Questions: 4 Slow queries: 0 Opens: 93 Flush tables: 2 Open
tables: 69 Queries per second avg: 0.000
```

The `resolve_stack_dump` is a utility program that resolves a numeric stack dump to symbols. To analyze the root cause of where the `mysqld` server process died, we find in the stack trace error logs. It can be resolved with the `resolve_stack_dump` program. It must be noted that it is possible that variable values found in the error logs may not be accurate.

Corrupted data or index files can cause the MySQL server to crash. These files are updated on the disk using the `write()` system called upon the execution of each SQL statement and before the client is notified about the result. It means that the contents in the data files are safe even in the event of a `mysqld` crash. The writing of the unflushed data on the disk is taken care of by the operating system. The `--flush` option can be used with `mysqld` to force MySQL to flush everything to disk after every SQL statement execution.

One of the following can be the reason for MySQL corrupted tables:

- If the data file or index file crashes then it contains corrupted data.
- A bug in the MySQL server process caused the server to die in the middle of an update.
- An external program manipulated the data and index files at the same time as `mysqld` without table locking.
- In the middle of an update, the MySQL server process was killed.
- Many `mysqld` servers are running on the system. The servers use the same data directory. The system does not have good filesystem locks or the external locking is disabled.
- It is possible that a bug is found in the data storage code. We can try to change the storage engine by using `ALTER TABLE` on the repaired copy of the table.

Handling MySQL full disk

This section focuses on the response from MySQL to disk-full errors and quota-exceeded errors. It is more relevant to writes in MyISAM tables. It can be applied to writes in binary log files and an index file. It excludes the references to rows and records that should be considered an event.

MySQL performs the following when a disk-full condition occurs:

- MySQL ensures that there is enough space available to write the current row.
- The MySQL server writes an entry in the log file every 10 minutes. It warns about the disk-full condition.

The following actions should be taken to remedy the problem:

- The disk space should be freed to make sure enough space is available to insert all records.
- We can execute the mysqladmin kill command to abort the thread. The next time it checks the disk, the thread is aborted.
- It may happen that a few threads are waiting for the table that caused the disk-full situation. Out of several locked threads, killing the thread that is waiting on the disk-full condition will enable other threads to continue.
- The REPAIR TABLE or OPTIMIZE TABLE statements are exceptions to the preceding condition. Other exceptions include indexes created in a batch after the LOAD DATA INFILE or ALTER TABLE statements. These SQL statements can create temporary files with large volumes. This may create big problems for the rest of the system.

MySQL temporary files storage

The value of the TMPDIR environment variable is used by MySQL on the Unix as the path name of the directory to store temporary files. MySQL uses a system default, such as /tmp, /var/tmp, or /usr/tmp if the TMPDIR is not set.

The values of the TMPDIR, TEMP, and TMP environment variables are checked by MySQL on Windows. If MySQL finds one set, it uses that value and does not check for remaining values. If none of these three variables are set, MySQL uses the system default, which is C:\windows\temp\.

If the temporary file directory in the filesystem is too small, we can use the mysqld --tmpdir option to specify a directory on the filesystem with enough space. For the replication, on slave machines, we can use --slave-load-tmpdir and specify the directory for holding temporary files during the replication of LOAD DATA INFILE statements. It is possible to set a list of several paths used in a round-robin fashion with the --tmpdir option. On the Unix system, the paths can be separated by the colon character(:), whereas on Windows, the semicolon character(;) can be used to separate the paths.

 To effectively distribute the load, multiple temporary directory paths should belong to different physical disks and not the different partitions of the same disk.

For the MySQL server working as a replication slave, we must take care of setting the --slave-load-tmpdir option so as not to point to a directory in the memory-based filesystem or to a directory that is cleared upon server or server host restarts. To replicate the temporary tables or LOAD DATA INFILE operations, the replication slave requires its temporary files on the machine restart. The replication fails if the files in the temporary file directory are lost.

MySQL takes care of removing the temporary files when the mysqld server process is terminated. On Unix-like platforms, it can be done by unlinking a file after opening it. One of the major disadvantage of this is that the name does not appear in directory listings. It also happens that we cannot see a big file that occupies the filesystem.

ibtmp1 is the name of the table space file that the InnoDB storage engine uses to store temporary tables. The file is located in the data directory of MySQL. If we want to specify a different filename and location, the innodb_temp_data_file_path option can be used on the server startup.

If the ALGORITHM=COPY technique is used by the ALTER TABLE operation on the InnoDB table, the storage engine creates a temporary copy of the original table in the same directory. The temporary table filenames start with the #sql- prefix. They only appear briefly while the ALTER TABLE operation is being performed.

If the InnoDB table is rebuilt by the ALTER TABLE SQL statement using the ALGORITHM=INPLACE method, the InnoDB storage engine creates an intermediate copy of the original table in the same directory as that of the original table. The intermediate table filenames start with the #sql-ib prefix. They only appear briefly while the ALTER TABLE operation is being performed.

The `innodb_tmpdir` option cannot be applied to intermediate table files. These intermediate files are always created and stored in the same directory as that of the original table.

The `ALTER TABLE` SQL statements that rebuild the `InnoDB` table with the `ALGORITHM=INPLACE` method create temporary sort files in the default MySQL temporary directory. The default temporary directory is denoted by `$TMPDIR` on Unix, `%TEMP%` on Windows, or the directory mentioned by the `--tmpdir` option. `tmpdir` may need to be reconfigured if the temporary directory is not large enough to store such files. As an alternative, we can define another temporary directory for online `InnoDB ALTER TABLE` statements using the `innodb_tmpdir` option. The `innodb_tmpdir` option can be configured at runtime, using the `SET GLOBAL` or `SET SESSION` statements.

Replicating an `innodb_tmpdir` configuration should be considered in replication environments if all the servers have the same operating system environment. In other cases, an `innodb_tmpdir` setting replication can result in a failed replication while executing online `ALTER TABLE` operations. It is recommended to configure `innodb_tmpdir` for each server separately if the operating environments are different.

MySQL Unix socket file

The MySQL server uses `/tmp/mysql.sock` as a default location for Unix socket files for communication with local clients. It may be different based on the distribution formats, such as `/var/lib/mysql` for RPMs.

On several Unix versions, it is possible to delete files stored in the `/tmp` directory and similar other directories used to store temporary files. It may cause problems if the socket file is stored in such a directory on the filesystem.

It is possible to protect the `/tmp` directory so as to ensure that the files can only be deleted by the owners or the root superuser. This is possible on almost every version of Unix. This can be done by setting the sticky bit on the `/tmp` directory while logged in as a root user. The following is the command to do the same:

```
chmod +t /tmp
```

Using the `ls -ld /tmp` command, it can also be checked if the sticky bit is set. The bit is set if the last permission character is `t`. A sticky bit is used to define the file permissions in Unix systems.

An alternative approach is also possible in which we should change the place of the Unix socket file. If we change the location of the Unix socket file, we must ensure that the client programs also know the new location of the file. The following are the ways to do it:

- The path can be set in the global or local option file, as follows:

```
[mysqld]
socket=/path/to/socket

[client]
socket=/path/to/socket
```

  - We can also specify a `--socket` option to `mysqld_safe` on the command line and also when we run client programs.
  - The `MYSQL_UNIX_PORT` environment variable can be set to the path of the Unix socket file.
  - The MySQL can also be recompiled from source so as to use a different Unix socket file location as a default.

Using the following command, it can be ensured that the new socket location works:

```
mysqladmin --socket=/path/to/socket version
```

Time zone problems

The MySQL server must be told the user's current time zone if we have problem with `SELECT NOW()` returning a value in UTC instead of the user's current time zone. It is also applicable if `UNIX_TIMESTAMP()` returns a wrong value. It should be done for the environment running the server; for example, `mysqld_safe` or `mysql.server`.

We can also set the server time zone by using the `--timezone=timezone_name` option with `mysqld_safe`. It can also be set by assigning the value to the `TZ` environment variable before the `mysqld` is started.

The allowed list of values for `--timezone` or `TZ` depends on the system.

MySQL 8 client errors

This section focuses on errors that occur on the MySQL 8 client. The job of a MySQL client is to connect to the MySQL server so as to execute the SQL queries and get the results from the MySQL 8 database. This section lists errors related to execution of the queries.

Case sensitivity in string searches

The string searches use the logical sequence of comparison operands for non-binary strings, such as CHAR, VARCHAR, and TEXT. The comparisons of binary strings, such as BINARY, VARBINARY, and BLOB use the numeric values of the bytes in the operands. It essentially means that the comparison will be case sensitive for the alphabetic characters.

The comparison of a non-binary string with a binary string will be treated as a comparison between binary strings.

The comparison operations such as >=, >, =, <, <=, sorting and grouping depend on the sort value of each character. The characters with a similar sort value are considered the same character. Consider an example of e and é. These characters have the same sort value in the provided logical sequence. These are considered equal.

utf8mb4 and utf8mb4_0900_ai_ci are the default character set and collation, respectively. As a default, the non-binary string comparisons are case insensitive. This means that we will get all the column values starting with A or a if we search with col_name LIKE 'a%'. To make it case sensitive, we have to ensure that one of the operands has a binary or case sensitive collation. For example, if a column is compared to a string and both have the utf8mb4 character set, the COLLATE operator can be used to cause either operand to have the utf8mb4_0900_as_cs or utf8mb4_bin collation. The following is an example:

```
col_name COLLATE utf8mb4_0900_as_cs LIKE 'a%'
col_name LIKE 'a%' COLLATE utf8mb4_0900_as_cs
col_name COLLATE utf8mb4_bin LIKE 'a%'
col_name LIKE 'a%' COLLATE utf8mb4_bin
```

In order to change the non-binary case-sensitive strings comparison to be case insensitive, we should use COLLATE to name a case-insensitive collation. The following is an example of how COLLATE changes the comparison to be case sensitive:

```
mysql> SET NAMES 'utf8mb4';
mysql> SET @s1 = 'MySQL' COLLATE utf8mb4_bin, @s2 = 'mysql' COLLATE
utf8mb4_bin; mysql> SELECT @s1 = @s2;
+-----------+
| @s1 = @s2 |
+-----------+
|         0 |
+-----------+
mysql> SELECT @s1 COLLATE utf8mb4_0900_ai_ci = @s2;
+--------------------------------------+
| @s1 COLLATE utf8mb4_0900_ai_ci = @s2 |
+--------------------------------------+
|                                    1 |
+--------------------------------------+
```

Problems with DATE columns

In MySQL, the default format of a DATE value is YYYY-MM-DD. Standard SQL does not permit any other format. This is the format that should be used in the UPDATE expressions and in the WHERE clause in a SELECT statement. The following is an example of the date format:

```
SELECT * FROM table_name WHERE date_col >= '2011-06-02';
```

When a constant string is compared to DATE, TIME, DATETIME, or TIMESTAMP using <, <=, =, >=, >, or BETWEEN operators, MySQL converts the string into an internal long integer value. MySQL does this so as to achieve a faster comparison. However, the following exceptions are applicable to this conversion:

- Comparing two columns
- Comparing a DATE, TIME, DATETIME, or TIMESTAMP column to an expression
- Use of a comparison method other than those just listed, such as IN or STRCMP()

The comparison is done by converting the objects into string values and performing a string comparison in case of these exceptions.

Problems with NULL values

A NULL value is often a point of confusion for new programmers. The NULL value is by mistake interpreted as an empty string ' ' in the case of strings. This is not correct. The following is an example of completely different statements:

```
mysql> INSERT INTO my_table (phone) VALUES (NULL);
mysql> INSERT INTO my_table (phone) VALUES ('');
```

In the preceding example, both statements insert the value in the same column (phone column). The first statement inserts a NULL value, whereas the second statement inserts an empty string. The first value can be considered as the phone number is not known, whereas the second value indicates the person is known to have no phone, and thus no phone number.

When a NULL value is compared to any other value, it always evaluates to be false. The expression containing the NULL value always results in a NULL value. The following example returns a NULL value:

```
mysql> SELECT NULL, 1+NULL, CONCAT('Invisible',NULL);
```

If the purpose of an SQL statement is to search for NULL column values, we cannot use expression = NULL. The following is an example that returns no rows, as expression = NULL is always false:

```
mysql> SELECT * FROM my_table WHERE phone = NULL;
```

To make a NULL value comparison, IS NULL should be used. The following example demonstrates the use of IS NULL:

```
mysql> SELECT * FROM my_table WHERE phone IS NULL;
mysql> SELECT * FROM my_table WHERE phone = '';
```

MySQL 8 troubleshooting approach

In this section of the chapter, we will focus on the MySQL 8 troubleshooting approach. Why do we need to troubleshoot MySQL 8? The reasons for troubleshooting are as follows:

- Faster execution of SQL queries
- Performance enhancement
- Efficient use of resources

The primary set of resources include CPU, disk IO, memory, and network. There are two approaches to measure MySQL performance:

- In a query focused approach, it is important to measure how fast the queries get executed
- In resource focused approach, it is important that the queries use fewer resources.

Let us take a deeper look at ways to troubleshoot MySQL problems.

Analyzing queries

EXPLAIN is the SQL statement that provides information for the way MySQL executes the SQL statements. The EXPLAIN statement works with INSERT, UPDATE, REPLACE, DELETE, and SELECT statements. The output of the EXPLAIN statement is a row of information for each table mentioned or used in the SELECT statement. The output lists the tables in the order of MySQL's reading these tables while executing the statement. All joins are resolved using the nested-loop join method. In the nested-loop join method, MySQL reads a row from the first table in the list and then finds the matching row in the second table in the list, then the third table, and so on. Once all the tables in the list are processed, MySQL processes the results of the selected columns and backtracks them through the list of tables until it finds a table with more matching rows. It reads the next row from this table. This way the process continues.

The following are the columns from the EXPLAIN output:

- id: This denotes the sequential number of SELECT within a query. It is also known as the SELECT identifier. It is possible that the value can be NULL when the row belongs to union result of other rows. The output shows <unionM, N> in the table column. It means that the row refers to union of ID values M and N.
- select_type: This output column indicates the type of SELECT statement. The possible list of values include SIMPLE, PRIMARY, UNION, DEPENDENT UNION, UNION RESULT, SUBQUERY, DEPENDENT SUBQUERY, DERIVED, MATERIALIZED, UNCACHEABLE SUBQUERY, and UNCACHEABLE UNION.
- table: This column indicates the name of the table referred in the output. It can have values such as <unionM, N>, <derivedN>, and <subqueryN>.
- partitions: This identifies the partitions from which the query matches the records. For non-partitioned tables, the value is NULL.

- `type`: This indicates the type of JOIN.
- `possible_keys`: This output column indicates possible indexes that MySQL may choose to fetch the rows in the table. If there are no matching indexes, the return value would be NULL.
- `key`: This output column indicates the key index that MySQL actually uses to fetch the rows from a table.
- `ref`: The `ref` output column indicates the columns or constants used to compare with the index mentioned in the key output column to select table rows.
- `rows`: The rows output column indicates the number of rows to be examined in order to successfully execute the query.

The following are the types of joins in EXPLAIN:

- `system`: This means that the table has only one row. It is a special case of `const` join type.
- `const`: This means that the table has at least one matching row. The row is read at the beginning of the query. As only one matching row is found, the rest of the optimizer regards the values from the column in this row as constants. As const tables are read only once, it is very fast. The const is used when all parts of a PRIMARY KEY or UNIQUE index are compared to constant values. The following is an example where `tbl_name` is used as a const table:

```
mysql> SELECT * FROM tbl_name WHERE primary_key=1;
mysql> SELECT * FROM tbl_name WHERE primary_key_part1=1 AND
primary_key_part2=2;
```

- `ref`: For each combination of rows from the earlier tables, all rows with matching index values are read from the `ref` table. If the join uses only the leftmost prefix of the key, the `ref` is used.

Real-world scenario

MySQL query optimization is referred to as improving the time of query execution. For example, when a query is not performing well means that the query is taking a longer time than expected for execution. The time of the query execution is important but there are other matrices as well that are used to measure performance. This section explains what should be measured and how it should be done as precisely as possible.

The following question arises: why should we optimize the query? Does it really require optimization if it only takes a hundredth of a second? Yes, it does require optimization unless the query is executed rarely. We should optimize the queries that are most expensive.

Let's discuss a real-time example. In one of the applications, we had a report that was generated based on a complex query and was taking too much time. The execution time was in minutes. To optimize such a complex query, we considered the following approach:

1. **Analyze the query plan using** EXPLAIN: MySQL provides two ways to analyze the performance of a query. One is the EXPLAIN method, which we have already learned about in the preceding section of this chapter. Another tool is SHOW STATUS. Usually, we should prefer to use EXPLAIN to understand the query plan of a SELECT query. In the case of the report query, we convert a few of the non-SELECT queries to SELECT queries. This helps us in understanding the query execution plan for non- SELECT queries as well. For example, rewriting an UPDATE query to SELECT can be done by using the WHERE clause in the UPDATE query, which is passed on to the SELECT query. We could also find few missing indexes on the tables.

2. SHOW STATUS: The SHOW STATUS statement outputs the internal counters for MySQL. The counters are incremented by MySQL upon every query execution. With the help of these counters, we could understand the types of operations performed by the server in aggregate. It also helps in indicating the work done by each individual query.

The following are the measurements performed for MySQL server variables:

- Select_: This counter is incremented whenever a SELECT query is executed. This counter can also be used to identify if a table scan is performed.
- Key_read: This variable provides additional information on the usage of the key index.
- Last_query_cost: This value indicates how expensive the last executed query was.

The following are the steps to perform query optimization:

1. Query the execution a few times to ensure it returns the same result.
2. Execute SHOW STATUS. The output should be saved.
3. Execute the query.
4. Execute SHOW STATUS to observe the differences from the previous execution.
5. Execute EXPLAIN if required.

The following parameters should be analyzed for query performance optimization:

- Table index
- Sorting
- Overall performance
- Row level operations
- Disk I/O operations

Summary

In this last chapter of the book, we learned an important aspect of any database: troubleshooting errors that we may encounter using the MySQL server or client. We started the discussion by understanding what troubleshooting is. We discussed different ways for initial diagnostics of the error. We understood common MySQL errors and what the error messages mean. We also learned about the ways to fix these errors. We also learned about the MySQL server and client errors and fixes for these errors. In the later part of the chapter, we learned about the MySQL troubleshooting approach and looked at a real-world scenario. Pretty important stuff for the last chapter, huh? That's it for the book.

Other Books You May Enjoy

If you enjoyed this book, you may be interested in these other books by Packt:

MySQL 8 for Big Data

Shabbir Challawala, Jaydip Lakhatariya, Chintan Mehta, Kandarp Patel

ISBN: 978-1-78839-718-6

- Explore the features of MySQL 8 and how they can be leveraged to handle Big Data
- Unlock the new features of MySQL 8 for managing structured and unstructured Big Data
- Integrate MySQL 8 and Hadoop for efficient data processing
- Perform aggregation using MySQL 8 for optimum data utilization
- Explore different kinds of join and union in MySQL 8 to process Big Data efficiently
- Accelerate Big Data processing with Memcached
- Integrate MySQL with the NoSQL API
- Implement replication to build highly available solutions for Big Data

MySQL 8 Cookbook
Karthik Appigatla

ISBN: 978-1-78839-580-9

- Install and configure your MySQL 8 instance without any hassle
- Get to grips with new features of MySQL 8 like CTE, Window functions and many more
- Perform backup tasks, recover data and set up various replication topologies for your database
- Maximize performance by using new features of MySQL 8 like descending indexes, controlling query optimizer and resource groups
- Learn how to use general table space to suit the SaaS or multi-tenant applications
- Analyze slow queries using performance schema, sys schema and third party tools
- Manage and monitor your MySQL instance and implement efficient performance-tuning tasks

Leave a review - let other readers know what you think

Please share your thoughts on this book with others by leaving a review on the site that you bought it from. If you purchased the book from Amazon, please leave us an honest review on this book's Amazon page. This is vital so that other potential readers can see and use your unbiased opinion to make purchasing decisions, we can understand what our customers think about our products, and our authors can see your feedback on the title that they have worked with Packt to create. It will only take a few minutes of your time, but is valuable to other potential customers, our authors, and Packt. Thank you!

Index

J

JavaScript Object Notation (JSON) 395
JSON data type
  about 145, 146
  partial updates 147

K

KEY partition management 301
KEY partitioning 297
keyring plugin
  about 365
  installing 365
  variables 365
keyring service 410, 411

L

Least Recently Used (LRU) 400
limitations, MySQL 8
  data dictionary 29
  group replication 30
  InnoDB storage engine 28
  joins 27
  number of databases 26
  number of tables 26
  partitioning 30
  row size 27
  table column count 27
  table size 26
  Windows platform 27
LINEAR HASH partitioning 296
Linux Apache MySQL PHP (LAMP) 25
Linux
  MySQL 8, installing on 55
LIST COLUMN partitioning 295
LIST partition management 299, 300
LIST partitioning 290, 291, 292
lock types, InnoDB storage engine
  AUTO-INC locks 207
  exclusive lock 207
  gap locks 207
  insertion intention locks 207
  intention locks 207
  next-key locks 207
  predicate locks 207

record locks 207
  shared locks 207
locking operations
  optimizing 378, 379, 380
locking service 409
logging 343

M

memcached
  best practices 428
  used, for scaling MySQL 8 322
memory storage engine 14
MEMORY storage engine
  about 197, 198, 199
  indexes 233
MEMORY tables
  optimizing 398
MERGE storage engine 202
merge storage engine 15
metadata 173
Microsoft Windows
  MySQL 8, installing on 41
mixed-format replication 267
multiple tables
  optimizing 389, 390
multiple-column indexes 233
My SQL 8
  absence of suffix 38
  Release Candidate (rc) 38
MyISAM 14
MyISAM index statistics collection 230
MyISAM key cache 400
MyISAM storage engine 195, 196, 197
MyISAM tables
  optimizing 398
myisam_ftdump 75, 107
myisamchk 75, 108
myisamlog 75, 108
myisampack 75, 109
MySQL 5.7
  upgrade prerequisites 65, 66
MySQL 8 client errors
  about 463
  case sensitivity, in string searches 463
  DATE columns issue 464

---

[480]

S

CPSIA information can be obtained
at www.ICGtesting.com
Printed in the USA
LVHW020336110723
752022LV00007B/749